MCSE
THE CORE EXAMS
IN A NUTSHELL

A Desktop Quick Reference

MCSE
THE CORE EXAMS
IN A NUTSHELL

A Desktop Quick Reference

Michael Moncur

O'REILLY™

Beijing · Cambridge · Köln · Paris · Sebastopol · Taipei · Tokyo

MCSE: The Core Exams in a Nutshell

by Michael Moncur

Copyright © 1998 O'Reilly & Associates, Inc. All rights reserved.
Printed in the United States of America.

Published by O'Reilly & Associates, Inc., 101 Morris Street, Sebastopol, CA 95472.

Editor: Tim O'Reilly

Production Editor: Jane Ellin

Printing History:

> June 1998: First Edition.

This book is printed on acid-free paper with 85% recycled content, 15% post-consumer waste. O'Reilly & Associates is committed to using paper with the highest recycled content available consistent with high quality.

ISBN: 1-56592-376-6   [10/98]

Table of Contents

Part 2: Windows NT Workstation

Part 3: Windows NT Server

Part 4: NT Server in the Enterprise

Part 5: Windows 95

Preface

The MCSE (Microsoft Certified Systems Engineer) program is a rigorous testing and certification program for Windows NT system and network administrators. This book is a concise, comprehensive study guide to the areas covered on the core MCSE exams.

If you're an experienced system administrator—whether the experience is with Windows NT, UNIX, NetWare, or another system—this book will help you codify your knowledge, understand Microsoft's view of the universe, and prepare for the MCSE exams.

If you are a beginner, this book should also prove useful. Of course, you'll need real-world experience, which no book can provide. Depending on your needs, you may also need help from other books or classes. Nevertheless, this book will provide a useful framework for your studies.

If you have already made some progress along the MCSE path, you probably have a number of MCSE-related books lining your shelves. While this book can't replace all of them, it can remain on your desk as a handy reference to the subjects covered in the core MCSE exams. It also includes several features—such as review items and practice tests—that will help you prepare to take the actual exams.

Contents

This book covers the core (required) exams for the Windows NT 4.0 MCSE certification, including the two alternatives for the desktop operating system requirement. The book is divided into Parts corresponding to each of the exams.

About the MCSE Exams
   Introduces the MCSE and other Microsoft certifications, with information about the content of the exams and study tips.

Part 1, Networking Essentials
   Covers required exam 70-058, *Networking Essentials*.

Part 2, Windows NT Workstation

Covers exam 70-073, *Implementing and Supporting Microsoft Windows NT Workstation 4.0*, one of the two choices for the desktop operating system requirement.

Part 3, Windows NT Server

Covers required exam 70-067, *Implementing and Supporting Microsoft Windows NT Server 4.0*.

Part 4, NT Server in the Enterprise

Covers required exam 70-068, *Implementing and Supporting Microsoft Windows NT Server 4.0 in the Enterprise*.

Part 5, Windows 95

Covers exam 70-064, *Implementing and Supporting Microsoft Windows 95*, the other choice for the desktop operating system requirement.

The MCSE certification requires passing four required exams and two elective exams. This book's companion volume, *MCSE: The Electives in a Nutshell*, covers the full spectrum of available elective exams.

Conventions Used in This Book

Each Part within this book corresponds to a single MCSE exam, and consists of five sections:

Exam Overview

This is a brief introduction to the exam's topic and two lists of objectives to help direct your preparation. *Need to Know* lists areas you should understand in-depth because they will more than likely be on the exam. *Need to Apply* lists tasks you should be able to perform, and should practice during your studies. The objectives in both of these lists include cross-references into the Study Guide.

Study Guide

This, the largest portion of each Part, is a comprehensive study guide for the areas covered on the exam. It can be read straight through, or referred to for areas in which you need further study.

Suggested Exercises

This is a numbered list of exercises you can perform, usually with a small test network, to gain experience in the exam's subject areas.

Practice Test

This section includes a comprehensive practice test in a format similar to the actual exam questions. Answers to the questions are provided with detailed explanations.

Highlighter's Index

Here we've attempted to compile the facts within the exam's subject area that you are most likely to need another look at—in other words, those you might have highlighted while reading the Study Guide. This will be useful as a final review before taking an exam.

Within the Study Guide section, the following elements are included:

Exam tips

These boxed tips provide information about areas you should focus your studies on for the exam.

In the Real World

These tips provide informative asides in cases where reality and the MCSE exams don't necessarily coincide.

The following typographical conventions are used in this book:

`Constant width`

is used to indicate keyboard keys, commands, and other values to be typed literally.

Italic

is used for URLs, to introduce new terms, and to indicate menu and dialog box options.

Other MCSE Resources

Depending on your current knowledge and experience, you may need resources beyond this book for your MCSE studies. The one resource all MCSE candidates should be aware of is Microsoft's Training and Certification web page:

http://www.microsoft.com/train_cert/

I recommend that you refer to this page regularly during your certification progress, since changes may be announced that will affect your exam choices.

A wide variety of MCSE study guides are available from other vendors, chief among them the MOC (Microsoft Official Curriculum) study guides. If you need a book for further study, choose the one that best fits your needs.

Another set of useful resources, while not specifically for the MCSE curriculum, are the various Resource Kits published by Microsoft. These are available for Windows NT Workstation, Windows NT Server, and Windows 95, and go into great detail about each product. Each also includes a CD-ROM with useful utilities, some of which are described in this book.

A number of practice MCSE test programs are available. See Microsoft's web page listed above for information about one such program, the PEP tests. See this book's web site (listed in the next section) for links to several third-party test software providers.

How To Contact Us

We have tested and verified all the information in this book to the best of our ability. If you have an idea that could make this a more useful study tool, or if you find an error in the text or run into a question on the exam that isn't covered, please let us know by writing to us at:

O'Reilly & Associates
101 Morris Street
Sebastopol, CA 95472
1-800-998-9938 (in the U.S. or Canada)
1-707-829-0515 (international/local)
1-707-829-0104 (FAX)

You can also send messages electronically. To be put on our mailing list or to request a catalog, send email to:

nuts@oreilly.com

To ask technical questions or comment on the book, send email to:

mcsenut@oreilly.com

Acknowledgments

I would like to thank everyone involved in the production of this book. Tim O'Reilly, the editor of the "in a Nutshell" series, came up with the original concept and has provided much useful input as the book has evolved. Troy Mott and Katie Gardner made sure the project and I moved along smoothly, not always an easy task.

Eric Pearce provided early technical feedback that helped shape this book, and contributed many useful comments for later drafts. The manuscript was also reviewed for technical accuracy at various stages by Walter Glenn, Mitch Tulloch, Robert Bruce Thompson, Paul Robichaux, Frank GoBell, Phil Scarr, David Kelman, and Brian Zeitz. Their input has helped make this a better book.

Thanks also go to the O'Reilly production staff: Jane Ellin, the Production Editor; Mike Sierra, who converted the book and provided much-needed tools support; Nancy Priest, the interior designer; Edie Freedman, who designed the cover; Seth Maislin, the indexer, with assistance from Marie Rizzo; Sebastian Banker, who provided production support; Mary Anne Weeks Mayo and Sheryl Avruch for quality control; and Robert Romano, who provided the figures.

Finally, I would like to thank Brian Gill, David Rogelberg, and Sherry Rogelberg of Studio B for their help with this project. As always, thanks go to my family and friends for their support, particularly my wife, Laura.

About the MCSE Exams

Microsoft's MCSE (Microsoft Certified Systems Engineer) program is rapidly gaining popularity as Windows NT is used for more and more networks. While Novell's CNE (Certified Novell Engineer) program was previously considered the necessary credential for network administrators, it's quickly losing ground to the MCSE program.

You must pass six exams to attain the MCSE certification: four required exams and two electives. This volume covers the available required exams. The full spectrum of available choices for elective exams are covered by *MCSE: The Electives in a Nutshell*, also from O'Reilly and Associates.

This section describes the MCSE and other certification credentials offered by Microsoft, summarizes the exams covered in this book and its companion volume, and provides information about the examination process.

Microsoft Certification Programs

Microsoft offers several certification options with varying levels of difficulty, from the Microsoft Certified Professional (MCP) (one exam) to MCSE+Internet (nine exams). The following sections describe each certification in detail.

On the Exam

For several of these programs, you are able to choose between two or more exams covering different versions of a software product. Since older exams are eventually retired, I recommend taking the exam for the most current product. This book and its companion volume cover the most recent exam currently available for each product.

The descriptions of certification programs and their requirements in the sections below are current at the time of this writing. For a list of the current requirements for these and other certifications, see Microsoft's Certification Online web site:

http://www.microsoft.com/train_cert/

MCP (Microsoft Certified Professional)

The MCP certification only requires passing a single exam. Depending on the exam, you are certified as an MCP with that specialty. You can attain multiple MCP certifications; in fact, you will attain several in the process of earning the MCSE certification.

In the past, the MCP certification was available only for certain exams. Microsoft has recently revised the program. You can now earn an MCP certification by passing any current (not scheduled to be retired) exam. The one exception is Exam 70-058, *Network Essentials,* which counts toward the MCSE but does not earn an MCP certification.

MCP+Internet (MCP with Internet Specialty)

Microsoft recently enhanced the MCP program to include a new certification category: MCP with a specialty in the Internet. This certification requires passing three specific exams dealing with Windows NT and the Internet. The current exams include the following:

- Exam 70-067: Implementing and Supporting Microsoft Windows NT Server 4.0 (Part 3)
- Exam 70-059: Internetworking with TCP/IP on Microsoft Windows NT 4.0
- Exam 70-087: Implementing and supporting Microsoft Internet Information Server 4.0

The first of these exams is one of the MCSE requirements, and is covered in Part 3 of this book. The remaining exams are MCSE electives, and are covered by *MCSE: The Electives in a Nutshell.*

MCSE (Microsoft Certified Systems Engineer)

The MCSE certification is currently the most sought-after credential for network administrators, and is the subject of this book. The MCSE requires passing six exams: four core requirement exams and two electives.

Core Requirement Exams

The core MCSE exams include the following:

- Exam 70-058: Networking Essentials (Part 1)
- Choose one of these desktop operating system exams:
    - Exam 70-073: Implementing and Supporting Windows NT Workstation 4.0 (Part 2)
    - Exam 70-064: Implementing and Supporting Windows 95 (Part 5)

- Exam 70-098: Implementing and Supporting Windows 98

- Exam 70-067: Implementing and Supporting Microsoft Windows NT Server 4.0 (Part 3)

- Exam 70-068: Implementing and Supporting Microsoft Windows NT Server 4.0 in the Enterprise (Part 4)

This book covers all of these exams. The exams are described in more detail later in this chapter, and in their corresponding chapters.

Elective Exams

You can choose your two MCSE electives from a pool of available exams. We have included coverage of nine exams in this book's companion volume, which includes all of the possible electives except for old versions that are likely to be retired. The following exams are included:

- Exam 70-059: Internetworking with TCP/IP on Windows NT 4.0

- Exam 70-087 Implementing and supporting Microsoft Internet Information Server 4.0 (Exam 70-077, IIS 3.0, is also accepted)

- Exam 70-081: Implementing and supporting Microsoft Exchange Server 5.5

- Exam 70-088: Implementing and supporting Microsoft Proxy Server 2.0

- Exam 70-086: Implementing and supporting Microsoft Systems Management Server 2.0

- Exam 70-026: System Administration for Microsoft SQL Server 6.5 or 70-029: System Administration for SQL Server 7.0

- Exam 70-027: Implementing a Database Design on Microsoft SQL Server 6.5 or 70-029: Implementing a Database Design on SQL Server 7.0

- Exam 70-085: Implementing and Supporting Microsoft SNA Server 4.0

- Exam 70-079: Implementing and Supporting Microsoft Internet Explorer 4.0 by Using the Internet Explorer Administration Kit

The current versions of all of the above exams are covered by *MCSE: The Electives in a Nutshell*.

MCSE+Internet (MCSE with Internet Specialty)

Until recently, the MCSE certification, with six exams, was the most advanced networking certification offered by Microsoft. The latest addition to the program is the MCSE+Internet, or MCSE with a specialty in the Internet. This is basically a combination of the MCSE and MCP+Internet certifications.

The MCSE+Internet certification requires a total of nine exams: seven core requirements and two electives. The required exams include the following:

- Exam 70-058: Networking Essentials (Part 1)

- Choose one of these desktop operating system exams:

  - Exam 70-073: Implementing and Supporting Windows NT Workstation 4.0 (Part 2)

- Exam 70-064: Implementing and Supporting Windows 95 (Part 5)
- Exam 70-098: Implementing and Supporting Windows 98

- Exam 70-067: Implementing and Supporting Microsoft Windows NT Server 4.0 (Part 3)

- Exam 70-068: Implementing and Supporting Microsoft Windows NT Server 4.0 in the Enterprise (Part 4)

- Exam 70-059: Internetworking with Microsoft TCP/IP on Microsoft Windows NT 4.0

- Exam 70-087: Implementing and Supporting Microsoft Internet Information Server 4.0 (Exam 70-077, IIS 3.0, is also accepted)

- Exam 70-089: Implementing and Supporting Microsoft Internet Explorer 4.0 by Using the Internet Explorer Administration Kit

The first four core exams are the same as the required exams for the MCSE certification, and are covered by this book. The TCP/IP, Internet Information Server and Internet Explorer exams are covered by the companion volume.

The two electives can be chosen from the following exams, all of which are covered by *MCSE: The Electives in a Nutshell*:

- Exam 70-026: System Administration for Microsoft SQL Server 6.5 (or 70-028 for SQL Server 7.0)

- Exam 70-027: Implementing a Database Design on Microsoft SQL Server 6.5 (or 70-029 for SQL Server 7.0)

- Exam 70-081: Implementing and Supporting Microsoft Exchange Server 5.5

- Exam 70-088: Implementing and Supporting Microsoft Proxy Server 2.0

If you plan to pursue the MCSE+Internet certification after completing the MCSE, be sure your MCSE electives are chosen to correspond with required or elective exams for the MCSE+Internet; otherwise, you may end up taking more than 9 exams total.

MCSD (Microsoft Certified Solution Developer)

This certification is aimed at software developers rather than network administrators. It requires four exams, two required and two electives. The two required exams are Exam 70-160, Windows Architecture I, and Exam 70-161, Windows Architecture II.

The elective exams can be chosen from various exams related to programming languages and databases. One of the electives, Exam 70-027: Implementing a Database Design on Microsoft SQL Server 6.5, is also an MCSE elective, and is covered by this book's companion volume.

MCT (Microsoft Certified Trainer)

The MCT certification is for individuals who intend to teach Microsoft's authorized courses on the MCP and other exams. To become an MCT, you must first register with Microsoft and prove that you have attended a class in instructional skills, or that you are an experienced trainer. (Microsoft holds instructor training courses for this purpose.)

After being approved as an MCT, you have to be separately approved to teach each MCP exam. To do this you must pass the exam and any related exams, and may be required to attend a Microsoft Official Curriculum (MOC) course for each subject you wish to teach.

Refer to Microsoft's MCT web site for details about the MCT program:

http://www.microsoft.com/train_cert/mct/

MCSE Core Exams

The MCSE is the most popular of the MCP programs. It requires six exams, the first four of which are core requirement exams. You can choose different exams for some of these, but this book covers the most useful or popular choices (most of the alternate choices are for previous operating system versions, and may not remain available).

The MCSE core exams covered in this book are described in the sections below.

Networking Essentials

The Networking Essentials exam, exam 70-058, is the only choice for the Networking requirement. This exam covers basic networking knowledge. This includes the various network media, architectures, and protocols, and the basics of network administration. This exam is covered in Part 1.

If you're experienced with networks already, this may be the easiest exam to pass. If you have been certified by Novell or Banyan, you can waive this exam entirely. See Part 1 for details.

Windows NT Workstation 4.0

This exam, number 70-073, is one of the available choices for the desktop operating system requirement. The other choices are Windows 95 and Windows 3.1, although the Windows 3.1 exam is scheduled to be retired.

This exam covers the basics of installing, using, and administering Windows NT Workstation 4.0. There's a lot of material here, ranging from installation choices to security to network types and disk configurations. This exam is covered in Part 2.

Windows 95

This exam, number 70-064, is the other current choice for the desktop operating system requirement. This exam was released in March 1998 to replace the previous Windows 95 exam, 70-063, which has been retired.

This exam covers Windows 95's architecture as well as details of installation, administration, and technical support. This exam addresses many of the same topics as the NT Workstation exam, but from a Windows 95 standpoint. This exam is covered in Part 5. When released, Exam 70-098 (Windows 98) will be an alternate choice.

Windows NT Server 4.0

This required exam, number 70-067, covers more advanced topics about Windows NT, centered on Windows NT Server 4.0. Since NT Server and NT Workstation are similar in some ways, there is some overlap in the content of this exam and the Workstation exam.

The emphasis in this exam is on features unique to Windows NT server, and on features that are likely to be used in larger networks, such as domain-based security. However, many of the objectives for the Workstation exam are also included in the potential questions for this exam. Part 3 covers the Server exam, and includes cross-references to Part 2 for the appropriate material.

Windows NT Server 4.0 in the Enterprise

This required exam is number 70-068. The emphasis in this exam is on Enterprise networking using domains and trusts, multiple platforms, and higher-level services such as IIS and DHCP.

This exam includes many of the same objectives as the Server and Workstation exams. Part 4 covers this exam, with cross references to Parts 2 and 3 for some topics.

The Examination Process

All of the MCSE exams are similar in format, and a certain amount of preparation will help you pass any of them. The following sections look at ways to prepare for the exams and the actual process of taking the exams.

Choosing Exams

Before beginning the certification process, you should choose the required and elective exams you will take, and the order in which you will take them. Here are some thoughts on making these choices.

Required Exams

There are a limited number of choices for the MCSE requirements. The two exams you can actually choose between are the NT Workstation and Windows 95 exams. These both have their advantages:

- The Windows 95 exam will be easier to learn if you already have experience with Windows 95. In addition, Windows 95 is more widely used on desktops.

- The NT Workstation exam covers some more difficult topics, but you'll need to learn most of these topics for the NT Server exam regardless of your desktop exam choice.

The NT Workstation exam is the most popular choice; it's a good foundation for the other MCSE exams, most of which are centered on Windows NT.

Having decided which desktop exam to take, you can decide which order to take the core exams in. You can take the exams in any order, but the logical choices for a first exam are Network Essentials or the desktop OS exam (NT Workstation or Windows 95), since these are generally the easiest.

While the Network Essentials exam covers more basic and fundamental topics, your experience may be more in line with the desktop OS exam. For example, someone who has worked as a Windows NT network administrator for a year would find the NT Workstation exam easy to pass.

On the other hand, the same person would most likely need to study for the Network Essentials exam, because they probably don't have experience with network topologies and protocols other than those used in their employer's network.

There is also a potential career advantage to passing a desktop OS exam first, since these exams result in an MCP certification. If you are trying to start a career quickly, the MCP may help you qualify for a job in network administration or technical support. (Aside from financial advantages, having a job that requires day-to-day work with Windows NT will be very helpful in passing the remaining MCSE tests.)

Once you've passed the Network Essentials exam and a desktop OS exam, you will probably want to take the remaining exams in order: NT Server, then NT Server in the enterprise.

Elective Exams

There are many more choices for elective exams. Your choice of two elective exams should be based on three considerations:

- Which topics do you already have experience with, or plan to learn?
- Which topics will be most useful in a career?
- Which exams provide other certification options? For example, choosing the TCP/IP and IIS exams will give you the MCP+Internet certification as well as the MCSE, and prepare you for the MCSE+Internet certification.

While choosing easier exams, or those you have experience with, can get you the MCSE certification faster, choosing more specialized topics can help you stand out from other certified applicants in your career pursuits.

Preparing for Exams

The exams currently cost $100 apiece to take, and the cost applies whether you pass or fail. Thus, it's a good idea to prepare as thoroughly as possible before attempting to take an exam. It's best to concentrate on a single exam at a time.

This book will obviously be helpful in preparing for exams. Depending on your understanding of the subject matter, it may be useful to study other materials.

Microsoft's documentation, such as the Windows NT Resource Kits, the online books, and the help files included with various utilities, may be helpful.

It is also very important to have real-world experience with the items covered in each exam. It's nearly impossible to pass a Microsoft exam just by studying. You should have access to a network with a minimum of two Windows NT computers to experiment with, and access to a larger network would be even more useful.

A number of free practice exams are available, including the PEP test free for download from Microsoft. These are not comprehensive and may not cover all of the exam topics, but can be a good barometer to test your preparedness. Commercial tests are available from several third-party companies. A practice test is also included in each of the parts of this book.

Scheduling and Payment

Microsoft's exams are administered by Sylvan Prometric. Call (800) 755-3926 to schedule an exam. Online registration is also available at the Prometric web site (*www.prometric.com*).

You can register entirely over the phone with a credit card. If you pay by check, you must first mail the check to Sylvan Prometric, then call to schedule the exam. Call the number listed above for the address to send payments to.

Your registration ID is your social security number, or a number assigned by Prometric if you are outside the U.S. Use this number in all communications with them, and write it on any checks you send.

You usually need to schedule an exam at least 24 hours in advance. Once you've scheduled an exam, you must call 24 hours before the scheduled time if you wish to cancel or reschedule.

How the Exams Work

You take the exams at a local Sylvan Prometric testing center. The tests are administered by computer. Most of the answers are multiple choice, but many are complex and include detailed scenarios and diagrams. Some of the newer exams include simulation questions, requiring you to perform a task with a simulated utility.

You are given a set time limit for the test (usually 1.5 hours) and must answer a number of questions (between 40 and 100). You can mark questions to return to later if you're not sure of the answers.

When you complete the exam, you are shown a review screen allowing you to examine and change your answers for any of the questions. When you are finished, you are given a passing or failing score. Each exam has its own passing percentage between 60% and 85%.

The questions generally fall into four categories, described below.

Single Answer

These are basic multiple-choice questions requiring a single answer, and are generally the easiest. Here is an example:

How many nodes can be used on a single segment in an Ethernet 10Base2 network?

a. 1

b. 32

c. 30

c. 90

Answer: **C**

These questions often address facts and figures included in the exam objectives. While these are relatively easy questions, many of them are worded to be confusing or to encourage jumping to conclusions. Be sure to read the questions carefully and double-check your answer.

Multiple Answer

These are multiple-choice questions where one or more of the answers is correct, and you must choose all that apply. The following is an example:

Which network connectivity devices operate at the physical layer of the OSI model? (check all that apply)

a. Hubs

b. Routers

c. Transceivers

d. Repeaters

Answer: **A, C, D**

These questions can be tricky. While they often address the same type of definitions and facts as the simpler questions, the multiple answers increase the possibility of mistakes. In addition, these questions often describe a network and ask you to answer questions based on its configuration.

Rather than look for one or more obvious answers to these questions, you may find it useful to consider them as a series of true/false questions, and evaluate each of the possible choices separately. Otherwise, it's easy to overlook a correct answer.

Be sure to read these questions carefully. Many of them explicitly state the number of correct answers, such as "Check the 3 items that apply." If you mark the incorrect number of items, the question is considered incorrect.

Scenario

These questions present a scenario about a need or problem and the steps taken to resolve it. You have to determine whether the solution meets the required result or the optional results. Here is a sample of this type of question:

> You are installing a network in a training room, to be used temporarily for a period of 30 days. You must connect 10 workstations running Windows NT Workstation and 2 servers running Windows NT Server.
>
> *Required result*: The network must have a transmission speed of 10 Mbps or higher.
>
> *Optional result*: The network should be inexpensive.
>
> *Optional result*: The network should be easy to install.
>
> *Solution*: Install 10Base2 Ethernet in a bus topology.
>
> a. The solution meets the required result and both of the optional results.
>
> b. The solution meets the required result and only one of the optional results.
>
> c. The solution meets the required result only.
>
> d. The solution does not meet the required result.

Correct Answer: **A**

These are the most complex questions, and can be difficult. They present a complex scenario which you will need to analyze and understand before you answer the question.

As with the multiple answer questions, these are best regarded as a series of true/false questions. Analyze the scenario and the proposed solution, then compare the required result and the optional results to see which ones are satisfied.

Be sure to double-check your answers to these questions—not only to check your work, but to ensure that you've selected the choice that matches the appropriate set of results.

It is also helpful to look for key phrases in these questions. For example, the question above mentions that the network is temporary, and one of Ethernet 10Base2's strong points is that it can be quickly set up and taken down. The 10-Mbps transmission speed mentioned in the required result is also an indication that Ethernet is the correct choice.

Most of these questions come in sets of two or more questions using the same scenario and different proposed solutions. You may find it helpful to examine all of the questions for a scenario before answering them.

Simulation Questions

Some of the newest exams include simulation questions. These provide a simulated version of a utility, and require you to perform a task (for example: create a user or copy a file). Simpler simulations show a dialog from a utility and ask you to click the appropriate button for a particular function.

These questions should be easy if you are experienced with the exam's subjects. You cannot mark these questions to return to them later, so be careful to perform the task correctly the firstne time.

Test-Taking Tips

It's best to study and prepare for one test at a time. Schedule the test on a day when you won't be under stress due to your job or other factors, and give yourself plenty of time to study for the test. Rest well the night before, and review your test preparation materials (such as this book) one last time before taking the test.

Use test preparation software, or have someone ask you questions, to be sure you're prepared for the test. Don't be satisfied if you merely know 95% of the topics the exam covers. As few as 5–10 incorrect answers can lead to a failing score, and you will make mistakes.

Since the MCSE exams are timed, pacing is important for success. The testing program includes Forward and Back buttons to review the questions and change your answers if necessary; in addition, you can check a box to highlight a question for later review.

Using these tools, a good strategy is to first review all of the questions, answering those you are sure of. Then take a second pass through the questions, answering all you can. Mark the questions that you may be able to answer with more time.

The exam scoring process does not deduct points for wrong answers, so it's beneficial to guess rather than leaving an answer blank. You can usually eliminate some of the choices to make your guess more educated. Be aware of the time limit and set aside the last 5–10 minutes to double-check your answers and guess if necessary.

Don't let the scenario questions take too much of your time: remember, they count for the same score as the other types of questions. You may wish to mark these and come back to them later.

You may not bring any material (papers, calculators, books, etc.) into the exam room with you. However, you are allowed to use the Windows Calculator program for some exams. You are also provided with a writing surface. If you have memorized critical items for the test, it may be helpful to write these down when you enter the testing room for reference during the exam.

If you should fail a test, ask the test administrator for a detailed report. This lists the topics of the questions you missed, and will be useful for further study. In addition, write down the questions you remember having trouble with so you can study those areas more carefully.

Continuing Education

To maintain your MCSE certification, you must continue to meet the MCSE requirements as they are updated by Microsoft. Existing exams are often retired or replaced with new versions, and exams for new products are added.

Retired Exams

Microsoft usually retires (discontinues) an exam when the product it refers to becomes obsolete, or is replaced by a new version. For example, the Windows NT 3.51 exams are scheduled to be retired when Windows NT 5.0 is released.

When one of the exams you took for the MCSE is retired, you are given time (usually six months to a year) to take a new exam to keep your certification. This can be the exam for a new version of the same product, or another exam in the same category (i.e., elective exam).

When you need to take the new version of an exam to replace a retired exam, Microsoft usually offers a 50% discount if you take the new exam within 6 months.

New Exams

Microsoft periodically releases new exams. These may cover new products, or new versions of old products. Microsoft may require that new exams be taken for MCSEs to retain their certification status.

If you take a new version of an exam you passed the previous version of within 3 months after it is released, you are given a 50% discount on the price.

Beta Exams

When a new exam is first developed, it is offered as a beta exam. These exams are available for 50% of the normal price. They include a large list of questions; after the beta period, some of these questions will be compiled into the real exam.

You receive credit for passing a beta exam, but you don't receive the results immediately; they are sent to you by mail after the beta period ends. Microsoft uses the results to develop the scoring to be used in the final version of the exam.

PART 1

Networking Essentials

Exam Overview

Networks of personal computers have largely replaced mainframes for information management in small and large companies. Today's networks range from small three-user setups to wide-area networks of thousands of computers that span the globe.

Microsoft's MCSE Exam 70-058, titled *Networking Essentials,* covers the basics of networking, including the various standards and protocols, types of connections, and basic network administration. This exam is not really specific to Windows NT, although some NT-specific terms are used. Although this is considered one of the easier exams, it does present some complex details for the uninitiated.

If you hold Novell's CNE-3, CNE-4, or Master CNE certification or Banyan's CBS or CBE certification, you can waive this exam. To receive credit for this exam, you must send proof of your existing certification to Sylvan Prometric after passing at least one other MCSE test. This exam is roughly equivalent to Novell's Networking Technologies CNE test.

In order to prepare for this chapter and the Networking Essentials exam, you should understand the basics of computers, and be familiar with PC architecture (memory, interrupts, etc.). You should also be familiar with at least one current Microsoft operating system (Windows 95 or Windows NT).

Objectives

Need to Know	Reference
Definitions of common terms relating to networks	"Media Types" on page 27; other terms introduced throughout chapter
Difference between peer-to-peer and client-server networks	"Network Types" on page 20
Types of servers	"Network Types" on page 20

Need to Know	Reference
The layers of the OSI model and their functions	"The OSI Reference Model" on page 21
The function of the IEEE 802.2, 802.3, and 802.5 standards	"IEEE 802 Standards" on page 24
The NDIS and ODI standards	"NDIS and ODI" on page 26
Characteristics of network media	"Media Types" on page 27
Common PC IRQ settings	"Network Cards" on page 32
Connectivity devices (routers, hubs, etc.) and their OSI model layers	"Connectivity Devices" on page 37
Specifications of various LAN architectures (Ethernet, Token Ring, etc.)	"LAN Topologies and Architectures" on page 34
Difference between connectionless and connection-oriented communications	"Common Network Protocols" on page 45
Specifications of various WAN architectures (X.25, ISDN, etc.)	"Common WAN Architectures" on page 49
Differences between user-level and share-level security	"User Accounts, Shares, and Security" on page 53
Types of fault tolerance and RAID levels	"Fault Tolerance" on page 55
Software tools for monitoring network performance	"Monitoring Performance" on page 58
Uses of various hardware troubleshooting tools	"Devices for Troubleshooting" on page 61

Need to Apply	Reference
Determine which media types to use in a given network.	"Media Types" on page 27
Install network cards in PCs, and resolve conflicts with other devices.	"Network Cards" on page 32
Determine the network topology to use in a given network.	"Network Topologies" on page 34
Choose the appropriate connectivity device (router, hub, etc.) for a given purpose.	"Connectivity Devices" on page 37
Choose the protocols to use in a given network.	"Common Network Protocols" on page 45
Choose the appropriate dial-up protocol (SLIP or PPP) for TCP/IP networks.	"SLIP and PPP" on page 47
Choose a WAN service (ISDN, X.25, etc.) for a given situation.	"Common WAN Architectures" on page 49
Plan a network for a given situation.	"Planning and Administration" on page 53

Need to Apply	_Reference_
Plan a NetBIOS naming scheme for a network.	"NetBIOS Names" on page 54
Choose fault tolerance methods to use on a network.	"Fault Tolerance" on page 55
Monitor network performance with the appropriate tools and identify performance problems.	"Monitoring Performance" on page 58
Resolve common problems with network connections.	"Connection Problems" on page 60
Prevent or resolve broadcast storms in a network.	"Broadcast Storms" on page 63

Study Guide

This chapter includes the following sections, which address various topics covered on the Networking Essentials MCSE exam:

Networking Basics and Standards

Introduces various terms relating to networking and the basic types of networks. This section also introduces the OSI reference model and the IEEE 802, NDIS, and ODI standards.

Network Media and Interface Cards

Discusses the various network media in common use today (such as twisted-pair cable, coaxial cable, and fiber optic media) and Network Interface Cards (NICs), used to interface between computers and network media.

LAN Topologies and Architectures

Describes the common network topologies (star, bus, ring, and mesh); hardware devices used to assemble networks (routers, hubs, repeaters, etc.); and common LAN architectures (such as Ethernet and Token Ring).

Common Network Protocols

Introduces the network protocols supported by Microsoft operating systems: TCP/IP, IPX/SPX, NetBEUI, AppleTalk, and DLC.

Common WAN Architectures

Describes the various standards and architectures for wide-area networking (X.25, ISDN, ATM, Frame Relay, etc.).

Planning and Administration

Introduces some of the basic administration tasks required for a network, including user accounts and security, naming schemes, and fault tolerance.

Troubleshooting

Introduces various methods of monitoring the performance of networks, and describes common network problems and their solutions.

Networking Basics and Standards

A network is a group of two or more computers that communicate through a transmission medium (cable or wireless media). The main purpose of networking is to share files, printers, and services. Networks range from small to large-scale:

- *Local Area Networks* (LANs) connect computers in a small area (usually a single building).

- *Metropolitan Area Networks* (MANs) use long-distance links, such as telephone lines or dedicated media, to connect two or more locations within a single city or metropolitan area.

- *Wide Area Networks* (WANs) use the same technologies as MANs to connect computers in distant locations, typically in different cities or even different countries.

Terminology

The following are some basic terms used to describe network functions and components:

Account
> A username and password given to each user of a network. Networks grant access to files and services based on the rights given to the user's account.

Administrator
> The person responsible for a network's operations, including installing network components, providing access to users, and troubleshooting.

Authentication
> The process of granting access to network services. Users are required to enter their account information (log on) to be authenticated.

Centralized processing
> A type of network in which all of the processing is done by one powerful central computer. This is typical of mainframe systems.

Client
> A computer that connects to a network and accesses files, printers, or other services offered by a server.

Distributed processing
> A type of network in which processing is done by individual workstations. This is typical of PC-based networks.

Internet
> The global network that evolved from the U.S. Department of Defense's ARPANET project. Many modern networks include some degree of Internet connectivity.

Internetwork
> A large network consisting of various small networks connected together by WAN links or faster local links. This type of network is also referred to as an internet (not to be confused with the Internet).

Network Operating System (NOS)
> A piece of software, such as Windows NT Server or Novell NetWare, that enables a computer to act as a network server.

Node
> Any computer or other device connected to a network. Nodes include workstations, servers, and occasionally devices such as printers.

Protocol
> A set of rules for communication between network components. A functioning network requires that all nodes understand the same set of protocols.

Server
> A computer that offers one or more services to the network, and runs a NOS.

Sharing
> The process of making files, printers, or other resources or services available across a network.

Transmission media
> The wire, cable, or wireless media that network nodes use to communicate with each other.

Workstation
> A nonserver computer attached to a network.

On the Exam

You should be familiar with all the above terms for the Network Essentials exam, as well as other terms introduced throughout this chapter.

Network Types

There are two basic types of networks: client-server networks, which use dedicated servers, and peer-to-peer networks, which share files between workstations. These are explained in the sections below.

Server-Based Networks

Server-based networks, also called *client-server networks*, use a dedicated server machine. Files and printers on this computer are made available to network workstations, called *clients*. Client machines are simply used by network users, and usually do not share files or printers.

A server-based network's main benefit is in centralization. The server provides a central control point for network access, security, and management. The disadvantages of a server-based network are the higher cost of dedicated servers and network operating systems, and the greater administrative effort required.

Windows NT Server is typically used as a server for this type of network. Windows NT's model for server-based networks is called the *domain model*. Servers are

---

organized into domains, with a single computer (the primary domain controller) providing centralized authentication.

Servers in a network can provide different functions. The typical server that shares files and printers is called a *file and print server.* The other common type of server is an *application server,* which provides back-end processing for complex applications (such as database access).

Peer-to-Peer Networks

A peer-to-peer network (sometimes simply called a peer network) consists solely of workstations called peers. Each workstation can be used by a user, and can also make shared files or printers available to users at other workstations. This system is best suited to smaller networks. Microsoft's term for peer-to-peer networks is *workgroups.*

The main disadvantage of peer networks is the lack of central control. Each user controls access to their own workstation's shared files and printers. In a large network, this is difficult to manage without compromising security. A workstation that is being accessed by peers can also be slowed down, inconveniencing the user at the workstation.

The advantages of peer networks include their ease of installation and use. They are also less expensive than server-based networks because a dedicated server is not required. If users are able to manage resource sharing, an administrator may not be required.

On the Exam

Microsoft generally draws the line between peer-to-peer networks and client-server networks at 10 workstations. Exam questions that ask which type of network should be used in a given situation are often easily answered based on the number of users. Be sure to take other factors, such as network growth, security, and administration, into account.

The OSI Reference Model

The OSI (Open Systems Interconnect) reference model, developed by the ISO (International Standards Organization) in 1977, is a conceptual model for network communications. The model consists of seven layers.

The OSI model is useful to help understand the process of network communication. It also provides a division of responsibility for network hardware and software components.

Each layer includes a number of protocols that are used to communicate with protocols at the same layer on other nodes of the network. Upper-layer protocols use the services offered by lower-layer protocols to transmit and process data. Figure 1-1 shows how these layers are used in communication between two nodes.

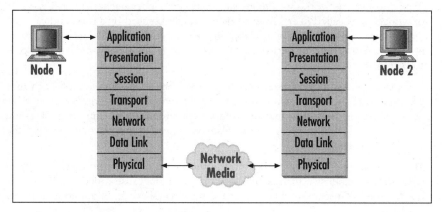

Figure 1-1: The OSI model's layers in action

Data is sent across the network in the form of *packets*. A packet contains data and header information. Different headers are added to the packet as it passes through the layers of the OSI model.

The seven layers of the OSI model are described below, from lowest to highest (physical to application).

Physical Layer

The physical layer deals with the network media and the hardware that supports it: repeaters, hubs, connectors, network interface cards, transceivers, and cables. The transmission media, connectors, and topologies used by various network architectures (such as Ethernet) are defined at the physical level.

This layer is responsible for translating bits of binary data from the upper layers into signals to be sent over the transmission media, and converting incoming signals into bits to be sent to the data link layer.

This layer also defines signaling methods to be used on the network media. Analog, or *broadband*, signaling modulates the signals into frequencies; different frequencies can be used simultaneously as data channels. Digital, or *baseband*, signaling uses high and low voltage levels to represent binary 1s and 0s. Most LAN architectures use baseband signaling.

The physical layer also deals with bit synchronization. Communications can be *asynchronous* (bits are sent in a single channel, and transitions from high to low voltage levels indicate the division between bits) or *synchronous* (a separate clock signal is sent to indicate when each bit arrives in the data channel).

Data Link Layer

While the physical layer deals strictly with bits of data, the data link layer organizes data into groups called *frames*. Frames include a header that defines the hardware address of the node. This address is also called a MAC (media access control) address, or a physical address.

Hardware addresses are set in network interface cards (NICs). Most NICS have a unique hardware address preprogrammed into them by the manufacturer. Some models allow you to set the hardware address using switches or a configuration utility.

In the Real World

Although some network cards allow you to change the MAC address, this is rarely necessary. In addition, changing MAC addresses may result in duplicated addresses, which cause network communication problems.

The data link layer is also responsible for error and flow control between nodes. Error control involves adding a checksum (cyclic redundancy check, or CRC) to the data so that it can be verified at the other end. Flow control ensures that data is sent only when the receiving device is ready to receive it.

The data link layer is further subdivided by the IEEE 802 standards, as described later in this section. A bridge is a hardware device that works at the data link layer to filter information and send it between network segments.

Network Layer

The network layer forms frames from the data link layer into packets, adding additional headers. The network layer headers define a logical address (such as an IP address or IPX address). This layer also translates between physical (MAC) and logical (network) addresses.

The other major responsibility of the network layer is routing. Routing consists of forwarding packets to the network segment of their destination, possibly through one or more intermediate nodes. Routers are hardware devices that work at the network layer.

Transport Layer

The transport layer is responsible for assembling packets into their proper sequence, checking them for errors, and passing them on to the session layer. Acknowledgments are sent to indicate that the data has been received, and retransmissions are requested for packets that are not received correctly.

When transmitting, this layer breaks large messages into packets of the appropriate size for the network, and passes them on to the network layer.

Session Layer

The session layer maintains a *session*, or connection, between two nodes on the network. This layer is responsible for requesting connections, sending periodic messages to maintain the connection, and tearing down the connection when communication is finished.

Protocols at the session layer also determine which nodes are currently allowed to send data. Services required to establish connections, such as name resolution and security, are also handled by the session layer.

Presentation Layer

The presentation layer is responsible for translating data sent by the application layer into the proper format for network communication, and translating data received from the network into a format the application can understand. If used, compression and encryption are also handled at this level.

The presentation layer is handled in Windows NT by the *network redirector*, a software driver that allows applications to access network files and printers in the same manner as local files and printers.

Application Layer

The application layer is the interface network-aware applications use to access the network. This layer controls access by applications to the network, and is responsible for informing an application when a network error has occurred.

Certain higher-level protocols that can be used by simple client applications (such as FTP and NFS) also operate at this level.

IEEE 802 Standards

The IEEE (Institute of Electrical and Electronics Engineers), in cooperation with the ISO, created a set of draft networking standards in 1980 under Project 802. Some of these have become the definitive standards for certain types of networks. Table 1-1 summarizes the 802 standards.

Table 1-1: IEEE 802 Standards

Standard	Description
802.1	Internetworking and the OSI model
802.2	Logical link control (LLC)
802.3	CSMA/CD (Ethernet) media access method
802.4	Token bus media access method
802.5	Token Ring media access method
802.6	Metropolitan Area Networks (MANs)
802.7	Broadband technologies
802.8	Fiber optic technologies
802.9	Hybrid (voice and data) networking
802.10	Network security
802.11	Wireless Networking (Draft)
802.12	High-speed LANs

On the Exam

You should know what the 802 standards are and the types of information they include for the exam, but you should only need to know the details of 802.1, 802.2, 802.3, and 802.5. These are described in detail in the following sections.

802.1: Internetworking

The 802.1 standard enumerates the layers of the OSI reference model. It also suggests further dividing the data link layer into two sublayers:

- Logical link control (LLC) handles error correction and flow control between network devices. LLC is defined by IEEE 802.2.

- Media access control (MAC) controls access to the network interface card. Different network types use different media access methods. The media access methods for Ethernet and Token Ring networks are defined by IEEE 802.3 and 802.5.

802.2: Logical Link Control (LLC)

The 802.2 standard defines the LLC sublayer within the data link layer. The LLC sublayer maintains a connection between two nodes on the network and provides service access points (SAP) for communication with upper layers.

802.3: CSMA/CD

CSMA/CD stands for Carrier Sense Multiple Access with Collision Detection. This is the media access method used by Ethernet networks. The three components of this access method are as follows:

Carrier Sense

When a node has information to send across the network, it first checks for a carrier on the network media, indicating that it is already in use. Data is not sent until the carrier drops.

Multiple Access

This refers to the fact that multiple devices can attempt to send data over the network at the same time. Although a node has to wait for the carrier to drop before sending, it doesn't have to wait until its turn, as with token-passing methods (explained below).

Collision Detection

Ethernet networks have no way to prevent collisions, or multiple devices sending data at the same time. If a collision occurs, both nodes detect the collision and wait a random interval before making another attempt.

802.5: Token Ring

The 802.5 standard defines the media access method used by Token Ring networks. This type of network uses a token-passing access method. While the nodes on an Ethernet network all monitor the media and can send data at any time, the nodes on a Token Ring network take turns sending data.

A special data frame called a *token* is passed between the nodes in an orderly fashion, and the node with the token is the only one allowed to transmit. Because the token is passed to all nodes, a node that has gone down can be easily detected and bypassed. Token Ring networks are explained in detail later in this chapter.

NDIS and ODI

The Network Device Interface Specification (NDIS) is a standard developed by Microsoft and IBM to define the communication between protocols and network card drivers. The purpose of NDIS is to abstract the functions of the network driver so that protocols can work with any driver. NDIS works within the data link layer of the OSI model.

NDIS allows software components to be written in a modular fashion, and components that conform to a version of the NDIS specification are guaranteed to communicate with each other. The current version of NDIS is 4.0.

The process of assigning a protocol to a network card is called *binding*. NDIS allows multiple protocols to be bound to a single network card, and multiple network cards to be bound to a single protocol (or multiple protocols).

ODI (Open Datalink Interface), developed by Novell and Apple, is an implementation of the same functionality. While designed primarily for the IPX protocol, ODI can be used with any protocol. NetWare clients and servers can have multiple network cards bound to multiple protocols. Microsoft's implementation of the IPX protocol, NWLink, also supports the ODI standard.

Network Media and Interface Cards

Each network uses a transmission medium: a wire, cable, fiber, or radio or light waves used to transmit data. Network interface cards (NICs) at each node act as an interface between the network medium and the computer.

Terminology

The following terms are used in discussing network media:

Attenuation
> The gradual weakening of a signal as it passes through a wire or other medium. The greater the distance, the greater the attenuation. Different cable types have different levels of attenuation, and thus different maximum distances.

Bandwidth
> The amount of data that can be transmitted over a network cable at one time, usually expressed in Mbps (millions of bits per second).

Baseband (digital signaling)
> A signaling method that uses high and low voltage levels on a cable to indicate binary 1s and 0s in network transmission.

Broadband (analog signaling)
> A signaling method that modulates data into frequencies before sending it across a network cable or other medium.

Crosstalk
> A type of interference that occurs when a network cable picks up a signal from an adjacent cable.

Emissions
> The tendency of some network media to transmit the network data in an undesired manner. For example, some cable types generate radio frequency signals. Unauthorized parties can "eavesdrop," or monitor network data, by picking up these signals.

EMI (Electromagnetic Interference)
> A type of interference that occurs when a network cable picks up a spurious signal induced by a magnetic field. This can be caused by power cables, fluorescent lights, and other devices.

Impedance
> A measure of attenuation in cables. Impedance is measured in ohms, the unit of electrical resistance.

Media Types

Common network media include twisted pair cable (UTP and STP), coaxial cable, fiber-optic cable, and wireless transmissions via infrared and radio waves. Network media are usually chosen based on several criteria: their cost, their vulnerability to EMI and eavesdropping, their bandwidth, and the maximum distance at which they can be used.

Table 1-2 summarizes the characteristics of the various network media. These are described in detail in the sections below.

Table 1-2: Network Media Characteristics

Media	Cost	Bandwidth (typical)	EMI	Snooping	Max. Distance
UTP	Low	10–100 Mbps	Medium	Medium	100 meters
STP	Medium	16 Mbps	Low	Low	100 meters
Coaxial (thick)	Medium	10 Mbps	Low	Low	500 meters
Coaxial (thin)	Medium	10 Mbps	Low	Low	185 meters
Fiber optic	High	100 Mbps–2 Gbps	None	None	100+ kilometers
Infrared	Medium to high	1–16 Mbps	None	Low	Varies
Radio	High	1–10 Mbps	High	High	25 meters–1 kilometer
Microwave	High	10 Mbps	Medium	Medium	Global

In the Real World

The bandwidth values listed in Table 1-2 are not theoretical maximum values, but the rates provided by the typical implementations of each type of media.

Unshielded Twisted Pair (UTP)

UTP is the most common type of network cable in use today. UTP consists of one or more pairs of insulated copper wires. The wires are twisted together to reduce crosstalk, and enclosed in a plastic insulator. UTP is the type of cable used in telephone systems.

UTP cables are generally wired using RJ-45 jacks and plugs. These are 8-conductor connectors similar to the RJ-11 connectors used in telephone cables. UTP is inexpensive and easy to install compared with other types of cable, although the different types of UTP vary in cost.

Copper wire has a high level of attenuation. UTP cable is limited to transmission distances of 100 meters or less. UTP is more susceptible to interference (EMI) than most types of cable, and is vulnerable to eavesdropping since its own emissions are not shielded.

Types of UTP cable are defined by the EIA standards, which specify three categories of cable. Category 3 is the minimum requirement for networking, and Category 5 is the highest-quality network cable. The UTP categories and the bandwidth they can support are summarized in Table 1-3.

Table 1-3: Standards for UTP Cable

Category	Maximum Data Transfer Rate	Description
3	10 Mbps	Least expensive network cable; commonly used
4	16 Mbps	Medium quality; rarely used
5	100 Mbps	Highest quality

Shielded Twisted Pair (STP)

STP cable is similar to UTP, but includes a foil or wire mesh shield between the wire pairs and the outer insulation. The shield is electrically grounded, and reduces emissions and susceptibility to EMI.

STP cable is used in some Token Ring and AppleTalk networks. STP is more expensive than UTP, and its thickness and rigidity make it more difficult to install. It also uses special grounded connectors, adding to the expense.

STP uses the same copper wire as UTP and has the same level of attenuation, and therefore the same maximum distance of about 100 meters. However, it is much less susceptible to EMI and eavesdropping. The reduced interference allows for a higher bandwidth, potentially as high as 500 Mbps.

Coaxial

Coaxial cable consists of a single thick copper wire surrounded by an insulator. A shield surrounding the insulator is used as the second conductor, and is encased in an outer insulation. One type of coaxial cable is that used for cable television.

The shielding makes coaxial cable less susceptible to EMI and emissions than UTP. The cable used in most networks is either Thick Ethernet (RG-8) or Thin Ethernet (RG-58).

Thin coaxial cable is less expensive than the highest quality (Category 5) UTP, but is more difficult to install due to its thickness, its lack of flexibility, and the connectors used. The generally available types of coaxial cable are described in Table 1-4.

Table 1-4: Types of Coaxial Cable

Type	Impedance	Common Use
RG-8	50 ohms	Thick Ethernet (thicknet)
RG-11	50 ohms	Thick Ethernet (thicknet)
RG-58	50 ohms	Thin Ethernet (thinnet)
RG-59	75 ohms	Cable TV
RG-62	93 ohms	ARCnet

Fiber Optic

A fiber optic cable consists of a thin glass or clear plastic fiber encased in a protective jacket. Signals are sent through the cable in the form of light.

There are two types of fiber optic cable: single-mode, which uses a single wavelength, and multimode, which uses multiple wavelengths in the same cable.

Fiber optic cable is completely invulnerable to EMI, and has no detectable emissions. It and its associated equipment are expensive compared to other types of cable, and the most difficult to install. Single-mode cable is much more expensive than multimode cable.

The advantages of fiber are high bandwidth (up to 2 Gbps [gigabits per second]) and extremely low attenuation. Fiber cables can reach distances ranging from several miles for multimode cable to hundreds of miles for single-mode cable.

Infrared

Wireless infrared networking systems use modulated beams of infrared light to transmit data. These types of networks require a line of sight, and are generally used for short distances, such as networks within buildings or between nearby buildings.

Infrared communications are not subject to EMI, but are vulnerable to obstructions (such as weather conditions) and bright light, and susceptible to eavesdropping. There are two types of infrared networks:

- *Point-to-point networks* use a focused beam, usually generated by a laser. They are less vulnerable to dispersion and can theoretically be used for long-distance networking, although the need for precise alignment between receiver and transmitter and the vulnerability to obstructions often makes this impractical. Bandwidth can be as high as 16 Mbps.

- *Broadcast networks* use a less focused beam that disperses rapidly. These systems can transmit to multiple workstations at once, but are much more vulnerable to dispersion, limiting their useful distance and bandwidth. Bandwidth is usually no more than 1 Mbps.

Radio

The most common type of wireless networks use radio waves. Radio-based networks have a reasonably high bandwidth, but are very sensitive to EMI and eavesdropping. Also, many radio frequencies are regulated by the FCC and are unavailable for use without a license. There are three basic types of radio links:

Low power single frequency
This type of system is best suited for small areas, such as within a building. It uses a lower-power transmitter on a single radio frequency. The available range is approximately 30 meters. This is the lowest-cost method of radio networking. Bandwidth may be as high as 10 Mbps.

High power single frequency
This system also uses a single frequency, but at a higher power. This allows for a much greater range, often covering an entire metropolitan area. Bandwidth is typically 10 Mbps. The greater range makes this type of network the most vulnerable to eavesdropping.

Spread-spectrum
These systems use multiple frequencies, primarily to avoid eavesdropping. This is done in two ways: *direct sequence modulation* sends packets sequentially over several different frequencies, while *frequency hopping* transmissions change frequencies at scheduled intervals known to both ends. Both of these are significantly less vulnerable to EMI and snooping than other radio networks.

Microwave

Another type of wireless communication uses microwaves, which are similar to radio waves but at a higher frequency. Higher frequencies are less vulnerable to interference and snooping, and can provide greater bandwidth. Two common types of microwave networks are in use:

Terrestrial
This method provides for line-of-sight communication, usually across a short distance. Bandwidth can be as high as 10 Mbps. Microwaves are still vulnerable to interference and eavesdropping, although not as much as conventional radio waves.

Satellite
This method relays microwave transmissions via a satellite, allowing for a nearly global range. The bandwidth can be as high as 10 Mbps, but the satellite relays do cause delays that may impair real-time communication. These systems are more expensive than other wireless media.

Network Cards

PCs and some other computers use *network interface cards*, or NICs, to connect to the network. A NIC is installed in a bus slot (ISA, EISA, or PCI) and provides one or more connectors to be attached to network media.

Network cards use a *transceiver* to communicate with network media. This is a device that translates between the card's digital output and the network media's signaling method. Most cards have the transceiver built in. Some cards, such as most 10Base5 Ethernet cards, require a separate transceiver.

Network cards in PCs require one or more resources. These can include the following:

Interrupt (IRQ)
> One of the available lines used by hardware to notify the processor when data is being transmitted or recieved. PC interrupts are numbered from 0–15.

I/O Address
> An address within the bottom 1 MB of memory to be used as a communication buffer for the hardware.

High Memory Address
> An area of memory above 1 MB. This is usually used when a larger area of memory is needed.

DMA Channel
> DMA (direct memory access) allows hardware to access the computer's RAM without using the CPU. This is often used for high-performance hardware.

Network cards typically require a single interrupt (IRQ) and an I/O address in low memory. Several NICs can be installed in a single computer for connection to different network segments, but this requires more available interrupts and addresses.

When you install a network card you must configure its settings. While older cards used DIP switches or jumpers for this purpose, most newer cards include a DOS or Windows-based configuration utility that can save the settings in non-volatile memory. Some of the typical settings for NICs are described in Table 1-5.

Table 1-5: Typical Network Interface Card Settings

Setting	Possible Values	Description	Possible Issues
Interrupt (IRQ)	0–15	Most cards require a single free interrupt.	This setting must be chosen carefully to avoid conflicts.
I/O address	0x100 to 0xEFF	Most cards require a 32-byte block of memory.	0x200–0x370 are typical settings. Conflicts are possible, but not common.
High memory address	Varies with memory size	Some cards use an additional area in high memory.	Rarely causes conflicts.

Table 1-5: Typical Network Interface Card Settings (continued)

Setting	Possible Values	Description	Possible Issues
DMA channel	0–2	High-performance cards may use a DMA address.	Conflicts are likely with sound cards or SCSI controllers.
Trans-ceiver/ Port	Coax, UTP, etc.	For combination NICs, specify which type of media is attached to the card.	Some cards set this automatically; otherwise, an incorrect setting will prevent network access.

Communications ports, printer ports, sound cards, and other devices may also be using IRQs and other resources. If two devices attempt to use the same resources, a conflict occurs. This usually results in one or both of the devices not functioning properly, and may prevent the computer from booting.

On the Exam

For the exam, you should be aware of all of the above resource settings. IRQ and I/O address settings are the ones most likely to cause conflicts, and the ones most likely to appear on the Networking Essentials exam.

The Device Manager in Windows 95 allows you to display a list of currently used interrupts and other resources to find an available setting. Older cards that are not supported by the OS may not be included in this listing. The Resources tab in Windows NT's WINMSD utility provides the same information.

Interrupts (IRQs) are the most likely cause of a conflict. Commonly available IRQs include 5, 9, 10, 11, and 15. Table 1-6 shows the interrupts in a typical PC and their typical assignments.

Table 1-6: Standard PC Interrupts and Availability

IRQ	Standard Function	Available?
0	System timer	Never
1	Keyboard	Never
2	Interrupt controller	Never
3	COM2 and COM4	Sometimes; may require disabling COM port
4	COM1 and COM3	Sometimes; may require disabling COM port
5	LPT2 or sound card	Often
6	Floppy disk controller	Rarely
7	LPT1	Sometimes; may require disabling printer port
8	CMOS/Real-time clock	Never
9	IRQ2 cascade	Usually

Table 1-6: Standard PC Interrupts and Availability (continued)

IRQ	Standard Function	Available?
10	Primary SCSI controller	Often
11	Secondary SCSI controller	Often
12	PS/2 (bus) mouse	Sometimes
13	Math coprocessor	Never
14	Primary IDE controller	Rarely
15	Secondary IDE controller	Often; may require disabling second IDE controller

---

On the Exam

A common type of Network Essentials exam question lists the devices installed in a computer and asks you to determine an available IRQ, or determine which device is conflicting with the NIC. You are expected to know the typical Interrupt settings given in Table 1-6.

LAN Topologies and Architectures

A network's *topology* is the configuration, or shape, of the wiring used in the network. Network *architectures* are standards for communication, such as Ethernet and Token Ring. This section describes the common topologies and architectures.

In the Real World

The terms *network architecture* and *network topology* are often used interchangeably, even in some Microsoft documentation. For clarity throughout this book, topology refers to the configuration of network wiring and communication (star, bus, ring), and architecture refers to standards (Ethernet, Token Ring, ARCnet).

Network Topologies

Different types of LANs are wired in different ways. The nodes might be connected to each other, to a central hub, or to a continuous cable (bus). The four major network topologies are illustrated in Figure 1-2.

Each type of network has a physical topology (the actual wiring) and a logical topology (the path data follows). In some types of networks these are identical. However, some networks use different physical and logical topologies. For example, Token Ring networks use a physical star topology and a logical ring topology.

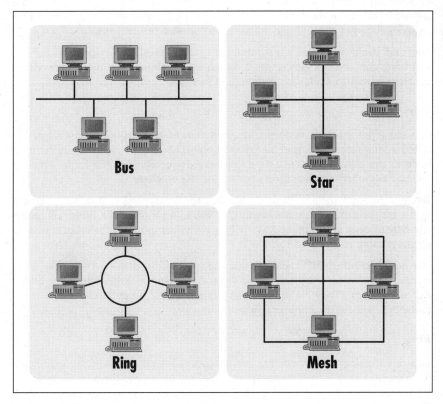

Figure 1-2: The common network topologies

On the Exam

For the exam, you should know the advantages and disadvantages of each of these topologies, as well as which network architectures (discussed later in this section) use each topology.

Bus

In a bus topology, a single cable supports an entire network segment. This cable is the *bus*, sometimes called a *backbone*. Nodes are attached at various points along the cable. Depending on the network architecture, nodes may be connected directly to the bus with T-connectors, or a cable called a *drop cable* can be connected between the bus and each node.

Bus networks typically use coaxial cable. Devices called *terminators* are used at either end of the bus. These absorb the signal to prevent signals from reflecting back and forth on the bus, which creates extra network traffic.

The bus topology is usually inexpensive for smaller networks, since no devices are required aside from the cable and connectors, and a minimum length of cable is required. Ethernet 10Base2 and 10Base5 are common bus networks.

The chief disadvantage of a bus topology is that a break at any point in the bus will bring the network down. Also, the coaxial cable used in these networks is generally harder to work with than twisted pair cable.

Star

In a star topology, each node is connected with its own cable to a central device called a *hub* (explained later in this section). The hub internally connects each node to the other nodes. Star-wired networks typically use UTP cable. Ethernet 10BaseT is the most common network with a star topology.

While a greater length of cable is required for this topology, it is more reliable than a bus because each node has its own cable. A problem in a cable will generally only affect a single node. Most hubs have visual indicators to make it easy to diagnose cable problems.

Star networks using UTP cable are often less expensive than bus networks using coaxial cable because the ease of wiring and inexpensive cable offsets the added expense of hubs. They are also easier to expand, since a new node can be wired to the hub without disconnecting other nodes.

Ring

In a ring topology, the nodes are connected to each other to form a circle. Each node receives signals from its upstream neighbor, and passes them on to its downstream neighbor. Ring networks often use token passing, as described in IEEE 802.5, for media access.

FDDI and Token Ring are two common networking systems that use ring topologies. Token Ring networks are actually physically wired as a star, but use a special hub that is wired internally as a ring, and function in a logical ring.

Ring topologies offer the advantage of equal access to the network media through token passing, so they are often used in networks with many clients or with high-speed requirements. The main disadvantage of a ring topology is the same as a bus: a single node's failure can disrupt the entire network. Ring networks can also be difficult to troubleshoot and expand.

Mesh

A mesh topology provides fault tolerance through redundant links. In this system, each node is connected to every other node with separate cables. Thus, a three-node network would use three cables; a four-node network would use eight cables; and a 10-node network would require 45 cables.

The main advantage of this system is a high degree of reliability. Any cable (or even several, depending on the size) could be severed without any nodes losing access to the network. The obvious disadvantage is that mesh topologies require large amounts of cable, making them very expensive to install and expand.

A mesh topology can use routers (described below) to choose the best path for each network transmission. This allows the redundant links to provide increased efficiency as well as reliability.

Hybrid

A hybrid topology is any combination of the above topologies. One common hybrid topology is a star bus, in which several star-wired network segments are interconnected with a bus. This topology is useful in networks where groups of workstations are close together, but several distant groups need to be connected.

Another hybrid topology is a star ring, or star-wired ring. This is the topology used by Token Ring networks. The wiring forms a star topology, but the hub is internally connected as a ring.

The mesh topology, while too expensive to be practical in itself, is useful in hybrid forms. For example, workstations might be connected by a star topology while three or four critical servers are wired in a mesh. This adds reliability to complex networks.

Connectivity Devices

The network topologies above can use several types of connectivity devices. Some are required (such as hubs for star networks) and others provide optional features; for example, a repeater can extend the length of a bus network segment. These devices are summarized by Table 1-7, and described in detail below.

Table 1-7: Network Connectivity Devices and Characteristics

Device	OSI Layer	Purpose
Repeater	Physical	Connects network segments to extend total length
Hub	Physical	Connects the nodes to a central point in a star topology
Switch	Physical, Data link	Connects nodes to a central point; sends packets to nodes based on MAC address
Bridge	Data link	Filters and moves data between segments based on MAC address
Router	Network	Filters and moves data between segments based on logical address
Brouter	Data link/Network	Combines bridge and router capabilities
Gateway	Application to Transport	Translates between protocols and data formats

---

On the Exam

The purposes of each of these devices are common topics for the Networking Essentials exam. You should also know the OSI layer(s) for each device.

Repeaters

A repeater is used to connect two network segments. Each network architecture has a maximum cable length due to attenuation. Repeaters extend the length of the network beyond this maximum by boosting the signal strength.

A simple device that boosts the strength of a signal is called an *amplifier*. Amplifiers are used in networks with analog (broadband) signaling. In digital (baseband) signaling, repeaters regenerate the signal. This reduces the level of noise on the cable as well as increasing signal strength.

Repeaters add delays to network transmissions, so each network architecture limits the number of repeaters that can be chained together, and thus the number of network segments.

Repeaters operate at the physical layer of the OSI model: they simply echo the signal, with no processing or filtering. Repeaters can be used between different media types (such as coaxial cable and UTP) but do not translate between network architectures (such as Ethernet and Token Ring).

Hubs

Hubs are used to connect the nodes in networks with star topologies. Each node is connected via a single cable to the hub, and the hub provides the connectivity between nodes. Hubs are sometimes referred to as *concentrators*.

Like repeaters, hubs operate at the physical layer of the OSI model. Hubs come with a fixed number of ports, typically 8 or 16. Hubs can be chained together to allow more nodes to attach to the network. There are three types of hubs:

- *Passive hubs* simply connect the nodes.

- *Active hubs* require power, and regenerate the signals between the nodes, acting as a repeater. These are occasionally known as *multi-port repeaters*.

- *Intelligent hubs* perform some processing or optimization on the data. For example, a *switching hub* performs a switching function, described in the next section. (In this case the hub functions at a higher OSI layer).

Switches

A switch, or switching hub, is a specialized type of hub that minimizes traffic over network segments. While a normal hub forwards all of the incoming traffic to each of the ports, a switch forwards each packet to the appropriate port based on its destination MAC address.

Switching hubs are often used to speed up crowded networks. Since each node receives only the packets it needs, more network bandwidth is available to each node. When switches are used with Ethernet, the network architecture is sometimes called *Switched Ethernet*.

Bridges

A bridge is used to connect two or more network segments. A bridge adds to the capabilities of a repeater by monitoring the MAC address of each packet, and

---

filtering packets that don't need to be sent to all segments. Thus, you can reduce network traffic by dividing the network into segments using a bridge.

If a packet's destination address is for the same segment as its source, it is discarded by the bridge. Otherwise, it is sent to the correct segment based on its destination. Network broadcast messages are forwarded to all segments. Bridges maintain a table of addresses and their appropriate network segments.

Bridges operate at the data link layer of the OSI model. Like repeaters, bridges can connect different transmission media, but they perform no translation on the packets.

Bridges are more expensive than repeaters, but can be used to increase network bandwidth by discarding unneeded packets. However, they do add a small delay to transmissions due to their need to examine the MAC addresses of packets.

Routers

Routers are similar to bridges in that they connect two or more network segments (also called *subnets*) and send packets to their appropriate destinations, and can thus be used to reduce network traffic in each segment. However, routers work at the network layer of the OSI model. Rather than the physical (MAC) address, routers use the logical (network) address, such as an IP or IPX address.

Unlike bridges, routers can connect networks using different architectures (such as Ethernet and Token Ring). There are two types of routers:

- *Static routers* use a fixed routing table entered by the administrator.

- *Dynamic routers* maintain a routing table intelligently. Multiple dynamic routers can use routing protocols to notify each other of routing table changes.

When a number of dynamic routers are in use, one of the following routing protocols is used for communication between the routers:

RIP (Router Information Protocol)
> RIP can be used in TCP/IP and IPX/SPX networks. This is a *distance vector routing protocol.* Its routing table lists the number of hops, or nodes a packet must be forwarded through, for each destination. Packets are sent by the route that requires the least number of hops.

OSPF (Open Shortest Path First)
> OSPF is a newer routing protocol used with TCP/IP networks. This is a *link state routing protocol.* Its main improvement over RIP is that while RIP routers frequently retransmit their routing table, adding traffic to the network, OSPF routers only broadcast notices of changes to the routing table.

While hubs, repeaters, and bridges are usually hardware devices, a router can be either a standalone device or a computer running routing software. A Windows NT computer with multiple network cards can act as a static or dynamic router.

Routers are more sophisticated than bridges, and work better for larger-scale networks. Their disadvantages include higher cost and less available bandwidth due to the messages used by routing protocols. Most modern routers add a negligible amount of delay to network transmissions.

Routers only work with certain network protocols, called *routable protocols*. Common routable protocols include IPX, TCP/IP, and AppleTalk. Microsoft's NetBEUI protocol, often used with Windows NT and Windows 95, is non-routable. Thus, a bridge is a better choice for connecting NetBEUI segments.

In the Real World

Some exam questions may ask what the appropriate connectivity device is to segment a particular network. If the network uses NetBEUI, a bridge is the obvious answer. In practice, however, NetBEUI is not really suitable for large networks. If network segmentation is necessary due to high traffic or number of nodes, it's probably time to consider a different protocol, such as TCP/IP or IPX/SPX.

Brouters

A brouter is a hybrid device that combines the functions of a router and a bridge. If a packet is sent using a routable protocol, it is routed based on its network address. If the packet is sent in a non-routable protocol, it is routed or filtered based on its MAC address.

Many of the hardware routers available today include a bridging function, and thus are actually brouters. Because they combine the functionality of routers and bridges, brouters operate at both the network and data-link layers of the OSI model. They are most useful when both routable and non-routable protocols are in use on the same network.

Gateways

A gateway is another type of device that connects network segments. Gateways are used to translate between protocols and data formats. Gateways can connect vastly different networks; for example, a common type of gateway connects PC networks with mainframe networks using the SNA architecture.

A gateway can perform a single translation or several. For example, one type of gateway might connect a PC LAN to a UNIX network and translate a large number of protocols. A more specialized gateway might be used to translate between different email systems (such as Exchange and SMTP).

Depending on their particular functions, gateways operate at layers of the OSI model ranging from the application layer to the transport layer. Gateways are usually software services running on computers rather than dedicated hardware devices.

Gateways provide functionality beyond that of a router in translating between networks, and should only be used when these features are necessary.

On the Exam

The term *gateway* is sometimes used as a synonym for router, even in some Windows NT configuration dialogs. For the exam, however, the term almost always refers to a device that translates data, or is used to connect to mainframes or other non-PC networks.

Ethernet

Ethernet is the most common network architecture worldwide. It was developed by Xerox, Intel, and DEC in the late 1960s, and revised as Ethernet 2.0 in 1982. Ethernet networks use the CSMA/CD (carrier sense multiple access with collision detection) media access method, defined in IEEE 802.3.

There are three 10-Mbps Ethernet standards for different media: 10BaseT (UTP cable), 10Base2 (thin coaxial cable, or thinnet), and 10Base5 (thick coaxial cable, or thicknet). The characteristics of these network types are summarized in Table 1-8. Each is discussed in further detail in the sections below.

Table 1-8: Ethernet Specifications

Specification	10BaseT	10Base2	10Base5
Max. segments	1024	5	5
Max. repeaters/hubs	4	4	4
Max. segments with nodes	1024	3	3
Max. segment length	100 meters (328 feet)	185 meters (607 feet)	500 meters (1640 feet)
Max. nodes/segment	1	30	100
Max. nodes/network	1024	90	300
Min. distance between nodes	N/A	.5 meters (1.6 feet)	2.5 meters (8.2 feet)

On the Exam

These statistics are often needed to solve scenario problems in the MCSE exam, particularly the length and node limitations. Be warned that measurements in the exam may be in feet or meters; you can convert meters to feet by multiplying by 3.28.

10BaseT

This is currently the most popular Ethernet implementation. 10BaseT Ethernet uses unshielded twisted pair (UTP) cable, Category 3 or Category 5. This system uses a physical star topology with a central hub, but the hub's internal wiring forms a logical bus topology. 10BaseT supports active and intelligent hubs.

10BaseT networks are easy to install because UTP is easy to handle. They are relatively inexpensive, and easy to troubleshoot, particularly with the diagnostic capabilities of active and intelligent hubs.

In the Real World

The 10BaseT standard does not actually specify a distance limitation; the widely known 100 meter limitation is based on the limitations of UTP cable (described earlier, in "Media Types"). The 100-meter figure may appear in the exam, however.

10Base2

10Base2 (thinnet) uses thin coaxial cable in a bus topology. The cable should be RG-58 A/U (standard) or RG-58 C/U (military spec) shielded cable. A third type, RG-58 /U, uses a solid rather than stranded core. This type of cable may work, but does not meet the IEEE specification and will be unreliable.

On the Exam

Be wary of exam questions that mention RG-58/U cable. This type of cable should not be used with thinnet networks.

A continuous cable is wired to form the bus. Sections of cable are connected with BNC connectors to a BNC barrel connector (to extend the segment) or a BNC T-connector (to attach a node). Both ends of the bus are terminated with 50-ohm BNC terminators. At least one of the terminators in each network segment should be connected to an electrical ground.

Thinnet is seldom used in large-scale wiring projects today due to the difficulty and expense of wiring coaxial cable. It also has the disadvantages of a bus topology—a single cable break can bring down the network. However, it is ideally suited for temporary networks (such as in a new office or training room) since it can be set up and taken down easily, and does not require any extra equipment (such as hubs).

Thin Ethernet is governed by the 5-4-3 rule: you can have no more than five segments in the network, connected by four repeaters, and only three of the segments can be populated with nodes. Since 30 nodes are supported per segment, this limits the total nodes on a network to 90. The number of collisions makes an Ethernet network with this many nodes impractical without a switch or separate segments, so this is not a major limitation.

10Base5

10Base5, also known as thick Ethernet or thicknet, uses RG-8 cable. This is a thicker and more expensive type of cable. Thicknet is rarely used in current networks, although it does have some advantages over thinnet: it supports a greater maximum segment length (500 meters) and more nodes per segment. For this reason, thicknet is sometimes used as a backbone to interconnect thinnet segments.

Due to the thickness of the cable, thicknet cable uses taps that pierce the bus rather than connectors that require cutting the cable. Taps are attached to an external transceiver, which in turn connects to the AUI port on a network card.

The thicknet bus is terminated with 50-ohm RG-8 terminators on either end, one of which should be grounded. Thicknet follows the same 5-4-3 rule as thinnet, but allows up to 100 nodes per segment, providing for a total of 300 nodes per network.

Fast Ethernet

Fast Ethernet, also known as 100BaseT, is a new standard for 100 Mbps Ethernet. Fast Ethernet can use two-pair Category 5 cable or four-pair Category 3–5 cable.

100BaseT uses a physical star topology identical to that used by 10BaseT, but requires that all equipment (hubs, NICs, and repeaters) support 100-Mbps speeds. Some NICs and hubs can support both standards, but all devices on the network need to be configured to use the same standard.

Several manufacturers developed 100-Mbps Ethernet devices before 100BaseT became a standard. The most popular of these, 100VG-AnyLAN, is still widely used. This standard uses a demand priority access method rather than CSMA/CD, and supports networks that combine Ethernet and Token Ring packets.

Token Ring

The Token Ring architecture is defined in IEEE 802.5. IBM has further defined the standard to include particular types of devices and cables. Token Ring uses a logical ring topology and a physical star topology. The hubs used for Token Ring are called multistation access units, or MAUs.

The Token Ring standard supports either 4-Mbps or 16-Mbps speeds. Cable can be STP, UTP, or fiber. One popular wiring scheme uses Category 5 cable. There are also a variety of cable types defined by IBM (referred to as Type 1 through Type 9). Distances between nodes can range from 45 meters for UTP to a kilometer or more for fiber optic cable.

Token Ring networks use a token-passing access scheme. A token data frame is passed from one computer to the next around the ring. Each computer can transmit data only when it has the token. This access method provides equal access to the network for all nodes, and handles heavy loads better than Ethernet's contention-based method.

The nodes in a Token Ring network monitor each other for reliability. The first computer in the network becomes an Active Monitor, and the others are Passive Monitors. Each computer monitors its nearest upstream neighbor. When an error occurs, the computer broadcasts a *beacon* packet indicating the error.

The NICs in all computers respond to the beacon by running self-tests, and removing themselves from the network if necessary. Nodes in the network can also automatically remove packets sent by a computer that is having a problem. This makes Token Ring a reliable choice for networking.

ARCnet

ARCnet, developed in 1977 by Datapoint Corporation, is an older standard that has largely been replaced by Ethernet in current networks. ARCnet uses RG-62 coaxial cable in a star, bus, or hybrid physical topology. This networking scheme supports active hubs and passive hubs, which must be connected to an active hub.

ARCnet requires 93-ohm terminators at the end of bus cables, and on unused ports of passive hubs. It supports a maximum of 255 nodes per network. ARCnet supports UTP, coaxial, or fiber-optic cable. The distance between nodes is 400 feet with UTP cable, and higher for coaxial or fiber-optic cable.

ARCnet uses a token-passing scheme similar to that of token ring. ARCnet networks support a bandwidth of 2.5 Mbps. Newer standards (ARCnet Plus and TCNS) support speeds of 20 Mbps and 100 Mbps, but have not really caught on.

FDDI

FDDI (Fiber Distributed Data Interface) is a high-speed, reliable, long-distance networking scheme often used for network backbones and networks that require high bandwidth. FDDI uses fiber optic cable wired in a true ring. It supports speeds up to 100 Mbps and a maximum distance between nodes of 100 kilometers (62 miles).

FDDI uses a token-passing scheme wired with two rings, primary and secondary. The primary ring is used for normal networking. When a failure is detected, the secondary ring is used in the opposite direction to compensate for the failure of the primary ring.

The advantages of FDDI networks are their high speed, long distance, and reliability. The token-passing scheme used by FDDI is also more sophisticated than that of Token Ring; it allows multiple packets to be on the ring at once, and allows certain nodes to be given a higher priority than the rest. The disadvantage of FDDI is its high cost and the difficulty of installing and maintaining fiber optic cable.

LocalTalk

AppleTalk is the network architecture developed by Apple to work with Macintosh computers. AppleTalk actually supports three network transports: Ethernet, Token Ring, and a dedicated system called LocalTalk.

LocalTalk is traditionally wired in a star or hybrid topology using custom connectors and STP cable. A popular third-party system allows ordinary phone cable to be used instead of STP. LocalTalk supports up to 32 nodes per network. The implementations of Ethernet and Token Ring (EtherTalk and TokenTalk) support more sophisticated networks.

LocalTalk uses the CSMA/CA access method. Rather than detect collisions as with Ethernet, this method requires nodes to wait a certain amount of time after detecting an existing signal on the network before attempting to transmit, avoiding most collisions.

Common Network Protocols

As mentioned earlier in this chapter, *network protocols* are sets of rules and standards for data communications over networks. A network architecture (such as Ethernet) can support multiple protocols, and even multiple protocols used concurrently.

Protocols are typically organized into protocol suites, or sets of compatible protocols. These are also referred to as *protocol stacks*. A stack includes protocols for several different layers of the OSI model. Lower-level protocols provide services for use by upper-level protocols. The highest level protocols communicate directly with applications.

Communications protocols can be divided into two basic types, connection-oriented and connectionless:

* *Connection-oriented protocols* establish a connection, or *virtual circuit*, before communicating, and disconnect it when finished. Connection-oriented protocols generally have a lower speed due to the bandwidth used for session maintenance.

* *Connectionless protocols* do not establish a virtual circuit. Data is sent without establishing a connection, and may be sent at any time. These protocols have low overhead, and are generally used where speed is a high priority.

Another distinction between protocols is their reliability. Some protocols send acknowledgments for each transmitted packet. This makes for a more reliable connection, but leaves less bandwidth for actual data transmission. These are called *reliable* protocols. Protocols without acknowledgments are known as *unreliable*, although this does not necessarily mean they are undependable.

On the Exam

While reliability is a separate criteria and can exist in both connection-oriented and connectionless protocols, some exam questions assume that connection-oriented protocols are reliable and connectionless protocols are unreliable.

The common protocols used in Windows NT networks are TCP/IP, NetBEUI, and IPX/SPX. Two vendor-specific protocols, AppleTalk and DLC, are also supported. The characteristics of these protocols are summarized in Table 1-9. The protocols are explained in detail in the sections below.

Table 1-9: Common Network Protocols and Characteristics

Protocol	Overhead	Routable?	Typical Application
TCP/IP	Medium	Yes	Large networks; Internet and UNIX compatibility
NetBEUI	Low	No	Small Windows-based networks
IPX/SPX	Medium	Yes	NetWare compatibility
AppleTalk	Medium	Yes	Apple Macintosh compatibility
DLC	Medium	No	IBM mainframe compatibility; some network printers

TCP/IP

The TCP/IP protocol suite was developed primarily for UNIX systems, and is the protocol used throughout the Internet. Windows NT's implementation of TCP/IP allows clients to access Internet services, and is also a popular transport protocol for Windows NT networks.

The TCP/IP suite includes a wide variety of protocols, including its namesakes, TCP (Transmission Control Protocol) and IP (Internet Protocol). The protocols in this suite are organized according to the DOD Reference model, a model similar to the OSI model but using only four layers.

The advantages of the TCP/IP protocol suite are the features provided by its wide array of protocols, its support for routing, and its standardization throughout the Internet and UNIX communities. Its main disadvantage is that it requires more effort in administration than other protocols.

On the Exam

The TCP/IP protocol suite is explained in more detail in *MCSE: The Electives in a Nutshell*, which includes coverage of the TCP/IP MCSE exam. For the Network Essentials exam, you should understand what TCP/IP is and the specific protocols mentioned in the following sections.

TCP and UDP

TCP and UDP are the main protocols in the DOD Host-to-Host layer, roughly equivalent to the OSI model's transport layer:

- TCP (Transmission Control Protocol) is a connection-oriented, reliable protocol with acknowledgements. It is dependable but has a high overhead.

- UDP (User Datagram Protocol) is a connectionless, unreliable protocol with a low overhead. It can transfer data faster but does not send acknowledgments.

NFS

NFS (Network File System) is the TCP/IP suite's equivalent of file sharing. This protocol operates at the Process/Application layer of the DOD model, similar to the application layer of the OSI model. NFS support is not included with Windows NT, but is available separately.

NFS provides access to entire file systems, or portions of them, on remote machines and makes them act as a subdirectory on the client machine. In Windows NT networks, NFS can be used to interconnect with UNIX hosts for file sharing.

SLIP and PPP

SLIP (Serial Line Internet Protocol) and PPP (Point-to-Point Protocol) are two protocols commonly used for dial-up access to the Internet. They are typically used with TCP/IP; while SLIP works only with TCP/IP, PPP can be used with other protocols. These are commonly used with RAS (Remote Access Service) in Windows NT networks.

SLIP was the first protocol for dial-up Internet access. It operates at the physical layer of the OSI model, and provides a simple interface to a UNIX or other dial-up host for Internet access. SLIP does not provide security, so authentication is handled through prompts before initiating the SLIP connection.

PPP is a more recent development. It operates at the physical and data link layers of the OSI model. In addition to the features of SLIP, PPP supports data compression, security (authentication), and error control. PPP can also dynamically assign network addresses.

Since PPP provides easier authentication and better security, it should be used for dial-up connections whenever possible. However, you may need to use SLIP to communicate with dial-up servers (particularly older UNIX machines and dedicated hardware servers) that don't support PPP.

IPX and SPX

IPX and SPX are protocols developed by Novell for use in NetWare networks. They were based on protocols used in Xerox's XNS network architecture. IPX (Internetwork Packet exchange) is a connectionless protocol that works at the network layer of the OSI model, and SPX (Sequenced Packet exchange) is a connection-oriented protocol that works at the transport layer.

Microsoft's implementation of IPX and SPX for Windows NT is called NWLink. IPX and SPX are commonly used in Windows NT networks that require connectivity with Novell NetWare networks. However, these protocols are easier to configure than TCP/IP and are routable, so they make a good alternative for some Windows NT networks, particularly small peer-to-peer networks. However, TCP/IP is more suitable for larger LANs and WANs.

Frame types are one aspect of IPX networks that sometimes does require configuration. The frame type determines the order and type of data included in a packet. Typical frame types used in NetWare networks are 802.2 and 802.3. Windows NT and Windows 95 can detect frame types automatically, but you may need to manually configure the frame type if a computer is unable to communicate with other IPX/SPX nodes.

NetBEUI

NetBEUI (NetBIOS Extended User Interface) is a transport-layer protocol developed by Microsoft and IBM. NetBEUI was mainly intended as a basic protocol to support NetBIOS (Network Basic Input/Output System), the Windows standard for workstation naming, communication, and file sharing.

NetBEUI is a fast protocol with a low overhead, which makes it a good choice for small networks. However, it is a non-routable protocol. Networks that use NetBEUI can use bridges for traffic management, but cannot use routers. Another disadvantage is its proprietary nature: NetBEUI is supported by few systems other than Windows.

On the Exam

Although NetBEUI was developed by Microsoft and was the default protocol for some operating systems (such as Windows for Workgroups and Windows 95), Microsoft recommends TCP/IP over NetBEUI for most Windows NT networks.

AppleTalk

AppleTalk is Apple's suite of protocols for networking, file sharing, and printer sharing between Macintosh computers. AppleTalk can function on Ethernet, Token Ring, or LocalTalk networks. Windows NT Workstation and Server include an implementation of AppleTalk.

Microsoft Services for Macintosh (SFM), included with Windows NT Server, provides additional support for Macintosh computers. SFM allows Macintosh clients to access Windows NT servers as if they were Macintosh servers, and to access Windows NT's shared files and printers.

DLC

DLC (Data Link Control) is a transport protocol developed by IBM for SNA (Systems Network Architecture), a protocol suite used for network communication with mainframe computers. Particular versions of DLC are called SDLC (Synchronous Data Link Control) and HDLC (High-level Data Link Control).

Along with its uses in mainframe communication, DLC is the protocol used by many network-aware printers, such as Hewlett-Packard's JetDirect interface. Windows NT includes support for DLC that can be installed to use these printers as NT printers.

Common WAN Architectures

While LANs typically use cable wired specifically for the network in a single location, WANs and MANs (Metropolitan-Area Networks) usually use public or leased lines provided by a third-party carrier.

WAN services can be provided by dedicated lines or switched (shared) networks. Public networks are characterized by their switching methods, the methods in which data is routed between points in the network. Three switching methods are commonly used:

Circuit switching
> Circuit switching is a connection-oriented method of communication. A circuit is dedicated to the connection, and a connection must be specifically established when needed and disconnected when not needed.

Message switching
> Message switching is a connectionless method of communication. Individual message units are sent across the network with routing information without establishing a dedicated circuit.

Packet switching
> Packet switching is a more efficient connectionless communication method. Packets (smaller than message units) are sent individually and can follow different routes to their destination. Some packet switching systems use virtual circuits for a logical connection, but don't use a dedicated physical connection.

On the Exam

The Networking Essentials exam may require you to choose switched or non-switched WAN links based on their advantages. Switched links are generally less expensive and allow networking with multiple locations; non-switched links are usually dedicated between two locations and provide a more consistent available bandwidth.

WAN connections typically require different (and more expensive) hardware than LAN connections. Typical WAN equipment includes specialized types of routers, CSU/DSUs (Channel Service Unit/Digital Service Unit), and *multiplexers*, which combine multiple signals (such as voice and data) for transmission on a single WAN connection.

A number of WAN technologies and public networks are available. FDDI, explained earlier in this chapter, can also be used for wide-area networks. The common WAN technologies are described in detail in the sections below.

PSTN

The PSTN (Public Service Telephone Network) is the telephone system used throughout the U.S. and many other countries. Although never intended for networking, telephone lines can be used for communications between computers.

A modem (modulator/demodulator) is used to interface between a computer and the telephone system. Modems convert data into audible tones and back. The fastest two-way modems currently available support a speed of 33.6 Kbps (kilobits per second).

On the Exam

Current modems advertise speeds up to 56 Kbps. These modems rely on digital equipment being used in the phone company's central office and in the facility (such as an Internet Service Provider) you are dialing into. The 56K speed also works in only one direction; the other direction supports 33.6-Kbps speeds.

RAS (Remote Access Service) under Windows NT and Dial-up Networking under Windows 95 provide networking over the PSTN through dial-up lines. This type of connection is usually only useful for temporary access that does not require high speeds. RAS also supports ISDN, described later in this section.

You can also lease dedicated analog phone lines to connect locations in a WAN. These are often used for voice communications between company locations, but can also support data through modems. This alternative allows continuous connections at modem speeds. Higher quality ("data grade") analog lines support speeds up to 56 Kbps.

Using the *multilink* feature of Windows NT RAS, you can use two or more modems to dial two or more modems at the same server. RAS aggregates the two connections into a single, faster connection. For example, two 28.8-Kbps modem connections could be combined for 56 Kbps of bandwidth.

DDS and Switched 56

DDS (Digital Data Service) is a type of dedicated digital line provided by phone carriers. DDS lines are more expensive than dedicated analog lines, but support a more consistent quality. DDS lines support a speed of 56 Kbps. A device called a CSU/DSU (Channel Service Unit/Digital Service Unit) is used to connect the network to the dedicated line.

Switched 56 is an alternative to DDS that provides the same type of connection, but in a circuit-switched format. The line is available on demand rather than continuously, and you are billed for the hours you use it. ISDN has largely replaced Switched 56 for this purpose.

ISDN

ISDN (Integrated Services Digital Network) was originally developed as a digital alternative to the standard PSTN telephone system for voice communications. It was introduced in 1984, but is only now being widely implemented in the U.S. There are two available ISDN packages:

- BRI (Basic Rate Interface) includes two B channels (64 Kbps apiece) for voice or data transmissions, and a D channel (16 Kbps) for call control. This is the ordinary consumer ISDN service.

- PRI (Primary Rate Interface) is a more expensive alternative that includes 23 B channels and one D channel. This is the equivalent of a T1 line, explained below.

ISDN's B channels are typically used for packet-switched data transmission, and the D channel is typically used for call control and switching; however, the D channel can also be used for data transmission in low-bandwidth applications.

T1-T4

A T1 line is a high-speed, dedicated, point-to-point leased line that includes 24 separate 64-Kbps channels for voice or data. Other lines of this type, called T-carrier lines, support larger numbers of channels. T1 and T3 lines are the most commonly used. T-carrier lines are summarized in Table 1-10.

Table 1-10: T-Carrier Lines

Carrier	Channels	Total Bandwidth
T1	24	1.544 Mbps
T2	96	6.312 Mbps
T3	672	44.736 Mbps
T4	4032	274.176 Mbps

While the specification for T-carrier lines does not mandate a particular media type, T1 and T2 are typically carried on copper wires, and T3 and T4 typically use fiber optic media. DS1, DS2, DS3, and DS4 are an alternate type of line equivalent to T1-T4, and typically use fiber optic media.

X.25

X.25 is a protocol developed in the 1970s for packet switching, allowing customers to share access to a PDN (Public Data Network). These networks, such as Sprintnet and Tymnet, were the most practical way to connect large companies at the time, and are still used by some companies.

PDNs are networks that have local dial-up access points in cities throughout the country, and use dedicated lines to network between these cities. Companies would dial up in two locations to connect their computers.

Computers, routers, or other devices that access a PDN using the X.25 protocols are called data terminal equipment, or DTEs. DTEs without built-in support for X.25 are attached to an external device called a packet assembler/disassembler, or PAD.

The X.25 protocol supports speeds up to 64 Kbps. This makes it impractical for many networks, but it is an inexpensive alternative for low-bandwidth applications. X.25 is a protocol with a relatively high overhead, since it provides error control and accounting for users of the network.

Frame Relay

Frame relay is a protocol used with leased lines to support speeds up to 1.544 Mbps. Frame relay uses packet switching over a phone company's network. Frame relay connections use a virtual circuit, called a PVC (private virtual circuit), to establish connections. Once established, connections use a low overhead and do not provide error correction.

A frame relay compatible router is used to attach the LAN to the frame relay line. Frame relay lines are available in speeds ranging from 56 Kbps to 1.544 Mbps, and varying proportionally in cost. One advantage of frame relay is that bandwidth is available on demand: you can install a line at 56K and later upgrade it to a higher speed by ordering the service from the carrier, usually without replacing any equipment.

SONET

SONET (Synchronous Optical Network) is a leased-line system using fiber optic media to support data speeds up to 2.4 Gbps. SONET services are sold based on optical carrier (OC) levels, as listed in Table 1-11. These are calculated as multiples of the OC-1 speed, 51.840 Mbps. OC-1 and OC-3 are the most commonly used SONET lines.

Table 1-11: SONET Optical Carrier Levels

Level	Bandwidth
OC-1	51.840 Mbps
OC-3	155 Mbps
OC-12	622 Mbps
OC-24	1.2 Gbps
OC-48	2.4 Gbps

ATM

ATM (Asynchronous Transfer Mode) is a high-speed packet switching format that supports speeds up to 622 Mbps. ATM can be used with T1 and T3 lines, FDDI, and SONET OC1 and OC3 lines.

ATM uses a technology called *cell switching*. Data is sent in 53-byte packets called cells. Because packets are small and uniform in size, they can be quickly routed by hardware switches. ATM uses a virtual circuit between connection points for high reliability over high-speed links.

Planning and Administration

When installing a new network, you should carefully consider several options. Planning begins with documenting the existing network (if any) and the requirements of users and management. The following factors should be considered in the planning of a network:

Network topology, architecture, and media
> The size of the building, the ease of wiring in walls and ceilings, and the need for WAN links should be considered to determine the appropriate network architecture and media. The limitations of the network media and architecture are the main factors in this decision.

NOS and server
> Choose a network operating system for workstations and servers, and choose whether to use a server-based or peer-to-peer network. The main factors here are the size of the network, future growth, and the type of security needed.

Server hardware
> If one or more servers will be used, determine the hardware requirements for the servers. This decision will be based on the number of users, the amount of disk storage needed, and the speed required.

Additional tasks involved in planning a network include planning security and user accounts, creating a naming scheme, and planning for fault tolerance. These are explained in the sections below.

User Accounts, Shares, and Security

Accounts must be created for each user who will access the network. An account consists of a user name and password. In a workgroup (peer-to-peer) network, a separate user account is created for each user at each workstation the user needs to access. In a server-based network, a single account provides access to the entire network.

In Windows NT, users are almost always given rights based on the groups they belong to. Groups range from the Users group, which contains all users, to the Administrators group, which gives administrative privileges to users. The default Windows NT Administrator account is a member of this group. You can also create groups for specific purposes and assign users to them.

Another security feature in Windows NT is *auditing*. This allows you to select categories of events to be logged to a file. For example, you can audit login attempts or disk accesses to a certain file. The Event Viewer utility, described later in this chapter, displays information collected by an audit.

Workgroup networks often use *shares*, or disk directories made available across the network. In Windows 95 and Windows NT, shares are accessed through the Network Neighborhood icon. They can also be accessed with a UNC (Universal Naming Convention) name. UNC names include a computer name and a share name:

```
\\computer\share
```

There are two methods of securing network shares, described in the sections below.

Share-Level Security

Share-level security is a basic level of security for shared files. A user who makes a directory (or printer) available as a share can assign a password to the share. Any other user who attempts to access the shared file or printer must know the password.

This level of security provides some protection from unauthorized access, but does not identify the user who is accessing the share. It is also an all or nothing security method. You can assign separate passwords for read-only or full access, but you cannot assign more specific permissions. This method is available in Windows 95 and Windows for Workgroups, but not in Windows NT.

The main disadvantage of share-level security is its lack of centralized control. Shares must be managed separately from the machines they are located on, and users must remember separate passwords for each share. As with peer-to-peer networking, share-level security works best in networks with 10 or fewer users.

User-Level Security

User-level security is a more sophisticated level of security requiring a user account at the workstation or a domain account in a server-based network. Each user has a unique account name and password used when they log on. Share access is granted to a list of user accounts.

This type of security also allows you to assign permissions to the share for each user. You can specify one or more of several permissions: Read, Change, Full Control, which grants all permissions, and No Access, which specifically overrides any other access and denies access to the user.

In a typical workgroup network, each workstation has a separate database of user accounts. User-level security can also be used in a client-server (domain) network; in this case, there is a central database of accounts for the entire network.

While user-level security can be used in either client-server or peer-to-peer networks, it requires a machine to store a list of user accounts. Since Windows 95 does not keep a user account database, at least one Windows NT or NetWare machine is required.

NetBIOS Names

Computer names in Windows networks are called NetBIOS names. A NetBIOS name can include up to 15 characters. (A 16th character is used by Windows to indicate the type of resource the name represents.) NetBIOS names are used to identify other computers when accessing shared information over the network.

NetBIOS also supports a scope ID, which identifies particular computers that can communicate. Only computers with the same scope ID as the current machine are reachable on the network.

NetBIOS names can be translated, or *resolved*, into IP or hardware addresses by the WINS (Windows Internet Name Service) service. In the absence of these servers, names are resolved by broadcasting queries over the network.

NetBIOS names must be unique. Since these names are not maintained by a central computer, it's possible to define the same name for multiple machines. This can cause one or both machines to have difficulty accessing the network.

Part of the process of planning a network includes choosing a standard format for NetBIOS names. There are two basic goals when choosing names: to make sure that each name is unique, and to include useful information (such as the location of the computer) in the name.

A common scheme is to combine various codes to make the NetBIOS name. For example, a typical name might be WKSWEST31: WKS indicates that the computer is a workstation, WEST is the building it is physically located in, 3 is the floor, and 1 is a unique number assigned to the workstation. Be sure to take the 15-character limit into account when developing a NetBIOS naming scheme.

Fault Tolerance

Another factor that should be planned for is *fault tolerance*. This encompasses various methods for keeping data safe from hard drive crashes, natural disasters, accidental erasure, and security violations resulting in loss of data. The main types of fault tolerance are described in the sections below.

On the Exam

Specific steps to implement each type of fault tolerance are described in Parts 2 and 3. For the Network Essentials exam, you should have a basic idea of which disk configurations are fault tolerant, and the speed and reliability of each.

Backups

All networks should include some kind of backup system, in addition to any other fault tolerance measures used. Backup systems make a copy of critical data onto a backup medium (typically a tape) at scheduled intervals. Multiple tapes should be used and rotated to maintain several backups. At least one recent backup should be stored off-site in case of disaster.

Most file systems support a file attribute called the *archive bit,* which is used to mark files that have been backed up. There are three basic types of backups:

- *Full backups* copy all of the files to a tape every time, and clear the archive bits. This is the most comprehensive backup and is easier to restore files from, but may be too slow or impossible depending on the amount of disk storage and the capacity of the backup device.

- *Differential backups* include all of the files that have changed since the last full backup. Thus, any data can be restored with a maximum of two tapes: the last full backup and the last differential backup. Depending on the amount of files modified, these backups may be nearly as large as full backups. Differential backups do not modify the archive bits.

- *Incremental backups* copy only the files that have changed since the last backup, whether full or incremental; the archive bits are cleared. This makes for smaller tape storage needs, but restoring files might require several tapes.

On the Exam

The exam may refer to two additional backup types supported by the Windows NT Backup utility: a *copy* backup is similar to a full backup but does not clear the archive bits (and thus does not affect incremental and differential backups). A *daily copy* backup includes files modified on the current date, and also does not clear the archive bits.

Disk Mirroring and Duplexing

Disk mirroring and duplexing are methods of storing data on two drives at the same time. Mirroring refers to systems that use a single disk controller, and duplexing refers to systems with a separate controller for each drive.

While the hardware hookups for these fault tolerance methods are different, Windows NT uses the term *mirroring* to refer to both methods. You can create a mirrored set from any two equally sized partitions on different physical drives.

Both of these systems provide significant fault tolerance. Duplexing is slightly more fault tolerant because a controller failure can be recovered from. The disadvantage of these systems is that only 50% of the total disk capacity of both drives is available. For example, a mirror set using two 500-MB drives would have a total capacity of 500 MB.

Another disadvantage of mirroring and duplexing is that disk writes are also slower than with a normal drive, since data must be written to both mirror copies. Reading from the disk can use a single copy. Since two reads can potentially be performed at the same time, disk read performance is faster.

Volume Sets and Striping

A volume set is two or more drives (or portions of drives) that have been configured to act as a single drive. The capacity of the volume set is the sum of the

---

capacity of the two drives. Volume sets actually decrease fault tolerance, because one drive's failure could make the entire volume set inaccessible.

A related technology is disk striping. Disk striping uses two or more drives, and treats them as a single drive. Rather than write to one drive until it's full before writing to the next, disk striping writes equal amounts of data to each drive. This provides for fast read and write access, since all drives can be working with different portions of a file at the same time.

As with a volume set, disk striping by itself reduces fault tolerance. A single drive failure not only disrupts the stripe set, but likely causes the loss of portions of every file on the volume.

An alternative is *disk striping with parity*. This is a variation that requires at least three drives, and uses a portion of each for checksum information. The checksums can be used to recreate data that is lost if a drive fails.

Disk striping with parity uses an amount of space equal to one drive's capacity for the checksum information. Thus, a striped set with parity made of four 200-MB disk drives would use 200 MB for parity information, and would have an available capacity of 600 MB.

On the Exam

For the exam, remember that disk striping with parity and disk mirroring or duplexing are the only fault tolerant disk configurations. Disk striping and volume sets do not provide fault tolerance.

RAID Levels

RAID (Redundant Array of Inexpensive Disks) is a set of standards for fault tolerance using multiple disks. Numeric RAID levels are assigned to types of multi-disk storage. The RAID levels commonly available with Windows NT are 0, 1, and 5, described in Table 1-12.

Table 1-12: RAID Levels

Level	Description	Fault Tolerant?
0	Disk striping without parity	No
1	Disk mirroring or duplexing	Yes
5	Disk striping with parity	Yes

All three of these RAID types are implemented in software by Windows NT Server. Windows NT Workstation supports only disk striping without parity. Dedicated hardware RAID devices are also available. These are generally faster than software methods, but more expensive and more difficult to configure.

Uninterruptible Power Supplies

Another import form of fault tolerance is an uninterruptible power supply, or UPS. These are power supplies with battery backups that allow a server to continue functioning after a power failure for a limited time (usually between 10 and 20 minutes).

While an expensive UPS that allows hours of operation can be used with critical equipment, the more common type of UPS is used to simply allow enough time to take the server down properly. Most UPS models can communicate with the server via a serial port. When the UPS detects a power failure, the server automatically closes all files and shuts down.

Virus Protection

A final aspect of fault tolerance is virus protection. Computer viruses are malicious programs that copy themselves by various means between computers. While the majority of viruses are relatively harmless, others can cause damage.

Most viruses are transmitted through executable files, particularly when users run executable files they downloaded from the Internet or brought on a diskette from home. If these are frequent practices, one of the popular virus scanning utilities should be used to prevent problems.

Troubleshooting

Network troubleshooting includes monitoring the performance of the network and servers as well as dealing with hardware and software problems. The most common tasks involved in network troubleshooting are explained in the sections below.

Monitoring Performance

Network troubleshooting is simpler if you have documented the network's usual performance. This is called a *baseline*. Once you have a baseline for the network, you can monitor trends; for example, the hard drive is getting busier, or the network is becoming less responsive.

You can monitor network and server performance with various Windows NT utilities, described in the sections below.

Event Viewer

Event Viewer is a basic utility that displays a log of events for the server and network. The events include such items as the server going up or coming down, network errors, hardware errors, and disk problems.

You can also enable auditing for more detailed events: accesses to files, login attempts, actions by certain users, and many other items.

Performance Monitor

The Performance Monitor utility, shown in Figure 1-3, is a Windows NT utility that monitors a wide variety of factors that affect network and system performance. The items that can be measured, called *counters*, are split into a number of categories, such as cache, disk, memory, and network.

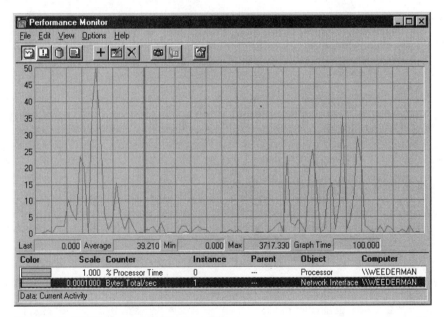

Figure 1-3: The Performance Monitor utility

You can display counters in four different ways:

Chart
   Displays a graph of the current and previous values of the counter.

Alert

Allows you to select a number of counters and maximum and minimum values, and alerts you when any one of the counters crosses the boundaries you have defined.

Log

Records a log of changing counter values. This option is useful for monitoring a counter over an extended period of time, and can be set to measure data from the moment Windows NT starts.

Report

Allows you to selectively display current counters in the form of a report.

A wide variety of counters are available in Performance Monitor. Some of the most useful include the following:

PhysicalDisk: %Disk Time

This is the percentage of time the disk drive is busy reading or writing data. If this value is high (25% or higher) a faster drive or disk striping may be beneficial.

Processor: %Processor Time

Indicates how busy the CPU in the computer is. If this number is frequently over 80%, a processor upgrade may be necessary.

Memory: Page faults/sec

Indicates the number of times each second the computer is unable to find a requested location in memory, indicating that it has been swapped to disk as virtual memory. If this number is high, a memory upgrade will improve performance.

SNMP

SNMP (Simple Network Management Protocol) is a large-scale tool for measuring and monitoring network performance. SNMP uses two components: an agent, which runs at client computers and monitors their status, and a manager, which polls clients and summarizes data.

Connection Problems

The most common problem that occurs on a network is when one or more workstations lose their connection to the network. This can be caused by a problem with configuration, with a network card, or with the network media. Common causes of connection problems are described in the following sections.

Network Cards

Network cards generally function well once configured. If a newly installed network card is unable to connect to the network, it may be due to incorrect configuration. Items you should check in the card's configuration include the following:

- Interrupt (IRQ) settings that may cause a conflict, especially if the network card or another device was recently installed.

- I/O address settings may conflict with other devices.

- Transceiver settings (such as Coax/UTP) set incorrectly appear the same as a disconnection.

- If the network card allows the MAC (hardware) address to be configured, be sure the address is unique. If two machines have the same MAC address, one or both will have trouble accessing the network.

A network card that is defective or configured with the wrong IRQ or I/O address will usually cause errors when the network drivers load at boot time. However, an incorrectly configured MAC address or transceiver setting will not cause an error.

On the Exam

If a network card does fail, it can sometimes send bad packets over the network, potentially causing problems with the entire network segment. However, network card failures are relatively rare.

Network Protocols

A lack of communication can often be caused by a protocol mismatch. This is a frequent issue in networks with multiple protocols. For example, a network may support IPX/SPX and TCP/IP protocols and include Windows NT, NetWare, and UNIX servers. If a new Windows machine can access the NT and UNIX servers but is unable to access the NetWare servers, chances are it has not been configured with the IPX/SPX protocol.

Configuration of nodes within a protocol can also cause communication problems. For example, a TCP/IP node may not be configured with a valid IP address. In an IPX/SPX network, the node may not be configured with the correct frame type.

Cables and Other Hardware

Cable problems, such as a severed cable, are usually sudden in nature. If a problem of this nature occurs, you should first check whether any recent changes (such as a new node or new network segment) could have caused the problem. Then check the cables and connectors, as described in the next section.

Devices for Troubleshooting

Network problems that occur suddenly are often the result of a cable problem. This can include a severed cable, a connector that has been unplugged, or a malfunctioning hub or other device. The next sections describe various devices that may be useful in diagnosing cable problems.

Cable Testers

Cable testers are dedicated devices designed to test particular types of network cable. One type, called a time-delay reflectometer or TDR, sends signals down the cable and times them to determine whether there is a break or short in the cable. These devices are generally expensive.

Terminators

You can perform simple troubleshooting with an extra terminator or two. This is particularly useful in a bus topology network, such as Ethernet 10Base2. Terminate the network at various points. If you can terminate a group of workstations and restore their connections, you know the problem lies in the section you've disconnected.

Protocol Analyzers

A *protocol analyzer*, or network analyzer, is a device that captures packets on the network media and analyzes them, providing useful statistics. For example, you can determine the bandwidth in use on the network. While hardware protocol analyzers are available, software-based network analysis is less expensive. Windows NT includes a utility called Network Monitor that performs this function.

Network Monitor consists of two components: the Network Monitor Agent, a service that runs on each computer that will be used to monitor the network, and Network Monitor Tools, the actual utility for capturing and analyzing packets. Network Monitor is explained in detail in Part 3.

Volt/Ohm Meters (VOMs)

These are sometimes called DVMs, or digital volt meters. These are devices that measure electrical properties: voltage (volts), resistance (ohms), and other values. Their main use in network troubleshooting is for measuring resistance in coaxial networks.

If you connect the DVM's probes to the inner and outer conductors of a network cable that is isolated from the network, you should get an infinite reading, indicating no connection. T-connectors and BNC connectors should also have an infinite reading between their inner and outer conductors. Terminators should read at a fixed resistance: 50 ohms for Ethernet, and 93 ohms for ARCnet.

Oscilloscopes

An oscilloscope measures voltage over time, and provides a visual display of a signal's frequency. These devices are most useful for diagnosing problems in networks that use analog signaling. Oscilloscopes are expensive, and not as useful as a dedicated device such as a cable tester.

Broadcast Storms

A common problem on networks is caused by network *broadcasts*. Broadcast messages are sent to resolve NetBIOS names and for other purposes. If there are many nodes on the network, broadcasts can seriously impede network traffic. A device or software service can also malfunction and start issuing excess broadcasts; this condition is called a *broadcast storm*.

Routers can usually be set not to forward broadcasts, which will prevent a broadcast storm from affecting any more than a single network segment. Bridges cannot prevent broadcast storms, since they forward all broadcasts. Non-routable protocols (such as NetBEUI) don't require these measures, since their packets are not routed to other segments in any case.

Suggested Exercises

For the most part, the Network Essentials exam is not operating system-specific. However, you should have experience with a Microsoft operating system, either Windows 95 or Windows NT.

Since the exam briefly covers certain Windows NT utilities (such as Performance Monitor), it's best to have a Windows NT machine available for studying. Experience with various network protocols and media is also helpful if possible.

While a single machine should be sufficient to prepare for this exam, this is a good time to begin to set up two or more computers in a network to use in preparation for future exams.

Performing the following exercises will help you prepare for the Network Essentials exam:

1. If you have access to a network at work or school, document the number of computers and the network media, topology, architectures, and protocols in use. If you are not the network administrator, ask an administrator to demonstrate the network's workings.

2. Document the IRQ and I/O address usage of one or more PCs. You will need to examine the system control panel (Windows 95) or WinMSD (Windows NT) and add any legacy devices (those without NT or Windows 95 drivers) to the list.

3. Install a network adapter (NIC) in a computer running Windows 95 or Windows NT. Attach it to a network and verify that it communicates properly. See the *Study Guide* and *Highlighter's Index* in this part for the details of configuring each operating system to work with the network adapter.

4. Choose a company you're familiar with (or invent one). Assume that the company does not currently have a network. Based on what you know about the company, plan a network using these steps:

    a. Choose a network architecture (Ethernet, Token Ring, etc.).

b. Choose a network topology (star, bus, ring, or mesh).

c. Based on the number of workstations in use, choose whether a server-based or peer-to-peer network is the most appropriate.

d. Choose one or more network protocols.

e. Assume that the company requires network connectivity with an equal-sized company across the country. Choose an appropriate WAN architecture.

f. Determine whether the network should use user-level or share-level security.

g. Create a NetBIOS naming scheme for the servers and workstations on the network.

5. On a Windows NT machine, create several user accounts using the User Manager utility. Only the basics of user accounts are covered on the Network Essentials exam; see the *Study Guide* for detailed information about Windows NT user accounts.

6. Run the Event Viewer utility on a Windows NT machine. This utility is located in the Administrative Tools menu under the Start menu. View the System log and determine the most recent time the machine was restarted.

7. Run the Performance Monitor utility on a Windows NT computer. Use the Chart view to monitor one or more CPU counters. Try running several applications on the machine and observe their impact on the chart.

8. If you've set up a small network at home to practice for the exams, disconnect one or more network cables, and observe the impact on the computers. If possible, ask another student or an experienced network administrator to disconnect the cable. Using the troubleshooting tools described in the *Study Guide*, attempt to pinpoint the problem.

Practice Test

Test Questions

1. A network with a Windows NT domain controller is which type of network?

    a. Peer-to-peer

    b. Server-based

2. Which of the following is *not* a disadvantage of peer-to-peer networks?

    a. Lack of centralized administration

    b. Low security

    c. High cost

3. You are installing a network to connect eight Windows NT Workstation computers in a single building and need to determine the network type to use.

    Required Result: The network should be inexpensive.

    Optional Result: The network should allow for centralized administration.

    Optional Result: The network should allow for growth (10 new workstations will be added over the next year).

    Solution: Install a peer-to-peer (workgroup) network.

    a. The solution meets the required result and both of the optional results.

    b. The solution meets the required result and only one of the optional results.

    c. The solution meets the required result only.

    d. The solution does not meet the required result.

4. You need to connect six workstations in a new network. No additional workstations are planned in the next few years. Security is not a major issue, and the management would like you to select the cheapest alternative. Which type of network should be used?

    a.   Server-based

    b.   Peer-to-peer

    c.   Domain-based

    d.   User-level

5. Which layer of the OSI model translates physical addresses to logical addresses?

    a.   Physical layer

    b.   Network layer

    c.   Transport layer

    d.   Session layer

6. Which layer of the OSI model maintains a connection between network nodes?

    a.   Session layer

    b.   Transport layer

    c.   Network layer

    d.   Physical layer

7. Which IEEE standard defines the LLC and MAC sublayers?

    a.   802.1

    b.   802.2

    c.   802.3

    d.   802.5

8. Microsoft's standard for network card and protocol bindings is called:

    a.   ODI

    b.   NDIS

    c.   IPX

    d.   OSI

9. Which of the following network measurements is expressed in Mbps?

    a.   Attenuation

    b.   Crosstalk

    c.   Bandwidth

10. What is the lowest category of UTP cable that can be used in an Ethernet 10BaseT network?

    a.   Category 2

    b.   Category 3

    c.   Category 4

    d.   Category 5

11. Which type of coaxial cable is used with Thin Ethernet networks?

    a.   RG-8

    b.   RG-57

    c.   RG-58

    d.   RG-62

12. Which type of fiber optic cable is generally more expensive?

    a.   multimode

    b.   single-mode

13. Which of the following network media are vulnerable to EMI? (check all that apply)

    a.   UTP

    b.   Infrared

    c.   Fiber optic

    d.   Radio

14. Which type of radio-based network is least vulnerable to eavesdropping?

    a.   Low Power Single Frequency

    b.   High Power Single Frequency

    c.   Spread-spectrum

15. You are installing a NIC in a computer that already has a printer attached to the LPT1 port, a sound card, and a SCSI disk drive. Which IRQ is most likely to be available for the NIC?

    a.   IRQ 7

    b.   IRQ 10

    c.   IRQ 11

    d.   IRQ 5

16. A network is wired using a single length of coaxial cable, with nodes connected at various points along the cable. Which network topology is in use?

    a.   Bus

    b.   Star

    c.   Ring

    d.   Mesh

17. Which network topology is generally the most reliable?

    a.   Star

    b.   Ring

    c.   Mesh

    d.   Bus

18. Which network connectivity device(s) operate at the physical layer of the OSI model? (check all that apply)

    a.   Hubs

    b.   Routers

    c.   Transceivers

    d.   Repeaters

19. Which network connectivity device(s) function at the network layer of the OSI model? (check all that apply)

    a.   Bridges

    b.   Routers

    c.   Hubs

    d.   Brouters

20. Which device is likely to be used only in wide-area networks?

    a.   Router

    b.   Bridge

    c.   CSU/DSU

    d.   Hub

21. Which hardware device can be used to prevent broadcast storms?

    a.   Bridge

    b.   Router

    c.   Hub

    d.   CSU/DSU

22. Which media access method is used in Ethernet networks?

    a.   Token passing

    b.   CSMA/CD

    c.   CSMA/CA

23. How many nodes can be used on a single segment in an Ethernet 10Base2 network?

    a.   1

    b.   32

    c.   30

    d.   90

24. Which Ethernet standard uses UTP cable?

    a.   10Base2

    b.   10Base5

    c.   10BaseT

25. Which terminators are used in an Ethernet 10Base2 network?

    a.   50 ohm

    b.   75 ohm

    c.   93 ohm

    d.   No terminators are used

26. Thin and thick Ethernets follow the 5-4-3 rule. What does the 5 refer to?

    a.   Network nodes

    b.   Network segments

    c.   Repeaters

    d.   Populated network segments

27. You must install a single network to support 80 computers: 70 running Windows NT Workstation and 10 running Windows NT Server. The computers are a maximum of 100 meters apart.

Required Result: The network must support the current computers in a single network.

Optional Result: The network should allow for 20 additional computers to be added over the next year without additional equipment purchases (aside from the computers and network cards).

Optional Result: The network should allow connectivity problems to be diagnosed easily.

Solution: Install 10BaseT Ethernet, using five 16-port hubs.

    a.   The solution meets the required result and both of the optional results.

    b.   The solution meets the required result and only one of the optional results.

    c.   The solution meets the required result only.

    d.   The solution does not meet the required result.

28. Which Ethernet standard supports the greatest number of nodes on a single network?

    a.   10BaseT

    b.   10Base2

    c.   10Base5

29. Which network architecture uses a dual-ring topology?

    a.   Ethernet

    b.   Token Ring

    c.   ARCNet

    d.   FDDI

30. You are installing a network in a training room, to be used temporarily for a period of 30 days. You must connect 10 workstations running Windows NT Workstation and 2 servers running Windows NT Server.

Required Result: The network must have a transmission speed of at least 10 Mbps.

Optional Result: The network should be inexpensive.

Optional Result: The network should be easy to install.

Solution: Install 10Base2 Ethernet in a bus topology.

    a.   The solution meets the required result and both of the optional results.

    b.   The solution meets the required result and only one of the optional results.

    c.   The solution meets the required result only.

    d.   The solution does not meet the required result.

31. Which of the following is a disadvantage of the TCP/IP protocol suite?

    a.   Non-routable

    b.   Proprietary

    c.   Difficult configuration

32. Which of the following protocols are used to support dial-up connections? (check all that apply)

    a.   NFS

    b.   SLIP

    c.   UDP

    d.   PPP

33. Microsoft's implementation of Novell's IPX/SPX protocol suite is called:

    a.   ODI

    b.   NDIS

    c.   NWLink

    d.   NetBEUI

34. Which of the following is a fast, basic, non-routable transport protocol developed by Microsoft and IBM?

    a.   NDIS

    b.   NetBEUI

    c.   NetBIOS

    d.   IPX

35. The DLC protocol is primarily used for which purposes? (check all that apply)

    a.   Network-aware printers

    b.   NetWare networks

    c.   Mainframe communication

    d.   Dial-up Internet service

36. Which type of WAN media uses a modem?

    a.   PSTN

    b.   DDS

    c.   ISDN

    d.   Frame Relay

37. Which of the following WAN technologies offers the highest bandwidth?

    a.   T1

    b.   T3

    c.   OC-3

    d.   ISDN

38. Which of the following WAN technologies use packet switching? (check all that apply)

    a.   ISDN

    b.   ATM

    c.   SONET

    d.   Frame Relay

39. You are planning a WAN between an office in New York and an office in Los Angeles, and must choose a WAN architecture for a continuous connection between the two locations.

Required Result: The WAN must have bandwidth of at least 1 Mbps.

Optional Result: The architecture chosen should be the least expensive method that meets the bandwidth requirements.

Optional Result: The WAN should be upgradable to higher bandwidth using the same type of equipment.

Solution: Install a leased T1 line, connected to the network with a CSU/DSU at both locations.

    a.   The solution meets the required result and both of the optional results.

    b.   The solution meets the required result and only one of the optional results.

    c.   The solution meets the required result only.

    d.   The solution does not meet the required result.

40. Which of the following WAN types typically use fiber optic media?

    a.   ISDN

    b.   SONET

    c.   DS3

    d.   T1

41. A user requires access to resources located on three different computers in a peer-to-peer network: two running NT Server and one running NT Workstation. How many user accounts must be created?

    a.   1

    b.   2

    c.   3

42. Which of the following is not a valid NetBIOS name?

    a.   SRV_WEST_19

    b.   WORKSTATION_WEST_2

    c.   SERVER1

    d.   SERVER-A

43. What type of fault tolerance is specified by RAID 5?

    a.   Disk striping

    b.   Disk striping with parity

    c.   Disk mirroring

    d.   Disk duplexing

44. You need to install disk striping with parity on a computer with four drives: one with 400 MB of free space, one with 200 MB, and two with 250 MB. If you make the largest possible stripe set with parity, what will be the amount of available disk space?

    a.   800 MB

    b.   1100 MB

    c.   600 MB

    d.   400 MB

45. Which of the following disk configurations can use 3 physical drives to store a single volume? (check all that apply)

    a.   Disk mirroring

    b.   Disk duplexing

    c.   Disk striping

    d.   Disk striping with parity

46. Which of the following disk configurations is *not* fault tolerant?

    a.   Disk mirroring

    b.   Disk striping

    c.   Disk striping with parity

    d.   Disk duplexing

47. Which of the following Windows NT utilities can display a graph of CPU performance?

    a.   Event Monitor

    b.   Performance Monitor

    c.   Event Viewer

    d.   System Monitor

48. You have just installed a network card in a Windows NT computer. The card is using the NetBEUI and NWLink protocols, and has Client Services for NetWare installed. The computer is able to communicate with other Windows NT machines, but cannot access files on a NetWare server. What is the most likely problem?

    a.   Incorrect IRQ setting

    b.   Bad network card

    c.   Invalid frame type setting

    d.   Broken network cable

49. What device is useful to determine if a coaxial cable terminator is faulty?

    a.   Oscilloscope

    b.   VOM/DVM

    c.   TDR

    d.   Network analyzer

50. You are installing two NICs in a computer that has three available IRQ settings: 5, 10, and 11. Which of the following combinations of IRQ settings would allow both cards to function? (check all that apply)

    a.   Card #1: IRQ 5; Card #2: IRQ 5

    b.   Card #1: IRQ 10; Card #2: IRQ 11

    c.   Card #1: IRQ 5; Card #2: IRQ 10

    d.   Card #1: IRQ 10; Card #2: IRQ 7

Answers to Questions

1. B. A server-based network uses a dedicated server, such as a domain controller.

2. C. While peer-to-peer networks do have a lack of central administration and low security, their low cost is a benefit.

3. C. The solution meets the required result (is inexpensive). However, a peer-to-peer network does not allow for centralized administration or for growth beyond 10 workstations.

4. B. A peer-to-peer network is ideal for six workstations when security is not an issue.

5. B. The network layer deals with network addresses and routing.

6. A. The session layer maintains a connection (session) between network nodes.

7. B. The 802.2 standard divides the OSI model's data link layer into LLC and MAC sublayers.

8. B. NDIS allows binding between network cards and multiple protocols. ODI (choice A) is a similar standard, but was originated by Novell and not Microsoft.

9. C. Bandwidth is expressed in Mbps (megabits per second).

10. B. Category 3 is the lowest category of cable for a 10BaseT network.

11. C. RG-58 cable is used with thinnet networks. RG-8 (choice A) is used with thicknet, and RG-62 (choice D) is used with ARCNet.

12. B. A single-mode fiber optic cable is generally more expensive.

13. A, D. UTP and radio transmissions are vulnerable to electromagnetic interference (EMI). Infrared and fiber optic transmissions use light, and thus are not vulnerable.

14. C. A spread-spectrum network uses frequency hopping, or regular frequency changes. An eavesdropper cannot read the signal without knowing the frequencies used and the switching interval.

15. C. IRQ 11 is typically used for a second SCSI controller, not listed in the question, and would thus be available. The printer uses IRQ 7 (choice A); the first SCSI controller uses IRQ 10 (choice B); the sound card is likely to use IRQ 5 (choice D).

16. A. A bus topology uses a single length of cable with nodes attached at various points.

17. C. A mesh topology uses redundant links to provide fault tolerance, and thus is more reliable than the others.

18. A, C, D. Hubs, Transceivers, and Repeaters operate at the OSI physical layer. Routers (choice B) operate at the network layer.

19. B, D. Routers and brouters operate at the OSI network layer. Bridges (choice A) operate at the data link layer, and hubs (choice C) operate at the physical layer.

20. C. A CSU/DSU is typically used to interface a network with a WAN connection. Routers, bridges, and hubs can be used in single-location LANs.

21. B. A router can be set to not forward broadcast storms between network segments. The other devices do not perform this function.

22. B. Ethernet uses the CSMA/CD (Carrier sense multiple access with collision detection) access method. Token passing (choice A) is used by Token Ring networks; CSMA/CA (choice C) is used by AppleTalk networks.

23. C. A 10Base2 network allows 30 nodes per network segment.

24. C. The 10BaseT standard uses UTP cable. The others use coaxial cable.

25. A. Ethernet 10Base2 uses 50-ohm terminators.

26. B. The 5-4-3 rule refers to 5 network segments, 4 repeaters, and 3 populated segments.

27. B. The solution meets the required result (support the current computers) and one optional result (allows connectivity problems to be diagnosed easily). It does not allow 20 additional computers to be installed without additional equipment, since additional hubs would be required.

28. A. 10BaseT allows up to 1024 nodes per network.

29. D. FDDI uses two rings, rotating in opposite directions, to provide fault tolerance. Token Ring (choice B) uses a single ring only.

30. A. The solution meets the required result (10 Mbps) and both optional results: since the network is temporary and has only 12 nodes, 10Base2 Ethernet is easy to install and relatively inexpensive.

31. C. While TCP/IP is routable and non-proprietary, it does require more configuration and planning than other protocols.

32. B, D. SLIP and PPP are the only protocols used to support dial-up connections.

33. C. Microsoft's implementation of IPX/SPX is called NWLink.

34. B. NetBEUI is a fast, basic, non-routable transport protocol developed by Microsoft and IBM. NetBIOS (choice C) is the communication and naming standard used over NetBEUI or other networks.

35. A, C. DLC is used for communication with network-aware printers and with mainframes.

36. A. Modems are used with PSTN (phone lines). ISDN (choice C) uses devices called terminal adapters, sometimes mistakenly referred to as modems.

37. C. OC-3 offers a bandwidth of 155 Mbps.

38. A, B, D. ISDN, ATM, and Frame Relay use packet switching.

39. A. The solution meets the required result and both optional results: T1 supports a bandwidth of 1.544 Mbps. It is usually the least expensive line of this speed, and higher-speed alternatives (T2–4) are available.

40. B, C. SONET and DS3 typically use fiber-optic media. ISDN and T1 typically use copper cable.

41. C. Since the network is peer-to-peer, the user will need an account on each of the computers.

42. B. NetBIOS names allow up to 15 characters.

43. B. RAID level 5 is disk striping with parity.

44. C. The largest possible stripe set would use 200 MB from each of the four drives. This is a total of 800 MB of space. Since 200 MB of space is used for parity information, 600 MB remains available.

45. C, D. Disk striping (with or without parity) can be used with three drives. Disk mirroring and duplexing (choices A and B) use only two drives.

46. B. Disk striping (without parity) is not fault tolerant.

47. B. Performance Monitor can display a graph of CPU performance.

48. C. Since the computer is able to communicate with other machines, the network card, cable, and IRQ must not be the problem. An invalid frame type can cause communication problems with NetWare servers.

49. B. A VOM/DVM can be used to measure the terminator's resistance, which should be 50 ohms for Ethernet or 93 ohms for ARCnet.

50. B, C. The cards could use IRQ 10 and 11 or 5 and 10. Choice A uses the same IRQ for both cards, which would cause a conflict. Choice D includes IRQ 7, which was not listed as available.

Highlighter's Index

Network Basics

Server-Based (Domain) Networks
One or more dedicated servers

Centralized administration

Higher security

Peer-To-Peer (Workgroup) Networks
Consist solely of workstations

Easy to configure

Require separate administration for each computer

Users require separate passwords for each computer

Recommended for networks with 10 workstations or fewer

Network Scales
Local-area networks (LANs) consist of a single location.

Wide-area networks (WANs) include two or more locations, usually in different cities, states, or countries.

Metropolitan-area networks (MANs) use WAN protocols but operate in a smaller area (such as a single city).

OSI Reference Model
A model for understanding network communications

Consists of seven layers; data travels from layer to layer

Higher-level layers use services provided by lower-level services

Physical layer

Communicates directly with hardware, and converts digital data into analog signals (NICs, transceivers, repeaters, and hubs).

Data link layer

Organizes data into frames; handles hardware addressing. Bridges operate at this layer.

Network layer

Forms frames into packets, adds headers, and translates between physical and logical addresses. Routers operate at this layer.

Transport layer

Sequences packets, acknowledges transmissions, and checks for errors.

Session layer

Establishes and maintains a connection (session) between two nodes.

Presentation layer

Translates data between network and application formats. Compression and encryption are performed at this layer.

Application layer

Provides network services to applications, and informs applications in the event of network errors.

Mnemonic for first letter of each layer: "People Don't Need To Study Preposterous Abbreviations."

IEEE 802 Standards

802.1

Internetworking and the OSI model

802.2

Logical link control (LLC)

802.3

CSMA/CD (Ethernet) media access method

802.5

Token Ring media access method

NDIS and ODI

NDIS is Microsoft's standard for protocol bindings

ODI (Open Datalink Interface) is Novell's similar architecture

Both allow multiple protocols to be used with a single network adapter

Network Media and NICs

Network Media

UTP

Low cost; 10–100 Mbps; vulnerable to EMI and snooping; 100 meters maximum

STP

Medium cost; 16 Mbps typical; less vulnerable to EMI and snooping; 100 meters maximum

Thick Coax

Medium cost; 10 Mbps typical; low vulnerability to EMI and snooping; 500 meters maximum

Thin Coax

Medium cost; 10 Mbps typical; low vulnerability; 185 meters maximum

Fiber optic

High cost; very high speeds; no vulnerability; 100 Km or greater distance

Wireless Media

Infrared (point-to-point)

High cost; 16 Mbps or greater; vulnerable to obstructions; long distance

Infrared (broadcast)

Low cost; 1 Mbps; high rate of dispersion; short distance

Radio (LPSF)

Low cost; 10 Mbps; vulnerable to EMI and snooping; 30 meters maximum

Radio (HPSF)

High cost; 10 Mbps; very vulnerable to EMI and snooping; long distance

Radio (spread spectrum)

High cost; 10 Mbps; less vulnerable to snooping; distances vary

Network Adapters

Also called network interface cards (NICs)

May require configuration of interrupt (IRQ); I/O address; high memory address; DMA channel; transceiver (port) type

Interrupts are the most common cause of conflicts

Interrupts (IRQs)

0: System timer

1: Keyboard

2: Interrupt Controller

3: COM2 and COM4 (occasionally available)

4: COM1 and COM3 (occasionally available)

5: LPT2 or sound card (often available)

6: Floppy disk controller

7: LPT1 (occasionally available)

8: CMOS/Real-time clock

9: IRQ2 cascade (often available)

10: Primary SCSI controller (often available)

11: Secondary SCSI controller (often available)

12: PS/2 (bus) mouse (sometimes available)

13: Math coprocessor

14: Primary IDE controller

15: Secondary IDE controller (often available)

Network Topologies and Architectures

Topologies

Bus
Nodes are connected at various points along a single cable segment, or *bus*. This type of network is often used as a backbone. Typically uses coaxial cable.

Star
All nodes connect to a central hub. This type of network provides for easier troubleshooting. UTP or STP cable is typically used.

Ring
Nodes are connected to one another in a circle. Nodes pass a *token* through the ring and take turns transmitting data. Token Ring networks use a logical ring topology, but are physically wired as a star.

Mesh
Each node is connected to all other nodes. This type of network is very reliable but requires a large number of connections.

Hybrid
A network that combines one or more topologies.

Network Connectivity Devices

Repeater
Connects network segments to extend total length (physical layer)

Hub
Connects the nodes to a central point in a star topology (physical layer)

Bridge
Filters and moves data between segments based on MAC address (data link layer)

Router

Filters and moves data between segments based on logical address (network layer)

Brouter

Combines bridge and router capabilities (data link/network layers)

Gateway

Translates between protocols and data formats (application to transport layers)

Ethernet

Most commonly used network architecture

Uses the CSMA/CD (carrier sense multiple access with collision detection) access method

Supports 10-Mbps bandwidth

Three standards with different specifications:

Specification	10BaseT	10Base2	10Base5
Max. segments	1024	5	5
Max. repeaters/hubs	4	4	4
Max. segments with nodes	1024	3	3
Max. segment length	100 meters (328 feet)	185 meters (607 feet)	500 meters (1640 feet)
Max. nodes/segment	1	30	100
Max nodes/network	1024	90	300
Min. distance between nodes	N/A	.5 meters (1.6 feet)	2.5 meters (8.2 feet)

Token Ring

Defined in IEEE 802.5

Uses a logical ring topology and a physical star topology

Uses a token-passing access method

Hubs are called multistation access units (MSAUs)

Supports speeds of either 4 or 16 Mbps

ARCnet

An older standard that has largely been replaced by Ethernet

Uses RG-62 coaxial cable

Star, bus, or hybrid physical topology

FDDI

Uses fiber optic cable wired in a true ring

Communicates in two logical counter-rotating rings

Supports speeds up to 100 Mbps

Maximum distance between nodes: 100 kilometers (62 miles)

LocalTalk

Supports AppleTalk networking

Supports up to 32 nodes per network

Uses CSMA/CA (collision-avoidance) access method

AppleTalk can also use Ethernet or Token Ring networks

Network Protocols

TCP/IP

Named for Transport Control Protocol and Internet Protocol

Routable

Used for UNIX and the Internet

Main protocols: TCP (connection-oriented); UDP (connectionless)

Dial-up Protocols

SLIP (Single line internet protocol)
   Simple; Physical layer

PPP (Point-to-point protocol)
   Supports authentication and error control; Physical and Data link layers

IPX/SPX

Used for NetWare connectivity or as a general network transport

Main protocols: IPX (connectionless); SPX (connection-oriented)

Routable

Supported in Windows NT by NWLink

NetBEUI

Used to support NetBIOS

Low overhead

Non-routable; used for small networks

AppleTalk

Used for Macintosh support

Works over Ethernet, Token Ring, or LocalTalk

Services for Macintosh (SFM) provides Macintosh file and printer sharing for Windows NT

DLC

Developed by IBM

Versions: SDLC and HDLC

Used for mainframe (SNA) support

Supported by many network-aware printers and interfaces (i.e., HP JetDirect)

WAN Architectures

PSTN

Regular telephone lines

Modems operate at up to 33.6 Kbps two-way; 56 Kbps download-only

Supported by RAS under Windows NT

DDS and Switched 56

Dedicated 56-Kbps digital lines

Uses a CSU/DSU

Switched 56 uses circuit switching

ISDN

Packet switched digital line

BRI: Two 64-Kbps B channels (total: 128 Kbps): one 16-Kbps D channel

PRI: 23 B channels (total: 1.4 Mbps); one D channel

T1-T4

Point-to-point leased line

T1: 24 64-Kbps channels (1.544 Mbps)

T2: 96 channels (6.312 Mbps)

T3: 672 channels (44.736 Mbps)

T4: 4032 channels (274.176)

Fiber optic versions: DS1-DS4

X.25

64-Kbps packet-switched protocol

Uses PDNs (Public Data Networks)

High overhead; developed in 1970s

Frame Relay

Packet-switched leased line

Uses CSU/DSU

Speeds from 56 Kbps to 1.544 Mbps

SONET

Synchronous fiber optic leased lines

OC-1: 51.840 Mbps

OC-3: 155 Mbps

Sold in higher multiples of OC-1 up to OC-48 (2.4 Gbps)

ATM

High-speed packet (cell) switching network

Can be used with T1-T4, FDDI, SONET

Uses virtual circuits

Also useful as a high-speed LAN backbone

Planning and Administration

Share-Level Security

Supported by Windows 95

Can only use read-only or full access

Administered at each machine that shares files

User-Level Security

Uses user names and passwords

Allows centralized administration

Rights can be assigned per user or group: Read, Execute, Write, Delete

NetBIOS Naming

Up to 15 characters

Each node must have a unique name

Converted to hardware addresses by WINS

Backups

Full backup copies all of the files every time; clears archive bits

Differential backup includes all of the files that have changed since the last full backup; does not clear archive bits

Incremental backup copies files that have changed since the last backup, whether full or incremental; clears archive bits

Copy includes all files; does not modify archive bit

Daily copy includes files modified on the current date; does not modify archive bit

Disk Mirroring and Duplexing

Requires two disks and one (mirroring) or two (duplexing) controllers

Duplicates data on both drives

Writes are slightly slower than a normal volume; reads are faster

RAID level 1

Volume Sets

Two or more drives (up to 32)

Capacity is total of all drives

Decreases fault tolerance

Disk Striping

Two or more drives; data is interspersed between drives

Basic disk striping decreases fault tolerance

Disk striping with parity uses the equivalent of one drive's available space to store parity information; provides fault tolerance

RAID 0 is disk striping; RAID 5 is disk striping with parity

Troubleshooting

Monitoring Performance in Windows NT

Event viewer displays system and error logs

Performance Monitor tracks system performance counters; includes Chart, Alert, Log, and Report options

Network analyzers such as Network Monitor capture and examine packets

SNMP is a large-scale performance monitoring tool

Troubleshooting Devices

Cable testers are dedicated devices designed to test particular types of network cable

Terminators are useful for simple troubleshooting

VOM/DVM can be used to test cables, terminators

Terminator resistance should be 50 ohm (Ethernet) or 93 ohm (ARCnet)

Oscilloscopes display a graph of voltage over time

Broadcast Storms

NetBIOS and other protocols use broadcasts

Malfunctioning devices (i.e., NICs) can send large volumes of broadcasts

Routers can block broadcasts

NetBIOS is non-routable, and thus less vulnerable to broadcast storms

---

PART 2

Windows NT Workstation

Exam Overview

Windows NT Workstation is Microsoft's less expensive Windows NT offering, designed to work as a standalone workstation or network client. Although NT Workstation is similar to Windows NT Server, it has a more restrictive license and does not include some features.

MCSE Exam 70-073, titled *Implementing and Supporting Microsoft Windows NT Workstation 4.0,* covers basic aspects of Windows NT in general, and NT Workstation in particular. The emphasis is on NT 4.0 as a desktop operating system and network client.

While this exam is the most popular choice to fulfill the MCSE desktop operating system requirement, other operating system exams can also apply. You may wish to consider Exam 70-064, *Implementing and Supporting Microsoft Windows 95.* At this writing exams are available for Windows 3.1 and Windows for Workgroups, but both are scheduled to be retired.

There is a significant overlap between the NT Workstation, NT Server, and NT Server in the Enterprise exam objectives. This Part covers the common material and the material unique to the Workstation exam, while Parts 3 and 4 cover the more advanced knowledge required for the Server and Enterprise exams.

In order to prepare for this chapter and the exam, you should be familiar with the concepts introduced in Part 1, "Networking Essentials." You should also have experience using and administering Windows NT in a small network. Additionally, since NT Server features are occasionally mentioned in NT Workstation exam questions, a review of Part 3 may be helpful.

Objectives

Need to Know	Reference
Differences between Microsoft operating systems	"Operating Systems" on page 93
Differences between NT Workstation and NT Server	"Windows NT Server" on page 95
Windows NT architecture and components	"NT Architecture" on page 96
Steps in the NT boot process	"The Boot Process" on page 99
Various methods of installing Windows NT	"Installation Methods" on page 107
BOOT.INI file syntax	"The BOOT.INI File" on page 114
Basic syntax of answer files and UDF files	"Server-Based Installation" on page 116
NetWare frame types and their support in Windows NT	"NetWare Frame Types" on page 123
Basic concepts of TCP/IP	"TCP/IP" on page 124
Common TCP/IP protocols and their uses	"TCP/IP Protocols and Services" on page 126
Purpose of the various icons in the NT Workstation control panel	"Using the Control Panel" on page 133
The five main registry subtrees and their purposes	"Editing the Registry" on page 137
NT Disk Architecture, and how volume sets and stripe sets work	"Managing Disk Storage" on page 145
NTFS permissions and their purposes	"NTFS Security" on page 146
Share permissions and their purposes	"File Sharing and Permissions" on page 148
Components involved in printing	"Configuring Printers" on page 149
Default local users and groups	"Default Users and Groups" on page 139

Need to Apply	Reference
Start applications with default and specific priorities in Windows NT.	"Starting Applications" on page 101
Access remote network resources.	"Network Browsing" on page 102, "UNC Paths" on page 103, and "Mapping Network Drives" on page 103
Plan the installation of Windows NT Workstation.	"Installation Planning" on page 103
Choose the file system for a particular Windows NT configuration.	"File Systems" on page 106
Install Windows NT Workstation.	"Steps for Installation" on page 110

Need to Apply	_Reference_
Upgrade an existing OS to Windows NT Workstation.	"Upgrading to Windows NT" on page 113
Configure Windows NT and another OS for dual boot.	"Configuring a Multi-Boot System" on page 113
Uninstall Windows NT Workstation.	"Removing Windows NT" on page 116
Configure server-based installation of Windows NT.	"Server-Based Installation" on page 116
Add, manage, or remove network components.	"Managing Network Components" on page 120
Install client software for NetWare connectivity.	"NetWare Client Software" on page 121
Configure TCP/IP client software.	"TCP/IP" on page 124
Install and manage Peer Web Services.	"Peer Web Services" on page 128
Install and manage dial-up networking.	"Remote Access Service (RAS)" on page 130
Use the control panel to install and configure hardware devices.	"Using the Control Panel" on page 133
Modify the registry with the REGEDIT or REGEDT32 utility.	"Editing the Registry" on page 137
Create and manage local users and local groups.	"Adding and Modifying Users" on page 140
Install or configure a local or remote printer.	"Configuring Printers" on page 149
Use appropriate tools to monitor performance of a system.	"Monitoring Performance" on page 152
Troubleshoot common Windows NT problems.	"Troubleshooting Procedures" on page 156

Windows NT
Workstation

Study Guide

This chapter includes the following sections, which address various topics covered on the Windows NT Workstation MCSE exam:

Windows NT Basics
> Describes Windows NT and compares it with other Microsoft operating systems. Windows NT's architecture and boot process are described in detail. This section also describes the basics of using Windows NT.

Installing NT Workstation
> Discusses planning steps necessary before installing Windows NT, methods of installing, the installation process itself, and methods for automating installation.

Managing Network Components
> Discusses the network protocols, services, and other components used with Windows NT, including Peer Web Services, a simple web server, and Remote Access Service (RAS).

Configuring NT Workstation
> Introduces the Windows NT Control Panel and registry. This section also discusses users and groups, disk configurations, and printing.

Optimization and Troubleshooting
> Describes several useful utilities for monitoring the performance of Windows NT, and methods for optimizing performance. Typical troubleshooting procedures are described along with solutions to common problems.

Windows NT Basics

Windows NT (New Technology) was initially developed by Microsoft as an alternative to Windows 3.1. The latest version, 4.0, is a robust system suitable for networking, and is available in Workstation and Server versions. Unlike earlier

Windows versions, Windows NT does not rely on DOS for any of its functionality, although it can run many DOS applications.

This section compares Windows NT with other Microsoft operating systems, and provides basic information about Windows NT architecture and networking.

Terminology

The following terms relating to operating systems will be useful in understanding the remainder of this section:

Cooperative multitasking
> A system for allowing multiple applications to execute at the same time in an operating system. Applications must cooperate, periodically giving up control of the processor for use by other applications.

Memory protection
> In an operating system, a feature that prevents applications from accessing memory belonging to other applications or the operating system itself. Windows NT provides a greater degree of memory protection than other Windows versions.

Multiprocessing
> The ability of an operating system to use multiple processors (CPUs) in a computer at the same time. Windows NT is the only version of Windows that supports multiprocessing.

Multithreading
> The ability of an operating system to allow multiple tasks (threads) within an application to execute at the same time. In a multiprocessor system, these may be executed on different processors.

Preemptive Multitasking
> A system for allowing multiple applications to execute at the same time in an operating system. Unlike cooperative multitasking, preemptive systems are able to assign equal amounts of time to all applications, regardless of the application's behavior.

On the Exam

You should know all of these terms for the NT Workstation MCSE exam, and understand whether they apply to various Windows versions (described in the next section).

Operating Systems

Microsoft has produced a variety of operating systems, ranging from DOS to Windows NT. These are summarized in Table 2-1, and the current ones are described in the sections below.

Table 2-1: Operating System Requirements and Key Features

Operating System	RAM	Disk Storage Required	Multi-tasking	Multi-processing	Plug and Play
DOS	256K	None	No	No	No
Windows 3.x	2 MB	10 MB	Cooperative	No	No
Windows 95	4 MB	40 MB	Preemptive	No	Yes
Windows NT Workstation	12 MB	117 MB	Preemptive (protected)	Yes (2 processors)	No
Windows NT Server	16 MB	124 MB	Preemptive (protected)	Yes	No

On the Exam

The NT Workstation exam focuses on Microsoft's products, particularly Windows. You should be aware of the differences between NT Workstation and Server, their requirements, and their advantages over other Windows versions.

Windows 3.1x

Windows 3.1 was the first version of Windows to gain widespread popularity, and was the first with specific support for Intel's 16-bit 80386 processor. Two additional versions were released: 3.11, a version with minor corrections, and Windows for Workgroups, a version with support for workgroup networking.

Windows 3.x is a 16-bit operating system with support for cooperative multitasking. It can run DOS or 16-bit Windows applications. It requires a minimum of 2 MB of RAM, although 4 MB is a more realistic minimum. About 10 MB of disk storage is required for the OS (Windows for Workgroups requires about 20 MB).

Windows 95

Windows 95, introduced in August 1995, is a 32-bit operating system with a new user interface. It can run DOS, 16-bit Windows, and 32-bit Windows applications. Windows 95 officially requires 4 MB of RAM, but 8 MB or more is recommended for a reliable system.

Windows 95's main improvements over Windows 3.1x include an improved graphical user interface (GUI), support for preemptive multitasking (although multitasking between 16-bit Windows applications is cooperative), and support for multithreading.

Windows 95 also introduced the Plug and Play specification, allowing hardware to be automatically detected and assigned to computer resources (such as IRQs). Another important feature is built-in support for dial-up networking.

At this writing a new version called Windows 98 is planned for release. This version will include additional Internet support and bug fixes, but is not a major revision.

Windows NT Workstation

Windows NT is Microsoft's business-oriented operating system. The basic version, NT Workstation, is a 32-bit operating system that supports multitasking with memory protection, multiprocessing, and multithreading. Windows NT is designed for networking, and is generally more reliable than other versions of Windows.

Unlike other versions of Windows, Windows NT is multiplatform. It supports Intel 486/33 and higher processors as well as Digital Alpha, MIPS, and PowerPC processors. Windows NT supports 32-bit Windows applications, 16-bit Windows, DOS, and has limited support for OS/2 and POSIX applications.

On the Exam

In addition to x86 and Alpha processors, Windows NT versions 3.51 and 4.0 include support for PowerPC and MIPS processors. However, support for these processors may not be included in Windows NT 5.0.

The user interface in Windows NT parallels other Windows versions. Windows NT 3.51 and earlier versions use the Windows 3.1x user interface, while Windows NT 4.0 and later versions use the Windows 95 interface.

Unlike Windows 95, Windows NT does not support the Plug and Play specification for automatic detection of hardware, although some hardware can be detected automatically.

On the Exam

At this writing, Windows NT Workstation 4.0 is the current version, and the MCSE exams refer to this version. Windows NT 5.0, expected in late 1998, will include additional features such as support for Plug and Play.

Windows NT Workstation requires a minimum of 12 MB of memory on Intel systems, although Microsoft recommends at least 16 MB. RISC systems require at least 16 MB. Upgrading to 32 MB or more will almost always improve performance, however. NT Workstation requires approximately 117 MB of hard disk storage for the operating system.

Windows NT Server

Windows NT Server is the fuller-featured, more expensive version of Windows NT. Internally, NT Server and Workstation are nearly identical; the main differences are in licensing and additional software included with the Server version. The key features of NT Server include the following:

- Supports unlimited network connections (NT Workstation supports only 10).

- Supports multiprocessing with up to 4 processors (NT Workstation is limited to 2 processors). Up to 32 processors can be supported with custom software provided by the system vendor.

- Supports up to 256 simultaneous incoming dial-up remote access (RAS) sessions (NT Workstation is limited to one session).

- Supports fault tolerance: disk mirroring, disk duplexing, and disk striping with parity.

- Can act as a domain controller (PDC or BDC). NT Workstation computers can participate in a domain but cannot act as a controller.

- Includes Microsoft Services for Macintosh (SFM).

- Includes Gateway Services for NetWare (GSNW).

- Includes DHCP, DNS, and WINS servers.

- Includes Internet Information Server (IIS).

Windows NT Server's hardware requirements are slightly steeper than those of NT Workstation. A minimum of 16 MB of memory is required, although servers in all but the smallest networks will require at least 32 MB. NT Server also requires a minimum of 124 MB of hard disk storage. Optional services, such as IIS, will require additional disk space.

On the Exam

For the NT Workstation exam, you should know Windows NT Server's hardware requirements (especially where they differ from NT Workstation) and its advantages over NT Workstation. Other than that, you should focus your studies on the capabilities of NT Workstation.

NT Architecture

The Windows NT operating system consists of several modular components. These are grouped into two main modes of operation: the *kernel mode* components work directly with memory and hardware, and the *user mode* components work with users and applications.

Figure 2-1 illustrates the modules comprising Windows NT and the communication between them. These are described in detail in the sections below.

Kernel Mode Components

The kernel mode components of Windows NT provide access to the CPU, memory, and other hardware. These components are also referred to as *Executive Services*. There are three main kernel mode components:

- The *Hardware Abstraction Layer* (HAL) encapsulates many of the hardware-specific tasks performed by the operating system; other layers access hardware through this layer. This component is specific to each supported motherboard and CPU.

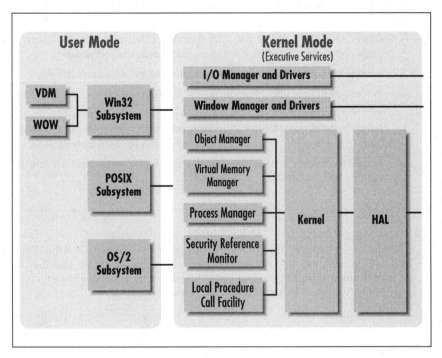

Figure 2-1: The components of the Windows NT OS

On the Exam

You don't need to entirely memorize this diagram for the NT Workstation exam, but you should know the various components (discussed below) and whether they run under user mode or kernel mode.

- *I/O Manager* handles communication with disk storage devices and network adapters. This component uses disk and network drivers to communicate directly with hardware, bypassing the HAL.

- *Window Manager* handles the video display for the graphical user interface (GUI). This component uses video drivers to communicate directly with the video adapter, bypassing the HAL. This is a new feature of Windows NT 4.0; in version 3.51 and earlier, these functions were provided in user mode. Handling screen output in kernel mode provides a speed increase, but increases the possibility of a GUI-related crash.

- The *kernel*, or *microkernel*, is the main hub of the operating system. The kernel handles synchronization between multiple processors, and prioritizes threads and assigns them to processors for execution. It also supports the remaining executive services, which communicate with hardware via the kernel and HAL:

- *Object Manager* handles the correspondence between objects (such as users and printers) and object names, and handles object security.

- *Virtual Memory Manager* handles virtual memory (discussed below).

- *Process Manager* allows applications to start, stop, or communicate between processes (threads).

- *Security Reference Monitor* communicates with the security subsystem (part of the Win32 subsystem) in user mode to provide logon security.

- *Local Procedure Call Facility* provides a set of procedures that can be used by applications.

On the Exam

You don't need to know the detailed workings of these systems for the NT Workstation exam, but you should be able to list them, be aware that they are kernel mode components, and know whether they access hardware directly (I/O Manager, Window Manager) or through the HAL.

User Mode Components

The user mode components of Windows NT handle the user interface, security, and the execution of user applications. User mode components have no direct access to hardware. There are two main components of user mode:

- The *security subsystem* handles logon security: a user name and password are required for access to system resources. Windows NT security is described in more detail later in this chapter.

- The *environment subsystems* allow the execution of various types of applications. These include the following:

  - The POSIX subsystem supports POSIX version 1 applications in text mode (these are rarely used).

  - The OS/2 subsystem, also rarely used, supports OS/2 1.x text-mode applications.

  - The Win32 subsystem supports 32-bit Windows applications (Windows 95 or NT) and provides the main user interface, communicating with the Window Manager in kernel mode for screen displays. The subsystems described below are also managed by the Win32 subsystem.

  - The DOS subsystem allows execution of DOS applications within VDMs (virtual DOS machines). Each of these has its own memory space.

  - The Windows-on-Windows (WOW) subsystem supports 16-bit Windows applications. By default, all 16-bit applications share a memory space and a virtual DOS machine. Applications can be executed in separate memory spaces if desired.

Virtual Memory

Windows NT uses a linear memory model: memory is handled as one contiguous block rather than divided into sections, such as conventional and extended memory in DOS. NT also supports *virtual memory*: swapping portions of memory to disk.

Windows NT makes memory available to applications in a 4-GB virtual memory address space. DOS applications each have a separate memory space; 16-bit Windows applications share a memory space; 32-bit Windows applications each have their own memory space. 2 GB of the virtual address space is used by the system, and 2 GB is available for the application.

The Virtual Memory Manager (VMM) within the NT Executive handles virtual memory. A file on the disk called a *paging file* stores the swapped memory. Applications see the memory as one large area, and are unaware of the swapping. Memory used by user mode applications and the NT Executive can be swapped.

When the physical memory space begins to run out, areas of memory that have not been used recently are swapped to disk to make room for current applications' needs. This system is called *demand paging*.

Unlike Windows 95, Windows NT's paging file can be split between multiple disk partitions. To configure paging, click the Change button in the Performance tab of the System control panel. You can configure a maximum and minimum paging file size for each drive letter. Splitting the paging file in this manner can provide a performance increase.

The Boot Process

As with other PC-based operating systems, the Windows NT OS is stored on disk, and loaded each time the computer is booted. NT's boot process is more complex than that of earlier versions of Windows. The following are the processes involved when Windows NT boots on an Intel-based computer:

1. The computer's BIOS (in ROM) reads the master boot record (MBR) from the hard disk. This contains the NT OS loader, NTLDR. If a SCSI controller without its own BIOS is in use, a driver is loaded from the NTBOOTDD.SYS file at this point.

2. NTLDR reads the BOOT.INI file and displays a menu of available operating systems. Configuring this file is described in the installation section of this chapter.

3. If DOS or a previous version of Windows was chosen, a DOS boot sector is read from the BOOTSECT.DOS file and executed. Otherwise, Windows NT begins to load.

4. NTLDR calls NTDETECT.COM. This program tests and detects the computer's hardware, and displays an error message if any hardware problems are found.

5. NTLDR then transfers control to NTOSKRNL.EXE, the Windows NT kernel. This in turn starts the user mode subsystems and user interface. A module that handles the hardware abstraction layer, HAL.DLL, is loaded by the kernel.

On the Exam

On a RISC computer, the boot process is similar. The main difference is that a single program, OSLOADER.EXE, handles the function of NTLDR and NT-DETECT. You should not need to know any RISC-specific boot information for the NT Workstation exam.

The boot process uses two special disk partitions, referred to as the *boot partition* and the *system partition*. These may be the same volume. These names are misleading: The boot files used in Steps 1–4 above are stored on the system partition, and NTOSKRNL.EXE and other operating system files are stored on the boot partition. Table 2-2 summarizes the files found on each of these partitions.

Table 2-2: Files Contained in the Boot and System Partitions

System Partition	Boot Partition
NTBOOTDD.SYS	NTOSKRNL.EXE
NTLDR	HAL.DLL
BOOT.INI	\WINNT files
BOOTSECT.DOS	
NTDETECT.COM	

On the Exam

For the NT Workstation exam, you should be aware of the steps involved in the boot process. You should also know which files are on the boot and system partitions. The names of the partitions may be confusing: the partition that contains the boot record is called the system partition. The "Optimization and Troubleshooting" section at the end of this chapter covers potential problems with the files listed here.

Using Windows NT

Windows NT 4.0's user interface is nearly identical to that of Windows 95. The initial Windows NT display includes a desktop with various icons. The My Computer icon provides access to the computer's disk drives through the Windows NT explorer, and the Start menu allows access to installed applications.

Starting Applications

Applications can be started in Windows NT using a variety of methods:

- From a shortcut (link) in the Start menu
- From a shortcut on the desktop
- From the Start menu's *Run* command
- From the command prompt

Windows NT internally supports 32 levels of priority for applications and processes (32 is the highest priority). You can use the `start` command at the command prompt to start an application with a specific priority:

```
start /priority application
```

The priority used in this command can be one of the following: *low* (4), *normal* (8), *high* (13), and *realtime* (24). The realtime priority can only be used by administrators. Using the realtime priority can devote up to 100% of the CPU's processing time to the application, effectively shutting down any background applications.

The priority affects the amount of CPU time available to the application. The priorities higher than 24 are reserved for operating system components. The system also changes priorities dynamically to allow for efficient multitasking.

On the Exam

The Task Manager utility, described in "Optimization and Troubleshooting" at the end of this chapter, allows you to change the priority of background processes; however, you cannot change the priority of an application without stopping and restarting it.

Windows NT supports several types of applications, supported by the various subsystems introduced earlier in this chapter:

DOS

Each DOS application runs in its own virtual DOS machine (VDM). The AUTOEXEC.NT and CONFIG.NT files provide configuration information for DOS applications, equivalent to AUTOEXEC.BAT and CONFIG.SYS in DOS. Applications that attempt to access hardware directly or use their own extended memory managers are not supported by Windows NT. Preemptive multitasking is supported for multiple DOS programs in separate VDMs. Each

DOS application has its own memory space, and DOS applications cannot communicate with other applications.

Win16 (16-bit Windows)

16-bit Windows applications are run in the WOW (Windows-on-Windows) subsystem, which also uses a VDM. These applications share a VDM and memory space by default, and are thus cooperatively multitasked. You can optionally specify that an application runs in its own VDM. This prevents crashes from affecting other running applications, and allows preemptive multitasking. 16-bit Windows applications can communicate with each other and with 32-bit applications.

Win32 (32-bit Windows)

32-bit Windows applications written for Windows NT are supported, along with the majority of those written for Windows 95. The exception: Windows 95 applications that access hardware in non-standard ways (such as some games). 32-bit applications each have their own memory space, but can communicate with each other and with 16-bit applications.

POSIX

Only POSIX version 1 applications are supported, and only in text mode. This limits support to very few available applications.

OS/2

Like POSIX, OS/2 support is limited. Only OS/2 1.3 and earlier applications are supported, and Presentation Manager, OS/2's window environment, is not supported. Therefore, only text-mode applications can be used. A separate extension called PMSHELL is available for download from Microsoft; this allows support for OS/2 1.3 or earlier Presentation Manager applications.

On the Exam

For the MCSE exam, you should know all of the types of applications that can run under Windows NT, and the types of non-Win32 applications that are unable to run under Windows NT.

Network Browsing

If Windows NT Workstation is used in a network environment, it can access network resources (chiefly files and printers) by browsing. Clicking the Network Neighborhood icon on the desktop opens an Explorer window that displays available network resources.

A list of resources offered by computers in the local workgroup or domain is displayed, and the Entire Network option provides access to nonlocal resources.

The contents of the Network Neighborhood window are obtained by accessing the Windows NT browser service. This service operates within networks to maintain a list of available resources. This list comes from a computer acting as a master browser or backup browser. Browser roles are described in more detail in Part 3.

UNC Paths

Universal naming convention, or UNC, is a standard for referring to network resources on the local network. UNC paths are an extension of file system paths, and use a similar format. The format of a UNC path is:

```
\\servername\share
```

Servername refers to the server offering access to the resource, and *share* refers to the name of the shared resource. The path can continue to refer to subdirectories under the shared directory if the user is allowed access. File and printer sharing is described in more detail later in "Configuring NT Workstation."

On the Exam

The specific syntax of UNC pathnames is often covered in MCSE test questions. Be sure you're familiar with the format; it may be helpful to experiment with names on a network to be sure you're using them correctly.

Mapping Network Drives

Right-clicking on the Network Neighborhood icon allows access to the *Map Network Drive* option. This allows you to define a UNC path to a network share and assign a local drive letter to the directory. Drives can be automatically mapped each time Windows NT Workstation is started.

Installing NT Workstation

Windows NT's installation process is largely automated and relatively simple. This section looks at the Windows NT installation process, from simple installations to large-scale server-based installation.

On the Exam

The following information about installation applies to both Windows NT Workstation and NT Server, and is included in both exams. Part 3 covers installation concerns unique to Windows NT Server.

Installation Planning

Before installing Windows NT on a computer, you should determine its compatibility with Windows NT. You should also have an idea of the type of network and file systems that will be used and the method of installation. These considerations are discussed in the sections that follow.

Hardware Requirements

Before installing Windows NT, be sure the computer meets the minimum hardware requirements. The minimum requirements for NT Workstation on Intel-based computers are described in Table 2-3.

Table 2-3: Windows NT Workstation Requirements

Item	Requirement
CPU	486/33 or higher (Pentium recommended)
RAM	12 MB (16 MB recommended)
Display	VGA, Super VGA, or better
Hard disk	SCSI or IDE; 117 MB of space required for OS
Floppy disk	3.5", 1.4 MB
CD-ROM	SCSI or IDE (not required for network installations)
Network interface card	Any supported by NT; only required for network access

There are more specific requirements for each of these devices: for example, certain CD-ROM drives or video adapters may not be supported by Windows NT. Each version of Windows NT includes a hardware compatibility list (HCL) that describes hardware that has been tested and verified to work with Windows NT.

The HCL is included on the Windows NT Workstation CD-ROM as HCL.TXT in the \SUPPORT directory. An updated version is always available from Microsoft's web or FTP sites.

On the Exam

Windows NT's hardware requirements are a common subject for MCSE test questions. Be sure you know all of the information above, and know where to access the HCL for specific information.

Windows NT also includes a utility called the NT Hardware Qualifier (NTHQ) that tests a computer for compatibility and detects supported devices. To use this utility, make an NTHQ disk by executing the MAKEDISK.BAT file in the \SUPPORT\HQTOOL directory of the Windows NT CD-ROM.

To use the NTHQ disk, insert it into a floppy drive and boot the computer. After booting, NTHQ starts a graphical interface. It offers two main options: Comprehensive detection (checks for all devices) and Safe detection (limits checking to avoid crashes). If the comprehensive option fails, try the safe option.

NTHQ spends several minutes analyzing the system. When finished, it displays a summary dialog and allows you to display information about various categories of the system (Motherboard, Network, Video, Storage, and Others). A complete report of the devices detected and their compatibility is stored in NTHQ.TXT on the floppy when you exit the utility.

Disk Partitions

Windows NT can be installed in a FAT or NTFS partition. The installation program is able to create either of these if there is empty space available on a hard disk. If you have existing partitions on the disk, you can delete them from the installation program, or with the DOS or Windows 95 FDISK utility before installing Windows NT.

Network Connection

If the computer you are installing Windows NT Workstation on will be used in a network, you should connect the network adapter to the network media before beginning the installation. This allows the network and any existing servers to be detected.

Network Planning

When planning one or more Windows NT installations, you should also have an idea of what type of network will be used and how its resources will be distributed. Areas of consideration for network planning are described in the sections below.

Network Types

As mentioned in Part 1, there are two basic types of Windows NT network:

- *Workgroup*, or peer-to-peer networks, in which each workstation can share resources and handle its own user authentication. This type is best suited for small networks with 10 computers or less.

- *Domain*, or client-server networks, in which one or more dedicated servers are used for resource sharing and network-wide user authentication. This type of network can handle large numbers of users.

On the Exam

As mentioned in Part 1, Microsoft recommends that peer-to-peer networks be used only in networks with 10 or fewer computers. A domain-based network may be useful even for small networks if central administration or security is required.

Within a workgroup network, each workstation is simply a member of the workgroup. Within a domain, Windows NT Server computers can serve several roles: Primary Domain Controller (PDC), Backup Domain Controller (BDC), member servers, or standalone servers. These roles are discussed in detail in Part 3. Windows NT Workstation can act only as a standalone server.

File Systems

Another factor in planning Windows NT installations is the file system or systems to be used. Several file systems are currently used in PC-based systems:

- FAT (file allocation table) is the file system originally implemented by DOS. It is limited to eight-character file names with three-character extensions and supports partitions up to 2 GB.

- VFAT (virtual FAT) is a modified implementation of the FAT system. The main differences are that it supports long file names and raises the maximum partition size limit to 4 GB. This system is backward compatible with FAT. This is the implementation of the FAT system used in Windows NT and Windows 95.

- FAT32 is a new version of the FAT system implemented by recent versions of Windows 95 (OSR2 and later). This system is not backward compatible with FAT. It provides for more reliable storage and more efficient use of space, and raises the partition size limit to 4 TB (terabytes). FAT32 is currently supported only by Windows 95.

- NTFS (NT file system) is an improved file system, supported only by Windows NT 4.0 and later. NTFS is not based on the FAT system. It supports long filenames, partitions as large as 16 EB (exabytes). and supports fault tolerance, security, and compression.

- HPFS (high-performance file system) is a 32-bit, secure file system developed by IBM for use with OS/2. Windows NT supported HPFS up to version 3.51, but does not support it in version 4.0 or later.

- CDFS (compact disc file system) is a read-only file system for compact discs. The CD-ROM support in Windows 95 and Windows NT uses the CDFS standard. This supports the ISO 9660 standard for DOS-compatible file names as well as extensions that allow for long filenames and bootable CD-ROMs.

On the Exam

It's easy to confuse the abbreviations HPFS and NTFS, which may appear as different possible answers in an NT Workstation exam question. Be sure to read the questions carefully. Remember that HPFS is not supported in Windows NT 4.0, and its use is not supported or recommended by Microsoft.

When installing Windows NT, you will need to choose between the two supported hard disk formats: FAT and NTFS. There are a variety of reasons to choose each one:

- FAT should be used for dual-boot systems, since it can be accessed by DOS or earlier versions of Windows. It also has a lower overhead than NTFS and is more efficient for small volumes; Microsoft recommends that FAT be used for partitions of 400 MB or smaller.

- NTFS has many advantages. It stores files more efficiently, supports file-level security, is more reliable, and supports Windows NT's more advanced fault

---

tolerant features, such as disk striping. NTFS is particularly more efficient with larger drives; Microsoft recommends using NTFS exclusively with partitions 400 MB or larger.

Another factor to consider is the ability to convert between file systems. Windows NT includes a utility, CONVERT.EXE, to convert FAT partitions to NTFS without loss of data. There is no way to convert NTFS partitions to FAT without backing up data and reformatting (and permissions will be lost in this process).

On the Exam

When you choose to create an NTFS partition during installation, the partition is actually created as a FAT partition. When Windows NT reboots to begin the graphical portion of installation, the partition is converted to NTFS.

Installation Methods

The Windows NT operating system is provided on a single CD-ROM disk. The OS can be installed using two basic methods, depending on the existing configuration:

- By creating and booting installation disks. This is the only method that works if another OS is not already installed on the computer. This method requires a CD-ROM drive compatible with the Windows NT hardware compatibility list (HCL), described earlier in this chapter.

- By running the installation program (WINNT or WINNT32) manually. This method works only if a previous OS is available on the computer. You can use this method with the /b switch to install without using floppy disks, providing for a faster installation. In addition, installation files on a local disk or network share can be used, eliminating the need for an HCL-compatible CD-ROM drive.

A third method is possible on some systems: booting the Windows NT CD-ROM directly. The CD-ROM conforms to the El Torito standard for bootable CDs; currently, this is not supported on a majority of systems.

Several specific installation procedures using these two basic methods are described in the following sections.

In the Real World

The sections below refer to the WINNT and WINNT32 installation programs. These programs are identical in function; the choice of which to use depends on the computer's existing operating system. These programs are described in detail later in this section.

Boot Disks/CD-ROM

If no previous OS is installed on the computer but the CD-ROM drive is compatible with the HCL, you can boot Windows NT installation floppy disks and continue the installation using the CD-ROM. You can create the installation disks from a different computer using the **WINNT** /OX command, described later in this section.

If the computer has a previous OS installed, you can use the **WINNT** /OX command to create installation disks and begin the installation immediately.

CD-ROM with Previous OS

If the computer has an existing operating system with access to the CD-ROM drive, you can install Windows NT directly from the CD-ROM. Use the WINNT or WINNT32 program, as described later in this section. The CD-ROM must be compatible with the Windows NT HCL.

From Hard Disk

If the CD-ROM drive is not HCL compatible, you can use an existing OS with access to the CD-ROM to copy the installation files to the hard disk, and run the installation program from there. The only files that need to be copied are in the OS-specific directories (such as I386) described below.

Over the Network

Windows NT can also be installed from a network share containing the appropriate platform-specific installation directory. This can be shared directly from the CD-ROM or from a hard disk copy of the files. Network shares are explained later in this chapter.

The Installation Program

The Windows NT Workstation CD-ROM includes separate installation directories for specific microprocessors: ALPHA (Digital Alpha) and I386 (Intel 386-series processors).

On the Exam

The Windows NT Workstation exam deals mainly with the Intel version of the operating system. You should be aware of the other systems, but you don't need to know the details of non-Intel installations for the exam.

The actual Windows NT installation program for Intel computers is WINNT.EXE or WINNT32.EXE. These programs perform the same function, but run under different operating systems:

- WINNT is a 16-bit version for use under DOS, Windows, or Windows 95.

- WINNT32 is a 32-bit version for use with Windows NT. This version does not work with Windows 95.

If you install using boot disks, WINNT32 is launched automatically (as you have effectively booted Windows NT). If you are starting the installation manually or creating installation disks, choose the correct version for the OS you are using. The specific options available for these utilities are described below.

In the Real World

The exam focuses on installation for Intel-based systems. To install Windows NT on a RISC computer, use the RISC setup menu. An *Install Windows NT* option may be available; if it is not, choose the *Run a Program* option and run the SETUPLDR program on the CD-ROM.

---

winnt, winnt32

winnt [*options*]

winnt32 [*options*]

Installs Windows NT. The Windows NT installation program can be run with one or more command-line parameters to control the specifics of the installation. The options are the same for WINNT and WINNT32, except where noted below.

Options

/B

Installs without using boot disks. Files to boot Windows NT are copied to the hard disk. This option can be used to speed up the installation process when installing from a previous OS.

/C

(WINNT only) Eliminates the check for free space when creating boot disks.

/E:command

Specifies a program to be executed when the installation has completed.

/F

(WINNT only) When used with the /O or /OX option, copies the files to the boot disks without write verification.

/OX

Creates boot disks, but does not start the installation. This option is useful if you are creating disks for use on a computer with no existing OS.

/S:path

Uses path as the source directory for the installation. This should be the I386 directory on the CD-ROM, a copy of it, or a network share. The directory containing WINNT is used by default.

/T:drive

Uses drive to store temporary files used for the installation. Approximately 104 MB of free space is required on the temporary drive.

/U

Unattended installation. See the "Server-Based Installation" section later in this chapter for details.

/UDF

Specifies that a uniqueness database file (UDF) will be used in an unattended installation.

Steps for Installation

When you run WINNT or WINNT32 from the appropriate location to install Windows NT on an Intel-based computer, you are prompted for several categories of information about the computer and the network as the installation progresses. The installation program uses five main phases, described below.

On the Exam

For the exam, you should be familiar with all of the installation steps, although you don't need to know exact details. You should also know which steps are performed in each of the phases described below. You should install Windows NT Workstation at least once to familiarize yourself with the process.

Pre-Copy Phase

This first phase takes place only if you run the WINNT program from an existing operating system. If you use boot disks for the installation, the next phase starts after the disks are booted.

1. From a Windows or DOS command prompt, type WINNT or WINNT32 to begin the installation. Use WINNT /B or WINNT32 /B to install without creating boot disks. You can use the /OX option instead to create installation disks for use on another computer.

2. You are prompted to enter the path for the Windows NT installation files (usually \I386). Files are now copied to the hard disk to boot Windows NT.

3. After the file copy finishes, shut down the current OS and restart the computer.

Phase 0 (Text-Based Phase)

In this phase, the computer loads the Windows NT kernel, but does not yet start the GUI. The following tasks are performed:

1. Windows NT checks the computer's hardware and indicates any problems.

2. The Windows NT OS now loads.

3. The setup options screen is displayed. This prompts you to press Enter to continue the installation, or press R to repair an existing installation.

4. A list of detected SCSI and IDE disk and CD-ROM controllers is displayed. You can press S to specify additional controllers. Otherwise, press Enter to continue.

5. The Windows NT Workstation license agreement is displayed. Read it using the Page Up and Page Down keys. Press F8 to indicate your agreement, or Esc to disagree and abort the installation.

6. The detected components of your computer are displayed: computer type, display, keyboard, and mouse. You can change any of these entries, or press Enter to continue.

7. A list of installed disk drives and their partitions is displayed. You can choose an existing FAT or NTFS partition or press C to create a new partition in a free area.

8. You are prompted as to whether to format the disk partition as FAT or NTFS, or leave it as-is for existing partitions. Depending on the size of the partition, formatting may take several minutes.

9. Specify the location for the Windows NT Workstation files. The default is the \WINNT\ directory on the partition you chose above.

10. Windows NT will now scan the hard disk for errors. If you press Enter, an exhaustive scan is performed and may take several minutes. Press Esc to skip the exhaustive scan and continue.

11. Windows NT files are now copied to the directory you specified. This may take several minutes.

12. A final screen is displayed indicating that this portion of the installation is complete. Press Enter to restart the computer and begin the next phase.

Phase 1 (GUI Phase)

When the computer restarts this time, Windows NT Workstation is booted including the graphical user interface. The prompts described below are presented in graphic dialogs by the Windows NT Setup Wizard. You can use the Next and Previous buttons on most dialogs to move forward or backward in the installation process.

1. Choose an installation option (*Typical, Portable, Compact,* or *Custom*). This determines the software components to be installed later in this phase. You are offered additional choices throughout this phase if you choose the *Custom* option here.

2. You are prompted for the computer user's name and organization.

3. Enter the CD key. This is a 10-digit number printed on the certificate accompanying the installation CD-ROM.

4. Enter a name for the computer. This is a NetBIOS name, described in Part 1.

5. Enter a password for the Administrator account, which will be created automatically during installation.

6. You are asked whether to create an emergency repair disk (ERD). If you choose not to, you can create one after installation. Emergency repair disks are described in the "Optimization and Troubleshooting" section at the end of this chapter.

7. Select the optional operating system components to be installed. These are displayed in several categories: Accessibility Options, Accessories, Communications, Games, Multimedia, and Windows Messaging. This dialog is only displayed if you chose the *Custom* installation option.

Phase 2 (Network Setup)

The Setup Wizard continues with this phase, which asks questions relating to network components. Depending on whether a network is used and the protocols used, the prompts in this phase may vary.

1. Specify whether the computer is connected to a network, and whether any network will be accessed remotely using a modem. If you indicate that no network is to be used, skip to Phase 3.

2. Choose a network adapter. Use the Start Search button to search for an installed adapter, or the Select from List button to choose one from a list.

3. Specify the network protocols to install. Network protocols are discussed later in this chapter. (This choice is only offered if you chose the *Custom* installation option.)

4. Choose whether the computer will be a member of a workgroup or a domain, and enter the workgroup or domain name. If you specify a domain, the domain must already exist and the domain controller must be online. You will be required to enter an Administrator password to create a computer account in the domain, or specify an account name if you already created one.

5. Depending on the settings you chose, you may be prompted for additional information, such as settings for the network adapter and properties for network protocols.

6. The installation program now warns you that it is about to start the network. Press Next to continue. This searches the network for existing domains and workgroups.

7. After copying additional files, the installation process completes. Press the Finish button to continue.

Phase 3 (Final Phase)

This phase completes the installation.

1. You are prompted for the current date and time and the computer's time zone.

2. The Display Properties dialog is now displayed. Choose the settings for the computer's video adapter.

3. If you chose to create an emergency repair disk, you are prompted to insert a blank disk, and files are copied to the disk.

4. Installation is now complete. Press the Restart Computer button to restart and boot Windows NT. (If you have a bootable CD-ROM drive, be sure to remove the CD-ROM before restarting.)

Upgrading to Windows NT

You can upgrade a computer to Windows NT Workstation 4.0 if it has a previous version of Windows NT. The current version of Windows NT supports installing over a Windows 95 installation, but this is not a true upgrade: very few settings are imported. Windows NT does not support upgrading from Windows 3.1, previous Windows versions, OS/2, or other operating systems.

On the Exam

Windows NT can import user accounts and other information from a NetWare server. However, this process is called *migrating* rather than upgrading, and almost always requires an additional computer to run Windows NT. The NetWare migration tools are introduced in Part 3.

Use the WINNT32 program, described above, to upgrade a previous version of NT. The installed version is detected during the text-based phase of installation, and you are prompted whether to upgrade that version or install Windows NT Workstation in a separate directory.

If you upgrade, the following settings are preserved from the previous Windows NT installation:

- Control Panel settings, including network configuration
- Registry settings
- Start menu contents and desktop layout
- Preferences for some Windows NT utilities
- Users, groups, and other security settings

If you are upgrading an existing version of Windows NT with an HPFS partition, it can not be automatically converted to NTFS by the installation program. You can use the ACLCONV utility, available from Microsoft, to convert these partitions.

Configuring a Multi-Boot System

The Windows NT OS loader, NTLDR, includes the ability to display a menu of operating systems at boot time. This allows you to configure a dual-boot system, typically with Windows NT and DOS or a previous Windows version. Multiple versions of Windows NT on the same computer can also be selected.

Installation

If you install Windows NT on a computer with DOS, Windows 3.1x, or Windows 95 already installed and use a separate directory (or a separate partition) for the Windows NT files, the installation program automatically configures the computer for dual boot. Run the WINNT installation program from the existing OS to install Windows NT.

The BOOT.INI File

The entries in the boot menu are based on the BOOT.INI file, located in the system partition. A typical Windows NT Workstation BOOT.INI file is listed below:

```
[boot loader]
timeout=30
default=multi(0)disk(0)rdisk(0)partition(1)\WINNT4
[operating systems]
multi(0)disk(0)rdisk(0)partition(1)\WINNT4="Windows NT Workstation
    Version 4.00"
multi(0)disk(0)rdisk(0)partition(1)\WINNT4="Windows NT Workstation
    Version 4.00 [VGA mode]" /basevideo /sos
C:\="MS-DOS"
```

The file consists of the [boot loader] section with information about defaults, followed by the [operating systems] section with individual entries for each operating system.

The [boot loader] section can include two entries:

timeout
> The number of seconds before the default OS will be selected. A timeout of 0 causes the default OS to boot immediately; a timeout of -1 causes the boot loader to wait indefinitely for a selection.

default
> An entry in the same format as the OS entries below for the default OS.

The entries in the [operating systems] section can include bootable FAT partitions (such as C:\ in the example) for DOS or earlier versions of Windows, and ARC (Advanced RISC Computing) entries for Windows NT. ARC is a standard also used for booting other operating systems on RISC machines. ARC entries use the following format:

> adapter(x)disk(x)rdisk(x)partition(x)\directory = description

adapter
> Specifies the disk controller the boot volume is attached to. This value is always either multi(x) or scsi(x). The multi keyword is used for most disks, including most SCSI drives; the scsi keyword is used strictly for SCSI controllers without a built-in BIOS. The value in parenthesis is the adapter number or slot on the motherboard.

disk
> For scsi entries, this value indicates the boot drive's SCSI ID number. For multi entries, this value is unused and should be set to zero.

rdisk
> For multi entries, specifies the SCSI ID or IDE unit number of the boot drive. This entry is unused with scsi entries, and should be set to zero.

partition
> Specifies the partition within the hard disk. Partitions are numbered sequentially from 1.

directory

Specifies the path within the boot partition for the system files. This is typically \WINNT for Windows NT.

description

A description of the operating system corresponding with the boot entry. These descriptions are displayed in the boot loader menu.

On the Exam

You should know what each field in an ARC path refers to for the NT Workstation exam. You may be expected to identify the purpose of a particular ARC entry, or describe how to change one to correspond with a change in hardware configuration.

ARC entries for Windows NT can be followed by one or more of the following options:

/basevideo

This and the following options can be used after an OS entry. This option forces Windows NT to use VGA mode instead of the defined video driver. The VGA mode entry in the default BOOT.INI file uses this option.

/baudrate=number

Specifies a baud rate for external debugging.

/crashdebug

If specified, debugging is activated when an error occurs.

/debug

Forces debugging on. Debug messages are sent to a computer or terminal attached to the serial port indicated below.

/debugport=port

Specifies a serial port (COM1–COM4) for external debugging.

/maxmem:number

Limits the amount of memory visible to Windows NT to the specified number of bytes.

/nodebug

Explicitly turns off debugging.

/noserialmice=device

Prevents Windows NT's usual scan of the indicated serial device (COM1–COM4). This is useful for a port connected to an uninterruptible power supply (UPS) as the scan can inadvertently cause the UPS to shut down or indicate an error.

/sos

Specifies verbose mode for device drivers.

Removing Windows NT

Removing Windows NT is reasonably simple. If Windows NT was installed on a FAT partition, you can simply boot another operating system and remove the \WINNT directory and other files associated with NT (listed below), or delete the partition entirely if desired.

If Windows NT is installed on an NTFS partition, you can remove that partition using the DOS or Windows 95 FDISK utility (for primary partitions) or the Windows NT installation boot disks (for extended partitions).

If you wish to continue using other operating systems installed on the computer, you can remove the NT boot loader. Boot DOS or Windows 95 and use the SYS C: command to rewrite the boot sector.

After removing Windows NT, the following files may remain in the root directory of the boot drive and can be deleted to reclaim disk space:

    BOOT.INI
    BOOTSECT.DOS
    NTBOOTDD.SYS
    NTDETECT.COM
    NTLDR
    PAGEFILE.SYS

Server-Based Installation

Although Windows NT's installation process is simple, it does take time and requires continuous attention to answer queries. If you need to install Windows NT on several computers, you can automate the installation using the features described below.

Unattended Installation

The Windows NT installation program supports the use of an unattended installation file, also called an *answer file*. This is an ASCII text file that includes the information that the installation program would normally prompt for during installation. An example answer file is included on the Windows NT CD-ROM as UNATTEND.TXT.

On the Exam

Although the unattended installation answer file can have any legal filename, questions in the NT Workstation exam may refer to this file as UNATTEND.TXT.

The answer file includes sections corresponding to each portion of the installation process:

[Unattended]
> Includes information usually prompted for in the text-based phase of installation. This includes upgrade options, file system options, and the path for the WINNT directory.

[UserData]
> Includes information about the registered user: name, organization, computer name, and CD Key.

[GuiUnattended]
> Includes information normally prompted for in the GUI phase of installation, including the Administrator password and the computer's time zone.

[Display]
> Includes configuration details for the video adapter.

[Network]
> Includes information about installed network adapters and desired protocols and services. This may specify additional sections to be read for detailed information about network protocols and services.

On the Exam

You don't need to know all the available answer file options for the exam, but you should be familiar with the purpose of this file, what it can and cannot do, and how to use it in an installation.

The specific parameters used in answer files are listed in the Windows NT Workstation Resource Kit. You can create the answer file manually with a text editor, or use the Setup Manager utility, described below. Once you've created the answer file, use the WINNT or WINNT32 program to begin the installation:

```
WINNT /U:path\unattend.txt /S:path\I386
```

The /U option specifies the path to the answer file, and the /S option (required) specifies the path to the installation files.

The Setup Manager Utility

The Setup Manager utility provides an alternative to manually creating unattended installation answer files. This utility is included on the Windows NT installation CD-ROM as \SUPPORT\DEPTOOLS\I386\SETUPMGR.EXE. (For non-Intel systems, replace I386 with MIPS, ALPHA, or PPC).

Setup Manager includes three main options, each of which displays a tabbed dialog to prompt for detailed information:

General Setup
> The settings in this dialog include most of the options in the Unattended, Userdata, GuiUnattended, and Display sections of the UNATTEND.TXT file.

Networking Setup
> These settings correspond to the [Network] section of the answer file.

Advanced Setup
> This dialog includes advanced settings, such as converting FAT partitions to NTFS. Nonstandard keyboards or pointing devices are also defined here.

Once you've specified the desired options, use Setup Manager's Save button to save the answer file. The New button allows you to create another file with new settings.

UDF Files

Unattended answer files are very specific, including items such as user information that will vary from computer to computer. You can avoid creating separate answer files for each computer by using a separate file called a uniqueness database file (UDF).

The UDF is a text file similar in format to the answer file. This file can define two or more IDs for separate computers, and specify the unique settings for each one. The following is a simple example:

```
[UniqueIds]
west1=UserData
west2=UserData,GuiUnattended

[west1:UserData]
Full Name="Andrew Jackson"
ComputerName=West1

[west2:UserData]
Full Name="Thomas Jefferson"
ComputerName=West2

[west2:GuiUnattended]
OemSkipWelcome=1
```

The first section of the UDF file, UniqueIds, assigns IDs to each computer and lists the sections of the answer file that will be overridden for each computer. The remaining sections contain the overriding information. If an item is not defined in this file, the default value in the UNATTEND.TXT file is used.

The SYSDIFF Utility

If you need to install applications beyond the Windows NT installation at each computer, you can use the SYSDIFF utility to automate this process. This utility is included in the Windows NT installation CD-ROM as \SUPPORT\DEPTOOLS\ I386\SYSDIFF.EXE.

The basic steps for using SYSDIFF are as follows:

1. Install Windows NT on a computer.
2. Run SYSDIFF /SNAP to record the standard configuration.
3. Install the additional applications and files.
4. Run SYSDIFF /DIFF to create a difference file.
5. Use SYSDIFF /APPLY to apply the difference file to other computers after the Windows NT installation.

SYSDIFF's options are listed in detail below:

/snap snap_file
Creates a snapshot of the current computer's configuration to the file specified.

/diff snap_file diff_file
Creates a difference file that lists the differences between the current configuration and the base configuration found in the specified snapshot file.

/apply diff_file
Applies the specified difference file to the current computer's configuration.

/inf diff_file path
Creates an INF file to correspond with the specified difference file in the specified OEM path. This file can be used to further automate installation as described in Part 3.

/dump diff_file file
Creates a report of the difference file's contents to the filename specified.

Managing Network Components

Windows NT Workstation is a versatile network client. Protocols are included to interact with Microsoft, Novell, TCP/IP, and other networks. This section looks at several important network components included with Windows NT Workstation.

Network components are configured using the Network control panel. To access this dialog, right-click on the Network Neighborhood icon on the desktop and select *Properties*. This option is also available from the Control Panel, described in the next section. The Network control panel includes several tabbed categories:

Identification
> Specifies the NetBIOS computer name, and the workgroup or domain the computer belongs to.

Services
> Allows you to add or remove network services. Some network client software, such as the NetWare client described below, is installed here.

Protocols
> Allows you to configure protocols for use on the network. Common protocols include NWLink (IPX/SPX), NetBIOS, and TCP/IP.

Adapters
> Allows you to configure installed network adapters.

Bindings
> Allows you to configure the bindings (connections) between various network services, protocols, and adapters.

On the Exam

Windows NT includes a special network loopback driver that allows you to use software that requires a network adapter without an actual network connection. This may be useful in your studies or for testing software. To install this device, select *Add* from the Adapters tab of the Network control panel and select *MS Loopback Adapter* as the device to add.

The following sections describe the network clients and other components that you need to understand for the Windows NT Workstation exam in detail. Other protocols are described in Part 3.

Microsoft Network Components

A variety of network components are included with Windows NT. The sections below describe some of the most useful protocols and services.

Protocols

The following network protocols are available with Windows NT Workstation:

- NetBEUI (NetBIOS Extended User Interface) is Microsoft's protocol built to support NetBIOS (described below) over networks. NetBEUI has a low overhead compared with other protocols and is easy to configure, but is not routable.

- TCP/IP is the standard protocol of UNIX and the Internet. TCP/IP is described in more detail later in this section.

- NWLink is Microsoft's implementation of Novell's IPX and SPX protocols. This protocol is described in more detail later in this section.

- DLC (Data Link Control) is a non-routable protocol used for communication with IBM mainframes using the SNA architecture. It is also supported by some printers with network interfaces, such as Hewlett-Packard's JetDirect interface.

Services

The following are some of the network services available in Windows NT Workstation:

- The NetBIOS (Network Basic Input/Output Services) interface, which supports a basic set of function calls used by network-aware applications. NetBIOS can be used over any of the supported network protocols.

- The Workstation service enables a Windows NT computer to access network resources.

- The Server service enables a workstation (or server) to share files and printers.

- The Computer Browser service allows the computer to participate in network browsing, described earlier in this chapter.

NetWare Client Software

Windows NT includes software to act as a client in a NetWare network and access resources on NetWare servers. NetWare support is provided by four components:

- Client Service for NetWare (CSNW) is the NetWare client software.

- NWLink is the protocol used for NetWare connectivity.

- Gateway Service for NetWare (GSNW) allows a Windows NT Server computer to act as a gateway to a NetWare network, making NetWare resources available to Windows NT clients without installing NetWare client software. GSNW also includes the functionality of CSNW.

- File and Print Services for NetWare (FPNW) allows clients on the NetWare network to access shared files and printers in the Windows NT Network. Windows NT Server computers running FPNW can be accessed as if they were NetWare servers, with no additional client software. FPNW is not included with Windows NT, but is available from Microsoft at additional cost.

Two of these components, CSNW and NWLink, are included with Windows NT Workstation and are described below. GSNW is included only with Windows NT Server, and is covered in Part 3.

On the Exam

You should be able to identify all four of the services listed above for the NT Workstation exam, but you shouldn't need to know the details of GSNW and FPNW. The exam focuses on CSNW and NWLink, which you should study thoroughly.

Client Service for NetWare (CSNW)

Windows NT Workstation can use CSNW to access a NetWare network. This is a full-featured 32-bit NetWare client that allows access to NDS (NetWare Directory Services). This is Microsoft's implementation of a NetWare client, and is unrelated to NetWare's own product (Client32 for Windows NT).

You can install CSNW using the Add button in the Services tab of the Network control panel. Once installed, you can access the CSNW icon in the Control Panel. The following options are included in the CSNW configuration:

Preferred Server
> For bindery (NetWare 3.12 and earlier) connections, specify a preferred NetWare server. If this server is unavailable, the nearest available server will be used.

Default Tree and Context
> For NDS (NetWare 4.0 and later) connections, specify the NDS tree and default context. NDS supports a global directory for multiple NetWare servers.

Print Options
> These three options (Add Form Feed, Notify When Printed, Print Banner) can be modified to suit your printing preferences.

Login Script Options
> Specifies whether the NetWare login script for the user, group, or context is executed after login.

NWLink IPX/SPX Protocol

Novell NetWare networks include the IPX (Internetwork Packet Exchange) and SPX (Sequenced Packet Exchange) protocols. These protocols were developed by Novell and are the default protocols for NetWare networks, although NetWare does support other protocols.

NWLink is Microsoft's implementation of the IPX/SPX protocols, and is included with Windows NT. This protocol is automatically installed when you install CSNW, or can be installed manually with the Add button in the Protocols tab of the Network control panel.

NWLink can also be used as a protocol in Windows NT networks that don't require NetWare connectivity. Used in this fashion, NWLink is easier to configure than TCP/IP and is routable, unlike NetBEUI.

On the Exam

While NWLink is separate from CSNW, the CSNW installation automatically installs this protocol. Therefore, you will only need to specifically install NWLink if you are using it on a non-NetWare network. This topic may be covered in NT Workstation MCSE questions.

Selecting NWLink and choosing *Properties* from the Network control panel displays the NWLink configuration dialog. While you may be able to access the NetWare network without modifying these settings, you will need to change them for certain networks. The settings include the following:

Internal Network Number
Specify an IPX network number, which should match the one specified in the NetWare server's AUTOEXEC.NCF file. This is only necessary if you run certain types of software, such as IPX routing or File and Print Services for NetWare.

Adapter
Choose one of the network adapters in the computer. The settings below will affect the adapter you have selected here.

Auto Frame Type Detection
Specifies that frame types (described below) will be detected automatically.

Manual Frame Type Detection
Select this option and add one or more frame types to manually add support for NetWare frame types, as described in the next section.

NetWare Frame Types

NetWare networks use a variety of frame types (formats for network packets and headers). The following are common NetWare frame types:

802.2
The industry standard, used by default in Windows NT and NetWare 3.12 and higher.

802.3
A proprietary frame type used by Novell in NetWare 3.11 and earlier versions.

Ethernet SNAP
A modified version of the IEEE 802.3 standard widely used in non-Novell networks, particularly AppleTalk.

Ethernet II
A standard frame used by most TCP/IP networks, including NetWare networks with TCP/IP support.

802.5

The standard frame type for Token Ring networks.

Token Ring SNAP

The frame type used in Token Ring AppleTalk (TokenTalk) networks.

The vast majority of NetWare networks use the 802.3 or 802.2 frame types. In general, 802.3 is used in NetWare 3.11 and earlier, and 802.2 is used in NetWare 3.12 and later. However, NetWare supports multiple frame types; because Novell's standard frame type changed, many NetWare 4.x networks are configured for both 802.2 and 802.3.

In the Real World

Novell's frame type numbers don't match up with the IEEE's 802 standards (described in Part 1). Novell's 802.3 is proprietary and does not follow the IEEE 802.3 standard for CSMA/CD. Novell's 802.2 is the IEEE 802.3 standard (IEEE 802.2 defines Logical Link Control, which is also supported by Novell's 802.2).

NWLink's *Auto Frame Type Detection* option, described above, may have trouble detecting networks using frame types other than 802.2. If your NetWare network uses a different frame type, you may need to choose the *Manual Frame Type Detection* option and add one or more frame types to support to the list.

On the Exam

Remember that you may need to explicitly add support for any frame type other than 802.2. For example, NetWare 3.1x networks frequently use 802.3. This topic is frequently seen on Windows NT Workstation exam questions.

TCP/IP

TCP/IP (Transport Control Protocol/Internet Protocol) is a suite of protocols in widespread use on the Internet. These are also the protocols used with UNIX systems. Windows NT also installs TCP/IP support by default. This section describes TCP/IP and how to use Windows NT Workstation as a TCP/IP client.

On the Exam

This is a simple introduction to TCP/IP for the purposes of the Windows NT Workstation exam. Some advanced aspects of TCP/IP are explained in Part 4.

IP Addressing

TCP/IP uses a system of *IP addresses* to distinguish between clients on the network. Each node has its own unique IP address. The IP address is a 32-bit number, expressed in dotted decimal format, such as 198.60.22.1. The four divisions of the IP address are referred to as *octets*.

A portion of the address is a network address, and a portion is a host address. The division between these components depends on the address class. In class A addresses, the first octet is the network address and the remainder is the host. Class B networks use the first two octets as the network address, and class C networks use the first three. Each class is also identified by a unique range for the first octet. Table 2-4 summarizes the IP address classes.

Table 2-4: IP Address Classes

Class	First Byte Range	Network/ Host Octets	Number of Networks	Hosts per Network
A	1-126	1/3	126	16,777,214
B	128-191	2/2	16,382	65,534
C	192-223	3/1	2,097,150	254

A technique called *subnet masking* can be used to further subdivide the network and host addresses. A subnet mask is a 32-bit binary number with digits set to 1 representing the network address and digits set to 0 representing the host address. This allows a greater variety of possible numbers of hosts and networks.

In configuring a TCP/IP client computer, you will need to know its assigned IP address and subnet mask. For networks connected to the Internet, these consist of a network number assigned by the InterNIC and a host number assigned by the administrator. For private networks, the network and host numbers are assigned by the network administrator. Addresses can be automatically assigned by the DHCP protocol, described below.

In the Real World

Although the InterNIC traditionally assigns TCP/IP network numbers, there are very few available network numbers today, and it is very difficult to obtain a new number. Networks that require Internet connectivity today usually use a block of IP addresses leased from an ISP (Internet Service Provider).

Hosts on an IP network also have alphanumeric names corresponding to their IP addresses. These can be local names, such as *server*, or fully qualified names, such as *server1.company.com*. DNS (Domain Name Service) is used to translate between host names and addresses.

TCP/IP Protocols and Services

The TCP/IP suite includes a great many protocols. The following are some of the higher-level protocols and services typically used with Windows NT:

DHCP (Dynamic Host Configuration Protocol)
> This protocol allows clients to be dynamically issued IP addresses from a pool of available addresses. Windows NT Workstation can act as a DHCP client. DHCP can also dynamically assign DNS and WINS server addresses and default gateway information.

DNS (Domain Name Service)
> This is an Internet standard protocol that translates host names into their corresponding IP addresses. This process is called *name resolution.* DNS can also translate IP addresses to host names (known as Reverse DNS). Windows NT Workstation can act as a DNS client; NT Server includes a DNS server implementation.

WINS (Windows Internet Naming Service)
> This is Microsoft's alternative protocol for host name resolution. WINS translates between IP addresses and NetBIOS names, described in Part 1. NetBIOS names can be resolved without a WINS server through the use of broadcasts or a local LMHOSTS file.

SLIP (Serial Line Internet Protocol)
> This is a protocol used for dial-up connections to servers. This is typically used by Internet service providers, but can also be used to dial in to Windows NT computers.

PPP (Point-to-Point Protocol)
> This is an alternative protocol for dial-up connections. PPP is newer and includes more sophisticated configuration and security features. In addition, while SLIP supports TCP/IP connections only, PPP can support NetBEUI or IPX/SPX protocols.

HTTP (Hypertext Transfer Protocol)
> This is the protocol used for WWW (World Wide Web) servers. Windows NT Workstation includes Peer Web Services, a server for HTTP, FTP, and Gopher.

FTP (File Transfer Protocol)
> This is a protocol that allows for file transfers between computers, and is commonly used on the Internet as well as local TCP/IP networks.

Gopher
> This is an Internet distributed information service that predates the WWW. It is still in limited use, particularly by universities.

On the Exam

For the Windows NT Workstation exam, you only need to understand DHCP, DNS, and WINS from the client perspective. Windows NT Server can act as a server for these protocols, as described in Part 3.

You may have installed TCP/IP as part of the Windows NT Workstation installation. If not, you can add it by using the Add button in the Protocols tab of the Network control panel. Once TCP/IP is installed, highlight *TCP/IP* and select *Properties* to display the TCP/IP Properties dialog. This dialog includes three categories of settings, described in the sections below.

IP Address Configuration

The first tab of the TCP/IP Properties dialog includes options relating to IP addresses:

Adapter
> Selects one of the computer's installed network adapters. The settings below affect the selected adapter.

Obtain an IP Address from a DHCP Server
> If selected, the client sends DHCP broadcast messages when started, and the IP address, subnet mask, and default gateway are assigned by the DHCP server.

Specify an IP Address
> Select this option to manually specify values for the IP address, subnet mask, and default gateway fields. The Advanced button displays a dialog that allows the entry of multiple addresses and gateways. The default gateway is an IP address of a router or other device. Packets intended for a node outside the local subnet are sent to this address.

DNS Configuration

The second tab of the TCP/IP Properties dialog includes the following DNS options:

Host Name
> Specify the host name (optional) to identify the computer to the DNS server. By default, the NetBIOS computer name is used.

Domain
> Specify the DNS domain the computer belongs to (optional).

DNS Service Search Order
> Add one or more DNS server addresses to this list to enable DNS. Servers are queried in the order you specify here. If a server is unable to resolve the name within a four-second period, the next server on the list is tried.

Domain Suffix Search Order
> Optionally, list DNS domain suffixes that can be used if a nonqualified host name is specified for DNS lookup.

WINS Configuration

The third tab of the TCP/IP Properties dialog includes the following WINS options:

Adapter
> Choose one of the computer's network adapters. The WINS server settings below apply to each selected adapter.

Primary WINS Server
> Specify the IP address of the first WINS server to be accessed for NetBIOS name resolution.

Secondary WINS Server
> Optionally, specify a second WINS server IP address to be used when the primary WINS server is unavailable.

Enable DNS for Windows Resolution
> If this option is selected, names that are not found by the WINS server are referred to a DNS server for resolution.

Enable LMHOSTS Lookup
> Enables the LMHOSTS file, usually \WINNT\SYSTEM32\DRIVERS\ETC\ LMHOSTS. This file is a lookup table of NetBIOS names and IP addresses, and is searched before consulting the WINS server.

Scope ID
> Optionally, specify the NetBIOS scope ID for the current computer. NetBIOS scope IDS are text values that are used with the NetBIOS name to identify the machine to the network. If a scope ID is set, the computer can only communicate with other computers with the same scope ID.

Peer Web Services

Peer Web Services (PWS), included with Windows NT Workstation 4.0, is a server for HTTP, FTP, and Gopher protocols. This is actually a limited version of Internet

Information Server 2.0; the full version is included with Windows NT Server 4.0. PWS is limited to 10 incoming connections (as is Windows NT Workstation itself).

TCP/IP must be installed and configured before you install PWS. To install PWS, select the Services tab in the Network control panel. Select *Add* and choose *Microsoft Peer Web Services* from the list. The PWS setup program runs, and allows you to choose which services to install (FTP, WWW, etc.) and the location for the PWS files.

Next, you are prompted for directories for the content to be published by the three services. By default, an InetPub directory is created on the system drive, and three directories are created under it: wwwroot, ftproot, and gophroot. After you specify these directories, files are copied to complete the installation.

Once PWS is installed, you can use Internet Service Manager, available from the Start menu, to configure the services. This utility's initial display shows the status of WWW, FTP, and Gopher services. Start, Stop, and Pause buttons allow control over the services.

Detailed configuration dialogs are also available for each service; highlight the service name and select *Service Properties* from the Properties menu. The following categories of properties are available in this tabbed dialog:

Service
> Includes the TCP port the service answers on, the timeout and maximum limits for connections, and a user name and password that are used for anonymous access to the service. Depending on the service, additional parameters may be included.

Directories
> Allows you to modify the directory for documents to be served (specified at installation). You can also add additional directory aliases, which map directories requested by a client to particular directories on the computer.

Logging
> Includes options for logging access to the service. Log records can be written to a text file or to an available SQL or ODBC database server.

Advanced
> The first portion of this category relates to security. Select whether all computers are allowed access or denied access by default, and add one or more IP addresses as exceptions to the rule. The remaining option allows you to limit the network use (bandwidth) by the services.

Windows NT Workstation

Remote Access Service (RAS)

Windows NT includes RAS (Remote Access Services), a collection of services that allow dial-up access to and from Windows NT via modem. Windows NT Workstation has the ability to act both as a RAS client and a server, although the server is limited to one incoming connection.

RAS allows Windows NT clients to connect to a Windows NT or other network over a modem, ISDN, or X.25 connection. The RAS connection acts just like a network connection, although modem connections are typically slow compared to network adapters. The RAS client is similar to the remote access feature in Windows 95, and is also called Dial-up Networking (DUN).

In addition to single modems, Windows NT RAS includes a *multilink* feature, which allows multiple modems to be used for a single connection. Assuming that the computer you are dialing into has the corresponding number of incoming modems, the modem connections can be combined into a single higher-speed connection. For example, two 28-Kbps modems used with multilink would provide a bandwidth of 56 Kbps.

Installing and Configuring RAS

Before installing RAS, use the Modems control panel to install a modem. You can install RAS by selecting *Add* from the Services tab of the Network control panel and selecting *Remote Access Service*. You are prompted for a modem to use with RAS.

Once you've added a modem, use the Configure button to choose the role of the modem: *Dial Out only, Receive Calls only,* or *Dial Out and Receive Calls*. For a RAS client, choose the *Dial Out only* option.

Once RAS is installed, you can configure it by highlighting *Remote Access Service* and selecting *Properties*. The following options are available:

Dial Out Protocols

Specify one or more protocols to use to dial into a RAS server. TCP/IP is typically used.

Server Settings

Allows you to configure the protocols available for incoming RAS connections, and specify encryption options. These settings are detailed in Part 3.

Creating Phonebook Entries

After installing RAS, you can configure client connections for individual servers by opening the Dial-up Networking icon under My Computer. Create a new phonebook entry with the New icon. You can define the entry with the wizard (automatic prompts) or manually.

The properties for each phonebook entry are divided into five tabbed dialogs:

Basic

Defines identifying information for the connection, including a name, an optional comment, the phone number to dial, and the modem to use for this entry. Windows NT's dial-up networking supports a list of alternate numbers that are used if the primary number is busy.

Server

Includes options for setting the type of server: PPP, supported by Windows NT and most Internet providers, SLIP, supported by some Internet providers, or the proprietary protocol supported by Windows NT versions before 3.5 and Windows for Workgroups. Also includes checkboxes for supported network protocols (TCP/IP, IPX/SPX, and NetBEUI). The TCP/IP Settings button displays an additional dialog with TCP/IP-specific information: IP address, DNS and WINS addresses, and other options.

Script

Includes options to either display a terminal window for manual logon after dialing, or run a script. Script files are text files in a proprietary scripting language, and are documented by the Windows NT Resource Kit or the help system.

Security

Includes settings relating to encryption. See the section below for details.

X.25

Includes options related to the X.25 WAN protocol. If you connect to an X.25 provider, the correct information should be entered here for access.

RAS supports an autodial feature, which automatically dials an outgoing RAS phonebook entry when an application attempts to use the connection. To configure autodial, select *User Properties* from the More button in the Dial-up Networking window.

Dial-Up Security

The Security tab mentioned above includes options for different types of authentication supported by the PPP protocol. These relate to how authentication information (username and password) is transmitted over the network. The PPP authentication protocols used by RAS are described in Table 2-5.

Table 2-5: PPP Authentication Supported by RAS

Protocol	Description
PAP (Password Authentication Protocol)	The Internet standard for PPP authentication. Passwords are sent as clear (ASCII) text, and are vulnerable to snooping.
SPAP (Shiva PAP)	Shiva's improved version of PAP. Passwords are sent in encrypted form.
CHAP (Challenge Handshake Authentication Protocol)	A two-way protocol using encrypted passwords.
MS-CHAP (Microsoft CHAP)	Microsoft's proprietary version of CHAP, supported only by Windows and Windows NT.

The protocols you choose to support depend on the capabilities of the system you are dialing into. Highest security is obtained by avoiding PAP (clear text) authentication, but many servers (including most UNIX dial-up servers) support only this protocol.

Rather than specifying particular protocols, you can configure RAS to accept one of three levels of security from the Security tab. These are described below, including the authentication protocols they support.

Accept any authentication including clear text
Allows any type of password authentication. (PAP, SPAP, CHAP, MS-CHAP)

Accept only encrypted authentication
Requires that some type of encryption be used. This option is supported by Windows NT and some UNIX servers. (SPAP, CHAP, MS-CHAP)

Accept only Microsoft encrypted authentication
Specifies Microsoft Challenge and Response authentication, supported only by Windows NT RAS servers. (MS-CHAP only)

On the Exam

For the NT Workstation MCSE exam, you should be familiar with the three security options described above, know the protocols they support, and their relative levels of security. (According to Microsoft, MS-CHAP is the most secure.) If a test question mentions dialing into a non-NT server, however, MS-CHAP is not a valid option.

In addition, RAS supports a callback option, which hangs up on incoming callers and calls them back at a specified number, preventing access from unauthorized locations. This option is set per user in the Remote Access dialog from the User Properties dialog. The callback number can either be specified in the RAS configuration or entered by the user when dialing in. See the description of the User Manager utility in "Security and Auditing" later in this chapter for details.

Configuring NT Workstation

Windows NT Workstation is a complex operating system with a great variety of options and features. The sections below explain various methods of configuring and managing hardware, software, disk storage, printers, users, and access to the system.

Using the Control Panel

Windows NT includes a Control Panel, similar to that found in Windows 95 and Windows 3.1. This option is found in the Settings menu under the Start menu. The Control Panel window includes a number of separate dialogs, called *applets*, to configure various hardware devices and software services. A typical Control Panel display is shown in Figure 2-2.

Some Control Panel applets are used to install or remove drivers for hardware devices. Since Windows NT does not support Plug and Play, you must install a driver after installing each device. When removing a device from the system, remove or stop the driver first.

Many of the items found in the Control Panel are duplicated elsewhere; for example, the Network control panel is also the Properties dialog for the Network Neighborhood icon. The applets available in NT Workstation are described below. Several of these are explained in more detail elsewhere in this chapter.

Add/Remove Programs
> Allows you to add or remove software. This includes components of Windows NT as well as applications that support installation and uninstallation through the Control Panel.

Console
> Defines options for the console (MS-DOS emulation) prompt.

Date/Time
> Configures the computer's date and time and time zone settings.

Figure 2-2: The Windows NT Workstation Control Panel

Devices

Allows you to start, stop, and configure hardware device drivers. These include disk, mouse, keyboard, modem, and other drivers. The Startup button allows you to configure the default status of a service. When Windows NT starts, devices with Boot status are started, followed by those with System and Automatic status. The *Manual* status option requires user intervention to start the driver, and the *Disabled* option prevents the driver from starting entirely.

Display

Includes settings relating to the display adapter and monitor. These include the appearance of the screen, screen savers and backgrounds, and video drivers. Windows NT uses its own type of display drivers, and is not compatible with Windows 3.1 or Windows 95 drivers.

Fonts

Allows you to install and remove fonts. These are stored in the \WINNT\FONTS directory.

Keyboard

Allows you to configure the keyboard type, language, and speed settings.

Modems

Automatically detects or allows you to configure modems. Windows NT includes support for a wide variety of modems; some may require a driver provided with the modem.

Mouse

Allows you to configure the mouse type, mouse pointers, and other settings.

Multimedia

Includes configuration settings for sound cards, video playback, MIDI controllers, and CD audio.

Network

Configures network settings, as described earlier in this chapter.

PC Card (PCMCIA)

For computers with PC Card slots (typically notebooks), allows configuration of these devices. Some devices may require configuration in another control panel applet, such as Modems or Network. Windows NT does not support hot swapping (inserting or removing cards while the computer is running).

Ports

Configures settings for communication ports (COM1 through COM4).

Printers

Configures printers. Windows NT printing is described later in this chapter.

Regional Settings

Includes location-specific settings, such as currency and date formats.

SCSI Adapters

Configures settings for SCSI adapters. The Drivers tab allows you to configure additional SCSI controllers. Some newer IDE controllers are also supported by this application.

Server

Includes options for a computer that acts as a server (shares one or more files or printers). This dialog allows you to monitor the use of shared resources and disconnect them if needed.

Services

Lists services currently installed on the computer, and allows you to start, stop, or change the default status of each service. The startup options are *Automatic*, *Manual*, or *Disabled*, similar to the Devices applet described above. New services are not installed from this dialog, but from the appropriate section of the Control Panel (i.e., Network for network services).

Sounds

Allows you to assign sounds to system events.

System

Configures system settings, including the boot loader, hardware profiles, performance, and user profiles. The options available in this dialog are described in the next section.

Tape Devices

Allows you to install or configure tape drives for use with backup software (described later in this chapter).

Telephony

Includes basic dial-out settings for modems and general configuration for the telephony service.

UPS

Configures communication with an uninterruptible power supply (UPS). This allows you to select a COM port connected to the UPS and specify the signals it sends in the event of power failure and other events. This allows Windows NT to shut down properly while the backup batteries are online. Some models of UPS include custom software with more options than this dialog provides.

On the Exam

You should not attempt to take the NT Workstation exam without at least trying each of the control panel applets described above and testing their various functions.

The System Control Panel

The System applet of the Control Panel includes a variety of options. These include the following:

General

Displays information about the computer and the Windows version.

Performance

Allows you to modify the amount of performance boost (priority) for the fore-ground application. The Change button allows you to modify virtual memory settings.

Environment

Allows you to modify various system environment variables, such as temporary file directories.

Startup/Shutdown

Allows you to choose the default option and timeout for the boot menu; these values are stored in the BOOT.INI file, described earlier in this chapter. The Recovery section of this dialog includes options for STOP errors and memory dumps.

Hardware Profiles

Allows you to create separate hardware profiles. Each profile includes the currently installed hardware and settings. Multiple hardware profiles can be useful if the hardware configuration changes frequently, as on a notebook computer with a docking station. To select a hardware profile at boot time, press the space bar at the beginning of the boot process.

User Profiles

Allows you to create and modify user profiles (described in detail later in this chapter).

Editing the Registry

The Windows NT registry is a database of keys and values that are used to store the configuration of the hardware, user preferences, operating system settings, and settings for various applications. This is similar but not identical to the Windows 95 registry.

The registry is organized in a hierarchical structure of keys and subkeys, each of which can hold one or more values. Values include a text identifier as well as a binary, string, word, or multiple string value. The registry has five main (root) subtrees. These include the following:

HKEY_CLASSES_ROOT
> This subtree stores file associations, which specify the programs to be run when files with particular extensions are used.

HKEY_CURRENT_USER
> This subtree stores information about the current Control Panel settings, loaded from the appropriate user profile at login. User profiles are explained later in this chapter.

HKEY_LOCAL_MACHINE
> This subtree stores hardware-specific data such as drivers and interrupt settings, as well as software settings that do not change based on user profiles.

HKEY_USERS
> This subtree stores a default set of settings as well as settings for each separate user profile. The appropriate user's information is copied from here to the HKEY_CURRENT_USER subtree at login.

HKEY_CURRENT_CONFIG
> The keys in this subtree are used to store dynamic configuration information and temporary values used by some applications and device drivers.

HKEY_DYN_DATA
> This subtree stores dynamic hardware information, specifying the current settings for removable disk drives, PC cards, and other hardware that can be changed without rebooting.

On the Exam

You should know these six registry subtrees and their basic purposes for the NT Workstation exam. You should not need to know the function of specific registry keys within the hives, but you should know how to use the registry editing tools described below.

REGEDIT and REGEDT32

Although most of the keys in the registry are set by the OS or based on your Control Panel settings, you can manually edit the registry. As an incorrect setting can cause the system to be unusable, this should not be attempted without backing up the registry files.

There are two programs for editing the registry: REGEDIT and REGEDT32. Either of these can be run manually from a console prompt or the Run dialog. Both modify the same registry, but provide different feature sets:

- REGEDIT is similar to the program of the same name in Windows 95, and displays all of the subtrees in a tree structure. This program provides sophisticated search options. REGEDIT is shown in Figure 2-3.

- REGEDT32 displays each subtree in a separate window, making some operations difficult, and does not support searching the entire registry. However, it allows access to security features. You can set permissions on registry keys, allowing them to be modified only by certain users or groups. REGEDT32 also includes a view-only feature which is useful to prevent accidental changes.

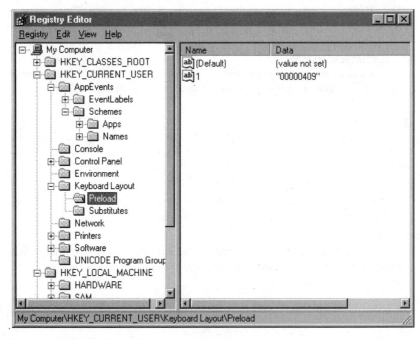

Figure 2-3: The Registry Editor

Security and Auditing

Windows NT uses a system of user names and passwords to allow access to a computer's resources. The logon dialog is displayed when Windows NT boots, and cannot be bypassed. This system is referred to as a *mandatory logon*. Logon information is used both for security and to store preferences specific to each user.

The CTRL-Alt-Del keystroke is required for logon because it is handled by the computer's BIOS, cannot easily be intercepted by a program that is not part of the OS, and cannot be generated remotely without the use of special software.

Users and Groups

Windows NT's user accounts can be given access to resources directly. However, a system of groups is provided for more efficient security management. Users can be members of zero or more groups, and are given the permissions assigned to each group.

Windows NT includes two types of groups: *local groups*, used to assign user rights to resources, and *global groups*, used to group users and allow trusts between domains. Windows NT Workstation supports only local groups; global groups are discussed in the next chapter. Both users and global groups can be members of a local group.

On the Exam

The NT Workstation exam focuses on local groups. However, be aware that a domain's global groups can be members of these local groups. This process is used to give a domain-wide group of users access to the local machine's resources.

Default Users and Groups

The following user accounts are created by default when Windows NT Workstation is installed:

Administrator
> This is the default administration account. You are asked to specify a password for this account at installation. This account cannot be disabled or deleted, and should be kept secure.

Guest
> This user cannot be renamed or deleted, but can be disabled. It has no password by default. Since this account is present on all systems and is a member of the Everyone group (explained below), it presents a significant security risk.

The following local groups are available by default:

Administrators
> The Administrator user is a member of this group. Members of this group are given full control to all resources of the computer.

Backup Operators
> Members of this group can access all files on the computer, regardless of file system security. No users are members by default.

Guests
> The Guest user is a member of this group. This group has a simple set of rights by default.

Power Users
> Users in this group can perform some system tasks; for example, managing printers or changing the computer's date and time. This group is created only on standalone servers and workstations.

Replicators
> This is a special group used by the file replication system, used to duplicate files between computers.

Users
> This group includes a basic set of rights, such as the right to log on locally or over the network. All users are members of this group by default.

In addition to these, the Everyone group is a virtual group that automatically contains all users of the system.

Adding and Modifying Users

You can create or modify users using the User Manager utility, accessed from the Administrative Tools menu under the Start menu. This utility is shown in Figure 2-4.

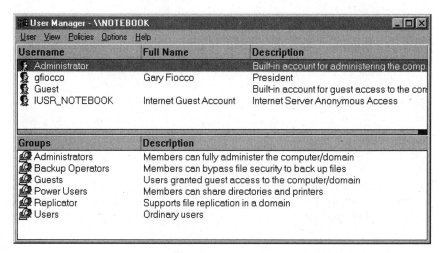

Figure 2-4: The User Manager utility

User Manager displays a list of users and groups on the system. Select *New User* from the User menu to create a user, or *New Local Group* to create a group. Select *Properties* from this menu to display properties for an existing user. Changes to a user's properties do not take effect until the next time the user logs in.

The User Properties dialog is displayed when you create or modify a new user. This dialog includes the following options:

Username
> A short name to identify the user. Usernames are limited to 20 characters.

Full Name
> The user's full name, displayed in file and user listings.

Description

An optional text field describing the user. This is displayed in User Manager, but is otherwise unused by the system.

Password

Specify a password for the user. Depending on system settings, the password may have a minimum length or may not be required. These settings are located in the Account Policy dialog, described later in this section.

User Must Change Password at Next Logon

Forces the user to change their password on the first logon. This setting is frequently used with new accounts to force users to choose their own passwords.

User Cannot Change Password

Prevents password changes except by the administrator.

Password Never Expires

If selected, this account is not subject to password expiration (described in the "Account Policy" section).

Account Disabled

Disables the account. This is useful for accounts that may be used again in the future. In addition, it can be used for employees that have left the company, since deleting the account entirely prevents its use in auditing and makes files created by the account owner difficult to access.

In addition to these options, three buttons at the bottom of the User Properties dialog display additional dialogs for other information about the user:

Groups

Displays a list of groups the user belongs to (by default, the Users group only) and allows you to add groups.

Profile

Includes options for logon script and home directory, as well as the directory for a user profile (described in the next section).

Dialin

Allows you to allow the user access via dial-in (RAS) connection. This also includes options for callback, described earlier in this chapter.

User Profiles

Windows NT supports *user profiles*, which allow users to maintain a set of desktop and other settings each time they log in. User profiles store desktop settings and some application settings for individual users. Windows NT supports three types of user profiles:

- *Local profiles* only work at a particular workstation.

- *Roaming profiles* are stored on a network server, and can be used from any Windows NT computer in the network. Roaming profiles can be configured from the User Properties dialog in User Manager. A default profile is stored in the \WINNT\Profiles\Default User directory on the server. Individual user profiles are stored in separate directories for each user by default.

- *Mandatory profiles* are roaming profiles that cannot be modified by users. Roaming profiles are stored in a file called NTUSER.DAT; to create a mandatory profile, rename the file to NTUSER.MAN.

To specify a user profile for the user, enter a filename in the User Profiles tab of the System control panel, described earlier in this chapter. Local user profiles are stored in the \WINNT\PROFILES directory on the local computer, in separate subdirectories for each user.

System Policies

Windows NT *system policies* affect many of the same settings as user profiles, but are controlled by the administrator. System policies can prevent users from changing settings, remove certain capabilities, and restrict some applications. System policy settings override user profile settings.

There are two basic types of system policy:

- *User policies* affect a user's environment. Policies can be specified for specific users or users in specific groups; a default user policy is used if the user has no user or group policy.

- *Computer policies* affect a particular computer. Policies can be created for specific computers on the network; a default computer policy is used for computers with no explicit policy.

The System Policy Editor utility, POLEDIT.EXE, allows you to create and modify system policies. This utility and the various options available within system policies are described in detail in Part 3.

Security Internals

Windows NT treats all secured resources as *objects*. Objects include files, printers, processes, and even keys within the registry. Each object has an access control list, or ACL, that lists the users or groups with permission to access the object in some fashion.

At logon, a valid user is issued an access token representing the username and the groups it belongs to. Each time the user attempts to access a resource, this token is compared with the object's ACL to grant or deny access. The Windows NT process that handles these tasks is called the security accounts manager, or SAM.

Users can be granted one or more permissions for an object, usually from the object's properties dialog. For example, the Security tab of a file's properties dialog lists users and groups with access to the file. Specific file permissions are listed in the "Managing Disk Storage" section, later in this chapter.

Account Policy

User Manager includes three options under the Policies menu. Each of these sets options that apply to the entire system. The first of these, Account Policy, specifies password options for all users. The following options are included:

Maximum Password Age
> If selected, users must change their password after the specified number of days has expired.

Minimum Password Age
> If this option is selected, the specified number of days must pass before users change their passwords. This prevents users from changing passwords repeatedly to defeat the uniqueness requirement (explained below).

Minimum Password Length
> Specify a minimum length for passwords. No minimum is required by default.

Password Uniqueness
> If a number is selected here, that number of previous passwords are stored for each user. Users are not allowed to use any of these when changing passwords.

Account Lockout
> If enabled, accounts will be disabled (locked out) after the specified number of incorrect logon attempts. You can specify a time after which the count starts over, and specify the duration of the lockout.

Users must log on in order to change password
> If selected, users can only change passwords before they expire; if a password expires, the password can be changed only by an administrator.

User Rights Policy

The User Rights Policy dialog manages a set of specific rights, which you can assign to users or groups. The following rights are included:

Access this computer from network
> Allows remote users to log on to and access the computer. This right is granted to all users (Administrators, Power Users, and Everyone) by default.

Backup files and directories
> Allows file system security to be bypassed to back up files (read only). Granted to Administrators and Backup Operators by default.

Change system time
> Users with this right can change the system date and time. Granted to Administrators and Power Users by default.

Force shutdown from a remote system
> Allows remote shutdowns. This right is not implemented in Windows NT 4.0.

Load and unload device drivers
> Allows hardware device drivers to be loaded, unloaded, started, and stopped. Granted to Administrators by default.

Log on locally
> Allows local access to the computer. This right is granted to all users by default.

Manage and audit security log
> Allows access to the security log, which stores events selected for auditing as well as security breaches. Granted to Administrators by default.

Restore files and directories
> Allows file system security to be bypassed to restore files (write access). This right is granted to Administrators and Backup Operators by default.

Shut down the system
> Allows use of the *Shut Down* command on the Start menu. This right is granted to all users by default.

Take ownership of files or other objects
> Allows users to change the ownership of files, printers, registry keys, and other objects.

Audit Policy

The final option in the Policies menu includes options for auditing. Events selected for auditing are stored in the system and security logs. These logs can be viewed with the Event Viewer utility, described later in this chapter.

Either the success, failure, or both can be audited for each event. The following events are included:

- Logon and Logoff
- File and Object Access
- Use of User Rights
- User and Group Management
- Security Policy Changes
- Restart, Shutdown, and System
- Process Tracking

Managing Disk Storage

Windows NT's disk architecture is similar to that found in other operating systems. The following are the components of Windows NT disk storage:

- *Drives* are actual installed disk drives.
- *Partitions* are portions of a drive set aside for use by an OS.
- *Volumes,* or *logical drives,* are blocks of disk storage available to the OS. Volumes usually coincide with partitions, but may include multiple partitions or multiple drives. Volumes must be formatted before use, and can be formatted as either FAT or NTFS.
- *Files and directories* are the actual elements of data storage on a volume. These are formatted differently depending on the file system.

This section looks at various aspects of disk management in Windows NT Workstation. The Disk Administrator utility, shown in Figure 2-5, is used for most disk management tasks.

Volume Sets

As mentioned above, a Windows NT volume can consist of multiple partitions. This type of volume is called a *volume set.* You can create a volume set by selecting two or more empty partitions in Disk Administrator and choosing *Create Volume Set* from the Partition menu.

You can also add partitions to an existing volume set without erasing current data. Select the volume set and one or more empty partitions and select *Extend Volume Set* from the Partition menu. A volume can include up to 32 partitions on as many physical drives. There is no way to remove partitions from a volume set aside from reformatting the drive.

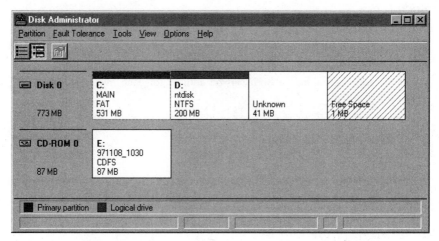

Figure 2-5: The Disk Administrator utility

Disk Striping

Disk striping is a more complex method of combining partitions into a volume. A volume set stores data sequentially, filling up one partition before moving on to the next. In a stripe set, data is interleaved between the partitions, so a single file written to the volume will be equally distributed among the partitions.

The advantage of disk striping is speed. Each partition in the stripe set must be on a separate physical drive; a stripe set requires at least 2 and up to 32 drives. Each drive added to the stripe set increases the risk of failure. If a single drive in the set fails, data on the entire volume becomes inaccessible.

On the Exam

Disk striping does not provide fault tolerance. RAID levels 1 and 5 (disk mirroring and disk striping with parity) do provide fault tolerance, but are not provided in Windows NT Workstation. These are described in Part 3.

NTFS Security

Windows NT supports a full range of security for NTFS partitions. FAT partitions do not support security. NTFS security treats files and directories as objects. Each file or directory has an ACL, and users or groups can be given permission to access it. The available NTFS permissions are described in Table 2-6.

Table 2-6: NTFS Permissions

Permission	Description
Read	View a directory's contents or open a file.
Write	Write data to a file, or create new files in a directory.

Table 2-6: NTFS Permissions (continued)

Permission	Description
Delete	Delete a file or directory.
Change Permissions	Modify the permissions assigned to the file or directory.
Execute	Execute a program file.
Take Ownership	Modify the ownership of a file or directory.

To modify permissions for a file or directory, right-click on it in Explorer. Select the Security tab, then click the Permissions button to display the permissions dialog.

These permissions can be assigned individually or in preset combinations, such as Full Control, which includes all of the permissions. Another available permission, No Access, explicitly denies the user or group access to the resource, regardless of other permissions.

A user may have one set of permissions granted explicitly for a resource, and one or more other permissions based on group membership. When this happens, the least restrictive permission becomes the effective permission unless one of the permissions is No Access.

Inheritance is not automatic in NTFS security: permissions or restrictions given to a user for a directory are not applied to its subdirectories unless you specify by selecting the *Replace Permissions on Subdirectories* option in the Permissions dialog. Permissions on files within a directory are not changed unless the *Replace Permissions on Existing Files* option is selected, but new files created in the directory inherit the directory's permissions.

The Everyone group is given Full Control access to NTFS volumes by default, effectively disabling NTFS security. This permission should be removed or restricted to secure the volume.

On the Exam

Some MCSE exam questions ask you to determine a user's abilities for a file or directory. Be sure you know the various NTFS permissions, and know what happens when user and group permissions are combined.

Copying and Moving Files

Files on NTFS partitions can be moved or copied in the same manner as local files, using Explorer (accessible from the My Computer icon on each computer) or over the network. Permissions are not always moved with the file, however:

- If the file is *moved*, the permissions of the original file are copied to the new location. Files can only be moved within a single NTFS volume. If you drag a file to a location on the same volume, a move operation is performed by default; for a copy, hold down the CTRL key.

- If the file is *copied*, the copied file inherits the permissions of the new directory. Dragging a file to a location on a different volume always results in a copy operation.

Of course, if the destination is on a FAT partition, NTFS permissions are lost. If a file from a FAT partition is copied to an NTFS location, it inherits the permissions of the new parent directory.

File Sharing and Permissions

Both Windows NT Workstation and Server support file sharing. A directory or volume can be shared using the Sharing tab of the file or directory properties dialog. Shared directories and volumes are listed by their share names when a user browses the Network Neighborhood, as described earlier in this chapter.

File sharing supports its own type of security, called *shared folder security*. Click the Permissions button in the Sharing tab to display the share permissions dialog. Shares have a simple set of permissions that provide a lesser degree of security than that provided by NTFS, but can be used even with shared FAT volumes. The share permissions are described in Table 2-7.

Table 2-7: Share Permissions

Permission	Description
Read	Allows read access to files or directory listings.
Change	Allows the user to create, write, or delete files.
Full Control	Includes both Read and Change permissions.
No Access	Explicitly denies access to the share.

As with NTFS security, the Everyone group is given Full Control rights to shares by default. To provide security, this permission should be removed or restricted.

Like NTFS security, a user may have permissions for a share assigned to the user as well as one or more groups. In this case the least restrictive permission is used, unless one of the permissions is No Access. If a user has both NTFS permissions and share permissions for a directory, the most restrictive permission is used.

Default Shares

In addition to user-created shares, Windows NT includes several shares that are available by default. Most of these have names ending in the dollar sign ($) character. Shares named in this manner are not shown in browse lists; the exact name must be used to access them. The default shares created in a typical NT installation are shown in Table 2-8.

Several of the default shares are called administrative shares. These include the ADMIN$ share, which points to the Windows NT root directory, and a share for each drive (i.e., C$). Administrative shares are accessible only to administrators by default.

Table 2-8: Windows NT Default Shares

Share name	Description
C$, D$, etc.	A share is created for each drive, pointing to the root directory.
ADMIN$	Points to the \WINNT directory. This share is used for remote administration.
IPC$	Used for IPC (inter-process communication).
NETLOGON	Used for logon to the network. Points to the \WINNT\system32\Repl\Import\Scripts directory.

Backing Up Files

Another important part of file system maintenance is regular backups. A tape drive or other device should be available for backups of important data. Windows NT includes a basic backup utility called NTBACKUP.EXE. This utility supports five basic types of backups:

Normal (Full Backup)
> This method backs up all of the files on the volume regardless of when files were modified, and clears the archive bits.

Incremental Backup
> This method backs up all of the files that have been modified since the last backup, and clears the archive bits.

Differential Backup
> This method backs up all of the files changed since the last full backup. It does not clear the archive bits, so each differential backup includes the same files as a previous one.

Copy
> This method is similar to a full backup, but does not clear the archive bits.

Daily Copy
> This method backs up all files modified on the current date.

On the Exam

For the Windows NT Workstation MCSE exam you should be familiar with NTBACKUP and these backup types, but you shouldn't need to know more specific details. System backups are covered in more detail by the Windows NT Server exam, discussed in Part 3.

Configuring Printers

Windows NT includes comprehensive support for printers. Printers installed on a computer are defined in the Printers folder, available under My Computer in Explorer. Several components are involved in the printing process:

Printer

The Windows NT object that corresponds with a hardware printer (print device) and stores jobs to be printed in a queue. Also called a logical printer.

Print Device

A physical printer. Remember that in Windows NT terms, Printers are software and Print Devices are hardware.

Print Job

A document sent to the printer. Print jobs are stored in a queue until they are sent to the printer.

Print Server

The server that controls a printer. This is usually the machine the printer is attached to.

Installing and Managing Printers

Select *Add Printer* from the Printers folder to install a printer. A Wizard prompts you for information about the printer. You can configure a local printer, or configure local access to a shared printer on another machine. You are asked to specify the port the printer is attached to, the printer manufacturer and type, and whether the printer will be shared.

Once a printer is installed, you can access its Properties dialog to configure it. This dialog includes the following tabbed categories:

General

Includes options for the printer's location and description, and allows you to choose the printer driver.

Ports

Specifies the ports the printer is connected to. You can also create a printer pool, described below, by selecting multiple ports. LPT (parallel), COM (serial), and UNC paths to shared printers can be used.

Scheduling

Specifies a time period when the printer is available. The priority for printer access is also set in this tab. When multiple logical printers are defined for one physical printer, documents are printed based on the priority. This allows you to give certain groups of users priority access to a printer.

Sharing

Specifies whether the printer is shared, and under what name. You can also install drivers for the printer for different operating systems from this dialog. Users running other systems (such as Windows 95) can then download a driver when they install a local icon for the shared printer.

Security

Allows you to set permissions for access to the printer, similar to those used with NTFS directories. Permissions affect both local and remote users.

Device Settings

Includes settings specific to the printer, defined by the printer driver software.

Print Pools

A logical printer can be assigned to two or more physical printers on different ports. This configuration is called a print pool. To create a pool, select the *Enable printer pooling* option in the Ports tab of the Printer Properties dialog, and select two or more ports.

Print pools should be used with identical printers, or at least compatible printers. A document is sent to the first available printer in the pool.

Scheduling and Priorities

In addition to configuring one Printer to access multiple print devices (print pool), you can configure one print device with several Printers. This technique is useful to assign different users or groups rights to a printer with a different available schedule or priority.

To assign schedules and priorities, use the Scheduling tab of the printer properties dialog. Configure a time period for the printer to be available if needed. Priority can be set between 1 and 99; 99 is the highest priority. Jobs from a higher-priority printer are always sent to the print device first.

Managing Print Jobs

Open a printer within the Printers folder to display print jobs currently printing or waiting to print. The options in the Document menu allow you to pause, resume, restart, or cancel the current document. Administrators can pause all printing or purge all print jobs from the Printer menu.

The print jobs list is managed by the print spooler service. Spool files are stored on the boot partition by default. If this partition has insufficient space, you can change the spool location by selecting *Server Properties* from the File menu of the Printers folder. Select the Advanced tab and specify a path to the new folder.

You can also create separate spool directories for one or more printers. To specify these directories, you will need to edit the registry. Each printer has an entry under the registry key:

```
HKEY_LOCAL_MACHINE\SYSTEM\CurrentControlSet\Control\Print\Printers
```

To modify a printer's spool directory, enter a value for the *SpoolDirectory* parameter under the printer's registry key.

On the Exam

You should be familiar with all aspects of Windows NT printing for the NT Workstation, NT Server, and NT Server in the Enterprise exams. You should also know how to troubleshoot common printing problems, as discussed in the next section of this chapter.

Optimization and Troubleshooting

Windows NT is a complex system, and the use of a server by several users running different applications at the same time complicates the use of memory and other resources. This section looks at methods of monitoring system performance, optimizing, and solving common problems.

Monitoring Performance

Windows NT includes a variety of tools for monitoring the performance of a computer:

- Event Viewer displays error messages and auditing messages.
- Task Manager displays information about current tasks and processes.
- Performance Monitor monitors a wide variety of performance information.

These are described in detail in the following sections.

On the Exam

You may have studied these utilities for the Network Essentials exam. For the NT Workstation exam, you should be familiar with the specific functions of each utility. Be sure to experiment with each of these on a Windows NT system and be sure you know their features and limitations.

Event Viewer

Windows NT system events, including errors, access violations, routine status messages, and auditing, are stored in three log files:

System
> Includes system error messages, and status messages for system reboots and other events. If system events are selected for auditing, these are also included in this log.

Security
> Includes messages relating to security. Security problems, such as incorrect logons, are included in this log if auditing is enabled. Security auditing is disabled by default.

Application
> Includes events logged by applications, and problems such as application crashes.

The Event Viewer utility, accessible from the Administrative Tools menu under the Start menu, displays information from these log files. Use the Log menu to select the file being displayed. You can change the order for viewing events or search for events matching a specific criteria.

The *Clear All Events* command under the Log menu clears the current log. This can prevent the log from using excess disk storage. You can also specify a maximum size for the log file using the Log Settings command.

Task Manager

The Task Manager utility displays information about current tasks. To access this utility, press CTRL-Alt-Del and click the Task Manager button. This utility consists of three tabbed dialogs:

Applications
Displays a list of currently running applications. The End Task button stops the selected application. Although you can change the priority of a process as described below, this utility does not allow you to change application priorities.

Processes
Displays a complete list of current processes, including those used by applications as well as system processes and services. The End Process button allows you to stop a process. You can right-click on a process name to change its priority.

Performance
Displays a graph of CPU and memory usage, as well as specific information about files, threads, and processes in use.

On the Exam

The Performance tab in Task Manager is one way to quickly determine if a system is slow due to lack of memory or processor speed. If all of the physical memory is frequently in use, the computer probably needs more memory; if the CPU Usage indicator is constantly 80% or higher, the CPU is probably the main bottleneck.

Performance Monitor

The Performance Monitor utility provides a graphical display of information about a wide variety of system performance factors. This utility is located in the Administrative Tools menu under the Start menu.

The items that can be displayed by this utility are called *counters*. Many counters are available in a variety of categories; the exact list of categories depends on the installed services and applications. The following are some of the most useful categories:

Processor
Includes counters related to the system processor (CPU). The %Processor Time counter is a good measure of processor load.

Memory
Includes counters that measure memory (RAM) performance.

PagingFile
> Includes counters that measure virtual memory performance.

PhysicalDisk
> Includes counters related to disk drives. The disk counters are disabled by default, as their use decreases system performance. To enable them, type the command `diskperf -y` at the command prompt.

LogicalDisk
> Includes counters related to logical disk drives (volumes). These counters are also disabled by default.

Process
> Allows you to view information about a specific process. Useful for monitoring server processes.

On the Exam

These are just a sampling of the counter categories included in Performance Monitor. The other categories available depend on the installed protocols and services; for example, several categories are devoted to TCP/IP performance.

Performance Monitor includes four possible views, each of which can be used with one or more of the available counters:

Chart
> Displays a graph of the value of the specified counters over time.

Alert
> Allows you to define maximum and minimum values for counters, and alerts you if a counter exceeds these boundaries.

Log
> Creates a log file with information from the selected counters. The log file can be loaded into Performance Monitor later and viewed using the *Chart* or *Report* options.

Report
> Generates a printable report based on the counters.

Network Monitor

Another useful Windows NT utility is Network Monitor, available from the Administrative Tools menu. This utility allows you to capture network packets over time and analyze them. This is useful for diagnosing network problems, and for analyzing the bandwidth use of the network.

Network monitor consists of two components: the Network Monitor Agent, a service that runs on each computer that will be used to monitor the network, and Network Monitor Tools, the actual utility for capturing and analyzing packets. Network Monitor is explained in detail in Part 3.

SNMP

In a complex network, it's impossible for an administrator to keep track of every aspect of every machine on the network. SNMP (Simple Network Management Protocol) is a protocol that automates some of these tasks.

SNMP allows data about the network and its nodes to be collected and monitored from a central location. SNMP supports two types of services:

- *Agents* run on nodes and maintain a database of information about the node in a database called the MIB (Management Information Base).

- *Management systems* are used to request, collect, view, and summarize the data from management agents. The management system sends messages to the MIB to request information. The available messages are GET, SET, and TRAP.

Windows NT includes a SNMP Agent service that can be installed from the Network control panel. Third-party software is required to act as the management system. However, installing the SNMP agent also provides several categories of TCP/IP counters that can be used with the Performance Monitor utility.

Optimizing Performance

Windows NT is designed to optimize performance automatically. However, there are some changes that can be made to eliminate bottlenecks and improve performance. Areas that can be improved are described in the sections below.

RAM

If Performance Monitor indicates that the paging file is being used constantly, this is an indication of insufficient physical RAM. Adding memory to the computer can dramatically improve performance.

Virtual Memory

The paging file can be managed from the Performance tab of the System control panel. You can display virtual memory status for each drive on the system. Unlike Windows 95 and previous versions, Windows NT allows you to use more than one drive for paging; this can improve swapping speed. You can also specify a minimum size for the paging file if it will be used frequently.

On the Exam

For the exam, you should know how to change and optimize Windows NT virtual memory settings. As a general rule, you should use paging files on as many separate disks (not partitions) as possible, with the exception of the disk containing the boot partition. Paging files should not be stored on stripe sets or volume sets.

Disk Storage

Use the PhysicalDisk counters in Performance monitor to check the performance of disk drives. Faster drives are one option; using disk striping also provides a dramatic increase in disk read performance.

Troubleshooting Procedures

In a complex system such as Windows NT, many things can go wrong. A number of basic techniques can be useful for a wide variety of problems; these are described in the sections below.

Last Known Good

Windows NT saves a copy of the registry and other critical files when a user logs on successfully. This is called the *last known good* configuration. Restoring this information is often sufficient to repair problems in the registry.

At the beginning of the NT boot process, the message "Press Spacebar NOW for last known good/hardware profile menu" is displayed. Press the space bar at this point to access this menu. You can then press L to restore the last known good configuration over the current settings.

The Last Known Good configuration can usually fix problems with the registry and with device drivers that do not function correctly. However, it cannot correct hardware configuration problems or disk problems such as missing files.

On the Exam

The "last known good" prompt is displayed by the NT OS loader (NTLDR). described earlier in this chapter.

Emergency Repair Disk

During the installation process, you were prompted to create an emergency repair disk. This disk includes a backup of critical portions of the registry and other system files. If you have a current emergency repair disk, you can use it to attempt to fix system problems.

The emergency repair disk includes backup copies of several registry keys and system files. These items are summarized in Table 2-9.

Table 2-9: Contents of the Emergency Repair Disk

Registry Key or File	Description
HKEY_LOCAL_MACHINE\SAM	The security manager (SAM) database
HKEY_LOCAL_MACHINE\SECURITY	Security-related settings
HKEY_LOCAL_MACHINE\SOFTWARE	Application software-related settings
HKEY_LOCAL_MACHINE\SYSTEM	System control panel settings

Table 2-9: Contents of the Emergency Repair Disk (continued)

Registry Key or File	Description
\WINNT\SYSTEM32\AUTOEXEC.NT	Batch initialization file used when a command prompt (DOS shell) is started
\WINNT\SYSTEM32\CONFIG.NT	Drivers and settings used when a DOS shell is started
SETUPLOG.TXT	A log file created during the setup of Windows NT, useful for diagnostic purposes
\WINNT\Profiles\Default User\NTUSER.DAT	The default user profile, used when a user without a specific profile logs in

---

On the Exam

This complete list of files is provided for your information. For the NT Workstation MCSE exam, you should only need to know the purpose of the emergency repair disk, how to create or update it, and how to use it to repair the system.

The ERD is not a boot disk and must be used in conjunction with installation boot disks. To use the repair disk, boot the installation disks as if you were reinstalling Windows NT, and choose the R (repair) option. You are prompted to insert the repair disk.

You can create an updated repair disk using the RDISK /S command at the command prompt. This disk should be updated frequently. Attempting to repair the system using an older disk can cause more problems than it solves.

Replacing Damaged Files

As a last resort, you can use the upgrade option in the Windows NT installation to replace all of the system files. This can fix a variety of problems, and preserves most of the registry settings, users, and groups. For details about this procedure, see "Upgrading to Windows NT," earlier in this chapter.

WARNING

This procedure is drastic, and may cause applications to stop working. It should only be used if the system is completely unstable.

Windows NT Diagnostics

Windows NT includes a simple diagnostic utility called WinMSD, or Windows NT Diagnostics. This utility provides a tabbed display with various categories of information about the computer:

Version

Displays Windows NT version and build information, along with the user name, company name, and CD key entered at installation.

System

Displays the PC type and the HAL version currently in use, and information about each currently installed processor. This is a good way to test whether the processors in a multi-CPU system were detected properly.

Display

Displays information about the display driver in use, current screen resolution, and color depth.

Drives

Displays a list of disk drives (floppy, hard disk, and CD-ROM) in the computer. Double-click on a drive entry for specific information.

Memory

Displays the amount of available physical and virtual memory, as well as current threads, file handles, and processes in use.

Services

Displays a list of services installed on the computer (the same list as the Services control panel) and their current status.

Resources

Displays a list of IRQs, I/O addresses, DMA addresses, memory addresses, and device drivers in use. This dialog is extremely useful in installing and debugging network cards.

Environment

Displays environmental variables currently in use, including those set in the system profile and those set by individual user profiles.

Network

Displays network information, including current access level, the currently attached workgroup or domain, and the current username.

Most of the information available in WinMSD is also available in Task Manager or a control panel. In addition, WinMSD only displays information—it does not allow any changes. The advantage of this utility is that it can be used over the network to view information about any computer running Windows NT.

Common Problems and Solutions

There are a large number of potential problems and error messages in Windows NT. The sections below describe some of the most common problems and give potential solutions.

Installation Problems

The following are common problems that may occur during the installation of Windows NT:

Out of disk space
> The installation program requires nearly 100 MB of temporary storage along with the space needed for Windows NT itself. Be sure you have plenty of free space and try the installation again. You can also use the WINNT /D option to specify a drive for the temporary storage.

Video problems
> If the GUI fails to display on the first reboot after installation, you probably have an incorrectly configured video driver. Reboot and choose the VGA mode option from the boot loader menu, then select a different driver or resolution.

CD-ROM problems
> If the installation stops after booting from floppies, the CD-ROM may not be compatible with the HCL. Try copying the installation directory (I386 for Intel systems) to a hard disk and running WINNT from there.

Boot Problems

The following are common error messages encountered while booting Windows NT:

Non-System disk or disk error
> This message usually indicates a problem with the boot sector. It can also be caused by a floppy disk left in the drive.

Boot: Couldn't find NTLDR
> Indicates that the NTLDR program is not found on the system drive. This could indicate a disk problem or a corrupt file.

I/O Error accessing boot sector file
> Indicates that the boot sector for DOS, or another OS selected from the boot menu, is corrupt or missing.

Inaccessible boot device
> Indicates that a drive referenced in a BOOT.INI entry is malfunctioning or not correctly configured.

Resource Access Problems

If a user is unable to access a network resource, check the following items:

- Verify that the network connection is working. Try accessing a different resource or using the ping utility (TCP/IP) to test the connection to the server.
- Make sure both NTFS and shared folder permissions are set correctly.
- Check the Security log in the Event Viewer utility (described above) for failed attempts to access resources; the error message will include detailed information on why the user was denied access.
- If the user is attempting to access NetWare resources, check for a frame type mismatch.

Printing Problems

If a user gets error messages indicating that a printer does not exist or is not responding, there is probably a network problem or permission problem as described above. The following are items you should check in the event of a printer problem:

- Check the printer's print job list, as described earlier in this chapter. If jobs are not reaching the list, the problem is most likely the user's workstation or the network connection. If jobs are reaching the list but not printing, the problem is most likely with the printer or print server.
- The spooler process can sometimes lock up. Stop and restart this service on the computer attached to the printer.
- A lack of free space in the print spool directory on the computer attached to the printer can also prevent jobs from reaching the job list.
- If the printer (or the user) has been recently added to the system, check the printer's permissions to ensure that the user is allowed access.
- Use the auditing feature to log unsuccessful print jobs. Audit entries are written to the System log, accessible through the Event Viewer utility. Events related to printer security (for example, if a user was denied access to the printer) are listed in the Security log.

Application Problems

The vast majority of application-related problems fall into two categories: improperly set permissions for running the application, and system configuration issues that cause application crashes. If you are configuring a new application or user and the user is unable to access the application, check these items:

- Make sure the user has the proper permissions for the application's executable file, any associated files (such as DLLs), and the data directory used by the application.

- If the user is trying to run a DOS or 16-bit Windows application, try it on another computer to ensure that it supports Windows NT. Modifying DOS settings may reduce the possibility of a crash.

- 16-bit Windows applications can be run in their own memory space, which may prevent or lessen the consequences of a crash.

- Make sure the computer has sufficient memory (both physical and virtual) for the OS and for the application. Exit any concurrently running applications to release memory.

- Note that RISC-based versions of Windows NT cannot run 32-bit Windows applications unless they are specifically compiled for that processor, and cannot run DOS or 16-bit Windows applications.

If the user has previously been able to access the application but it fails to run or crashes, check these items:

- Restart the computer. If memory corruption was caused by a previous application's crash, it may prevent another application from running correctly.

- Make sure there have been no changes to the permissions of the application's directory and data directories.

- Check for file corruption or missing files in the application's directory. If files are missing, check for a user with excessive permissions in the directory who may have inadvertently deleted a file.

On the Exam

Application troubleshooting is sometimes covered in scenario questions in the NT Workstation MCSE exam. In addition, issues relating to which operating systems can run which types of executable files are often covered. See the "Operating Systems" section at the beginning of this chapter for information about the various versions of Windows and their abilities.

System Troubleshooting

While previous versions of Windows are vulnerable to general protection faults (GPFs) and other types of crashes, Windows NT is relatively stable. Nonetheless, it does have occasional problems.

Problems in the NT operating system kernel itself usually result in a STOP error, also called a "blue screen" error. The screen is switched to text mode and information is displayed on a blue screen. This screen includes a hexadecimal dump of the memory area involved in the crash and other information that may be useful for technical support professionals.

Application errors happen far more often than system errors. In particular, 16-bit Windows applications can crash just as they do in their native system, although Windows NT does not allow the crash to affect the OS or other applications.

Windows NT includes a utility called Dr. Watson, which is executed when an application crashes. This utility displays detailed information about the crash and allows you to create a log file. You can run Dr. Watson yourself by typing DRWTSN32 at the Run dialog or command prompt to display a configuration dialog.

You may wish to change Dr. Watson's configuration to improve response to crashes. You can specify a log file directory, a filename for application memory dumps, a soundfile to be played in the event of a crash, and various other options.

On the Exam

For the NT Workstation exam, you should be familiar with the types of crashes that can occur and their symptoms. You should also know the purpose of the Dr. Watson utility and be familiar with its configuration dialog. More detail about crashes and debugging is covered in Part 4 for the NT Server in the Enterprise exam.

Suggested Exercises

Since the NT Workstation exam is the first of the Windows NT exams, it includes many questions about the operation of Windows NT in general, its architecture, and the various administrative utilities. You should have as much experience as possible installing and using NT Workstation for the exam.

While it's possible to study and practice for this exam using a single computer running Windows NT Workstation, I recommend that you have access to at least two Windows NT computers in a network.

This exam emphasizes the various control panels, configuration dialogs, and utilities included with Windows NT Workstation. In addition to the steps, you should run and become familiar with all of the utilities described in the *Study Guide*.

Performing the following exercises will help you prepare for the exam:

1. Install Windows NT Workstation on a computer:

    a. Use the HCL, NTHQ, and the hardware requirements listed in Chapter 8 to determine whether the computer can run Windows NT.

    b. If you will be attaching the computer to a network, install a network card. Be sure the settings (IRQ, etc.) will not conflict with other components of the computer.

    c. Based on the available hardware and its compatibility, determine the appropriate installation method.

    d. Perform the Windows NT installation. As you proceed through the installation steps, follow along with the list of steps in the *Study Guide*. Use an NTFS partition so that you'll be able to use the security features.

    e. Because it's important to be familiar with the installation process, install Windows NT Workstation several times in different configurations.

2. If you have an earlier version of Windows NT available, try an upgrade installation of Windows NT 4.0 over the older version. Notice which settings are maintained.

3. Install Windows 95 after Windows NT is already installed and create a multi-boot configuration. You will need to manually edit the BOOT.INI file.

4. Use the Setup Manager utility to create an unattended installation answer file, and perform the unattended installation.

5. Once you have Windows NT running on a computer, try running various types of applications (DOS, Windows 16-bit, Windows 32-bit). Experiment with different priority levels for Win32 applications.

6. Create several users and assign them different combinations of NTFS permissions. Log on using the accounts you created and verify that the permissions are being enforced.

7. If you have at least two Windows NT workstations on a network, perform these exercises:

   a. Ensure that the computers are set up with compatible network protocols.

   b. Configure the machines to belong to the same workgroup.

   c. Share one or more directories on one machine, and verify that they are visible from the other machine's Network Neighborhood window.

   d. Create a user with specific permissions for a share. Log on to the other workstation as that user and access the share.

   e. Try moving several files from one computer to a shared directory on the other computer. Notice how permissions are affected.

   f. Map a drive letter on one computer to a network share on the other computer.

   g. Configure both computers for TCP/IP support, and assign them IP addresses.

8. Install CSNW on a computer. If you have a NetWare server available, verify that you can access resources on the server.

9. Install and configure Peer Web Services (PWS). If you have another computer on the network, try using Internet Explorer to access the web server.

10. Install RAS and configure a dial-up phonebook entry. If you have access to a remote network or ISP, configure dial-up networking to communicate with the network.

11. Use the REGEDIT and REGEDT32 utilities to view and modify the Windows NT registry.

12. If you have two or more disk drives in the computer, configure them as a volume set. If you have three or more drives, try configuring a stripe set.

13. Experiment with the NTBACKUP utility. This utility will run even if you do not have a backup device.

14. Install support for one or more printers.

15. View information using the Event Viewer, Performance Monitor, and Task manager utilities.

16. Create an emergency repair disk (ERD) and use it to restore system files.

Practice Test

Test Questions

1. Which of the following terms refers to an operating system's ability to run portions of an application concurrently on the same processor?

    a. Multitasking

    b. Multithreading

    c. Multiprocessing

    d. Memory protection

2. You want to install Windows NT Workstation on a machine. The machine is a 100-MHz Pentium with 8 MB of memory, a double-speed SCSI CD-ROM drive, and a 2-GB hard disk drive. Which of these components is inadequate for NT Workstation?

    a. Hard disk space

    b. RAM

    c. CD-ROM drive

    d. CPU

3. You are installing high-end machines for users in the design department, who use complex CAD applications. The machines you have chosen have four Pentium processors, 64 MB of memory, and 4-GB hard disks. Which operating system will take the best advantage of these resources?

    a. Windows 95

    b. Windows 3.11

    c. Windows NT Workstation

    d. Windows NT Server

4. Which of the following operating systems supports preemptive multitasking and multiprocessing?

    a.   Windows 3.1

    b.   Windows for Workgroups

    c.   Windows 95

    d.   Windows NT

5. You are choosing a network operating system for several machines on your network.

Required Result: The OS must support DOS, Windows 3.1, and Win32 applications.

Optional Result: The OS should support preemptive multitasking.

Optional Result: The OS should support a secure file system

Solution: Install Windows 95.

    a.   The solution meets the required result and both of the optional results.

    b.   The solution meets the required result and only one of the optional results.

    c.   The solution meets the required result only.

    d.   The solution does not meet the required result.

6. Which of the following features is supported by Windows 95 but not by Windows NT Server?

    a.   Multitasking

    b.   Multiprocessing

    c.   Plug and Play

    d.   Memory protection

7. You are installing a group of new computers in a domain-based network. These machines need to be able to share files and printers.

Required Result: The OS must support file and printer sharing in a domain, and must support two processors.

Optional Result: The OS should be able to act as a domain controller.

Optional Result: The OS should support fault tolerance through disk mirroring.

Solution: Install Windows NT Workstation.

    a.   The solution meets the required result and both of the optional results.

    b.   The solution meets the required result and only one of the optional results.

c. The solution meets the required result only.

d. The solution does not meet the required result.

8. Which of the following portions of the Windows NT operating system are able to communicate directly with hardware? (choose all that apply)

    a. Window Manager

    b. Object Manager

    c. Security Reference Monitor

    d. I/O Manager

9. Which mode contains Windows NT's executive services?

    a. User mode

    b. Kernel mode

    c. Hardware mode

10. Which of the following types of applications are not supported at all by Windows NT?

    a. OS/2

    b. POSIX

    c. UNIX

    d. DOS

11. Which of the following application types require the use of a VDM? (select all that apply)

    a. 32-bit Windows

    b. 16-bit Windows

    c. DOS

    d. OS/2 Presentation Manager

12. You are installing several computers to run a custom DOS accounting suite, and need to choose the appropriate OS. Some users need to run reports in the General Ledger program and have access to the Accounts Receivable program while the report is running in the background.

Required Result: The OS must support DOS applications.

Optional Result: The OS should be able to run a DOS application in the background while another application executes.

Optional Result: The OS should also be able to run a DOS-based graphics program that accesses the video driver directly for fast performance.

Solution: Install Windows NT Workstation.

    a. The solution meets the required result and both of the optional results.

b. The solution meets the required result and only one of the optional results.

c. The solution meets the required result only.

d. The solution does not meet the required result.

13. Specify the correct order for the following steps in the Windows NT boot process.

    a. The BOOT.INI file is read.

    b. The MBR is read from disk and NTLDR starts.

    c. A menu of operating systems is displayed.

    d. NTDETECT analyzes the computer's hardware.

14. Which partition contains the NTLDR and BOOT.INI files?

    a. The default partition

    b. The root partition

    c. The system partition

    d. The boot partition

15. Which of the following is the correct command sequence to start an application called APP.EXE with a priority value of 13?

    a. Start /13 app.exe

    b. Start /high app.exe

    c. Start app.exe /high

    d. Run app.exe /priority=13

16. Environment settings for a DOS application can be changed by modifying which file?

    a. AUTOEXEC.BAT

    b. AUTOEXEC.NT

    c. CONFIG.SYS

    d. MSDOS.PIF

17. To look for shared files on a specific computer on the network, which window should be used?

    a. My Computer

    b. Network Neighborhood

    c. File Manager

    d. Network Share Explorer

18. You have configured a share called DOSFILES to point to the \APPS\SYSTEMS\DOS directory on the D: drive on the WEST3 server. Which of the following is a valid UNC path for this share?

    a.   \west3\apps\systems\dos

    b.   \\west3\dosfiles

    c.   \WEST3\DOSFILES

    d.   \\west3\dosfiles\apps\systems\dos

19. What is the correct procedure for running the NT Hardware qualifier utility?

    a.   Run C:\NTHQ from a Windows NT machine

    b.   Run MAKEDISK.BAT from the CD-ROM, then boot the disk

    c.   Run MAKEDISK.BAT from the CD-ROM, and type A:NTHQ at the DOS prompt

    d.   Boot the Windows NT CD-ROM

20. You are installing a new 600-MB SCSI disk drive and want to use file system security. Which file system should you install?

    a.   NTFS

    b.   FAT

    c.   HPFS

21. You are installing a new network with 8 Windows NT Workstation computers. Security is not a major issue. Which is the most appropriate network type?

    a.   Workgroup

    b.   Domain

    c.   Hybrid

22. You want to create Windows NT installation disks from an existing Windows 95 computer for booting on a computer with no existing OS. Which is the correct command to create the disks?

    a.   WINNT /OX

    b.   WINNT32 /OX

    c.   WINNT /O

    d.   MAKEDISK /O

23. Which is the correct command to install Windows NT from an existing Windows 95 installation, without using boot disks?

    a.   WINNT /B

    b.   WINNT32 /B

    c.   WINNT /O

    d.   WINNT32 /OX

24. Which of the following operating systems can be upgraded to Windows NT 4.0 with some settings from the original OS preserved? (choose all that apply)

    a.   Windows NT 3.51

    b.   Windows 95

    c.   Windows 3.11

    d.   OS/2 3.0

25. You are installing a new SCSI adapter with built-in BIOS on a Windows NT system, and want to be able to boot from the main partition on the first drive (SCSI ID 0) attached to the adapter. No other SCSI controllers are installed. Which is the correct ARC entry for this option?

    a.   scsi(0)disk(0)rdisk(0)partition(1)\WINNT4="Windows NT"

    b.   multi(0)disk(1)rdisk(0)partition(1)\WINNT4="Windows NT"

    c.   scsi(1)disk(1)rdisk(0)partition(1)="C:\WINNT4"

    d.   scsi(0)disk(0)rdisk(0)partition(1)\WINNT4="Windows NT"

26. Which file is *required* for an automated installation of Windows NT?

    a.   Unattended answer file

    b.   Uniqueness database file

    c.   SYSDIFF dump file

27. Where do you specify the NetBIOS name for a Windows NT computer?

    a.   NetBIOS control panel

    b.   Network control panel

    c.   AUTOEXEC.NT file

    d.   In the registry

28. Which service allows the computer to share files and printers?

    a.   Workstation

    b.   Server

    c.   Share

    d.   Computer Browser

29. Which of the following services is *not* provided by CSNW?

    a.   Access to NetWare files for NT clients

    b.   Access to NetWare printers for NT clients

    c.   Access to NT files for NetWare clients

30. Which CSNW setting may need to be set manually if NetWare 3.11 is in use?

    a.   Default Tree and Context

    b.   NWLink support

    c.   Frame types

31. Which frame type is typically used by NetWare 4.x?

    a.   802.2

    b.   802.3

    c.   SNAP

    d.   802.5

32. Which of the following is not a protocol related to TCP/IP?

    a.   SLIP

    b.   FTP

    c.   IPX

    d.   DHCP

33. A node's network address is 128.110.204.26. Which protocol is most likely being used?

    a.   IPX/SPX

    b.   NetBIOS

    c.   TCP/IP

    d.   SLIP

34. Which service can translate a TCP/IP host name into an IP address?

    a.   WINS

    b.   DNS

    c.   ARP

    d.   NetBEUI

35. How many incoming TCP/IP connections can be used with NT Workstation's Personal Web Server software?

    a.   20

    b.   10

    c.   16

    d.   256

36. Which of the following protocols is not supported by PWS?

    a.   HTTP

    b.   FTP

    c.   Gopher

    d.   Telnet

37. Which of the following PPP authentication protocols is the least secure?

    a.   CHAP

    b.   PAP

    c.   SPAP

    d.   MS-CHAP

38. Windows NT Workstation's RAS can be used to connect to which types of servers?

    a.   Windows NT servers only

    b.   UNIX or Windows NT servers

    c.   Any server running a compatible protocol

39. Which Control Panel applet is used to install a modem driver?

    a.   Devices

    b.   Modems

    c.   Drivers

    d.   Services

40. Which registry subtree stores hardware driver and interrupt settings?

    a.   HKEY_LOCAL_MACHINE

    b.   HKEY_HARDWARE

    c.   HKEY_CURRENT_USER

    d.   HKEY_CLASSES_ROOT

41. Which utility can be used to set user permissions to various registry keys?

    a.   REGEDIT

    b.   REGEDT32

    c.   REGUSER

    d.   User Manager for Domains

42. Which of the following user accounts cannot be deleted?

    a.   Guest

    b.   LOCAL_USER

    c.   Default

    d.   Administrator

43. If you wish to restrict users to passwords with a minimum of 6 characters, which dialog should be modified?

    a.   User Properties

    b.   User Rights Policy

    c.   Account Policy

    d.   User Restrictions

44. Which type of user profile allows a user to log into different workstations with the same desktop settings, and allows the user to change settings?

    a.   Local user profile

    b.   Roaming user profile

    c.   Mandatory user profile

    d.   Desktop user profile

45. A Windows NT Workstation computer has three 400-MB disk drives. If you combine the three drives into the largest possible volume set, how much space will be available on the volume?

    a.   '400 MB

    b.   800 MB

    c.   1200 MB

    d.   1600 MB

46. You are combining four 200-MB drives and wish to increase speed as much as possible. Fault tolerance is not required. What is the best configuration for the disks?

    a.   Volume set

    b.   Stripe set with parity

    c.   Stripe set

    d.   Mirror set

47. User PAUL has the Read permission for the APPS directory. He belongs to the Accounting group, which has Read and Write permissions, and the Users group, which has the No Access permission. What cumulative permissions does he have to the directory?

    a.   Read

    b.   Read and Write

    c.   Read, Write, and Change

    d.   No Access

48. If you want users to be able to write files to a directory using a network share and read files in the same directory, which permissions should be assigned?

    a.   Write and Read

    b.   Change and Read

    c.   Create and Read

    d.   Modify and Access

49. Which default share allows an administrator access to the D drive of a Windows NT Workstation computer?

    a.   D

    b.   NETLOGON\D

    c.   D$

    d.   ADMIN$

50. If a laser printer is attached to a Windows NT Workstation computer, the term Print Device refers to which object?

    a.   The actual hardware printer

    b.   The queue of jobs for the printer

    c.   The device driver for the printer

    d.   The computer attached to the printer

51. Which utility allows you to view the results of auditing?

    a.   Performance Monitor

    b.   Event Viewer

    c.   Task Manager

    d.   Audit Manager

52. Which Performance Monitor option can be configured to notify you when the CPU usage of a computer exceeds 80%?

    a.   Chart

    b.   Alert

    c.   Log

    d.   Graph

53. If the registry is corrupt on a Windows NT computer, which of the following troubleshooting methods should be tried first?

    a.   Emergency repair disk

    b.   Last known good

    c.   Upgrade installation

54. Which of the following capabilities is not included in the WinMSD utility?

    a.   Display available physical memory

    b.   Display information for a remote computer

    c.   Start and stop services

    d.   Display a list of disk drives

55. What is the most likely cause of an "Inaccessible boot device" message during the Windows NT boot process?

    a.   Missing DOS boot sector

    b.   Incorrect BOOT.INI entry

    c.   Missing NTLDR program

    d.   Corrupt boot sector

Answers to Questions

1. B. Multithreading is the process of running application subprocesses (threads) concurrently.

2. B. NT Workstation requires a minimum of 12 MB of RAM.

3. D. Windows NT Server supports up to 4 processors and would be the best choice.

4. D. Windows NT supports preemptive multitasking and multiprocessing.

5. B. The solution meets the required result (support for DOS, Win16, and Win32 applications) and one optional result (preemptive multitasking). Windows 95 does not support a secure file system.

6. C. Plug and Play is supported by Windows 95 but not by Windows NT.

7. C. The solution meets the required result only (support file and printer sharing and two processors). Windows NT Workstation cannot act as a domain controller, and does not support disk mirroring.

8. A, D. The Window Manager and I/O Manager components of Windows NT can communicate directly with hardware.

9. B. The executive services are part of Kernel mode.

10. C. UNIX applications are not supported by Windows NT.

11. B, C. Win16 and DOS applications use a VDM (virtual DOS machine).

12. B. The solution meets the required result (support for DOS applications) and one optional result (background processing of DOS application). Windows NT cannot run a DOS program that accesses the video driver directly.

13. B, A, C, D. The boot process begins with the MBR being read from the disk and starting NTLDR. Next, the BOOT.INI file is read. A menu of operating systems is displayed. Finally, NTDETECT analyzes the computer's hardware.

14. C. The system partition contains the NTLDR and BOOT.INI files.

15. C. The correct command is start /high app.exe.

16. B. The AUTOEXEC.NT file is executed when a DOS application starts and can be used to modify environment settings.

17. B. The Network Neighborhood window displays a list of computers on the network and allows you to browse shared files.

18. B. \\west3\dosfiles is the correct UNC path.

19. B. To run NTHQ, first run MAKEDISK.BAT to create the disk, then boot the disk.

20. A. NTFS supports file system security and is more efficient than FAT for a 600-MB drive.

21. A. A workgroup network works well for this size of network when security is not an issue.

22. A. WINNT /OX is the correct command. WINNT32 (choice B) is for use under Windows NT only.

23. A. WINNT /B is the correct command. WINNT is the utility to use under Windows 95, and the /B option specifies that boot disks will not be used.

24. A, B. Windows NT 3.51 can be upgraded with most settings preserved. An upgrade from Windows 95 to Windows NT preserves a small number of settings.

25. B. Since the SCSI adapter has a built-in BIOS, the ARC entry should begin with multi rather than scsi.

26. A. The unattended answer file is required for an unattended installation. The other files can be used but are not required.

27. B. The NetBIOS name is specified in the Identification tab of the Network control panel.

28. B. The Server service allows a Windows NT computer to share files and printers.

29. C. CSNW does not provide access to NT files for NetWare clients. (FPNW, available at extra cost, does provide this service.)

30. C. The Frame types setting may need to be configured manually, particularly for earlier NetWare versions.

31. A. NetWare 4.x typically uses Novell's 802.2 frame type.

32. C. The IPX protocol is unrelated to TCP/IP.

33. C. TCP/IP uses 32-bit network addresses in dotted decimal format.

34. B. DNS translates between TCP/IP host names and IP addresses. WINS (choice A) performs a similar service, but for NetBIOS names.

35. B. PWS is limited to 10 incoming connections.

36. D. Telnet is not supported by PWS.

37. B. PAP uses clear text authentication, and is the least secure.

38. C. RAS can connect to any server running a compatible protocol.

39. B. The Modems control panel is used to install or configure modem drivers.

40. A. The HKEY_LOCAL_MACHINE subtree stores hardware driver and interrupt settings.

41. B. REGEDT32 can set user permissions to registry keys. REGEDIT (choice A) is also a registry editor, but cannot set permissions.

42. A, D. Neither the Guest nor the Administrator user account can be deleted.

43. C. The Account Policy dialog allows you to modify password restrictions.

44. B. A roaming profile is available to different workstations, and allows the user to change settings.

45. C. A volume set simply combines the capacity of the drives used, so three 400-MB drives would result in 1200-MB of capacity.

46. C. A stripe set (without parity) provides the greatest speed increase, but does not provide fault tolerance.

47. D. The No Access permission given to the Users group overrides the permissions for the Accounting group and the user.

48. B. The Change and Read permissions should be assigned.

49. C. The D$ share allows administrator access to the D drive.

50. A. The term Print Device refers to the actual printer hardware.

51. B. The Event Viewer utility allows you to view logs that show the results of auditing.

52. B. The Alert option allows you to set thresholds for one or more counters and notifies you when the thresholds are exceeded.

53. B. The Last Known Good option should be tried first for a registry problem.

54. C. The WinMSD utility can display a list of services, but cannot start or stop them.

55. B. This message is most likely the result of an incorrect BOOT.INI entry.

Highlighter's Index

Operating Systems

Windows 3.x

Does not support preemptive multitasking, multithreading, multiprocessing, or Plug and Play

Requires approximately 2 MB RAM; 10-MB disk storage

16-bit

Runs DOS and Win16 applications

Windows 95

Supports preemptive multitasking; multithreading; Plug and Play

Requires 4 MB RAM (8 MB recommended); approximately 40-MB disk storage

32-bit

Runs DOS, Win16, and Win32 applications

NT Workstation

Supports preemptive multitasking; multithreading; multiprocessing; no support for Plug and Play

Intel 486/33 or higher, or Digital Alpha

Supports up to two processors

Requires 12 MB RAM (16 MB recommended); approximately 117-MB disk storage

32-bit

Runs DOS, Win16, Win32, OS/2 (limited), POSIX (limited) applications

Version 4.0: Windows 95 user interface

NT Server

Supports unlimited Network connections

Supports up to 32 processors

Supports up to 256 incoming RAS connections

Can act as domain controller (PDC or BDC) or as a member server

Supports fault tolerance (disk mirroring, striping with parity)

Includes additional software (SFM, GSNW, IIS)

Requires 16 MB RAM; approximately 124-MB disk storage

Other features same as NT Workstation

NT Architecture

Kernel Mode

HAL (Hardware Abstraction Layer)

I/O Manager

Window Manager

Kernel (Includes Object Manager, Virtual Memory Manager, Process Manager, Security Reference Monitor, Local Procedure Call Facility)

User Mode

Security subsystem

Environment subsystems (POSIX, OS/2, Win32, DOS, WOW)

Request services from kernel mode components

Virtual Memory

Memory not in current use is swapped to disk

Swap files can be used on multiple disks

4-GB virtual memory space (2 GB for applications; 2 GB for system)

Applications

DOS applications each use a VDM; each has a separate memory space

Win16 applications share a VDM and a single memory space by default

Win32 applications each have a separate memory space

NT Boot Process

1. BIOS reads MBR, starts NTLDR
2. NTLDR reads BOOT.INI, displays menu of operating systems
3. If DOS is selected, BOOTSECT.DOS is executed
4. NTDETECT.COM tests and detects hardware
5. NTOSKRNL.EXE starts Windows NT

Partitions

Boot partition contains system files (\WINNT, HAL.DLL, NTOSKRNL.EXE)

System partition contains files used in boot process (NTBOOTDD.SYS, NTLDR, BOOT.INI, BOOTSECT.DOS, NTDETECT.COM)

Planning and Installation

Hardware Requirements

CPU: 486/33 or higher (Pentium recommended)

RAM: 12 MB (16 MB recommended)

Display: VGA, Super VGA, or better

Hard disk: SCSI or IDE; 117 MB of space required for OS

Floppy disk: 3.5", 1.4 MB

CD-ROM: SCSI or IDE (not required for network installations)

Network interface card: Any supported by NT; only required for network access

Hardware Support Information

HCL (Hardware Compatibility List): Current list of supported hardware

NTHQ (NT Hardware Qualifier): Utility to check compatibility; use MAKE-DISK.BAT to create disk, then boot the disk

Network Types

* Workgroup (peer-to-peer) networks: Each workstation can share resources; each handles its own user authentication; best suited for small networks (10 workstations or less)

* Domain (client-server) networks: One or more dedicated servers; centralized administration; any number of users; requires PDC (NT Server only)

File Systems

FAT: DOS standard; 2 GB maximum; 8.3 filenames

VFAT: Windows 95 and NT; 4 GB maximum; long filenames

NTFS: NT 4.0 and later; 16 EB (exabytes) maximum; long filenames; security

HPFS: OS/2 and NT 3.51 and earlier; includes security; cannot be migrated to HPFS in NT 4.0

Installation Program

WINNT32 (Windows NT) or WINNT (Windows 3.1; DOS; Windows 95)

WINNT /B: Don't create boot disks

WINNT /OX: Create boot disks, but don't start installation

`WINNT /T:`*drive*: Specify temporary storage drive

`WINNT /U`: Use unattended answer file

Installation Phases

Pre-copy: Copies files to temporary directory or creates boot disks

Phase 0: Text-based phase

Phase 1: Beginning of GUI (Setup Wizard) phase

Phase 2: Set up network components

Phase 3: Final setup: time zone, display properties, etc.

Unattended Installation

Answer file: Contains answers to installation prompts

Uniqueness database file (UDF): Contains specific exceptions for one or more computers

SYSDIFF

`SYSDIFF /snap`: Create snapshot

`SYSDIFF /diff`: Create difference file

`SYSDIFF /apply`: Apply difference file to computer

`SYSDIFF /inf`: Create INF file based on difference file

`SYSDIFF /dump`: Create report of difference file contents

Network Components

TCP/IP

Named for Transport Control Protocol and Internet Protocol

Routable

Used for UNIX and the Internet

Main protocols: TCP (connection-oriented); UDP (connectionless)

IP address consists of network address and node address

Bytes for network address: 1 (Class A); 2 (Class B); 3 (Class C)

First octet: 1-126 (Class A); 128-191 (Class B); 192-223 (Class C)

Dial-up Protocols

SLIP (Serial line Internet protocol): Simple; TCP/IP only; UNIX servers

PPP (Point-to-point protocol): Supports authentication and error control; TCP/IP or other protocol; NT servers

IPX/SPX (NWLink)

Used for NetWare connectivity or as a general network transport

Main protocols: IPX (connectionless); SPX (connection-oriented)

Routable

NetBEUI

Used to support NetBIOS

Low overhead

Non-routable; used for small networks

DLC

Non-routable

Used for mainframe connectivity and network printers

NetWare Support

NWLink: IPX/SPX protocol

CSNW: Client for NetWare

GSNW: Gateway for NetWare (NT Server Only)

FPNW: File and print sharing for NetWare (add-on product)

RAS Security

PAP (Password Authentication Protocol): Internet standard; passwords sent as clear text; least secure

SPAP (Shiva PAP): Shiva's improved version of PAP; passwords sent in encrypted form

CHAP (Challenge Handshake Authentication Protocol): Two-way protocol using encrypted passwords

MS-CHAP (Microsoft CHAP): Microsoft's proprietary version of CHAP; supported only by Windows and Windows NT

Configuring Windows NT

Registry Subtrees

HKEY_CLASSES_ROOT stores file associations

HKEY_CURRENT_USER stores control panel settings; loaded from user profile at login

HKEY_LOCAL_MACHINE stores hardware-specific data

HKEY_USERS stores default user settings and settings for each user profile

HKEY_CURRENT_CONFIG stores dynamic configuration information

HKEY_DYN_DATA stores dynamic hardware information

Registry Utilities

REGEDIT displays entire registry in one window; allows complex searches

REGEDT32 displays subtrees in separate windows; allows changes to registry key security

User Profiles

Local profiles only work at a particular workstation

Roaming profiles work at any Windows NT computer in the network

Mandatory profiles are roaming profiles that cannot be modified by users

System Policies

User policy affects a particular user, or default user

Computer policy affects a particular computer, or default computer

System policies override user profile settings

Security Policies

Account Policy stores defaults for user accounts (password length, etc.)

User Rights Policy assigns rights to users or groups

Audit Policy enables or disables auditing

Volume Sets

Two or more partitions

Total capacity is sum of all partition sizes

Partitions can be added without erasing

Decreases speed

Not fault tolerant

Disk Striping

2–32 partitions on separate disks

Intersperses data between disks

Increases read and write speed

Not fault tolerant

NTFS Security

Rights: Read, Write, Delete, Change Permissions, Execute, Take Ownership, Full Control, No Access

Combining user and group rights: Least restrictive permission applies unless any right is No Access

Copied files inherit permissions of new directory

Moved files retain permissions

File Sharing

Rights: Read, Change, Full Control, No Access

Combining NTFS and share rights: Most restrictive permission applies

Default shares: NETLOGON; ADMIN$ for WINNT directory; shares for each drive (C$, etc.)

Backups

Full backup copies all of the files every time; clears archive bits

Differential backup includes all of the files that have changed since the last full backup; does not clear archive bits

Incremental backup copies files that have changed since the last backup, whether full or incremental; clears archive bits

Copy includes all files; does not modify archive bit

Daily copy includes files modified on the current date; does not modify archive bit

Printing

Printer is software representation; print device is actual hardware

Configured from Printers folder

Print pool: Printer with multiple assigned ports, attached to identical print devices

---

Troubleshooting

Event Viewer

System Log: System error messages and status messages

Security Log: Security errors and auditing

Application Log: Application-specific errors and messages

Task Manager

Applications: List of currently running applications

Processes: Complete list of current processes

Performance: Graph of CPU and memory usage; information about files, threads, and processes in use

Performance Monitor

Chart: Displays a graph of counter valuess over time

Alert: Alerts you if a counter exceeds defined boundaries

Log: Creates a log file with counter values

Report: Generates a printable report based on the counters.

PART 3

Windows NT Server

Exam Overview

Windows NT Server is Microsoft's higher-priced version of Windows NT, intended for use as a network server. It is similar to Windows NT Workstation, with two main functional differences: a less restrictive license, and a variety of bundled software (such as Internet Information Server). NT Server is also optimized for performing typical server duties.

Microsoft's MCSE Exam 70-067, titled *Implementing and Supporting Microsoft Windows NT Server 4.0*, covers various tasks involved in managing Windows NT networks. Although this exam covers more network- and server-related topics than the Workstation exam, the emphasis is still on simple networks (those with one domain, and usually a single location).

Because of the overlap between the NT Workstation and NT Server exams, you should study all of the *Study Guide* in Part 2 in conjunction with this Part, even if you've already passed the Workstation exam. Specific items to study in Part 2 are listed in this section's "Objectives."

In order to prepare for this chapter and the NT Server exam, you should be familiar with the concepts introduced in Part 1, "Networking Essentials." You should also have some real-world experience using and administering Windows NT Server in a network.

Objectives

Need to Know	Reference
Difference between fault tolerance methods and specific requirements for each	"Planning Fault Tolerance" on page 191
Differences between NT server roles (PDC, BDC, member server)	"Planning a Domain" on page 196

Need to Know	Reference
Various methods of installing Windows NT	Part 2, "Installation Methods" on page 107
BOOT.INI file syntax	Part 2, "The BOOT.INI File" on page 114
Basic syntax of answer files and UDF files	Part 2, "Server-Based Installation" on page 116
Network protocol advantages and disadvantages	"Selecting Network Protocols" on page 195
NetWare frame types and their support in Windows NT	Part 2, "NetWare Frame Types" on page 123
Computer browser types and their functions	"Network Browsing" on page 212
NT Disk Architecture, and how volume sets and stripe sets work	Part 2, "Managing Disk Storage" on page 145
NTFS permissions and their purposes	Part 2, "NTFS Security" on page 146
Share permissions and their purposes	Part 2, "File Sharing and Permissions" on page 148
Components involved in printing	Part 2, "Configuring Printers" on page 149
Distinctions between and uses of local and global groups	"Users and Groups" on page 220
Types of settings found in computer, user, group, and default policies	"System Policies" on page 224

Need to Apply	Reference
Choose the appropriate file system for a network.	Part 2, "File Systems" on page 106
Choose the appropriate network protocols for a network.	"Selecting Network Protocols" on page 195
Install Windows NT Server.	"The Installation Process" on page 198
Configure client installation with Network Client Administrator.	"Installing Network Clients" on page 201
Install and configure network adapters.	"Network Adapters and Protocols" on page 203
Install and bind network protocol.	"Installing Protocols" on page 203
Configure NT Server services.	"Network Services" on page 205
Install client software for NetWare connectivity.	Part 2, "NetWare Client Software" on page 121
Install Gateway Service for NetWare (GSNW).	"NetWare Connectivity" on page 206
Install Migration Tool for NetWare.	"NetWare Connectivity" on page 206
Install and manage dial-up networking (RAS) clients.	Part 2, "Remote Access Service (RAS)" on page 130
Install Remote Access Server (RAS) servers.	"Remote Access Server" on page 210

Need to Apply	Reference
Use the control panel to install and configure hardware devices.	Part 2 ,"Using the Control Panel" on page 133
Install or configure a local or remote printer.	Part 2, "Configuring Printers" on page 149
Configure NT Server hard disks for performance and fault tolerance.	"Managing Disk Storage" on page 214
Configure backups for critical files.	"Configuring System Backups" on page 215
Manage domain controllers and add computers to domains.	"Domains and Security" on page 219
Manage domain users and groups.	"Users and Groups" on page 220
Create and modify local, roaming, and mandatory user profiles.	"User Profiles" on page 223
Manage system policies.	"System Policies" on page 224
Use NT server tools for remote administration.	"System Policies" on page 224
Monitor performance of a system with Performance Monitor.	Part 2, "Monitoring Performance" on page 152; "Monitoring Performance" on page 228
Troubleshoot common Windows NT problems.	Part 2, "Troubleshooting Procedures" on page 156
Troubleshoot common network problems.	"Network Troubleshooting" on page 229

Study Guide

This chapter includes the following sections, which address topics covered on the Windows NT Server MCSE exam:

Installing Windows NT Server
> Introduces Windows NT Server's hardware requirements and the aspects of planning unique to NT Server, including licensing, fault tolerance, and domain controllers, and describes the installation process.

Managing Network Components
> Includes information about installing and configuring NT Server network components, including network adapters, protocols, services, NetWare features, RAS, and browsing services.

Configuring Disks
> Describes the various disk configurations available in NT Server, including fault tolerance, and the backup methods available.

Security and Administration
> Describes how users and groups are used in a domain-based network. This section also covers user profiles and system policies, which can be used to manage user preferences and settings, and describes the available remote administration tools for NT Workstation and Windows 95.

Optimization and Troubleshooting
> Describes methods of monitoring the performance of NT Server computers and networks, and describes common network problems and their solutions.

Installing Windows NT Server

Windows NT server's installation is similar to that of NT Workstation. However, there are additional choices available during the installation, and additional considerations when planning the installation. These are discussed in the sections that follow.

Hardware Requirements

NT Server is more demanding of hardware than NT Workstation. The minimum requirements for NT Server on Intel-based computers are described in Table 3-1.

Table 3-1: Windows NT Workstation Requirements

Item	Requirement
CPU	486/33 or higher (Pentium recommended)
RAM	16 MB (32 MB recommended)
Display	VGA, Super VGA, or better
Hard disk	SCSI or IDE; minimum 124 MB of space required for OS
Floppy disk	3.5", 1.4 MB
CD-ROM	SCSI or IDE (not required for network installations)
Network interface card	Any supported by NT

As with Windows NT Workstation, NT Server includes the NTHQ utility and the HCL to allow specific hardware to be checked for compatibility.

Planning Fault Tolerance

Unlike Windows NT Workstation, NT Server supports two fault-tolerant configurations for disks. These are software implementations of RAID (Redundant Array of Inexpensive Disks) standards. NT Server supports RAID 1 (disk mirroring or duplexing) and RAID 5 (disk striping with parity). Disk striping without parity is supported by NT Workstation and NT Server, but does not provide fault tolerance.

The sections below look at the following elements of fault-tolerant networking:

- *Disk mirroring and duplexing* store the same data on two separate physical drives.

- *Disk striping with parity* stores data across three or more drives and stores error-checking information.

- *Hardware RAID* solutions provide fault tolerance within a disk controller.

- *Tape backups* provide another degree of fault tolerance for any network.

- While not technically part of a fault-tolerant server, an uninterruptible power supply (UPS) can prevent power-related disk failures.

Disk Mirroring and Duplexing

Disk mirroring and duplexing use two identical partitions on separate physical disks, and write the same data to each one. The difference between these methods is the hardware used: disk mirroring uses a single drive controller for both disks, while disk duplexing uses two controllers. Since it can protect against a controller failure, duplexing is slightly more fault tolerant.

While the hardware controlling the drives may be different, Windows NT implements both of these techniques the same way. NT refers to a disk volume created using either of these methods as a *mirror set.*

If a disk in a mirror set fails, the remaining disk continues to work, but is not fault tolerant. To repair the mirror set, you must replace the failed drive and recreate the mirror with the existing drive. Mirror sets are the only method of fault tolerance that can be used on the boot or system partitions. Mirroring causes disk writes to be slightly slower, while disk reads are significantly faster.

If you plan to use disk mirroring or duplexing on the system drive, install the hardware before installing Windows NT. Use the normal procedure to install the OS on the first of the two drives. After installation is successful, create a mirror set with the two drives.

On the Exam

The "Managing Disk Storage" section, later in this chapter, describes how to implement and repair mirror sets and other fault tolerant disk configurations.

Disk Striping with Parity

Disk striping, introduced in Part 2, is a method of combining several partitions on separate physical drives into a single volume. Data is interspersed, or striped, among the drives. Basic disk striping is usually done to increase performance, and does not provide fault tolerance.

Disk striping with parity, available only in NT Server, adds parity (checksum) data to the stripe set. This allows the set to be reconstructed if a single drive fails. A failed drive should be replaced quickly, since there is no provision for recovery if two drives fail.

Disk striping with parity requires at least 3 drives, and can be used with up to 32 drives. An amount of space equal to the size of one of the drives is used for parity data, which is spread equally between the drives. For example, a parity stripe set consisting of five 400-MB partitions would use 400 MB for parity (about 80 MB per drive), and would have 1600 MB of available space on the volume. Figure 3-1 illustrates how data is distributed on a three-disk parity set; one file is shown to illustrate how files are stored.

As with regular disk striping, disk striping with parity provides faster read and write speeds. Unlike mirror sets, a stripe set cannot contain the system or boot

---

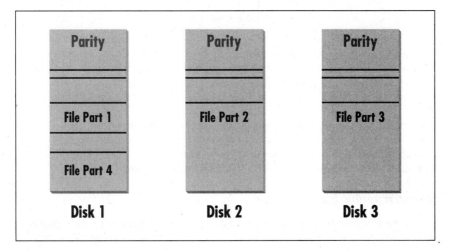

Figure 3-1: Disk striping with parity

partitions. Because of this, you will need to install Windows NT on a non-striped volume, then create the stripe set with parity on separate drives or partitions.

Windows NT Server

In the Real World

Some administrators find it practical to use a small (1 GB or less) IDE drive as the system/boot volume, and three or more large SCSI disks in a stripe set for actual data storage. This allows the full capacity of the SCSI disks to be used for the stripe set.

Hardware RAID

A variety of disk controllers are available with built-in RAID support, implementing fault tolerance entirely under hardware control. These are more expensive than Windows NT's software-based solution, but have the advantage of better performance. They can also be used on the system or boot drives, unlike disk striping with parity.

If you plan to use hardware RAID, be sure the product includes Windows NT support. Install the controller and drives as directed by the controller's instructions. When you install Windows NT, the drives will appear as a single device. You do not need to configure fault tolerance within the OS.

Tape Backups

Regardless of whether another type of fault tolerance is used, your server should include a backup device of some sort. Tape drives are the most common. These are available in a wide range of capacities in internal and external models. Backups can be performed over the network, so you may not need backup devices in all servers.

Most high-capacity tape drives use a SCSI interface. These can be hooked to the same controller as SCSI disk drives and CD-ROMS; however, the backup process will cause less system slowdown if it has a separate controller. Tape devices do not need to be configured during the NT installation process.

Uninterruptible Power Supplies

An uninterruptible power supply, or UPS, includes batteries to provide power to the server for several minutes in the event of a power outage. Windows NT includes basic UPS support, and most models of UPS include more sophisticated software.

Most UPS devices include a serial cable to connect to the server. This allows the server to detect when the power has gone out and close files. This cable should not be hooked up during the installation process, because it can be incorrectly detected as a serial device; in addition, the signals sent in the detection process may cause the UPS to shut down. A solution to this problem is to use the /noserialmice option in the BOOT.INI file, as described in Part 2.

Network Planning

Before installing any server, you should plan how the server will be configured and how it will be used. The following sections look at various aspects of planning the network installation.

On the Exam

Some of the aspects of network planning (such as selecting a file system) were introduced in Part 2, and are summarized here. The NT Server exam also emphasizes choosing protocols for a network, explained in this section.

Selecting a File System

As explained in Part 2, you should choose whether to use FAT or NTFS partitions as part of the installation process. Each has its advantages and disadvantages:

- FAT can be used for dual-boot systems, since it can be accessed by DOS or earlier versions of Windows. It also has a lower overhead than NTFS and is more efficient for small volumes; Microsoft recommends that FAT be used for partitions of 400 MB or smaller.

- NTFS stores files more efficiently, supports file-level security, is more reliable, and supports Windows NT's more advanced fault tolerant features, such as disk striping. NTFS is particularly more efficient with larger drives; Microsoft recommends using NTFS exclusively with partitions larger than 400 MB.

On the Exam

Since Windows NT Server is typically used for larger networks, which tend to have far more than 400 MB of storage and usually require file-level security, NTFS is almost always the logical choice for NT Server installations.

Selecting Network Protocols

Windows NT supports a number of network protocols, and your installation plan should address the protocols that will be used. In a new network, protocols can be chosen based on their speed and efficiency; for an existing network, the main issue is compatibility with existing components.

The following protocols are included with Windows NT. Details about installing and using each of these are explained later in this chapter.

NetBEUI and NetBIOS

NetBEUI (NetBIOS Extended User Interface) was developed by Microsoft and IBM. NetBEUI works with NetBIOS, a Microsoft standard for workstation naming, communication, and file sharing. NetBEUI has the advantages of low overhead and ease of use, but is not routable, and therefore not suitable for large networks.

IPX/SPX

These are protocols developed by Novell for use with NetWare. Windows NT includes NWLink, an implementation of these protocols. Although the main reason to use NWLink is for compatibility with NetWare, it can be useful on NT-only networks; IPX is a routable protocol, unlike NetBEUI, and is easier to configure than TCP/IP.

TCP/IP

TCP/IP is a suite of protocols that originated with UNIX systems and the Internet. While TCP/IP is often used for Internet connectivity, Microsoft also recommends it for NT-only networks. TCP/IP requires more administrative effort than NetBEUI or IPX, but is routable and works well with large-scale networks.

AppleTalk

AppleTalk is supported by Windows NT for compatibility with Macintosh clients, which have this protocol built-in. Separate software, Microsoft Services for Macintosh (SFM), provides full Macintosh connectivity. These services are discussed in Part 4.

DLC

DLC (Data Link Control) is IBM's protocol for mainframe communications. The main reason for Windows NT's support of DLC is that some stand-alone print servers and network-ready printers (such as those made by Hewlett-Packard) use DLC.

Installation Methods

As discussed in Part 2, there are two basic methods of installing Windows NT. This method should be planned before you begin the installation, based on the computer's available resources. The two methods are as follows:

- By creating and booting installation disks. This is the only method that works if another OS is not already installed on the computer. This method requires a CD-ROM drive compatible with the Windows NT HCL.

- By running the installation program (WINNT or WINNT32) manually. This method works only if a previous OS is available on the computer. This method can use files installation files from the CD-ROM, from a copy on a local disk, or a network share.

Planning a Domain

Windows NT supports two basic types of networks: the workgroup model, in which all workstations on the network have separate user account databases, and the domain model, which centralizes security and file sharing with one or more servers. Windows NT Server is usually associated with the domain model, although an NT Server computer can be configured to participate in a workgroup.

On the Exam

The NT Server exam focuses on single-domain networks. Issues involved in multi-domain networks are covered in the Enterprise exam, as discussed in Part 4.

The servers in a domain are called *domain controllers*. During installation, you must choose whether the computer will be a domain controller and which type. Only Windows NT Server computers can act as domain controllers. The three possible server roles are discussed in the sections below.

Primary Domain Controller (PDC)

The PDC stores the main copy of the security database for the domain. Each domain has exactly one PDC. When a client logs into the domain, the user name and password are authenticated by a PDC (or BDC, explained below). The PDC can also store shared files and directories for use by clients.

If you are installing several machines for a new network, the PDC must be installed first. This creates the domain security database and allows the remaining

---

installations to authenticate to the domain. If BDCs are used, they should be installed second.

Backup Domain Controller (BDC)

Along with the PDC, the domain can have one or more BDCs. These servers store a copy of the security database and update it regularly. This serves as a backup for the PDC. In addition, users can authenticate with the BDC. The BDC's database is read-only, so you must access the PDC to make changes to user accounts. BDCs can also store shared data.

Member Server

A member server is a stand-alone server that participates in a domain. (Stand-alone servers can also participate in workgroups, as described in Part 2.) A member server is not configured as a domain controller. It can be used to store shared files and directories, or provide a service (such as an Intranet server). Member servers do not store a copy of the security database.

In the Real World

You can't change a member server to a domain controller, or a domain controller to a member server, after installation. You also cannot move a domain controller to a different domain without reinstalling. However, you can promote a BDC to a PDC for the same domain.

Windows NT Licensing

Windows NT Server supports two license modes: per server and per seat. You are asked to choose a licensing mode during the installation of Windows NT Server. You must also specify the number of licenses you have purchased. You can change the licensing mode and number of licenses using the Licensing applet of the Control Panel. The two modes are explained below

Per Server

In this mode, a single license is required for each currently logged on user of the server, regardless of the number of computers attached to the network. These licenses only apply to one server.

The advantage of the Per Server mode is that computers with no user currently logged in don't require licenses. For example, if a company has desks and computers for 40 employees, but no more than 20 are on duty at a given time, only 20 licenses would be required. The disadvantage of this method is that if clients need to access more than one server, they use a license for each server they logon to.

If you're unsure which licensing method will turn out to be the most economical for your situation, Per Server is the best choice because NT Server allows a one-time switch from Per Server to Per Seat. Once you've selected Per Seat, the licensing mode cannot be changed.

Per Seat

In this mode, one license is required for each client computer attached to the network. A license is required for a computer whether a user is logged on there or not, but a client can logon to any number of servers using a single license.

This method is usually more economical for large networks with multiple servers. For example, if a company has 100 workstations and two servers, and all clients require resources on both servers, only 100 licenses are required—if Per Server licensing was in use, 200 licenses would be required.

On the other hand, the small company mentioned in the previous example has 40 workstations but only 20 employees on duty at a time. If the Per Seat mode was used there, 40 licenses would be required rather than 20.

As mentioned above, once the Per Seat mode is selected, the licensing mode cannot be changed to Per Server. You should only use this mode in new installations if you're sure it's the most efficient arrangement.

On the Exam

Licensing questions often appear on the NT Server MCSE exam. In general, the Per Server mode is most economical for a small network with a single server, and the Per Seat mode is better for most large, multiple-server networks.

The Installation Process

The sections below enumerate the steps involved in installing Windows NT Server. The process is the same as the installation of NT Workstation, with some added options. For clarity, the entire list is included here. Steps unique to NT Server are prefixed with (Server).

On the Exam

The "Troubleshooting" section at the end of Part 2 describes some problems that may occur during installation. The installation steps may vary depending on the configuration and any errors; you should have experience installing Windows NT Server in various configurations for the exam.

Pre-Copy Phase

This first phase takes place only if you run the WINNT program from an existing operating system. If you use boot disks for the installation, the next phase starts after the disks are booted.

1. From a Windows or DOS command prompt, type WINNT /B to begin the installation, along with any other options you need.

2. You are prompted to enter the path for the Windows NT installation files (usually \I386). Files are now copied to the hard disk to boot Windows NT.

3. After the file copy finishes, shut down the current OS and restart the computer.

Phase 0 (Text-Based Phase)

In this phase, the computer loads the Windows NT kernel, but does not yet start the GUI. The following tasks are performed:

1. Windows NT checks the computer's hardware and indicates any problems.

2. The Windows NT OS now loads.

3. The setup options screen is displayed. This prompts you to press Enter to continue the installation, or press R to repair an existing installation.

4. A list of detected SCSI and IDE disk and CD-ROM controllers is displayed. You can press S to specify additional controllers. Otherwise, press Enter to continue.

5. The Windows NT license agreement is displayed. Read it using the Page Up and Page Down keys. Press F8 to indicate your agreement, or Esc to disagree and abort the installation.

6. The detected components of your computer are displayed: computer type, display, keyboard, and mouse. You can change any of these entries, or press Enter to continue.

7. A list of installed disk drives and their partitions is displayed. You can choose an existing FAT or NTFS partition or press C to create a new partition in a free area.

8. You are prompted as to whether to format the disk partition as FAT or NTFS, or leave it as is for existing partitions. Depending on the size of the partition, formatting may take several minutes.

9. Specify the location for the Windows NT Workstation files. The default is the \WINNT directory on the partition you chose above.

10. Windows NT will now scan the hard disk for errors. If you press Enter, an exhaustive scan is performed and may take several minutes. Press Esc to skip the exhaustive scan and continue.

11. Windows NT files are now copied to the directory you specified. This may take several minutes.

12. A final screen is displayed indicating that this portion of the installation is complete. Press Enter to restart the computer and begin the next phase.

Phase 1 (GUI Phase)

When the computer restarts this time, Windows NT is booted including the graphical user interface. The prompts described below are presented in graphic dialogs.

You can use the Next and Previous buttons on most dialogs to move forward or backward in the installation process.

1. You are prompted for the computer user's name and organization.

2. Enter the CD key. This is a 10-digit number printed on the certificate accompanying the installation CD-ROM.

3. (Server) Select which licensing mode (Per Server or Per Seat) will be used, as described earlier in this chapter.

4. Enter a name for the computer. This is a NetBIOS name, described in Part 1.

5. (Server) Select whether the server will be a PDC, BDC, or member server.

6. For a PDC, enter the name of the new domain to be created. If you are installing a BDC or member server, enter the name of the domain the computer will participate in. The PDC must be running and attached to the network before you proceed with this step.

7. Enter a password for the Administrator account, which will be created automatically during installation.

8. You are asked whether to create an emergency repair disk (ERD). If you choose not to, you can create one after installation. Emergency repair disks are described in the "Optimization and Troubleshooting" section at the end of this chapter.

9. Select the optional operating system components to be installed. These are displayed in several categories: Accessibility Options, Accessories, Communications, Games, Multimedia, and Windows Messaging.

Phase 2 (Network Setup)

The Setup Wizard continues with this phase, which asks questions relating to network components. Depending on the services and protocols used, the prompts in this phase may vary.

1. Specify whether the computer is connected to the network or will access a network remotely using a modem. NT Workstation offers a "not connected to a network" option; this is not available in NT Server.

2. (Server) You are now asked whether to install Internet Information Server (IIS).

3. Choose a network adapter. Use the Start Search button to search for an installed adapter, or the Select from List button to choose one from a list.

4. Specify the network protocols to install. Network protocols are discussed later in this chapter.

5. Depending on the settings you chose, you may be prompted for additional information, such as settings for the network adapter and properties for network protocols.

6. The installation program now warns you that it is about to start the network. Press Next to continue. This searches the network for existing domains and workgroups.

7. After copying additional files, the installation process completes. Press the Finish button to continue.

8. If you chose to install IIS, the IIS setup program now runs and prompts for several settings. (IIS is described in detail in Part 4.)

Phase 3 (Final Phase)

This phase completes the installation.

1. You are prompted for the current date and time and the computer's time zone.

2. The Display Properties dialog is now displayed. Choose the settings for the computer's video adapter.

3. Installation is now complete. Press the Restart Computer button to restart and boot Windows NT.

On the Exam

You don't need to know the complete list of installation steps for the exam, but you should be familiar with the process, know the portions unique to NT Server, and the choices you can't change later (such as PDC/BDC/member server).

Automating Installation

Windows NT supports unattended installation, which can simplify the installation process for multiple computers. Windows NT Server and NT Workstation support the same method of automated installation, described in Part 2. Two files are used in the installation process:

- A unattended installation file, or *answer file*. This is an ASCII text file that includes the information that the installation program would normally prompt for during installation. The Windows NT CD-ROM includes an example answer file called UNATTEND.TXT.

- A uniqueness database file (UDF) is a text file similar in format to the answer file. This optional file defines two or more IDs for separate computers, and specifies unique settings for each one.

Installing Network Clients

Some client machines, such as Windows NT Workstation, include client software to connect to Windows NT Server. In addition, NT Server includes a utility called Network Client Administrator to assist in installing client software for various types of clients.

Network Client Administrator is found in the Administrative Tools menu in Windows NT Server. To use it, you will need access to the Windows NT Server installation CD-ROM or a shared copy of the \CLIENTS directory. This utility includes two main options, described below.

Over-the-Network Installation

The Create Network Installation Startup Disk option creates a bootable disk that can be used to begin the installation of an operating system. The Windows 95 installation files are included in the \CLIENTS directory of the Windows NT CD-ROM.

You can also install Windows for Workgroups, Windows NT Workstation, or Windows NT Server if you share a copy of the \CLIENTS directory and copy the installation disks to subdirectories of CLIENTS: WFW\NETSETUP for Windows for Workgroups, WINNT\NETSETUP for NT Workstation, and WINNT.SRV\NETSETUP for NT Server.

On the Exam

For the exam, you should know the distinction between Client Administrator's main features: the *Create Network Installation Startup Disk* option is used mainly to install entire operating systems, while the *Make Installation Disk Set* option is used to add networking capabilities to preexisting operating systems.

Installation Disks

The *Make Installation Disk Set* option allows you to create bootable disks that will install a network client or service on client machines. The following services are available using this option:

- LAN Manager for MS-DOS
- Remote Access for MS-DOS
- Microsoft Network Client for MS-DOS and Windows
- TCP/IP for Windows for Workgroups
- LAN Manager for OS/2

Managing Network Components

Windows NT Server includes a variety of network features. This section discusses the process of installing and configuring network adapters, protocols, and services, and covers two NT Server capabilities (remote access and NetWare connectivity) not supported to the same extent in Windows NT Workstation.

Network Adapters and Protocols

The Network control panel, introduced in Part 2, is used to configure network adapters, protocols, and bindings. To access this control panel, select Network from the Control Panel folder or right-click on the Network Neighborhood icon and select *Properties*.

Network Adapters

Network adapters, also called network interface cards (NICs), allow a computer to connect to network media. Any Windows NT computer on the network requires at least one network adapter. Adapters are available for a wide variety of network media types.

Network adapters use several of the computer's available resources: IRQs (interrupts), I/O addresses, and possibly other settings. Adapters should be installed and configured to avoid conflicts with other devices. If there is no conflict between them, a computer can have multiple adapters installed.

The Adapters tab in the Network control panel displays a list of adapters currently installed and allows you to add to or modify the list. The settings you specify when adding an adapter should match those set on the card itself (or using the configuration software included with the card).

Windows NT Server

On the Exam

You should have experience installing and troubleshooting network cards in clients and servers for the NT Server exam. Part 1 covers the basics of installation and conflict troubleshooting in more detail. The questions in the Server exam usually don't require as much detailed knowledge (such as exact IRQ numbers) as the Network Essentials questions.

Installing Protocols

The Protocols tab in the Network control panel displays a list of currently installed protocols. You can add a protocol using the Add button, or remove an existing protocol with the Remove button. Some protocols (such as TCP/IP) have an additional configuration dialog accessible with the *Properties* option.

Binding Protocols to Adapters

Windows NT maintains a list of connections between network adapters, network services (described below), and network protocols, called *bindings*. The Bindings tab in the Network control panel, shown in Figure 3-2, allows you to view or modify bindings.

The *Show Bindings for* option in this dialog allows you to change the sorting of the bindings: by service, by adapter, or by protocol. All of the possible bindings

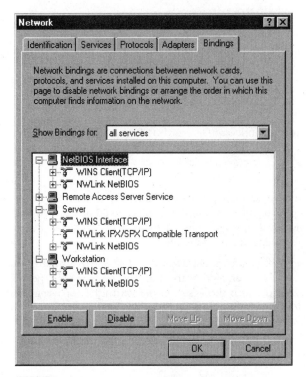

Figure 3-2: The Network control panel's Bindings tab

are included on the list; use the Enable or Disable buttons to control whether each binding is active.

When viewing the bindings by service, you can change the binding order of protocols. One way to improve performance is to rearrange the bindings for the workstation, since protocols are tried in the given order when communicating across the network.

Since the workstation usually initiates communication with the server, thus determining the protocol that will be used, changing the bindings of the Workstation service on workstations will provide a performance increase. The bindings of the Server service have little effect on performance.

To change protocol bindings, double-click on the icon for the Workstation or Server service. A list of protocols currently bound to the service is displayed; use the Move Up and Move Down buttons to change the bindings.

The most frequently used protocols should be at the top of the list. Protocols that are rarely used or use low bandwidth should be moved to the bottom of the list. Needless to say, removing unused protocols from the bindings list will also provide a performance benefit.

Network Services

Network services provide non-protocol-specific functions for Windows NT networking. The Services tab in the Network control panel lists installed network services and allows you to add, remove, or modify them.

Some of the most common network services are described in the sections below. Additional services, such as Computer Browser, Gateway Services for NetWare, and Remote Access Server, are described later in this chapter.

NetBIOS Interface

This service handles NetBIOS naming and communication. Windows NT supports NetBIOS over NetBEUI, the native protocol, as well as TCP/IP and IPX/SPX. This service is required for Windows NT networking regardless of the protocols in use.

Server

The Server service handles the protocols required for file and printer sharing over the network. This service is available on both NT Workstation and Server. The Properties dialog of the Server service allows you to optimize server use; the options include *Minimize Memory Used, Balance, Maximize Throughput for File Sharing,* and *Maximize Throughput for Network Applications.*

Since most of the server's use by clients is through this service, these optimization settings can affect the speed of the entire network.

The Server control panel applet is related to the Server service. This dialog, shown in Figure 3-3, displays information about the server including the shares currently available, files being shared, and users attached to the server.

The following dialogs are available from the server control panel:

Users
> Displays a list of currently attached users, and a list of resources currently in use by the highlighted user.

Shares
> Displays a list of the server's shares. Selecting a share displays a list of users currently accessing the share.

In Use
> Displays a list of open resources (files, printers, etc.) and the users currently accessing them.

Replication
> Provides a simple facility for automatic replication of files between servers.

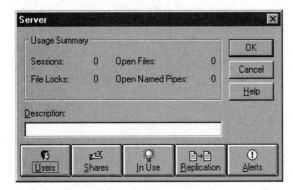

Figure 3-3: The Server control panel

Alerts

Maintains a list of users or computers that alerts are sent to in the event of a problem with the Server service.

Workstation

The Workstation service is the client software corresponding to the Server service. This service is included on both Windows NT Workstation and NT Server, and installed by default. This service is required for access to shared files and printers.

Directory Replicator

The Directory Replicator service is built into Windows NT Server, but not included with NT Workstation. This service allows simple replication of files between servers. This service is not listed in the Network control panel, but can be started or stopped using the Services control panel.

Once the Directory Replicator service is started, it can be configured using the Replication button in the Server control panel. Use the *Export Directories* and *Import Directories* options to configure directories to be copied.

The Directory Replicator service is somewhat limited: it cannot compare versions of files being copied, and it cannot copy open files.

License Manager

The License Manager service controls Windows NT licensing, discussed earlier in this chapter. The only options for this service are the *Per Server* and *Per Seat* options. These can be modified using the Licensing control panel.

NetWare Connectivity

Windows NT Server includes a variety of tools for NetWare connectivity. These include the following:

* NWLink, an implementation of the IPX/SPX protocols

* Gateway Services for NetWare (GSNW)

- Migration Tool for NetWare
- File and Print Services for NetWare (FPNW)

Client Services for NetWare (CSN) was introduced in Part 2, and is supported only by Windows NT Workstation. The sections below describe the NetWare features included with NT Server.

On the Exam

The main emphasis in the NT Server exam is on GSNW and Migration Tool for NetWare, although questions about these subjects rarely cover specific details. You should also be familiar with the NetWare features introduced in Part 2.

NWLink IPX/SPX Protocols

This protocol, introduced in Part 2, is Microsoft's implementation of Novell's IPX (Internetwork Packet Exchange) and SPX (Sequenced Packet Exchange) protocols. This protocol is automatically installed when you install CSNW, or can be installed manually. While primarily provided for NetWare support, NWLink can be used as a transport protocol in its own right.

The aspect of NWLink's configuration that most often causes confusion is the support for various IPX/SPX frame types. The *Auto Frame Type Detection* option works in most cases. In the event that it does not detect the frame type, frame types should be manually configured with the *Manual Frame Type Detection* option. The 802.2 frame type, supported by NetWare 3.12 and higher, is the most reliably detected.

Gateway Services for NetWare (GSNW)

CSNW, introduced in Part 2, is a full-featured 32-bit NetWare client included with Windows NT Workstation. Windows NT Server includes GSNW rather than CSNW. This service requires the NWLink protocol, which will be installed during the GSNW installation if it is not already present. GSNW also includes the features of CSNW, so the server does not require additional software to act as a NetWare client.

GSNW allows clients of the Windows NT network to access resources on a NetWare server. These resources appear as Windows NT shares to the clients. The clients do not require any NetWare client software. In addition, only a single NetWare user account (for the gateway server) is required regardless of the number of Windows-based clients.

GSNW does have its disadvantages compared to dedicated client software: since all users access the NetWare server in the same way, you cannot individually secure resources on the NetWare server. In addition, a single network connection (between the gateway server and the NetWare server) carries the NetWare traffic for all users, and can quickly become a bottleneck.

To install GSNW, use the Add button in the Services tab of the Network control panel. Choose Gateway Services for NetWare from the list. The files for GSNW are located in the I386 directory of the Windows NT Server CD-ROM. The server must be restarted after the installation is complete.

In addition to installing GSNW on the gateway server, you must configure the NetWare server to work with GSNW: create a group called NTGATEWAY, and assign it rights to the resources to be passed through the gateway. Create a user as a member of that group, and remember its name and password.

Once GSNW is installed, it can be configured using the GSNW applet within the Control Panel. The initial dialog includes the same client settings as the CSNW control panel. Press the Gateway button to set the following options:

Enable Gateway

Select this option to activate the gateway. If this option is not selected, GSNW acts as a NetWare client only.

Gateway Account

Enter the NetWare username that you assigned to the NTGATEWAY group here.

Password

Specify the password for the NetWare user account.

Share List

By default, no NetWare resources are shared. Use the Add button to browse the NetWare server's resources and add selected items to the list. These items will appear to Windows clients as NT shares with the same names.

On the Exam

You may not have access to a NetWare server to experiment with GSNW. In general, the MCSE exam does not go into the specifics of setting up the Net-Ware server to work with GSNW; however, you should know the basic steps described above (create the NTGATEWAY group, create a user, and assign the appropriate rights to the group).

Migration Tool for NetWare

The installation of GSNW includes a utility called Migration Tool for NetWare, available in the Administrative Tools menu. This tool copies users, groups, and files from one or more NetWare servers to one or more Windows NT servers.

This utility does not migrate NetWare passwords to Windows NT. In addition, ownership and rights settings for files and directories may not be entirely migrated.

When you run this utility, it prompts for a NetWare server name and a Windows NT server name. Both must be currently accessible over the network. You can add additional servers to migrate using the Add button. Before starting the migration, you should set two categories of options:

- *File Options* allows you to specify the files to be migrated and their destination path.

- *User Options* allows you to specify the method in which user and group names and default security settings (account policy) are migrated. This dialog includes the following options:

  Transfer Users and Groups
  > If selected, the users and groups from the NetWare server will be migrated to the NT server.

  Use Mappings in File
  > This allows you to specify a mapping file, which indicates how NetWare usernames are to be converted to Windows NT usernames.

  Passwords
  > The options in this tab relate to NetWare passwords. Since NetWare passwords are not migrated, you must specify a default password here: either no password, the username, or a specific password. You can also select the *User Must Change Password* option to require a password change at logon.

  Usernames
  > The options in this tab allow you to specify the action in the event of a conflict between NetWare usernames and existing usernames. You can choose to log the error, ignore the conflict, overwrite the existing user, or add a specified prefix to the name.

  Group Names
  > This is similar to the *Usernames* option, but applies to group names. Choose to log errors, ignore conflicts, or add a specified prefix.

  Defaults
  > This tab includes three options: *Use Supervisor Defaults* specifies that the NetWare server's default settings are copied to Windows NT's account policies. *Add Supervisors to the Administrators Group* specifies that all supervisor-equivalent NetWare users are added to the NT Administrators group. Finally, the *Migrate NetWare Specific Account Information* option specifies that certain NetWare user properties will be migrated to their NT equivalents.

After setting the options, use the Start Migration button in the main dialog to begin the migration. You can also use the Trial Migration button to perform a simulated migration (no changes are made to the NT Server computer). This is useful to eliminate any potential errors before the actual migration.

File and Print Services for NetWare

A final NetWare-related service is File and Print Services for NetWare (FPNW). This software performs the reverse function of GSNW: it runs on a Windows NT server, and allows NetWare clients to access Windows NT shares and printers.

Using this service, NetWare clients can access the NT server as if it were a NetWare server, with no additional client software. Services for NetWare is available at extra charge from Microsoft.

Remote Access Server

RAS, or Remote Access Server, allows computers to connect to the Windows NT
network over a modem. This service was introduced in Part 2. While the version
included with NT Workstation supports only one incoming connection, the NT
Server version supports up to 256 connections.

Server Configuration

To configure the RAS server, install the RAS service as described in Part 2. When
configuring the modem, choose the *Receive calls only* or *Dial out and receive calls*
option. After installation, you can configure the RAS server by choosing *Properties*
from the Network control panel. The options available depend on the protocols in
use, and are described below.

TCP/IP

RAS supports TCP/IP through the PPP (point-to-point protocol) dial-up protocol.
The SLIP protocol is not supported by the RAS server, although it is supported by
the RAS client for dialing into non-NT servers. The RAS TCP/IP options include the
following:

Allow remote TCP/IP clients to access
Specify whether TCP/IP clients can access network resources beyond the RAS
server, or strictly resources on the RAS server.

Use DHCP to assign remote TCP/IP client addresses
If selected, RAS clients are assigned IP addresses via DHCP, using the DHCP
server defined in the RAS server computer's TCP/IP properties.

Use static address pool
As an alternative to DHCP, you can select this option and specify a range of
IP addresses to be made available to RAS clients.

Allow clients to request a predetermined IP address
If selected, RAS clients can use a consistent IP address. This may be required
for certain network applications to work on the RAS client.

IPX

IPX, or NWLink, is also supported by the RAS server. The following options are available:

Allow remote IPX clients to access
Specify whether IPX clients can access network resources beyond the RAS server, or strictly resources on the RAS server.

Allocate network numbers automatically
If selected, IPX internal network numbers are assigned randomly to incoming RAS clients.

Allocate network numbers from
Alternatively, select this option and specify a range of IPX internal network numbers to be used for RAS clients.

Assign same network number to all IPX clients
If selected, a single IPX network number (defined in the From field above) is assigned to all incoming IPX clients.

Allow remote clients to request IPX node number
If selected, RAS clients can use a predetermined IPX network number rather than being assigned one.

NetBEUI

NetBEUI is a simple protocol, and its RAS configuration is simple. A single option is available: *Allow remote NetBEUI clients to access.* Select whether clients running NetBEUI as their sole protocol have access to resources beyond the RAS server, or only the resources on the server.

Remote Access Admin

When the RAS server is configured, the Remote Access Admin utility becomes available from the Administrative Tools menu under the Start menu. This utility allows you to manage the RAS services on the current server, or on another server.

This utility displays a list of servers on the network running the RAS service, whether the service is currently running, and the number of ports in use. The following menu options are available to manage the servers:

Server
The *Communication Ports* option allows you to define the serial ports (or internal modems) used for the RAS service. This menu also includes options to start, stop, or pause the RAS service, and to manage a different domain or server.

Users
The *Permissions* option displays a list of users of the server or domain. Select the *Grant dialin permission to user* option to enable RAS access for that user; all users are disabled by default. The *Active Users* option from the Users menu displays a list of currently connected users.

View

The *Refresh* option redisplays the list of servers and connections with the latest information.

Options

The *Low Speed Connection* option, available in this and other server utilities, sets the utility to update the display only when you use the *Refresh* option. This simplifies access over a slow connection (such as a RAS connection).

Network Browsing

A key feature of windows networks is the ability to browse lists of resources available on computers across the network. The lists are broadcast by individual computers with shared resources, and are maintained by a variety of machines that act as *browsers*. Windows NT, Windows 95, and Windows for Workgroups systems can act as browsers.

On the Exam

While browsing is managed automatically by Windows NT and other systems, and should only require intervention for larger networks, an understanding of how browsing works is essential for the NT Server exam.

Browser Types

There are five basic browser types in a Windows network:

Master browser

This computer receives broadcasts from sharing computers and compiles them into a browse list. This list is then distributed to backup browsers.

Domain master browser

In a domain with multiple subnets, a master browser is used in each subnet. The domain master browser collects information from each master browser and distributes it to the other master browsers. This machine is usually the PDC. In a single-subnet network, the PDC is both master browser and domain master browser.

Backup browsers

These machines keep a backup copy of the browse list. When a client browses the network, a backup browser is contacted to provide the list of resources.

Potential browsers

These are machines that can act as browsers, but are not currently participating in the browse process. All Windows NT, Windows 95, and Windows for Workgroups machines can be potential browsers.

Non-browsers

These are machines that cannot act as browsers, but can make shares available and broadcast their lists to the master browser.

Browser Elections

If the master browser is down, the first machine that fails to contact the master browser broadcasts a packet indicating that a browser election should occur. This causes all potential browsers to broadcast their status.

A new master browser is chosen based on browser role and OS version: backup browsers are most likely to be considered, followed by potential browsers. Windows NT Server machines are given the most consideration, followed by NT Workstation, Windows 95, and Windows for Workgroups.

If the domain master browser goes down or reboots, a similar election is held between the master browsers.

Changing Browser Types

You can modify the registry of a Windows NT computer to change its browser type. This may be useful to assign a specific master browser, or to prevent a busy application server from participating in browsing. Two registry keys must be modified to change browser status. These are both under the HKEY_LOCAL_MACHINE\SYSTEM\CurrentControlSet\Services\Browser\Parameters registry key.

MaintainServerList
> Set this value to *Yes* for a backup browser, which may be elected as master browser. Set the value to *Auto* for a potential browser, or *No* for a non-browser.

IsDomainMaster
> If this binary value is set to *True*, the computer will start an election when it boots, and will usually be assigned as the domain master browser. *False* is the default setting.

In the Real World

Windows NT maintains browser types automatically, and in theory the above values should rarely need to be changed. In practice, they often need to be modified to allow efficient and reliable browsing in complex networks.

The Browser Service

In Windows NT Workstation and Server, the Computer Browser service performs browsing-related functions. This service is installed and running by default. You can control this service using the Services control panel.

Configuring Disks

Windows NT Server's configuration is similar to that of Windows NT Workstation. Part 2 discusses using the Control Panel and configuring hardware devices and printing. The sections below discuss the disk management and backup functions you'll need to understand for the NT Server exam.

Managing Disk Storage

Windows NT supports a variety of disk volume types. Some of these, included only in NT Server, provide fault tolerance. The Disk Administrator utility in the Administrative Tools menu, described in Part 2, allows you to configure disks. The various capabilities of this utility for NT Server are described in the sections below.

Creating and Formatting Partitions

Disk Administrator displays a graphical list of available drives and partitions. Areas of free space are shown with a shaded box. You can create a new partition in any of these areas by highlighting it and selecting *Create* from the Partition menu.

After creating a partition, it can be formatted with either the FAT or NTFS file system. Use the *Format* option in the Tools menu to format the partition and create a simple volume.

Volume Sets

Volume sets, introduced in Part 2, combine two or more partitions on separate drives into a single volume. To create a volume set, select two or more empty partitions (hold down CTRL to select the second) and select *Create Volume Set* from the Partition menu.

You can also extend an existing volume set. Select the existing portions of the volume and an area of free space, and choose *Extend Volume Set* from the Partition menu.

Stripe Sets

Stripe sets, introduced in Part 2, combine partitions into a volume using an interleaved writing method, allowing for faster performance. To create a stripe set, select two or more partitions on separate drives. The partitions must be the same size. Choose *Create Stripe Set* from the Partition menu.

Mirror Sets

Mirror sets provide fault tolerance by storing two copies of data. To create a mirror set, select an existing volume and an area of free space at least as large as the existing volume. Choose *Establish Mirror* from the Fault Tolerance menu. The mirroring of data begins when you establish the mirror, and continues in the background.

To repair a mirror set after the second drive has been repaired or replaced, use the *Break Mirror* option from the Fault Tolerance menu. Delete the partitions on the repaired drive. Next, select the undamaged partition and the free space on the repaired drive, and select *Establish Mirror* from the Fault Tolerance menu.

Stripe Sets with Parity

Stripe sets with parity add fault tolerance to stripe sets by using an area of each disk to store parity information. To create a stripe set with parity, select at least three partitions of equal size on separate drives, and choose *Create Stripe Set with Parity* from the Fault Tolerance menu.

A stripe set with parity can be repaired if only one drive has failed. Windows NT will automatically remove the failed drive from the set. After replacing the drive, select the stripe set and the free space on the new drive, and choose *Regenerate* from the Fault Tolerance menu.

Configuring System Backups

Windows NT includes a basic backup utility called Backup (NTBACKUP.EXE), shown in Figure 3-4, which can copy files from one or more drives to a tape device. The following sections provide an overview of this program.

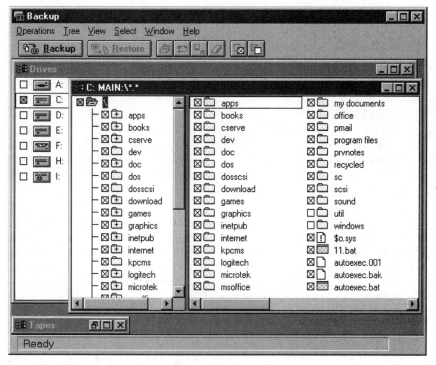

Figure 3-4: The Windows NT Backup utility

On the Exam

When the MCSE exam asks which type of fault tolerance is appropriate for a situation, backups may be one of the options. The chief advantage of backups is that, if well-configured, they can recover all files; their main disadvantage is that they must be explicitly restored by an administrator, often requiring network downtime.

Backup Devices

Before using Backup, you need to have at least one backup device (a tape drive, usually) installed. The drivers for tape drives are installed from the Tape Devices applet in the Control Panel. Backup should detect all properly configured devices when it first runs.

On the Exam

Backup only supports devices configured through the Tape Devices control panel. It does not support backup to hard disks, removable disks, or other media.

Backup Methods

The Backup utility supports a variety of backup methods. Depending on the size of your network and your needs, one or more of these strategies may be appropriate.

Normal (full backup)
> This method backs up all of the files on the volume (or the selected files), regardless of when files were modified. A file attribute called the archive bit is cleared for each backed up file; this can be used with other backup methods to back up changed files. If you have time and tape capacity to back up all files, this is the most reliable method.

Incremental backup
> This method backs up all of the files that have been modified since the last backup. This is done by reading the archive bits. These bits are cleared after backing up the files. This method is typically used with a weekly full backup and daily incremental backups. This allows for fast backups, but restoring data may require several tapes (one full backup and several incremental backups).

Differential backup
> This method backs up all of the files changed since the last full backup. It does not clear the archive bits, so each differential backup includes the same files as a previous one. This slows down backups, but allows any set of files to be restored with two tapes (the last full backup and the last differential backup).

Copy
> This method is similar to a full backup, but does not clear the archive bits. This allows extra backups to be made without affecting the status of regular backups.

Daily copy
> This method backs up all files modified on the current date. The files are found using the modification date attribute rather than the archive bit, and archive bits are not cleared.

Backing Up and Restoring Data

When you run Backup, it displays a list of volumes on the current computer. You can back up files on remote servers by mapping a drive to them. Check the box to the left of a volume to back up all files on the volume, or double-click a volume to select specific files.

In most networks, backing up specific files allows for adequate fault tolerance while using less tape storage. Files you may wish to exclude from the backup are temporary files, application files (these can be reinstalled from their original media), and the files in the WINNT directory and subdirectories (these can be restored using an emergency repair disk or upgrade installation).

Once files are selected, choose the *Backup* option. You are prompted for several options, including the backup method and the location of a log file. Use the *Backup Local Registry* option to back up the registry. The backup process begins immediately.

The Restore button allows you to restore files from an existing backup tape. Specify the path to store the restored files. The *Restore Local Registry* option allows the registry to be restored. The *Restore File Permissions* option copies the original file permissions from the tape rather than using the default permissions of the restored path.

Automating Backups

Backup does not support scheduled backups, but you can use a batch file to start a backup with command-line options. This can be used with a scheduling utility, such as the AT command built into Windows NT, for automated backups. For example, this command schedules a full backup for 12:00 midnight on the current day:

```
AT 12:00 "ntbackup BACKUP C:\ /t:normal"
```

The command-line options for NTBACKUP.EXE are listed below.

---

ntbackup ⠀⠀⠀⠀⠀⠀⠀⠀⠀⠀⠀⠀⠀⠀⠀⠀⠀⠀ ntbackup *operation* [*options*]

Starts an automated backup. *operation* should be BACKUP to perform a backup, or EJECT to manually eject a tape.

Options

/a

⠀⠀⠀⠀Appends data to the tape after the last existing backup set.

/b

⠀⠀⠀⠀Similar to the *Backup Local Registry* option in the graphical version of Backup, specifies that the registry will be included in the backup.

/d description

⠀⠀⠀⠀Provides an optional description for the current backup set.

/e

⠀⠀⠀⠀Restricts the backup log (described below) to exceptions only.

/hc:value

⠀⠀⠀⠀Turns hardware compression on or off. *value* should be "on" or "off."

/l filename

⠀⠀⠀⠀Specifies that a log of the backup process will be written to the specified filename. If the /e option is specified, this log includes errors only.

/r

⠀⠀⠀⠀Restricts access to the backup set. Restricted backups can be accessed only by the Administrators or Backup Operators groups.

/t:type

⠀⠀⠀⠀Specifies the backup type, as described above. *type* can be normal, incremental, differential, copy, or daily.

/tape:value

⠀⠀⠀⠀Specifies the tape device (numbered starting with 0) for the backup.

/v

⠀⠀⠀⠀Turns on write verify for the backup; the backup set will be read from tape and tested after the backup is complete.

> ### On the Exam
>
> You will not need to know all of these options for the NT Server exam, but you should know that NTBACKUP can be used on the command line in this fashion. Restoring from the command line is not supported.

Security and Administration

Windows NT Server is typically used in larger networks than NT Workstation, and requires greater attention to security. This section examines the domain model and the issues involved in securing users and groups within domains. We will also examine two tools for further securing systems, user profiles and system policies, and techniques for managing NT Server computers remotely from clients.

Domains and Security

Domains, introduced earlier in this chapter, are groups of computers that use a central security database for authentication. This database is stored on the primary domain controller (PDC), and replicated on one or more backup domain controllers (BDCs).

Domain Controllers

The domain requires one PDC, and Microsoft recommends that at least one BDC be used. Additional BDCs provide redundancy for the security database, and also allow a greater number of clients to use the network without slowing.

In the event of a PDC failure, the BDCs will still be available for authentication. However, changes cannot be made to the security database on the BDC. Before making changes to the database, you must either return the PDC to operation or promote a BDC.

If you are taking down the PDC permanently or if it will be down for some time, you should promote a BDC to act as PDC. Use the Server Manager utility in the Administrative Tools menu for this purpose. Highlight the BDC and select Promote to Primary Domain Controller from the Computer menu.

When you promote a BDC, the existing PDC is automatically demoted to a BDC. It can then be removed from the network without creating problems (provided the shared files and applications on this server have also been relocated).

Adding Computers to the Domain

When you install a BDC, you must specify the domain it will join. This process requires the administrator password for the PDC. For member servers, you can specify a domain at installation, but can also join the domain after installation, or change the domain the computer belongs to.

This information is stored in the Identification tab of the Network control panel. Select the *Change* option to modify this information. Select *Domain* to connect to a domain, and specify the domain's name. (The PDC must be available over the network when you do this.)

For a member server to access a domain, there must be a computer account on the PDC with the same name as the server. You can optionally create this account from the Change dialog by checking the *Create a Computer Account* in the *Domain* option. This requires the PDC's administrator account name and password, or another account with the appropriate rights (specifically, the Add Workstations to Domain user right).

On the Exam

For the exam, remember that one of the security advantages of the domain model over the workgroup model is that workstations cannot be added to the domain without a domain administrator account.

The Authentication Process

When a user logs on to the domain, the PDC (or BDC) authenticates the username and password. The password is encrypted before being sent over the network. If the name and password are valid, the user's workstation is returned an access token, which includes a security identifier for the username and for any group memberships.

This access token is sent back to the domain controller each time the user requests a resource, and used to determine whether the user is to be granted access.

The Windows NT service that manages security is called the security accounts manager, or SAM. The SAM keeps a database of user names, encrypted passwords, and security identifiers in the \WINNT\SYSTEM directory.

Security identifiers (SIDs) are numbers assigned to each user or group name for security purposes. They do not depend on the name of the object. For example, if a user is renamed, the security identifier remains the same. If a user is deleted and a new user is created with the same name, the new user has a new identifier and is not considered the same user for permissions and file ownership.

Users and Groups

Windows NT Server's system of users and groups is very similar to that of NT Workstation. The difference is that users and groups can be created on the PDC for access to the entire network. This is the principal advantage of the domain model, as it improves security and simplifies administration.

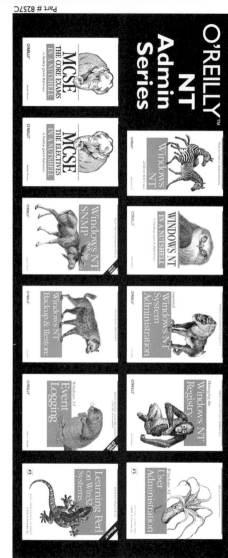

Creating and Managing Users

Part 2 introduced the User Manager utility, which is used to create users and groups. NT Server includes User Manager for Domains, a similar utility with access to domain-related groups and features. User Manager for Domains is automatically installed on PDCs or BDCs.

User Manager for Domains supports global user accounts, used for normal users of the domain, and local user accounts, used to provide access for a user from a remote, non-trusted domain. All users are global by default.

On the Exam

A version of User Manager domains is also available for Windows NT Workstation and Windows 95 to allow for remote administration. This is explained later in this chapter.

In addition to the user properties described in Part 2, User Manager for Domains supports the following additional dialogs, available by clicking their corresponding buttons in the User Properties dialog:

Hours
Allows you to specify the hours and days the user is allowed to log on. By default, users can log on at any time.

Logon To
Allows you to list the workstations the user is allowed to connect to the domain from. The names here are NetBIOS computer names.

Account
Allows you to specify an expiration date for the account. In addition, specify whether the account is global (default) or local.

Local and Global Groups

Windows NT Server supports two types of groups: local groups and global groups. In general, local groups are usually used to assign rights to a resource, while global groups are used to group similar categories of users. Here is a detailed description of these types of groups:

- Local groups on non-domain controllers are specific to one computer, and can be granted rights for that computer only. Local groups on the PDC or BDC exist on all domain controllers in the domain, and can be granted rights for any resource in the domain. This is the only type of group available in a workgroup network, and in Windows NT Workstation. Local groups can include users and global groups as members.

- Global groups exist only in a domain model, and are visible throughout the domain. Global groups are also visible to trusted domains (discussed in Part 4). Global groups can include only domain users as members.

Global groups can be given permissions for a resource directly. However, Microsoft recommends using local groups to control resource access, and using global groups to group users with similar functions. The global groups can be made members of one or more local groups to grant privileges to their members.

As an example, you might have a local group called Accounts Receivable with access to the AR directory, and one called Accounts Payable with access to the AP directory. The Accounting global group could be made a member of both local groups, giving its members rights for both directories. The advantage of this approach is that groups with less permissions can be created: for example, the Purchasing global group might need access to the AP files but not the AR files.

Windows NT Server includes the same local groups as NT Workstation: Account Operators, Administrators, Backup Operators, Guests, Power Users, Replicators, and Users. NT Server also includes a Server Operators group. If the server is a domain controller, these groups have the corresponding rights and permissions for all of the domain controllers rather than a single machine.

In addition to these, the following built-in global groups are available:

Domain Admins
> This global group is a member of the Administrators local group, thus having administrative privileges for all domain controllers. The Administrator account is a member of this group.

Domain Guests
> This group is a member of the domain's Guests local group. This group has no rights by default. The Guest user is a member of this group.

Domain Users
> All users of the domain are members of this group. By default, this includes the Administrator account. Any users created in the domain are made members of this group. This group is a member of the Users local group.

Permissions and User Rights

Domain users can be given permissions to files, directories, and other resources, and assigned rights through the User Rights Policy function in User Manager. These permissions and rights work as described in Part 2, but can be used throughout the domain controllers rather than at a single machine.

In addition, users receive rights and permissions given to any local or global groups they belong to. If the user and one or more groups both have rights to the same resource, the least restrictive right takes precedence. The only exception is the No Access right; if this is granted to the user or to any group containing the user, the user has no access.

User Profiles

Windows NT uses *user profiles* to store preferences and settings for the OS and for certain applications. This feature allows users to have the system colors, fonts, and other options they prefer each time they log into the system.

There are three types of profiles: *local profiles*, which only work at a particular workstation; *roaming profiles*, which work at any Windows NT computer in the domain; and *mandatory profiles*, which are roaming profiles that cannot be modified by the user.

On the Exam

User profiles are supported by NT Server and NT Workstation, but the Workstation exam focuses on local profiles. The Server and Enterprise exams both include objectives covering roaming and mandatory profiles.

Profiles are stored in a path set in the Profiles dialog from the User Properties dialog in User Manager. This dialog also allows you to configure user home directories and logon scripts. These features are explained in the sections below.

Local Profiles

Local user profiles are stored in the \WINNT\PROFILES directory on the local computer, in separate subdirectories for each user. Local profiles are used by default.

Roaming Profiles

Roaming profiles can be stored in a shared directory, typically the \WINNT\PROFILES directory on a domain controller. To configure a user to use a roaming profile, specify the path to the shared directory in the *User Profile Path* option in the User Environment Profile dialog.

You can set profiles to automatically use the user's name as a subdirectory by specifying \WINNT\PROFILES\%USERNAME% as the path. This is useful if you create users by copying an existing account.

Mandatory Profiles

After a roaming user profile has been created, you can convert it to a mandatory profile. This prevents the user from making further changes to settings. To do this, rename the file NTUSER.DAT in the profile directory to NTUSER.MAN. The configuration in the User Environment Profile dialog box is the same as for a roaming profile.

Windows 95 also supports roaming profiles, but they are not compatible with Windows NT profiles: a user will not receive settings from a NT user profile when logging on to a Windows 95 workstation, but a separate Windows 95 profile can be created. Part 5 explains Windows 95 profiles in detail.

Logon Scripts

Logon scripts are another method of providing specific settings each time the user logs on, although they have been replaced by user profiles in many networks. A logon script is a DOS batch file or Windows NT executable.

To use a logon script, specify the path to the script in the Logon Script Name field of the User Environment Profile dialog. Logon scripts can be stored on the local computer or in a shared directory.

Home Directories

The final setting in the User Environment Profile dialog box allows you to specify a home directory for the user. This directory is used as the default directory in some applications. In addition, the user is automatically given full rights to the specified directory.

You can either specify a local path for the directory, or a network share path. If a network share is used, a drive must be mapped to the path. Specify a drive letter and UNC path.

System Policies

Windows NT *system policies* affect many of the same settings as user profiles, but are strictly controlled by the administrator. Using system policies you can prevent users from changing settings, remove certain capabilities, and restrict some applications. System policy settings override user profile settings.

There are two basic types of system policy:

- *User policies* affect the user's environment. This policy includes keys found in the HKEY_LOCAL_USER registry subtree (described in Part 2). This section of the registry is replaced with the contents of the user policy at logon. Policies can be specified for specific users or users in specific groups; a default user policy is used if the user has no user or group policy.

- *Computer policies* affect a particular computer. These settings are found in the HKEY_LOCAL_COMPUTER registry subtree, and this section of the registry is replaced with the policy's settings at boot time. Policies can be created for specific computers on the network; a default computer policy is used for computers with no explicit policy.

No system policies exist by default. You can create policies using the System Policy Editor, available from the Administrative Tools menu. This utility is shown in Figure 3-5. System policies are available in both NT Workstation and NT Server.

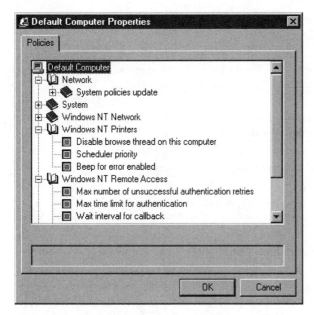

Figure 3-5: The System Policy Editor utility

To use System Policy editor, create a new policy file by choosing *New Policy* from the File menu. The policy includes a default user and default computer. Use the add user, add group, and add computer buttons to add specific entries. You can also open the current registry with the *Open Registry* command from the File menu.

To use a system policy, use the Save option in the File menu to save the policy in the NETLOGON share of the PDC or BDC.

When you select a user or computer policy entry, a hierarchical list of available settings and restrictions is displayed. The sections below describe the categories of settings available for users and computers.

On the Exam

You don't need to know exact policy settings for the NT Server exam, but you should know the difference between user and computer policies, and have an idea of what you can and cannot do with a system policy.

Computer Policy Options

Computer policies can include the following categories of settings:

Network
> Allows you to specify a network system policy file that the local policy file will be automatically updated from at each logon.

System
> Includes settings for SNMP (Simple Network Management Protocol, described in Part 4) and an option to run a list of programs at startup.

Windows NT Network
> Includes options to control whether hidden shares (such as ADMIN$ or C$) are created. These shares are described in Part 2.

Windows NT Printers
> Includes options for print spooling and scheduling.

Windows NT Remote Access
> Includes security settings for RAS, described earlier in this chapter.

Windows NT Shell
> Allows you to specify shared directories for the Programs folder, desktop icons, the Start menu, and the Startup folder.

Windows NT System
> Includes settings for logons and file system access. For example, you can disable the "Press CTRL+Alt+Del to logon" banner at startup and the display of the previously used username.

Windows NT User Profiles
> Includes settings relating to user profiles. You can specify settings to work with slow network connections, and force cached user profiles to be deleted at logout (if these are deleted, a mandatory profile will not be used unless the PDC is reachable).

User Policy Options

The following options are available in user policies:

Control Panel
> Allows you to restrict the user's use of the Display control panel. You can disable the Display icon completely or hide specific tabs within the Display Properties dialog.

Desktop
> Allows you to specify mandatory wallpaper and color scheme settings.

Shell
> Includes restrictions relating to the Start menu and Explorer. You can disable the *Run* and *Find* commands, hide drive letters in the My Computer window, restrict the available items in the Network Neighborhood window, disable the *Shutdown* command, and prevent the user's shell settings from being saved.

System
> Includes an option to disable access to registry editors (REGEDIT and REGEDT32). You can also specify a list of allowed Windows applications, preventing all other applications from being executed.

Windows NT Shell
> Allows you to enforce locations for the Start menu contents, Programs folder, Network Neighborhood, and other system folders.

Windows NT System
> Includes an option to include environment variables defined in a DOS AUTOEXEC.BAT file in the environment, and options relating to logon scripts.

On the Exam

It's easy to confuse user policies with user profiles, described earlier in this chapter. Although both can be used to enforce particular settings, policies are most often used to restrict a user's access to particular portions of the Windows NT shell.

Remote Administration

Windows NT Server includes a set of server tools. These are versions of server management utilities that can run from client operating systems. This allows you to perform many aspects of server administration from a client.

Separate server tools packages are available for NT Workstation and Windows 95. These are described in the sections below.

Windows NT Workstation

To install server tools for NT Workstation, you will need the NT Server CD-ROM or access to a shared copy. Run the SETUP.BAT file in the \Clients\Srvtools directory to install the server tools. The following tools are included:

User Manager for Domains
> Allows you to create and manage domain users and local and global groups (described earlier in this chapter).

Server Manager
> Allows you to manage server shares and services, and add or remove workstations from the domain (described in Part 2).

System Policy Editor
> Allows you to modify mandatory system policies (described earlier in this chapter).

Remote Access Admin
> Allows you to manage current incoming RAS settings and connections (described earlier in this chapter).

DHCP Manager
> Allows you to configure IP addresses for a DHCP server (described in Part 4).

WINS Manager
> Allows you to configure a WINS server (described in Part 4).

Remoteboot Manager
> Provides options for managing remote boot (diskless) computers.

On the Exam

Most of these utilities are the same ones installed during the Windows NT Server installation, but they are not available on NT Workstation computers without installing this version. Some NT Workstation tools (such as Event Viewer and Task Manager) will work equally well with a remote NT Server machine.

Windows 95

A more limited set of server tools is available for Windows 95. To install them, select Add/Remove Programs from the Control Panel. Select the Windows Setup tab and select the *Have Disk* option. Specify the \Clients\Srvtools\Win95\ Srvtools.inf installation file.

The tools available for Windows 95 include User Manager for Domains and Server Manager, described above. In addition, a version of Event viewer is included (NT Workstation already includes this utility). The installation program also adds an extension to the Windows 95 Explorer to display and modify security information for drives, folders, files, and printers.

Optimization and Troubleshooting

The sections below discuss optimizing and troubleshooting techniques specific to Windows NT Server and server-based networks. Basic Windows NT trouble-shooting techniques are introduced in Part 2.

Monitoring Performance

Part 2 introduced the Performance Monitor utility, which allows you to monitor various counters that indicate the performance of Windows NT and the network. NT Server includes the same version of this utility.

Since the performance of a server is more critical than that of a workstation, you should regularly use this utility to check performance. Some of the counters that are useful in identifying server bottlenecks are described below.

Processor
> The %Processor Time counter in the Processor category provides a basic measure of processor use. If this counter is over 80%, an upgraded processor (or additional processor) may improve performance.

Memory

In the Memory category, the Available Bytes counter tracks the amount of memory (physical and virtual) available. The Pages/Second counter tracks the amount of virtual memory paging. A value of one or more pages per second indicates that more memory would improve performance. The %Usage counter in the Paging File category tracks usage of the virtual memory file.

Disk

In the PhysicalDisk category, the %Disk Time counter tracks the percentage of time the disk drive is in use. The %Disk Read Time and %Disk Write Time counters divide disk use into reads and writes. If the drive is in use constantly, a faster drive or disk striping may improve performance.

Network

The Bytes Total/Sec counter in the Server category indicates the amount of network traffic the server is using. The Server Sessions counter measures the current activity of the server. Depending on the protocols in use, additional categories of counters are available: NWLink (IPX), NetBEUI, and NBT (TCP/IP).

On the Exam

The Windows NT Server exam may refer to specific counters other than the common ones listed here. It's best to run Performance Monitor and experiment with it, becoming familiar with the available counters. However, you should not need to memorize the list of available counters.

Network Troubleshooting

Inaccessible network resources are the most common problems encountered by users of a network. These problems can be caused by network card malfunctions, cable problems, or misconfigurations. Some of the most common problems are described below.

Network Adapter Problems

If a network adapter is newly installed and does not work, its configuration is most likely the problem. Check the following items:

- Interrupt (IRQ) settings

- I/O address settings

- Transceiver settings

- Frame types (these must match if you are using NWLink for NetWare connectivity; automatic detection does not always work)

Connectivity Problems

If a user whose network card was configured correctly loses the connection to the network, a cable problem should be suspected. While broken cables and loose connectors are often the cause of such problems, subtle problems are possible, and a wide variety of troubleshooting tools are available. See Part 1 for further information.

Configuration Problems

Resource access problems can also be caused by incorrect configuration at the workstation or server. Check the following items:

- The workstation and server should have the same protocols defined, or at least one common protocol.

- The binding order for protocols should be the same between workstation and server for maximum performance. The most heavily used protocol should be moved to the top of the list.

- Protocol-dependent settings, such as IP and IPX addresses, should be checked carefully.

- Be sure a router or other device is not preventing network communication (for example, NetBEUI is not routable).

Suggested Exercises

For the Windows NT Server exam you should have as much experience as possible with the features unique to Windows NT Server, most notably domains and domain controllers, incoming RAS, and fault tolerant disk configurations.

Beginning with this exam, it becomes vital to have at least two computers on a network available for practice. If you are setting up an in-home network on a low budget, it may be helpful to know that Windows NT will run comfortably on a relatively inexpensive computer. I recommend at least a low-end Pentium with 1 GB of disk storage and 32 MB of RAM.

You'll also need to be able to experiment with disk fault tolerance, which will require at least three drives. At this writing, 1-GB drives are very inexpensive; three of these would make an excellent practice setup. Be sure your controller can support the drives (SCSI controllers generally support 7 devices; most IDE controllers are limited to two drives, but multiple controllers can be used).

Performing the following exercises will help you prepare for. the exam. In addition, since many of the basic Windows NT topics covered in Part 2 are also objectives for the NT Server exam, you may wish to review the *Suggested Exercises* in Part 2. These exercises assume you have two computers already wired in a network.

1. Install Windows NT Server on a computer:

   a. If you have not installed NT Workstation or Server on the computer before, use the HCL, NTHQ, and the hardware requirements listed in the *Study Guide* to determine whether the computer can run Windows NT Server.

   b. Based on the available hardware and its compatibility, determine the appropriate installation method.

c. Perform the Windows NT Server installation. As you proceed through the installation steps, follow along with the list of steps in the *Study Guide*. Use an NTFS partition so that you'll be able to use the security features.

d. During installation, specify that the computer will be the PDC for the domain, and choose a domain name.

2. Install Windows NT Server on the second computer, and make this computer the BDC for the domain you created above. The PDC must be running while you install the BDC.

3. Copy the installation files for Windows NT Workstation or NT Server to the CLIENTS directory as described in the *Study Guide*. Use the Network Client Administrator utility to create a startup disk. Boot the disk and install the OS on a computer. (If you don't have a third computer, use the BDC computer and install into a different directory.)

4. Configure the machines on the network to use various protocols (TCP/IP, NetBEUI, IPX/SPX) and ensure that they communicate correctly.

5. If you have access to a NetWare server, perform these exercises:

   a. Install GSNW on a Windows NT Server computer and test it by attempting to access NetWare resources from another Windows NT computer.

   b. Use the Migration Tool for NetWare to copy users, groups, and files from the NetWare server to a Windows NT Server computer.

6. Install and configure the RAS server to accept incoming connections. If possible, test the server by dialing in from another phone line or another location.

7. If you have three or more disk drives available, create and test the following disk configurations:

   a. Configure the disks as a volume set.

   b. Configure two of the disks as a mirror set.

   c. Configure three or more disks as a stripe set (without parity). Note the available capacity.

   d. Configure the same disks as a stripe set with parity. Note the available capacity.

8. If you have a third computer available, try adding it to the domain as a member server.

9. Create the following user profiles for a user one at a time. Log on as that user and test their behavior.

   a. Local user profile

   b. Roaming user profile

   c. Mandatory user profile

10. Create a default user policy using the system policy editor. Log on and determine whether the policy is being enforced.

Practice Test

Test Questions

1. What is the amount of RAM required to install NT Server?

    a. 16 MB

    b. 32 MB

    c. 12 MB

    d. 44 MB

2. Which of the following disk configurations provides the least amount of fault tolerance?

    a. Disk mirroring

    b. Disk duplexing

    c. Disk striping

    d. Disk striping with parity

3. Your server has three 800-MB disk drives, all currently empty. If you create a stripe set with parity using the full capacity of the drives, what is the total capacity of the stripe set?

    a. 800 MB

    b. 1600 MB

    c. 2000 MB

    d. 2400 MB

4. You are setting up a backup strategy for a network. You will be creating a backup once a day to a tape device.

   Required Result: All files should be backed up.

   Optional Result: A minimum of tapes should be required for a restore.

   Solution: Use a full backup each Monday, and incremental backups on other weekdays.

   a.   The solution meets the required result and the optional result.

   b.   The solution meets the required result only.

   c.   The solution does not meet the required result.

5. Which of the following is not an advantage of the NTFS file system?

   a.   Higher security

   b.   Efficient for small disk capacities

   c.   Fault tolerance

   d.   Better use of large disk capacities

6. Which utility provides information about a computer's compatibility with Windows NT?

   a.   COMPAT

   b.   HAL.EXE

   c.   NTHQ

   d.   WinMSD

7. Which is the correct command to install Windows NT without the use of boot disks from an existing Windows 95 installation?

   a.   WINNT /b

   b.   WINNT32 /b

   c.   WINNT /ox

   d.   WINNT32 /ox

8. You have a UPS attached to serial port number 1 on a Windows NT Server computer. When you attempt to boot Windows NT, the UPS displays an error message or shuts down. What switch can be added to the BOOT.INI file to solve this problem?

   a.   /vgamode

   b.   /com1=0

   c.   /noserialmice

   d.   /UPS=1

9. Which of the following is a non-routable transport protocol developed by Microsoft?

    a.   TCP/IP

    b.   IPX

    c.   NetBEUI

    d.   NetBIOS

10. You are installing Windows NT Server on a new computer. The computer does not have an existing OS. You have checked the components against the HCL, and the computer appears to be compatible. What is the correct procedure for installation?

    a.   Run WINNT32 with the /B option.

    b.   Use WINNT /OX to create disks from another computer, then boot them on the new computer.

    c.   Boot the NTHQ disk to begin the installation.

    d.   Boot a DOS disk, then run WINNT32 from the CD-ROM.

11. You are installing a network with 7 computers. No other computers will be added for at least a year. Users want to manage access to their own files.

Required Result: The network should support 7 computers, and allow users to restrict access to files on their workstations.

Optional Result: The network should allow central administration from a single login.

Optional Result: The network should remain efficient with the addition of 5 more computers in a year.

Solution: Use a workgroup network.

    a.   The solution meets the required result and both of the optional results.

    b.   The solution meets the required result and one of the optional results.

    c.   The solution meets the required result only.

    d.   The solution does not meet the required result.

12. You are installing a BDC on a network. When you specify the domain name for the computer to participate in, the installation program pauses for several minutes and displays an error. Which of the following is a potential cause of this problem?

    a.   Windows NT Workstation is being installed.

    b.   The PDC is down, or not currently available on the network.

    c.   There is not enough disk space on the volume.

    d.   A BDC has already been installed for the domain.

Windows NT Server

13. Your network has one PDC and 3 BDCs. The PDC is down due to a cable failure. A technician is repairing the problem, but the cable will be down for several hours. What should you do to ensure that users can authenticate to the network?

    a.   Demote the PDC; a BDC will be promoted automatically.

    b.   Install a new NT Server computer to act as PDC.

    c.   Promote a BDC to act as PDC.

    d.   No action is necessary; a BDC will be automatically promoted.

14. Which of the following computer types are able to authenticate users for logon? (select all that apply)

    a.   PDC

    b.   BDC

    c.   Member server

    d.   Stand-alone server

15. Which of the following machines must be online in order for the administrator to create new domain accounts? (select all that apply)

    a.   PDC

    b.   BDC

    c.   Member server

    d.   Stand-alone server

16. A network is installed with one PDC and 4 BDCs. Which of the following operations are possible? (select all that apply)

    a.   Promote a BDC to a PDC

    b.   Move a BDC to another domain

    c.   Demote a BDC to a member server

    d.   Promote a member server to a BDC

17. A network has 500 client computers running Windows 95 and 10 servers running Windows NT Server. Most of the client computers are used regularly. Each user needs to use resources on at least 3 servers. Which licensing mode would be the most economical for this network?

    a.   Per Server

    b.   Per Seat

18. Which one of the following files can be used alone for unattended installation of Windows NT?

    a.   Answer file

    b.   UDF file

    c.   BOOT.INI file

    d.   SYSDIFF.TXT file

19. Which utility can be used to create a network installation boot disk for MS-DOS?

    a.   Network Administrator

    b.   MAKEDISK.BAT

    c.   Network Client Administrator

    d.   WINNT32 /OX

20. Which tab of the Network control panel would you use to move TCP/IP to the top of the bindings list for the server?

    a.   Services

    b.   Protocols

    c.   TCP/IP

    d.   Bindings

21. Which utility can be used to display a list of users currently logged onto the server?

    a.   Users control panel

    b.   Server control panel

    c.   User Manager for Domains

    d.   Task Manager

22. Which utility can be used to change the current licensing mode?

    a.   Server control panel

    b.   License Manager

    c.   Licensing control panel

    d.   This cannot be changed without reinstalling Windows NT.

23. You are running GSNW on a Windows NT Server computer attached to a NetWare network. What additional software needs to be installed for Windows 95 clients to access resources on the NetWare server?

    a.   FPNW on the NetWare server

    b.   CSNW on the Windows NT server

    c.   CSNW on the Windows 95 clients

    d.   No client software is needed

24. You are configuring a Windows NT Server computer that needs to access NetWare files, without acting as a gateway. Which of the following NetWare connectivity services should be installed on the server?

    a.   CSNW

    b.   GSNW

    c.   NWLink

    d.   FPNW

25. Which of the following are not migrated when you use Migration Tool for NetWare to migrate to a Windows NT Server computer?

    a.   Users

    b.   Groups

    c.   Passwords

    d.   Data files

26. Which of the following utilities allows NetWare clients to access a Windows NT Server computer's resources without additional client software?

    a.   GSNW

    b.   CSNW

    c.   FPNW

    d.   Migration Tool for NetWare

27. Which of the following protocols is not supported by the Windows NT RAS server?

    a.   TCP/IP

    b.   NetBIOS

    c.   SLIP

    d.   PPP

28. Which service can be used with RAS to assign IP addresses dynamically to dial-up clients?

    a.   DNS

    b.   DHCP

    c.   SLIP

    d.   IPX

29. You have installed the RAS server on a Windows NT Server computer, and configured modems for dial-up connections. You want to authorize several users to access the network via RAS. Which utilities can be used to grant users permission to dial up? (select all that apply)

    a.   User Manager for Domains

    b.   Server control panel

    c.   Remote Access Admin

    d.   Network control panel

30. A single domain network contains one PDC, three BDCs, two member servers, and a variety of clients. If a browser election occurs, which of the following computers is most likely to be chosen as the new master browser?

    a.   PDC running NT Server, configured as a non-browser

    b.   BDC running Windows NT Server, configured as a potential browser

c. Client machine running Windows 95

d. Client machine running Windows 3.1

31. Which of the following browser types causes an election each time it is rebooted?

a. Master browser

b. Backup browser

c. Non-browser

d. Potential browser

32. You need to configure a Windows NT Server computer to be a non-browser. Where is this changed?

a. The registry

b. Browser control panel

c. Services control panel

d. The BROWSER.INI file

33. Which of the following Windows NT utilities is used to change the partitioning of a disk?

a. FDISK.EXE

b. Disk Administrator

c. Disks control panel

d. Disk Properties dialog

34. You have installed four 1-GB disk drives in a Windows NT Server computer. You want to configure them as a single volume.

Required Result: The volume should provide fault tolerance.

Optional Result: The volume should provide an increase in speed.

Optional Result: The volume should allow the full 4 GB capacity of the drives to be used for data storage.

Solution: Create a stripe set with parity using the full capacity of all four disks.

a. The solution meets the required result and both of the optional results.

b. The solution meets the required result and one of the optional results.

c. The solution meets the required result only.

d. The solution does not meet the required result.

35. If you create a volume set using three 300-MB disks, what is the total available capacity?

    a.   300 MB

    b.   600 MB

    c.   750 MB

    d.   900 MB

36. Which of the following disk configurations provides the smallest degree of fault tolerance?

    a.   Mirror set

    b.   Stripe set with parity

    c.   Volume set

37. Which disk configurations can be used with only two drives? (select all that apply)

    a.   Disk mirroring

    b.   Disk striping with parity

    c.   Disk striping without parity

    d.   Disk duplexing

38. If you create a stripe set with parity with four 300-MB disks, what is the total available capacity of the volume?

    a.   300 MB

    b.   600 MB

    c.   900 MB

    d.   1200 MB

39. Which of the following capabilities are provided with the NTBACKUP.EXE utility? (select all that apply)

    a.   Back up local files

    b.   Back up remote files

    c.   Back up the local registry

    d.   Back up remote registries

40. Which of the following backup methods clear the archive bits of backed up files? (select all that apply)

    a.   Full backup

    b.   Incremental backup

    c.   Differential backup

    d.   Daily copy

41. A group of print devices that print from the same print job list is called:

    a.   A print queue

    b.   A print pool

    c.   A printer group

    d.   A printer set

42. What should be done before taking a PDC down permanently?

    a.   Demote it to a BDC

    b.   Change it to a member server

    c.   Promote a BDC to a PDC

    d.   Demote all BDCs to member servers

43. Which of the following statements are true of local and global groups? (select all that apply)

    a.   Local groups can contain global groups.

    b.   Global groups can contain local groups.

    c.   Local groups can contain users.

    d.   Global groups can contain users.

44. Which of the following are global groups created by default on Windows NT Server? (select all that apply)

    a.   Domain users

    b.   Backup operators

    c.   Administrators

    d.   Domain guests

45. John has the Read permission for the APPS directory. He also belongs to the Accounting group, which has the No Access permission for APPS, and the Payroll group, which has Read and Write permissions. What is John's effective access to the APPS directory?

    a.   Read

    b.   Read and write

    c.   Write

    d.   No access

46. Which type of user profile allows users to have the same settings each time they log on to a particular computer, but only affects that computer?

    a.   Local user profile

    b.   Roaming user profile

    c.   Mandatory user profile

47. You wish to assign each user a roaming profile in a subdirectory of the \WINNT\PROFILES directory, using the user name as a directory name. What is the correct value for the user's Profile setting?

    a.   \WINNT\PROFILES

    b.   \WINNT\PROFILES\%USERNAME%

    c.   \WINNT\PROFILES\%1

    d.   %USERNAME%

48. Which of the following allows you to prevent a user from accessing the Run command in the Start menu?

    a.   User profile

    b.   User policy

    c.   Computer policy

    d.   Desktop policy

49. Which software package allows you to use the User Manager for Domains utility to manage a Windows NT server from a Windows 95 workstation?

    a.   User tools for Windows 95

    b.   Server tools for Windows 95

    c.   Users control panel

    d.   No software allows this.

50. You have installed a new network adapter in a Windows NT Server computer. This computer will be used as a general-purpose server and to run GSNW. You have installed the TCP/IP and NWLink protocols and Gateway Service for NetWare. The computer is unable to access either Windows NT or NetWare resources. Another computer works when attached to the same network connection. What is the most likely problem?

    a.   CSNW needs to be installed

    b.   The network adapter is configured incorrectly.

    c.   There is a frame type mismatch.

    d.   The network wiring is faulty.

Answers to Questions

1. A. NT Server requires 16 MB of RAM.

2. C. Disk striping (without parity) provides no fault tolerance.

3. B. Three 800-MB drives allow 2400 MB of total space, but 800 MB of space is used for parity information. This leaves 1600 MB of available capacity.

4. B. The solution meets the required result (back up all files) only. The optional result states that a minimum of tapes should be required for a restore. Since restoring from an incremental backup may require several tapes, this result is not met.

5. B. NTFS is less efficient than FAT for small disk capacities.

6. C. NTHQ (NT Hardware Qualifier) analyzes a computer and determines its compatibility with Windows NT.

7. A. Since the installation will be run from Windows 95, the WINNT utility is used; the /b switch specifies that boot disks will not be used.

8. C. The /noserialmice switch in BOOT.INI prevents the scan of serial ports at boot time, which causes some UPS systems to shut down.

9. C. NetBEUI is a non-routable transport protocol developed by Microsoft. NetBIOS (choice D) is a standard for naming and file sharing. TCP/IP and IPX (choices A and B) are routable protocols.

10. B. Since there is no existing OS, you should create setup boot disks and use them to begin the installation.

11. C. The solution meets the required result only. The network supports 7 computers, and allows users to restrict file access. A workgroup network does not allow central administration, and would not be efficient with 5 more computers (total 12).

12. B. The BDC must authenticate with the PDC during the installation process. If the BDC is not available, installation cannot proceed.

13. C. Promote a BDC to act as PDC. While users can still authenticate using a BDC, no changes to the security database are possible until a BDC is promoted.

14. A, B. PDCs and BDCs provide logon authentication.

15. A. The PDC must be online to allow changes to the security database.

16. A. You can promote a BDC to a PDC. You cannot change the domain served by a BDC (choice B), demote a BDC to a member server (choice C), or promote a member server to a BDC (choice D) without reinstalling Windows NT.

17. B. Since the users need to access resources on multiple servers frequently, the Per Seat licensing mode is more economical.

18. A. The unattended answer file can be used alone for an unattended installation. The UDF file (choice B) can only be used in conjunction with an answer file.

19. C. Network Client Administrator can create a network installation boot disk.

20. D. The Move Up and Down buttons in the Bindings tab are used to reorder the bindings.

21. B. The Server control panel (also available from the Server Manager utility) can display a list of currently logged on users.

22. C. The Licensing control panel can be used to change the current licensing mode.

23. D. No additional client software is needed. The Windows 95 clients use Client for Microsoft Networks to access NetWare files through the GSNW server.

24. B. Although GSNW includes additional functionality, it is also the NetWare client software for use with NT Server. CSNW (choice A) provides the same function, but is included only with NT Workstation.

25. C.Passwords are not migrated from NetWare to Windows NT. You can specify that they are left blank or assigned a preset value.

26. C. FPNW (File and Print Services for NetWare) allows clients running NetWare client software to access the NT Server's resources.

27. C. SLIP is supported by the Windows NT RAS client, but not by the RAS server.

28. B. DHCP (Dynamic Host Control Protocol) can be used to assign IP addresses dynamically.

29. A, C. Dial-up permissions can be set in the User Manager for Domains or Remote Access Admin utilities.

30. B. Since the PDC is configured as a non-browser, the BDC would win the election.

31. A. The master browser causes an election each time it is rebooted.

32. A. Browser status changes are made in the registry.

33. B. The Disk Administrator utility can be used to change disk partitioning.

34. B. The solution meets the required result (provide fault tolerance) and one of the optional results (provide an increase in speed). Since a stripe set with parity would use 1 GB for parity information, the second optional result (allow 4-GB capacity to be used for data storage) is not met.

35. D. A volume set simply combines the capacities of the drives, for a total of 900 MB.

36. C. A volume set does not provide fault tolerance.

37. A, C, D. Disk mirroring, disk striping without parity, and disk duplexing can use two drives. Disk striping with parity (choice B) requires a minimum of three drives.

38. C. Since 300 MB is used for parity information, 900 MB remains as available capacity.

39. A, B, C. NTBACKUP can back up local or remote files and the local registry, but cannot back up remote registries (choice D).

40. A, B. Full and Incremental backups clear the archive bits. Differential backup (choice C) and daily copy (choice D) do not clear archive bits.

41. B. A group of print devices that print from the same print job list is called a print pool.

42. C. Before taking a PDC down permanently, promote a BDC to act as the new PDC.

43. A, C, D. Local groups can contain global groups or users; global groups can contain users. Global groups cannot contain local groups.

44. A, D. The Domain Users and Domain Guests global groups are created by default on Windows NT Server. The Backup Operators and Administrators groups (choices B and C) are created by default, but are local groups.

45. D. The No Access permission for the Accounting group overrides the permissions assigned to John and the other groups he belongs to.

46. A. A local user profile provides the same settings each time a user logs in to a particular computer.

47. B. The %USERNAME% value expands to the username.

48. B. A user policy can prevent a user from accessing the Run command in the Start menu.

49. B. Server Tools for Windows 95 includes a version of User Manager for Domains.

50. B. Since another computer attached to the same connection works, the network connection is not the problem. Since both NT and NetWare resources are affected, a frame type mismatch is unlikely. The most likely problem is an incorrectly configured network adapter.

Highlighter's Index

Planning and Installation

Hardware Requirements

CPU: 486/33 or higher (Pentium recommended)

RAM: 16 MB (32 MB recommended)

Display: VGA, Super VGA, or better

Hard disk: SCSI or IDE; 124 MB of space required for OS

Floppy disk: 3.5", 1.4 MB

CD-ROM: SCSI or IDE (not required for network installations)

Network interface card: Any supported by NT

Hardware Support Information

HCL (Hardware Compatibility List): Current list of supported hardware

NTHQ (NT Hardware Qualifier): Utility to check compatibility. Use MAKE-DISK.BAT to create disk, then boot the disk.

File Systems

FAT: DOS standard; 2 GB maximum; 8.3 filenames

VFAT: Windows 95 and NT; 4 GB maximum; long filenames

NTFS: NT 4.0 and later; 16 EB maximum; long filenames; security

HPFS: OS/2 and NT 3.51 and earlier; includes security; cannot be migrated to HPFS in NT 4.0

Computer Types

PDC: Primary domain controller (one per domain); must be installed first

BDC: Backup domain controller; PDC must be up when installing

Member Server: Participates in domain but is not a controller

Adding computers to domain requires Administrator password to create computer account

Installation Program

WINNT32 (Windows NT) or WINNT (Windows 3.1; DOS; Windows 95)

WINNT /B: Don't create boot disks

WINNT /OX: Create boot disks but don't start installation

WINNT /T:*drive*: Specify temporary storage drive

WINNT /U: Use unattended answer file

Installation Phases

Pre-copy: Copies files to temporary directory or creates boot disks

Phase 0: Text-based phase

Phase 1: Beginning of GUI (Setup Wizard) phase

Phase 2: Set up network components

Phase 3: Final setup: time zone, display properties, etc.

Unattended Installation

Answer file: contains answers to installation prompts

Uniqueness database file (UDF): Contains specific exceptions for one or more computers

SYSDIFF

SYSDIFF /snap: Create snapshot

SYSDIFF /diff: Create difference file

SYSDIFF /apply: Apply difference file to computer

SYSDIFF /inf: Create INF file based on difference file

SYSDIFF /dump: Create report of difference file contents

Network Components

TCP/IP

Named for Transport Control Protocol and Internet Protocol

Routable

Used for UNIX and the Internet

Main protocols: TCP (connection-oriented); UDP (connectionless)

Dial-up Protocols

SLIP (Serial line internet protocol): Simple; TCP/IP only; UNIX servers

PPP (Point-to-point protocol): Supports authentication and error control; TCP/IP or other protocol; NT servers

IPX/SPX (NWLink)

Used for NetWare connectivity or as a general network transport

Main protocols: IPX (connectionless); SPX (connection-oriented)

Routable

NetBEUI

Used to support NetBIOS

Low overhead

Non-routable; used for small networks

NetWare Support

NWLink: IPX/SPX protocol

GSNW: Gateway Services for NetWare

FPNW: File and Print sharing for NetWare (add-on product)

Migration Tool for NetWare

Copies files from NetWare server to NT Server

Migrates users and groups from NetWare to NT Server

Does not migrate passwords

May not fully migrate file ownership, permissions, and defaults

RAS Server

Up to 256 incoming connections under NT Server

Supports TCP/IP, NetBEUI, IPX/SPX

Configure and manage with Remote Access Admin utility

RAS Security

PAP (Password Authentication Protocol): Internet standard; passwords sent as clear text; least secure

SPAP (Shiva PAP): Shiva's improved version of PAP; passwords sent in encrypted form

CHAP (Challenge Handshake Authentication Protocol): Two-way protocol using encrypted passwords

MS-CHAP (Microsoft CHAP): Microsoft's proprietary version of CHAP; supported only by Windows and Windows NT

Network Browser Types

Master browser: Receives broadcasts from sharing computers; compiles browse list; distributes list to backup browsers; usually PDC or BDC

Domain master browser: Collects information from master browsers in different subnets and distributes it to the other master browsers; usually the PDC

Backup browsers: Maintain a backup copy of browse list; provides list to clients

Potential browsers: Can act as browsers, but are not currently participating in the browse process; all Windows NT, Windows 95, and Windows for Workgroups machines

Non-browsers: Cannot act as browsers, but can make shares available and broadcast share lists to master browser

Configuring NT Server

Registry Subtrees

HKEY_CLASSES_ROOT stores file associations

HKEY_CURRENT_USER stores control panel settings; loaded from user profile at login

HKEY_LOCAL_MACHINE stores hardware-specific data

HKEY_USERS stores default user settings and settings for each user profile

HKEY_CURRENT_CONFIG stores dynamic configuration information

HKEY_DYN_DATA stores dynamic hardware information

Registry Utilities

REGEDIT displays entire registry in one window; allows complex searches

REGEDT32 displays subtrees in separate windows; allows changes to registry key security

Volume Sets

Two or more partitions

Total capacity is sum of all partition sizes

Partitions can be added without erasing

Decreases speed

Not fault tolerant

Disk Mirroring and Duplexing

2 partitions on separate drives with identical capacities

Mirroring uses one controller; duplexing uses two controllers

Total capacity is equal to one drive's capacity

Increased read speed; slight decrease in write speed

Disk Striping

2-32 partitions on separate disks

Intersperses data between disks

Increases read and write speed

Not fault tolerant

Cannot contain system or boot partitions

Disk Striping with Parity

3-32 partitions on separate disks

Uses a portion of each drive for parity

Total capacity is (number of drives - 1) * (capacity per drive)

Total space used for parity is equal to one drive's capacity

Set of 3 600-MB drives uses 600 MB for parity (200 MB per drive)

Cannot contain system or boot partitions

File Sharing

Rights: Read, Change, Full Control, No Access

Combining NTFS and share rights: most restrictive permission applies

Default shares: NETLOGON; ADMIN$ for WINNT directory; shares for each drive (C$, etc.)

Backups

Full backup copies all of the files every time; clears archive bits

Differential backup includes all of the files that have changed since the last full backup; does not clear archive bits

Incremental backup copies files that have changed since the last backup, whether full or incremental; clears archive bits

Copy includes all files; does not modify archive bit

D*aily copy* includes files modified on the current date; does not modify archive bit

Printing

Printer is queue of jobs; print device is actual hardware

Configured from Printers folder

Print pool: Printer with multiple assigned ports, attached to identical print devices

Print priorities: 1-99; 99 is highest; default is 1 for all printers

Security and Administration

Users

Global user: Typical domain user (default)

Local user: Created for user from remote non-trusted domain

Local Groups

Equivalent to groups in NT Workstation

Used to control access to a computer or domain resource

Can contain users and global groups

Global Groups

Available in NT Server domain model only

Used to group users with similar functions

Can contain users only

Can be made members of local groups on trusted domains

NTFS Security

Rights: Read, Write, Delete, Change Permissions, Execute, Take Ownership, Full Control, No Access

Combining user and group rights: Least restrictive permission applies unless any right is No Access

Copied files inherit permissions of new directory

Moved files retain permissions

User Profiles

Local profiles only work at a particular workstation

Roaming profiles work at any Windows NT computer in the network

Mandatory profiles are roaming profiles that cannot be modified by users

System Policies

User policies affect user's environment

Computer policies affect a computer or all computers

Created with System Policy Editor (POLEDIT)

Stored in registry

Remote Administration

Server Tools available for NT Workstation and Windows 95

Windows 95 tools: User Manager for Domains, Server Manager, Event Viewer, Explorer extensions

NT Workstation tools: User Manager for Domains, Server Manager, Policy Editor, Remote Access Admin, DHCP Manager, WINS Manager, Remoteboot manager

Troubleshooting

Event Viewer

System Log: System error messages and status messages

Security Log: Security errors and auditing

Application Log: Application-specific errors and messages

Task Manager

Applications: List of currently running applications

Processes: Complete list of current processes

Performance: Graph of CPU and memory usage; information about files, threads, and processes in use

Performance Monitor

Chart: Displays a graph of counter valuess over time

Alert: Alerts you if a counter exceeds defined boundaries

Log: Creates a log file with counter values

Report: Generates a printable report based on the counters.

PART 4

NT Server in the Enterprise

Exam Overview

Microsoft's MCSE Exam 70-068, *Implementing and Supporting Microsoft Windows NT Server 4.0 in the Enterprise*, covers the use of NT Server in larger, more sophisticated networks: those with multiple servers, multiple domains, and often multiple platforms.

The NT Enterprise exam is generally considered the most difficult of the three Windows NT exams (Workstation, Server, and Enterprise). While its objectives encompass some of the material covered for the Workstation and Server exams, there is emphasis on multiple-domain issues (trusts, WAN models) and on several TCP/IP protocols and services (DNS, WINS, and IIS).

Because of the overlap between the three Windows NT exams, you should study the *Study Guide* and *Suggested Exercises* for Parts 2 and 3 of this book in conjunction with this chapter, even if you have passed the previous exams. This chapter covers the material unique to the NT Enterprise exam. Specific items covered in Parts 2 and 3 are referenced in this chapter's "Objectives" section.

In order to prepare for this chapter and the NT Server in the Enterprise exam, you should be familiar with the concepts introduced in Part 1, "Networking Essentials." You should also have some real-world experience using and administering Windows NT Server in an enterprise network.

Objectives

Need to Know	Reference
Difference between fault tolerance methods	Part 3, "Planning Fault Tolerance" on page 191
Differences between NT server roles (PDC, BDC, member server)	Part 3, "Planning a Domain" on page 196

Need to Know	Reference
Difference between trusted and trusting domains	"Trusted Domains" on page 259
Domain models, and the number of trusts they require	"Trust Models" on page 262
NetBIOS name resolution methods	"Configuring WINS Server" on page 268
TCP/IP name resolution methods	"Configuring DNS Server" on page 270
Features of Services for Macintosh	"Supporting Macintosh Clients" on page 270
Types of information displayed in a STOP error	"Advanced Troubleshooting" on page 285

Need to Apply	Reference
Choose the appropriate network protocols for a network.	Part 3, "Selecting Network Protocols" on page 195
Configure trusts to allow users to access resources in other domains.	"Trusted Domains" on page 259
Configure multiple domains to support a single logon account.	"Logons Across Trusts" on page 261
Choose a domain model for a particular network.	"Trust Models" on page 262
Configure NT Server services.	Part 3, "Network Services" on page 205
Install client software for NetWare connectivity.	Part 2, "NetWare Client Software" on page 121
Install Gateway Service for NetWare (GSNW).	Part 3, "NetWare Connectivity" on page 206
Install Migration Tool for NetWare.	Part 3, "NetWare Connectivity" on page 206
Install and manage dial-up networking (RAS) clients.	Part 2, "Remote Access Service (RAS)" on page 130
Install Remote Access Server (RAS) servers.	Part 3, "Remote Access Server" on page 210
Install or configure a local or remote printer.	Part 2, "Installing and Managing Printers" on page 150
Configure NT Server hard disks for performance and fault tolerance.	Part 3, "Managing Disk Storage" on page 214
Manage domain users and groups.	Part 3, "Users and Groups" on page 220
Create and modify local, roaming, and mandatory user profiles.	Part 3, "User Profiles" on page 223
Manage system policies.	Part 3, "System Policies" on page 224
Use NT server tools for remote administration.	Part 3, "Remote Administration" on page 227

Need to Apply	Reference
Configure a DHCP server.	"Configuring DHCP Server" on page 266
Configure a WINS server.	"Configuring WINS Server" on page 268
Configure a DNS serve.	"Configuring DNS Server" on page 270
Install Macintosh client support.	"Supporting Macintosh Clients" on page 270
Configure IP, DHCP, and IPX routing.	"Configuring Internet Services" on page 272
Install and configure IIS (Internet Information Server).	"Internet Information Server (IIS)" on page 274
Monitor performance of a system with Performance Monitor.	Part 2, "Monitoring Performance" on page 152; Part 3, "Monitoring Performance" on page 228
Troubleshoot common Windows NT problems.	Part 2, "Troubleshooting Procedures" on page 156
Troubleshoot common network problems.	Part 3, "Network Troubleshooting" on page 229
Establish a network or server baseline.	"Gathering Baseline Data" on page 278
Use Network Monitor to capture and analyze network packets.	"Monitoring Network Traffic" on page 279
Optimize a server's performance based on its primary use and number of users.	"Optimizing Server Performance" on page 281
Optimize various aspects of interdomain communication.	"Optimizing Domains" on page 281
Gather data for advanced Windows NT troubleshooting.	"Advanced Troubleshooting" on page 285

Study Guide

This chapter includes the following sections covering various topics in the NT Server in the Enterprise exam:

Directory Services
Introduces Windows NT's system of trusted domains, which allows wide-area networks with many users to be managed.

Advanced Network Configuration
Describes four components provided with Windows NT Server for network management and connectivity: DHCP Server, WINS Server, DNS Server, and Services for Macintosh.

Configuring Internet Services
Introduces Windows NT's routing capabilities for TCP/IP, DHCP, and IPX, and describes Internet Information Server (IIS).

Optimization and Troubleshooting
Describes techniques and utilities for monitoring server performance and network traffic, and discusses techniques for optimizing server and domain performance.

Directory Services

As you learned earlier in this book, Windows NT supports two basic networking models:

- In the *workgroup model*, each computer has a separate list of user accounts.

- In the *domain model*, a single account database (on the PDC) supports the entire domain.

A single Windows NT domain, with enough fast BDC machines, can support a theoretical maximum of 40,000 accounts, although the limit for user accounts is approximately 26,000. While this is sufficient for many organizations, larger companies need to use multiple domains. Even in an organization with less than 26,000 users, there are many benefits to using multiple domains, particularly where WAN links are concerned.

In the Real World

The 26,000 user limit referred to here is based on the SAM (security accounts manager) database's size. This does not take other factors into account: a domain with 26,000 users would be slowed down severely by network traffic and would be an administrative nightmare. In typical networks, 2,000–5,000 users per domain is a more manageable limit, although more can be supported in certain cases (for example, if only a fraction of the users are logged in at a time).

Windows NT supports resource access between domains by a system of *trusts* between domains. This allows users to access resources in other domains, and permits a user to logon to the network from any participating domain using a single logon account. Microsoft uses the term *directory services* to describe the use of interconnected domains.

On the Exam

Windows NT's system of domains isn't a true directory services architecture, such as Novell's NDS, Banyan's StreetTalk, or the X.500 standard. Nevertheless, if the term *directory services* appears in the exam, it most likely refers to trusted domains. Windows NT 5.0 is expected to replace the current system of domains and trusts with a system called the *Active Directory*. This is a true directory service, compatible with X.500 systems, and can theoretically support up to ten million users per domain. Active Directory is not covered in the current (NT 4.0) version of the Enterprise exam.

Trusted Domains

When multiple domains have been installed on a network, there is no built-in way for a user in one domain to access resources in another without logging on separately to the second domain. You can eliminate the need for a separate logon by establishing *trusts* between domains.

A trust relationship can be configured between any two domains. The two domains involved are called the trusting domain and the trusted domain:

- The *trusted domain* contains the user accounts that need resource access.

- The *trusting domain* contains the resources that access is granted for.

Although complex systems of trusts can be configured, they can be broken down into a number of simple trust relationships. Two limitations of trusts also make them easier to understand:

- Trusts only work one way. Users in the trusting domain have no access to the trusted domain's resources, unless an additional trust is configured in the opposite direction.

- Trusts are not transitive. For example, if the NORTH domain trusts the CENTRAL domain and the CENTRAL domain trusts the SOUTH domain, no trust relationship exists between NORTH and SOUTH domains. This trust must be explicitly defined if desired.

Trust Types

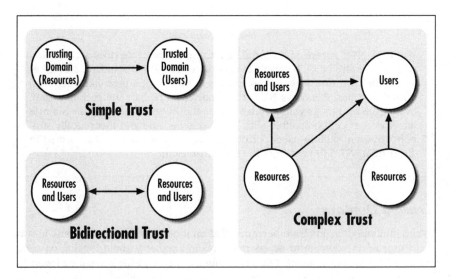

Figure 4-1: The three basic types of trusts

Figure 4-1 shows the three basic types of trust possible in Windows NT. These include the following:

Simple Trust
   A simple trust (or one-way trust) is a single trust relationship with one trusting domain and one trusted domain.

Bidirectional Trust

A bidirectional trust (or two-way trust) is a combination of two simple trusts between two domains, wherein each trusts the other.

Complex Trust

A complex trust is any combination of trusts between three or more domains. Each domain may be a trusted domain, trusting domain, or both. While this type of trust appears complex, it is really nothing more than a number of simple trust relationships.

On the Exam

Figure 4-1 uses arrows to describe trust relationships. Each arrow indicates a simple trust, and the arrow points from the trusting domain (resources) to the trusted domain (users). This is Microsoft's suggested notation for trust relationships, and is used in the Enterprise exam.

Creating Trusts

Trusts are created using the User Manager for Domains utility, included with Windows NT Server. Choose *Trust Relationships* from the Policies menu to display the Trust Relationships dialog. This dialog includes a list of trusted domains, and a separate list of trusting domains.

To create a simple trust, first logon to the domain to be trusted as an administrator, and add the trusting domain to the Trusting Domains list. You are asked for a password when you add the trusting domain; this is an optional password unrelated to any user account.

This password is used to establish the initial communication between the domains, and prevents the trust from being established without agreement between the administrators of both domains.

Next, logon to the trusting domain's PDC, and add the trusted domain to the Trusted Domains list. You must enter the same password you created while configuring the trusted domain.

If you configure the trust in the order given above, the trust is established immediately. You can perform these steps in the opposite order, but a delay of 15–20 minutes may be required for the domains to synchronize.

Logons Across Trusts

In addition to allowing users to access resources in other domains, trusts can be used to allow users to log onto the network with a single account regardless of the domain of their current workstation. This process is called *pass-through authentication.*

The Windows NT logon dialog includes a field for a domain name, which defaults to the name of the current domain. If a user specifies the name of a domain which is trusted by the current domain, an authentication request is passed on to a BDC or PDC for that domain.

If the user does not specify a domain but a trust relationship exists, the system automatically attempts to authenticate the user in each trusted domain using pass-through authentication.

A user logged on through pass-through authentication is given the same rights and permissions as the same user logged on directly to the domain containing the user account.

Trust Models

Using a combination of one-way and two-way trusts, an infinite number of complex trust relationships can be configured between domains. However, most useful domain configurations fall into one of the four categories, called *domain models*, defined by Microsoft. These are described in the sections below.

On the Exam

For the exam, you should know the advantages and disadvantages of each of these models, and the approximate number of users they can support. In addition, you may need to calculate the number of trust relationships required for a specific model. Formulas are given in the sections below.

Single Domain

The single domain model uses only one domain, and no trust relationships. This is the model defined in Part 3. Due to the limitations of the SAM database, there is a theoretical maximum of 40,000 accounts in this model, although the practical limit for users is much lower.

The single-domain model is most useful for small or medium-sized companies with single-location LANs, although it can be used with a WAN provided the number of users falls within the limit.

Master Domain

The master domain model uses a single trusted domain (the master domain) for user and group accounts, and one or more trusting domains (known as resource domains) to store resources. This allows true centralized user management, since all user accounts are in a single domain's security database; however, it has the same limitation on number of users as the single domain model.

This model is most often used with multiple locations or divisions, particularly when each has its own local administrator. The master domain controllers are stored in a central location, and the resource domain controllers in the various locations. Users must authenticate with the master domain's PDC, but can then access local resources without using a WAN link.

This model uses several one-way trust relationships. Each resource domain is a trusting domain, and the master domain is the trusted domain. The total number of trusts required is equal to the number of resource domains. The trusts involved in the master domain model are illustrated in Figure 4-2.

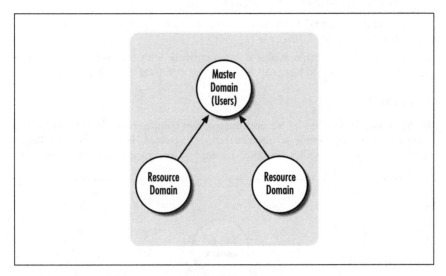

Figure 4-2: Trusts in the master domain model

Multiple Master Domains

The multiple master domain model uses two or more master domains, each with a separate database of user accounts, and a number of resource domains. This model is ideal for organizations with too many users for a single master domain. This model can support about 40,000 accounts per master domain. A simple multiple master domain model is illustrated in Figure 4-3.

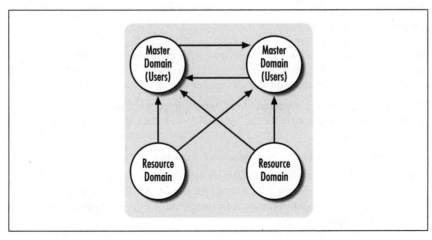

Figure 4-3: Trusts in the multiple master domain model

This model requires a complex trust arrangement: two-way trusts are established between each master domain and all other master domains to allow for authentication, and a one-way trust is established between each resource domain and each master domain. You can use the following formula to calculate the total number of trusts required (two-way trusts count as two trusts):

```
(master domains) * (master domains - 1) + (resource domains *
master domains)
```

As an example, a multiple master domain network with 3 master domains and 8 resource domains would have (3 * 2) + (8 * 3), or 30 total trust relationships.

Complete Trust

In the complete trust model, all domains contain both accountsand resources. This model is relatively simple to understand and versatile, but requires the largest number of trusts. Figure 4-4 illustrates a complete trust model with three domains.

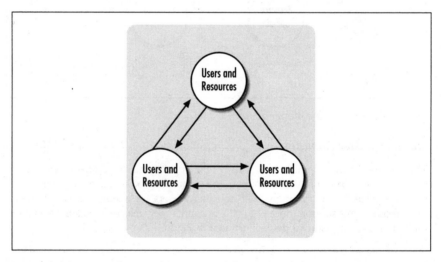

Figure 4-4: Trusts in the complete trust model

The complete trust model is best suited to wide-area networks with few domains and separate administrators for each domain. However, with as few as four or five domains, the number of required trusts makes this model impractical.

This model requires a two-way trust between each domain and every other domain. The following formula can be used to calculate the total number of one-way trusts required:

```
(number of domains) * (number of domains - 1)
```

For example, a complete trust model between 4 domains would use 4 * 3, or 12 trust relationships; a network with 5 domains would use 5 * 4, or 20 trust relationships. This domain model becomes increasingly difficult to manage as the number of domains increases.

Domain Users and Groups

Although trusts may have been established between domains, users still cannot access resources in the trusting domain until they are granted access. This is accomplished by using global and local groups.

To grant access, first create a global group in the trusted domain using User Manager for Domains, and make the appropriate domain users members of the group. This can be accomplished using the Properties dialog for the group, or from the Groups dialog within the user's properties.

Next, create a local group in the trusting domain. Grant the permission to access the needed resources to the local group. Finally, make the global group in the trusted domain a member of the local group. To do this, view the local group's properties in User Manager for Domains. Press the Add button, select the trusted domain in the pull-down list, and select the global group from the list.

Depending on the domain model in use, a more complex arrangement may be needed. In general, you should create one or more global groups in the trusted (user) domains, and make them members of one or more local groups in the trusting (resource) domains.

If your network uses member servers, they each have their own database of local groups. In order for a global group in a trusted domain to access resources on these servers, the global group must be made a member of a separate local group on each member server. If there are a large number of member servers in the network, this can be a tedious process.

Group permissions across trusts work in the same way as local group permissions: if a user is a member of one or more groups with permissions for the same resource, the least restrictive of the rights is used unless one of them is No Access.

NT Server in the Enterprise

Advanced Network Configuration

While the protocols described earlier in this book are sufficient for simple networks, an enterprise network may require the use of additional protocols and services. The sections below examine several of these:

- DHCP (Dynamic Host Configuration Protocol) allows the dynamic assignment of IP addresses to clients.

- WINS (Windows Internet Name Service) supports conversion of NetBIOS names to IP addresses.

- DNS (Domain Name Service) supports conversion of TCP/IP domain names to IP addresses.

- The AppleTalk protocols and Microsoft Services for Macintosh (SFM) provide support for Macintosh clients.

- The DLC (Data Link Control) protocol supports mainframe connectivity and print servers.

Several of these items (DHCP, WINS, and DNS) are related to the TCP/IP protocol suite. For a basic introduction to TCP/IP, see Part 2.

Configuring DHCP Server

DHCP (Dynamic Host Configuration Protocol) is an Internet-standard protocol for the assignment of IP addresses to client machines. While you can manually assign addresses, using DHCP allows ease of administration. In addition, if you have more computers than IP addresses, DHCP can be used to dynamically allocate addresses based on need. A DHCP server assigns addresses with limited duration, called *leases*. A lease can also be assigned with an unlimited duration.

To use DHCP, you will need to configure at least one DHCP server per subnet or use a router that forwards DHCP packets. (or use DHCP relay, explained in the next section of this chapter). Windows for Workgroups, Windows 95, and Windows NT are all able to act as DHCP clients.

To configure a Windows NT client to use DHCP, select the Obtain an IP address from a DHCP server option in the IP Address tab of the TCP/IP properties dialog.

On the Exam

For the NT Enterprise exam, you should be familiar with the uses of DHCP and the process of configuring it using DHCP Manager. You do not need to understand the exact details of how DHCP works or its more complex options. DHCP is described in more detail in *MCSE: The Electives in a Nutshell.*

Installing DHCP Server

DHCP Server is included with Windows NT Server. To install DHCP Server, select the *Add* option from the Services tab of the Network control panel. Select *Microsoft DHCP Server* from the list.

The DHCP Server machine must itself have a manually configured IP address, to allow communication with DHCP clients. Be sure the *Obtain an IP address from a DHCP server* option in the TCP/IP properties dialog is disabled on the server machine.

Creating Scopes

DHCP assigns IP addresses from a range of available addresses called a *scope*. To operate, the DHCP server must have at least one scope configured. Scopes are configured using the DHCP Manager utility. This utility is installed with the DHCP service. To run it, choose *DHCP Manager* from the Administrative Tools menu under the Start menu. DHCP Manager can be used from the DHCP server or from a remote computer on the network.

On the Exam

DHCP scopes are unrelated to NetBIOS scopes, described earlier in this book. Scopes in DHCP are pools of available addresses.

Before you can configure a scope, you must add the DHCP server computer's IP address to the DHCP Manager utility's list. Choose *Add* from the Server menu, and enter the address.

To create a scope, choose *Create* from the Scope menu. The Create Scope dialog, shown in Figure 4-5, is displayed. This dialog includes the following categories of information:

IP Address Pool
Specify the start and end address of a range of available IP addresses. You can also specify one or more ranges of addresses to be excluded from the scope. Also enter the subnet mask corresponding to the address range.

Lease Duration
Specify the duration of the lease. This is the amount of time the IP address remains available after being issued. By default, this value is three days.

Name and Comment
Enter a name for the scope, and an optional comment. These are displayed in the list of scopes in DHCP Manager.

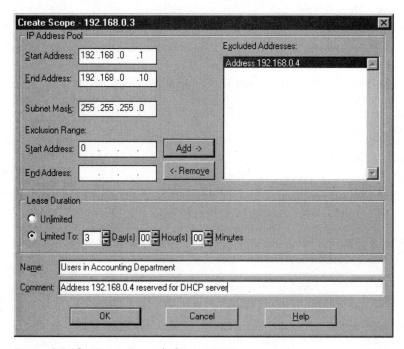

Figure 4-5: The Create Scope dialog in DHCP

Reserving IP Addresses

Some clients may require a consistent IP address. You can still use these clients with DHCP by adding a *reservation* to the scope. This reserves a specific address for a particular computer's MAC (hardware) address.

To add a reservation, choose *Add Reservations* from the Scope menu in DHCP manager. You must specify the MAC address (Unique Identifier) and the desired IP address. This address must be within the scope. You can also specify a name and comment to identify the computer the address is reserved for.

Setting Options

By default, DHCP assigns clients IP addresses and subnet masks. You can configure DHCP to send additional values to clients using the Scope option in the DHCP Options menu.

You can use DHCP options to specify a router (preferred gateway) as well as WINS and DNS information (explained below). The Options dialog in DHCP Manager includes a list of the available options.

Configuring WINS Server

NetBIOS computer names (the names defined in the Identification tab of the Network control panel) are often used in Windows networks. When TCP/IP is used, it is necessary to convert NetBIOS names to IP addresses. This process is called *NetBIOS name resolution*. NetBIOS resolution can use one of several methods:

- Each machine can have an optional LMHOSTS file in the \winnt\system32\ drivers\etc directory. This is an ASCII file that maps NetBIOS names to IP addresses.

- NetBIOS clients can use broadcasts for name resolution. Because this involves a number of messages sent to the entire network, broadcasts can cause heavy network traffic.

- A WINS (Windows Internet Name Service) server can be consulted. This is the most efficient and manageable method.

To configure a Windows NT client to use a WINS server, use the WINS Address tab in the TCP/IP Properties dialog. You can specify a primary server and a secondary server, which will be used when the primary server is unreachable.

Installing WINS Server

WINS Server is included with Windows NT Server. To install it, select *Add* from the Services tab of the Network control panel, and select *Windows Internet Name Service*.

The computer that runs the WINS server should have a manually configured IP address. This is the same address that will be entered in the client computers' TCP/IP properties dialog. An optional DHCP option can be used to send this value to clients automatically.

You do not need to configure a database to use the WINS server. The server maintains a database of NetBIOS names and IP addresses automatically by receiving broadcasts from clients.

Once the WINS server is installed, the WINS Manager utility is available from the Administrative Tools menu under the Start menu. To set options for the WINS Server in this utility, select *Add* from the Server menu to add the server's IP address, then select *Configuration* from the Server menu.

NT Server in the Enterprise

Configuring DNS Server

IP hostnames, introduced in Part 2, provide a user-friendly notation for IP node references. A process of name resolution is used to convert domain names to IP addresses:

- Each computer can have a HOSTS file in the \winnt\system32\drivers\etc directory. This is an ASCII text file that maps host names to IP addresses.

- DNS (Domain Name Service) is an Internet-standard service for resolving TCP/IP host names to IP addresses.

Installing DNS Server

A DNS server is included with Windows NT Server. To install it, select Add from the Services tab of the Network control panel. Select *Microsoft DNS Server.*

After the server is installed, you can use the DNS Manager utility in the Administrative Tools menu to configure the DNS server. As with the DHCP Manager and WINS Manager utilities, you must add the server's IP address to the list to manage it.

Creating a Zone

To use DNS, you must create at least one zone. A zone is a database consisting of names and addresses for a number of hosts. To create a zone, select *New Zone* from the DNS menu. Specify the IP domain name associated with the zone. You can then use the *New Host* command from the DNS menu to add hosts to the database.

Unlike WINS, the DNS server does not automatically update its database when a machine's IP address changes. However, you can configure DNS to use WINS to answer requests, eliminating the need for a separate database. To do this, double-click on a zone to display the zone properties dialog, and select the WINS Lookup tab. Select the *Use WINS Resolution* option, and specify one or more WINS server IP addresses.

On the Exam

Although this information should be adequate for the NT Enterprise exam, DNS includes many options not described here. These are described in *MCSE: The Electives in a Nutshell.*

Supporting Macintosh Clients

Microsoft Windows NT includes support for Apple Macintosh clients. This includes the AppleTalk protocol, which allows communication with standard Macintosh networks, and Services for Macintosh, a service that allows Macintosh clients to access Windows NT disk shares and printers.

Installing Services for Macintosh

Services for Macintosh is included with Windows NT Server. To install it, select *Add* from the Services tab of the Network control panel. Select *Services for Macintosh* from the list. This automatically installs the AppleTalk protocol. You can then modify the AppleTalk properties dialog. This dialog includes two categories of options:

(General) Default Adapter
> Specify a network adapter that is connected to the AppleTalk network.

(General) Default Zone
> Specify the AppleTalk zone to communicate with. Zones are groups of up to 255 networked Macintosh computers.

(Routing) Enable Routing
> Allows the computer to act as an AppleTalk router. This allows you to create a zone or route data between zones.

On the Exam

Macintosh computers do not require any additional client software to access Services for Macintosh. You do not need to be experienced with Macintosh computers for the NT Enterprise exam, but you should know how to configure NT Server to work with them.

Macintosh Disk Sharing

Unlike Windows or NetWare clients, Macintosh clients cannot access Windows NT shares directly. A special volume called a *Macintosh-accessible volume* must be created and made available to Macintosh clients.

Macintosh-accessible volumes are not actual disk volumes, but links to directories in the NTFS file system. The same directory can be shared for access by Windows clients. The FAT file system does not support Macintosh volumes.

The installation of Services for Macintosh adds a MacFile menu to the Server Manager utility (described in Part 3) with options for Macintosh volumes. To display the volumes available on a server, select *Volumes* from the MacFile menu.

From the Macintosh-Accessible Volumes dialog box, choose *Create Volume* to create a new volume or *Properties* to manage an existing volume. The following properties are available:

Volume Name
> Specify a name for the volume. This is the name that will appear to Macintosh clients.

Path
> Specify the drive and directory to be used as a Macintosh-accessible volume.

Password

Specify an optional password. If specified, Macintosh users will need this password to access the volume.

Volume Security

Choose whether the volume is read-only (Macintosh users cannot write to it) and whether guest users can access the volume.

User Limit

If selected, only the specified number of Macintosh users are allowed to access the volume concurrently.

Supporting AppleTalk Printing

Unlike disk volumes, shared printers are available to Macintosh clients with no additional configuration. The shared printers appear as Apple LaserWriter printers in the Mac Chooser. When a Macintosh user prints to this printer, the data is converted to the appropriate format for the actual printer.

Windows NT (Workstation or Server) computers with AppleTalk installed can print to AppleTalk printers without using SFM. Windows clients can also access Apple-Talk printers if they are specifically shared by the server running Services for Macintosh. To do this, choose *Add Printers* from the Printers dialog. Select the local printer option.

When prompted for the port the printer is attached to, select the *Add Port* option. Select *AppleTalk Printing Devices* from the list. Select the appropriate AppleTalk zone and printer.

When you configure the AppleTalk printer in this fashion, it becomes inaccessible to the Macintosh network. To make it available, share the printer. This will also make it available to Windows clients.

The computer running SFM can also share Windows printers, which will be available to Macintosh clients.

Configuring Internet Services

Windows NT includes several features that are useful on Internet-connected systems and other large networks. These include the following:

- Routing allows Windows NT to route packets between networks. Windows NT supports routing for TCP/IP, DHCP, IPX/SPX, and AppleTalk. Collectively, these services are referred to as the *multiprotocol router* or MPR.

- Internet Information Server (IIS), included with NT Server, provides Internet services: World Wide Web (WWW), File Transfer Protocol (FTP), and Gopher.

These items are explained in detail in the following sections.

IP Routing

Any Windows NT Workstation or Server computer that is connected to multiple networks (with multiple network cards, or dial-up connections) can act as a router.

Microsoft refers to a computer connected to two or more networks as a *multi-homed* computer.

There are two basic types of routing:

- *Static routing* uses a table of available IP addresses and the network card they can be reached through. This table is created manually by the administrator.

- *Dynamic routing* uses an intelligent protocol to communicate between routers and dynamically maintain routing tables. One such protocol, RIP (routing information protocol) is supported by Windows NT.

Configuring Static Routing

Static routing is built into all NT Workstation and Server computers. If a computer has multiple network cards, you can enable static routing by checking the *Enable IP Forwarding* option in the Routing tab of the TCP/IP properties dialog.

Once you've enabled routing, you must create a routing table. The table can be maintained using the `route` command at the command prompt. For example, type `route add` to add a route, or `route /help` to display a complete list of options.

On the Exam

You do not need to know the specific options of the `route` command for the NT Enterprise exam. These are covered in *MCSE: The Electives in a Nutshell.*

Configuring Dynamic Routing

NT Server includes an implementation of RIP to support dynamic IP routing. To install it, select *Add* from the Services tab of the Network control panel. Select *RIP for Internet Protocol* from the list.

Once RIP is installed on two or more multihomed computers, this protocol will be used to dynamically maintain a routing table. No additional configuration is required to use RIP, but the *Enable IP Forwarding* option described above must be enabled.

DHCP Relay Agent

DHCP is not normally supported by routers, requiring the use of a separate DHCP server for each subnet. Some routers allow DHCP (BOOTP) packets to be forwarded. Windows NT Server includes the DHCP Relay Agent, which can forward DHCP requests and responses between subnets.

Installing DHCP Relay

DHCP Relay should be used on a multihomed computer with access to both subnets; this can be the same server that is configured as an IP router. No installation process is needed to use DHCP Relay Agent; it is installed on all Windows NT Server computers.

To activate the DHCP relay, select the DHCP Relay tab from the TCP/IP properties dialog, and specify at least one DHCP server IP address.

Once the DHCP Relay is running, clients on the subnet without its own DHCP server can use DHCP. The DHCP broadcasts will be received by the DHCP Relay machine and forwarded to a DHCP server on the other subnet, and the result will be returned directly to the requesting client.

IPX Routing

Windows NT Server's implementation of the IPX protocol (NWLink) includes a facility for acting as an IPX router. Any NT Server computer that is connected to two or more networks that use the IPX protocol can be configured to act as a router.

Windows NT IPX routing is dynamic, and uses the RIP for IPX protocol. RIP for IPX is not the same protocol as RIP for IP, described earlier in this section, but serves a similar purpose.

To install RIP for IPX, Select *Add* from the Services tab of the Network control panel. Select *RIP for NWLink IPX/SPX Compatible Transport* from the list.

To configure RIP for IPX, select it from the list of services and choose *Properties*. This server has a single property: NetBIOS Broadcast Propagation. If enabled, NetBIOS broadcasts are forwarded between the IPX networks, which allows network browsing.

On the Exam

You may recall from Part 1 that one of the advantages of a router is the re-duction of broadcast traffic, since routers don't generally forward NetBIOS broadcasts. Enabling NetBIOS Broadcast Propagation lets some of this traffic through the router, which may cause traffic problems on the network.

Internet Information Server (IIS)

Part 2 introduced Peer Web Services (PWS), a simple Internet server included with Windows NT Workstation. The full version of this software is called Internet Infor-mation Server (IIS) 2.0 and is included with Windows NT Server.

IIS includes three basic services:

- The WWW (World Wide Web) service allows documents created in HTML (Hypertext Markup Language) to be published for viewing by web browsers.

- FTP (File Transfer Protocol) allows files to be transferred to and from client computers from the server.

- Gopher is an information service that predates the World Wide Web, but is still in use among some educational institutions.

Installing IIS

To install IIS, select *Add* from the Services tab of the Network control panel. Select *Microsoft Internet Information Server 2.0* from the list. The setup program now displays a list of IIS components to install. These include the following:

Internet Service Manager
> A utility (installed in the Microsoft Internet Server menu under the Start menu) for managing IIS services.

World Wide Web Service
> The WWW (World Wide Web) service.

WWW Service Samples
> Includes sample HTML documents for the web server.

Internet Service Manager (HTML)
> An HTML version of the Internet Service Manager that can be accessed using a web browser.

Gopher Service
> The Gopher information service.

FTP Service
> The FTP (File Transfer Protocol) service.

ODBC Drivers and Administration
> Optional drivers and tools for integrating database access with web publishing.

Select the OK button in this dialog to continue. You are now prompted for directories for the content to be published by the three services. These default to directories under the InetPub directory on the boot volume. These directories will be created if needed.

NT Server in the Enterprise

Configuring IIS

Once IIS is successfully installed, the Internet Service Manager utility is available in the Microsoft Internet Server menu under the Start menu. This utility allows you to monitor, control, and configure the three IIS services.

The Internet Service Manager window displays a list of installed services and their current status. The Start, Stop, and Pause buttons in the toolbar allow you to control the selected service. You can highlight a service and select *Service Properties* from the Properties menu to configure the service. The available property categories are described in their own sections below.

Service Properties

These properties allow you to specify the TCP port the service answers on, the timeout and maximum limits for connections, and a username and password for anonymous access to the service. Depending on the service, additional parameters may be included. The following options are included:

TCP Port
> Specify the TCP port the service will send and receive data through. Defaults are 80 for WWW, 21 for FTP, and 70 for Gopher.

Connection Timeout
> Specify the timeout (in seconds) for connections to this service. If there is no traffic for the specified number of seconds, the user is disconnected.

Maximum Connections
> Specify the maximum number of concurrent connections to the service. The default values are very large; be sure to specify lower limits if your server has heavy traffic.

Anonymous Logon
> Enter a username and password for anonymous access. This user is created when you install IIS and given permissions for the directories you specify.

Password Authentication (WWW Service only)
> Specify whether a password is required to access the server, and the type of authentication. You can choose the standard format or MS-CHAP, a proprietary but more secure scheme.

Comment
> Enter a comment if desired. This field is displayed in the main Internet Service Manager display.

Directory Properties

This category allows you to modify the publishing directories you specified at installation and other settings:

Directory
> Specify the directory path. You can specify a UNC path to a directory on another machine.

Home Directory
> If this option is selected, this directory acts as the home (root) directory for this service. Only one directory can be designated as the home directory.

Virtual Directory
Indicates that this directory will be used as a virtual directory. Specify an alias for the directory. The alias path begins with the root directory; for example, an alias of *pub* indicates the /pub directory.

Enable Default Document (WWW Service only)
If enabled, requests that do not specify a filename will be answered with the default file in the directory, typically index.html.

Directory Browsing Allowed (WWW Service only)
If the default document does not exist and this option is selected, a listing of the directory's contents will be sent as a document.

Account Information
If this directory is on another machine, you must specify a username and password with access to the directory. Using the Administrator password here can be a security risk; it's best to create a user specifically for the purpose.

Access
Select whether users are able to read from the directory, write to it, or both. The NTFS rights for the directory must match this setting.

Logging Properties

This category includes options for logging access to the service. Log records can be written to a text file or to an available SQL or ODBC database server. The following settings are available:

Enable Logging
Check this box to enable transaction logging. Logging is disabled by default.

Log to File
Enables logging to a disk file. This is a standard ASCII text file, with one line per transaction.

Log Format
Choose the format for log entries. For FTP and Gopher, only the Standard format is available. For WWW, you can choose Standard or NCSA log formats. (The NCSA web server was one of the first available, and many utilities are available for analyzing logs in this format.)

Automatically open new log
If this option is checked, IIS will automatically create a new log file at selected intervals. New logs can be created daily, weekly, monthly, or when the log file reaches a specified size.

Log file directory
Specify the directory in which IIS will create log files. Log files are named automatically based on the current date.

Log to SQL/ODBC Database
Enables logging to a database. Selecting this option disables the above options for file logging. Specify the Data Source Name (ODBC), table name (SQL), and the username and password for database access.

Advanced Properties

This category allows you to control access to the server and limit the network bandwidth used by the services:

Granted Access, Denied Access
Choose whether access is granted or denied to all computers by default. The *Denied Access* option is useful if you wish to grant access to specific machines exclusively.

Except those listed below
Use the Add, Edit, and Remove buttons to maintain this list of IP addresses that are exceptions to the above rule.

Limit Network Use by all Internet Services on the computer
Check this option and specify a number to limit the network bandwidth that can be used by Internet services. This option applies collectively to FTP, Gopher, and WWW services.

Optimization and Troubleshooting

Parts 2 and 3 introduced various aspects of optimizing and troubleshooting Windows NT. The sections below examine optimizing and troubleshooting techniques unique to the NT Server in the Enterprise exam. These include gathering and saving baseline data, monitoring network traffic, optimizing server performance and domain communication, and advanced troubleshooting issues.

Gathering Baseline Data

While there are some methods of optimizing the performance of a Windows NT Server computer, these changes should be made carefully. Any change has the potential to degrade the performance of a server. In order to ensure that changes have the desired effect, a *baseline* should be measured.

A baseline is a measure of the server's performance in various areas. This data can be saved and compared with recent results to determine if a change improved performance, or if a hardware malfunction or other problem is reducing performance.

You can create a baseline by using the Log option in Performance Monitor, described in Part 2, to write counter values to a file. Some suggested counters to baseline are those that were recommended for regular monitoring in Part 3.

In addition to these, a number of counters are available for the TCP/IP protocol. These are included as part of the SNMP (Simple Network Management Protocol) service. To install this service, select *Add* from the Services tab of the Network control panel. Select *SNMP Service* from the list. The following categories of counters are added:

IP
Counters related to the Internet Protocol (IP). This protocol is used for addressing and sending packets between computers.

ICMP

Counters for the Internet Control Message Protocol (ICMP). This protocol is used for diagnostic messages and error messages between network nodes.

TCP

Counters for the Transport Control Protocol (TCP). This protocol manages connection-oriented communication between computers.

UDP

Counters for the User Datagram Protocol (UDP). This protocol manages connectionless communication between computers.

On the Exam

You don't need to know the specific counters in these categories for the NT Enterprise exam, but you should know that some categories are installed with the SNMP service. SNMP itself is not covered on the Enterprise exam, but is covered in *MCSE: The Electives in a Nutshell*.

Monitoring Network Traffic

The Network Monitor utility, included with NT Server, is a network analyzer. This utility is able to capture packets being transmitted on the network, and allows you to view raw packets or statistics about the captured packets as a group.

The version of Network Monitor included with Windows NT Server is limited to capturing "legitimate" packets: those that are addressed to, or from, the monitored computer, and network broadcasts. The full-featured version of Network Monitor (included with SMS) is able to use *promiscuous mode* network drivers, which allow all packets passing through the network to be viewed, regardless of their origin and destination.

On the Exam

SMS, or Systems Management Server, is a component of the Microsoft Back-Office package that allows for network inventory and management. SMS is covered in this book's companion volume, *MCSE Electives in a Nutshell*.

Installing Network Monitor

There are two components of Network Monitor: the Network Monitor Tools, which you use to capture and view data, and the Network Monitor Agent, which captures data for analysis by the tools. You should install the Tools on the computer you will monitor the network from, and the Agent on one or more computers to monitor.

You can install either of these components using the Services tab in the Network control panel. Select *Add*, and select *Network Monitor Agent* for the agent only, or

Network Monitor Tools and Agent for the tools and agent. You must then restart the computer and use the Services control panel to start the Network Monitor Agent service.

Using Network Monitor

To start this utility, select *Network Monitor* from the Administrative Tools menu under the Start menu. The main Network Monitor window, shown in Figure 4-6, is now displayed.

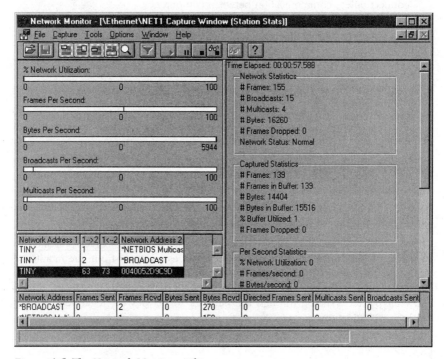

Figure 4-6: The Network Monitor utility

To begin capturing network packets, select *Start* from the Capture menu. As data is captured, statistics are displayed in the Network Monitor window. To capture data without displaying intermediate statistics, select *Dedicated Capture Mode* from the Capture menu.

To end a capture, select *Stop* from the Capture menu. The data captured is now stored in memory. You can save the data using the *Save as* command in the File menu, or display it using the *Display Captured Data* in the Capture menu.

Capturing data for an extended period of time can consume a large amount of memory. One way to reduce the required memory is to configure a filter. Select *Filter* from the Capture menu. You can filter captured data for a particular type of packet, for one or more specific computers (by hardware address), or by data matching a specified pattern.

Monitor Agent Controls

On each machine where you've installed the monitoring software, the Monitor Agent control panel is available to change the agent's settings. The following options are available:

Change Password
> Changes the password required to capture and display packets from this workstation. By default, there is no password.

Describe Net Cards
> Allows you to enter a description for each of the network adapters in the computer. While not required, this description is helpful when analyzing captured data.

Reset Defaults
> This option applies only if you are using the Network Monitor utility on this computer. It resets Network Monitor's display, protocols, and other options to their default values.

Optimizing Server Performance

Windows NT includes a simple method of optimizing the performance of a server. To access this option, select the Services tab in the Network control panel. Highlight the Server service and select *Properties*. Choose one of the following choices:

Minimize Memory Used
> Attempts to use the smallest amount of memory possible. Microsoft recommends this option for networks with 10 or fewer users.

Balance
> This option is a compromise between memory use and network throughput. This option is recommended for networks under 64 users.

Maximize Throughput for File Sharing
> This dedicates memory and processing to file sharing over other server activities. Microsoft recommends this option for large networks (64 users or more).

Maximize Throughput for Network Applications
> This is a specialized option for application servers. Servers that are infrequently used for file sharing and frequently used for client-server applications should use this option.

Optimizing Domains

Windows NT provides for efficient communication between domain controllers and between trusted domains with a minimum of administration. However, certain aspects of domains can be optimized, often providing dramatic increases in performance. Several areas that can be optimized are introduced in the following sections.

Database Size

If a domain has a large number of users and groups, the user account database (also called the directory services database) can be quite large. Aside from disk storage requirements, the size of this database affects several aspects of domain optimization.

If the network has already been set up and is in use, you can check the current size of the database. This is a single file called SAM in the \WINNT\SYSTEM32\ CONFIG directory of the PDC. Each domain has a separate user account database.

If you are planning a future network or growth of an existing network, you can calculate the database size based on the number of users, groups, and computer accounts in the domain. Values for these items are given in Table 4-1.

Table 4-1: Database Size Factors

Item	Size Calculation
User account	1K (User accounts always use this exact amount)
Global group	512 bytes plus 12 bytes per group member
Local group	512 bytes plus 36 bytes per group member
Computer account	512 bytes (A computer account is required for each computer in the domain)

Domain Controllers

To provide fault tolerance, each domain should have at least one BDC in addition to the PDC. The number of additional BDCs depends on the anticipated number of users and their location.

The number of users a domain can support depends on the processor speed and RAM of the domain controllers. Table 4-2 lists common RAM values and the database size they can support. (This table assumes that Pentium processors are used. The users value listed in the table is a maximum; the value will be lower when computer and group accounts are factored in, as described above.)

Table 4-2: RAM Versus Database Size

RAM	Database Size	Max. Users (approx.)	Notes
32 MB	10 MB	7,500	This is the minimum recommended RAM for NT Server.
64 MB	20 MB	15,000	A fast machine (Pentium Pro, Pentium 2, or RISC) is advised.
128 MB	30 MB	20,000	This is the maximum database size.

Since each domain controller stores the entire security database, each PDC and BDC should support the requirements listed above. As for the number of BDCs, Microsoft recommends using one BDC for every 2,000 user accounts.

The idea behind adding BDCs in this fashion is to distribute the work of authenticating users to several machines. The actual user database is not divided among the machines—each one stores a copy of the entire database. Be sure disk space is sufficient for the database size listed in the table above.

The location of BDCs is another factor. While a single powerful BDC may be able to handle all of the users of your network, distributing the load between several BDCs, one at each location, would increase the speed and efficiency of the network. Figure 4-7 shows a network using BDCs at each location.

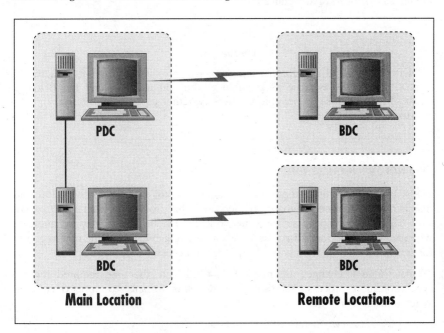

Figure 4-7: Using one BDC per location

Master Domains

Based on the specifications of the domain controllers and the number you plan to have in each domain, you can determine the maximum number of users a domain will support. If your network has more users than this number, you should use the multiple master domain model.

If you use an adequate number of domain controllers per domain, each master domain can support a maximum of 20,000 users. Thus, a network with three master domains could support 60,000 users. In practical terms, bandwidth and administrative overhead make networks any larger than five master domains (about 100,000 users) difficult to support.

WAN Issues

Users must authenticate with a BDC (or the PDC) of the domain that contains their user account to log on to the network. In a single master domain model, this means that users in any domain need to reach the BDC of the master domain.

In a single-location network, authentication is very fast. If this authentication crosses a WAN link, however, it can cause delays. One way to prevent these delays is to place a BDC for the master domain in each of the domains where users will logon.

The disadvantage of this approach is that synchronization traffic between the PDC and BDC uses some of the bandwidth of the WAN link. However, it is often worth the increased speed of authentication.

On the Exam

Here is a general rule for placing domain controllers in any network: the PDC should be as close as possible to the administrator, and the BDCs should be as close as possible to users (whether in the same domain or a trusting domain).

Domain Synchronization

PDCs and BDCs must periodically communicate to exchange information and maintain the same user database on each one. This process is called *synchronization*. This process does use some network bandwidth, which may be an issue when the BDCs are located across WAN links. You can calculate the time required for synchronization and optimize this process if necessary.

To determine if changes are needed, first calculate the time required for the synchronization process. Microsoft provides this formula to approximate the synchronization time per month per BDC:

```
time = (users * age/30) / (speed * 450)
```

The following values are used in this formula:

time
> The synchronization time required per month (in hours).

users
> The number of domain user accounts.

age
> The maximum password age. This is the Expires In value from the Maximum Password Age section of the Account Policy dialog in User Manager for domains.

speed
> The speed of the WAN links, measured in Kbps.

As an example, suppose a network has 3 BDCs located across 128-Kbps WAN links. The network has 5,000 users, and passwords are set to expire in 90 days. The formula would evaluate as follows:

```
time = (5000 * 90/30) / (128 * 450)
time = (5000 * 3) / (57600)
time = 15000 * 3 / 57600 = .78 hours
```

This network would require .78 hours (about 47 minutes) per month per BDC, or about 2.3 hours total, for synchronization.

On the Exam

You should not need to know the exact formula for synchronization time for the exam. However, you should know how to manage synchronization using the registry settings given below.

If the synchronization time is excessive, you can optimize the synchronization process by changing two registry settings, both located under the HKEY_LOCAL_MACHINE\SYSTEM\CurrentControlSet\Services\Netlogon\Parameters registry key:

ChangeLogSize
> This registry change is made on the PDC. The change log stores changes made to the user database on the PDC that need to be synchronized to PDCs. The log's size controls the number of changes that are transmitted in one synchronization session. The default size is 64K; you can change this value to anything between 32K and 4 MB. Higher values cause the database to be updated less frequently.

ReplicationGovernor
> This registry change is made on the BDCs. This value controls the percentage of time and bandwidth that can be used for replication. The default setting is 100 percent; using a lower value will ensure that synchronization does not create a network bottleneck. A value of 0 prevents replication entirely.

You can use the ReplicationGovernor value to control when synchronization occurs. The Windows NT Server Resource Kit includes a command-line utility called REGINI.EXE to set this value. By using a scheduler (such as Windows NT's AT command) you can set the value to 0, then have it set to 100 at an appropriate time (such as after business hours).

Advanced Troubleshooting

This section covers advanced aspects of Windows NT troubleshooting: STOP errors and memory dumps. Both of these come into play when the system crashes, and may be useful in determining the cause of the crash.

STOP Errors

Although Windows NT is more stable than any other version of Windows, system crashes do happen. When this happens, a STOP error or "blue screen" is displayed. This message includes the following information:

- The word STOP followed by a series of hexadecimal codes. The first of these codes indicates the type of error.
- An identifier for the system CPU and OS version.
- A list of currently running device drivers.
- A memory dump of the code that was executing.

On the Exam

For the exam, you don't need to be able to interpret blue screens on your own. You should be aware of the basic information they include, and be able to report it to Microsoft Technical Support if you contact them.

Memory Dumps and Notification

In addition to the memory dump displayed at the end of a blue screen, Windows NT can create a file containing the area of memory involved in a crash. Unfortunately, you must configure this option before a crash happens. To configure behavior at blue screens, select the Startup/Shutdown tab from the System control panel. The following options are available:

Write an event to the system log
> If selected, a system log entry is created with specifics about the STOP error. You can view this using the Event Viewer utility, introduced in Part 2.

Send an administrative alert
> If selected, administrators are notified when the crash happens.

Write debugging information to:
> Specify a file to store a memory dump at the time of the crash. This file can be used by Technical Support to determine the problem.

Automatically reboot
> If selected, NT will reboot upon display of the blue screen. This allows the server to return to useful operation, provided the STOP error is not a recurring problem.

In practice, most administrators find it useful to enable the system log or administrative alert options. While users may notify you when their machine crashes, they may not give you all of the details (and may reboot without telling you); this allows you to know when crashes are a problem. The memory dump option should not be enabled unless you know how to analyze the dump (or plan to send it to someone who does).

Suggested Exercises

The Windows NT Server in the Enterprise exam stresses many issues that affect only large networks, such as trusted domains and routing. You should ideally have experience in dealing with all of these issues on a wide-area network.

For this reason, this exam is difficult to prepare for on an in-home network. However, if you have at least three computers on the network, you should be able to experiment with most of the features. Installing multiple copies of NT Server in a multi-boot configuration will be helpful—for example, you may need one PDC and two BDCs for the same domain for study of some topics and three PDCs on separate domains for others.

Performing the following exercises will help you prepare for the exam. In addition, since some of the basic Windows NT features covered in Parts 2 and 3 are also objectives for the Enterprise exam, you should study the *Suggested Exercises* for Parts 2 and 3.

1. Configure two computers as PDCs for different domains and perform the following exercises:

   a. Configure a one-way trust between the domains.

   b. Create a local group on the trusting domain and give it permissions for several directories.

   c. Create a global group on the trusted domain and assign several users to the group.

   d. Make the trusted domain's global group a member of the trusting domain's local group.

   e. Log on using one of the user accounts in the trusted domain and verify that you can access the directories on the trusting domain.

   f. Add a second one-way trust relationship to form a two-way trust between the domains. Perform the steps above for the other trust to share resources in the other direction.

2. If you have access to three computers, configure them as PDCs for three separate domains and perform these exercises:

    a.   Choose one domain to act as a master domain. The other two domains will act as resource domains (trusting domains).

    b.   Create one-way trust relationships between each of the resource (trusting) domains and the master (trusted) domain.

    c.   Create a global group on the master domain and assign several users to the group.

    d.   Create a local group on each of the trusting domains and grant it permissions for several directories.

    e.   Make the master domain's global group a member of each of the trusting domains' local groups.

    f.   Log on to the master domain's PDC using a user account that belongs to the global group. Verify that you can access resources on both of the trusting domains.

    g.   Add the required trust relationships to create a complete trust model between the three domains. How many one-way trusts are required?

3. Install DHCP Server on a Windows NT Server computer. Add a scope of IP addresses (for a network that is not connected to the Internet, one set of addresses that will work is 192.168.0.1 through 192.168.0.3). Configure a client computer on the network to use DHCP, and verify that it is assigned an IP address at boot time.

4. Install WINS Server on a Windows NT Server computer. Configure a client computer with the WINS server's IP address and verify that you are able to resolve NetBIOS names. (Using the ping command with the NetBIOS name will display the IP address if WINS is working correctly.)

5. Install DNS Server on a Windows NT Server computer. Create a zone in the DNS database and add entries for the host names and IP addresses in your network. Configure a client to use the DNS server, and verify that name resolution works (use the nslookup command at the command prompt to display the IP address for a host name).

6. Install Services for Macintosh (SFM) on an NT Server computer and configure it. Create a Macintosh-accessible volume. (You can perform these steps without any Macintosh computers on the network. If you have a Macintosh computer on the network, verify that you can access the volume.)

7. Install RIP for Internet Protocol on a Windows NT Server.

8. Install RIP for NWLink IPX/SPX on a Windows NT Server.

9. Configure a Windows NT Server computer to act as a DHCP relay.

10. Install and configure IIS on an NT Server computer. Use the ftp command at the command prompt on another computer to access the FTP server.

11. Install the Network Monitoring Agent on an NT Workstation or Server computer, and Network Monitor on another computer. Capture a set of packets and view them.

Practice Test

Test Questions

1. If resources in the WEST domain are made available to users in the EAST and SOUTH domains, which domain(s) are the trusted domains?

    a.   EAST and SOUTH

    b.   WEST

    c.   EAST, WEST, and SOUTH

    d.   Not enough information to answer

2. You are configuring a directory services architecture for a network with five domains. Two of the domains contain users, and the remaining domains contain resources. Which domain model are you using?

    a.   Single domain

    b.   Single master domain

    c.   Multiple master domain

    d.   Complete trust

3. If a complete trust model is used between five domains, how many total trust relationships are required?

    a.   5

    b.   10

    c.   20

    d.   25

4. Trust relationships between domains are created using which utility?

    a.   Server Manager

    b.   User Manager for Domains

    c.   Trust Manager

    d.   Domain Manager

5. To ensure the fastest synchronization, which portion of a trust relationship should be created first?

    a.   Add the trusted domain to the list on the trusting domain

    b.   Add the trusting domain to the list on the trusted domain

    c.   Either a or b; there is no difference in synchronization time

6. Which of the following can be members of a local group? (select all that apply)

    a.   Global groups

    b.   Other local groups

    c.   Users

    d.   Trusted domains

7. Which protocol is used to support NetBIOS name resolution?

    a.   TCP/IP

    b.   DHCP

    c.   WINS

    d.   DNS

8. Which of the following services are *not* included in Services for Macintosh?

    a.   Macintosh clients can access Windows NT files

    b.   Macintosh clients can print to Windows NT printers

    c.   Windows clients can print to Macintosh printers

    d.   Windows clients can access files on a Macintosh

9. Which software allows DHCP to work across a router?

    a.   DHCP Server

    b.   IPX Router

    c.   IP Forwarding

    d.   DHCP Relay

10. Which of the following computers should not be configured to obtain an IP address through DHCP?

    a.   Windows 95 clients

    b.   Windows NT Workstation clients

c. DHCP servers

d. WINS servers

11. You are using DHCP to manage IP addresses on a network. 20 users are sharing a pool of 10 IP addresses, but no more than 10 users are online at a time. Users are receiving errors when they boot their machines and are not issued an IP address. Which of the following is a possible solution to this problem?

a. Reserve an IP address for each user

b. Decrease the lease duration in DHCP manager

c. Modify workstations to use a WINS server instead

d. Assign a fixed IP address to the DHCP server

12. Which file is a list of NetBIOS host names and IP addresses?

a. DNS.DAT

b. LMHOSTS

c. HOSTS

d. NETBIOS.LST

13. Which of the following is not consulted in the process of NetBIOS name resolution?

a. HOSTS file

b. LMHOSTS file

c. WINS server

d. Broadcasts

14. Which of the following are used for TCP/IP host name resolution? (select all that apply)

a. LMHOSTS file

b. HOSTS file

c. DNS

d. WINS

15. The database of names and addresses used by DNS server is called:

a. A zone

b. A scope

c. The LMHOSTS file

d. The HOSTS file

16. You need to support DNS on your network. You have installed a DNS server, but would like to avoid manually entering the database of host names and IP addresses. Which of the following may be a solution to this problem?

   a.   Configure DNS to use the HOSTS file

   b.   Configure DNS to use WINS resolution

   c.   Install a WINS server instead of DNS

   d.   Enable the Automatic Database Generation option in DNS Server

17. Which of the following is a Windows NT service that allows Macintosh clients to access Windows NT resources?

   a.   AppleTalk

   b.   LocalTalk

   c.   Services for Macintosh

   d.   Apple Services for NT

18. When the appropriate software is installed, Macintosh clients can access which files?

   a.   Files on a FAT volume

   b.   Files on any NTFS volume

   c.   Files on any Macintosh-accessible volume

   d.   Any files on the NT server

19. Macintosh-accessible volumes can be created on which types of volumes?

   a.   FAT

   b.   NTFS

   c.   Either FAT or NTFS

   d.   The system partition only

20. Which types of routing are supported by Windows NT Server? (select all that apply)

   a.   TCP/IP routing

   b.   DHCP forwarding

   c.   NetBIOS routing

   d.   IPX/SPX routing

21. You are managing a network with two subnets. You have recently installed the TCP/IP protocol, and need to set up one or more DHCP servers to assign IP addresses. You are using a scope of 20 IP addresses.

   Required Result: Workstations on both subnets must be able to use DHCP.

   Optional Result: The server(s) should support 20 users on a single subnet, 20 users on the other subnet, or 20 users distributed between the two.

Optional Result: The server(s) should support centralized administration of the DHCP address pool.

Solution: Install a single DHCP server on one of the subnets. Install DHCP Relay Agent on a server on the other subnet with the appropriate DHCP server specified.

    a. The solution meets the required result and both of the optional results.

    b. The solution meets the required result and one of the optional results.

    c. The solution meets the required result only.

    d. The solution does not meet the required result.

22. Which types of routing are supported by default on all Windows NT computers?

    a. Static IP routing

    b. Dynamic IP routing

    c. Static IPX routing

    d. Dynamic IPX routing

23. Which service should be installed from the Services tab of the Network control panel to add support for dynamic IP routing?

    a. Dynamic Router

    b. RIP for Internet Protocol

    c. RIP for NWLink

    d. Multiprotocol Router

24. You have a Windows NT Workstation computer with one network adapter. The computer is configured to use the TCP/IP and IPX protocols. What additional configuration is needed to make the computer function as a dynamic IP router?

    a. Install RIP for Internet Protocol

    b. Install the NetBEUI protocol

    c. Install an additional network adapter

    d. Upgrade to Windows NT Server

25. Which of the following is a protocol primarily used for communication with IBM mainframe computers and networked printers?

    a. NWLink

    b. TCP/IP

    c. DLC

    d. LocalTalk

26. You are installing a Windows NT Server computer for use as a web server. The machine will be backed up regularly and files are rarely changed, so fault tolerance is not a major issue. You want to install a disk configuration that allows for high speed when many users are accessing the web server.

Required Result: The disk configuration should allow the fastest possible read speeds using a maximum of five physical disks.

Optional Result: The disk configuration should also improve disk write speeds.

Optional Result: The disk configuration should provide at least 5 GB of storage space.

Solution: Install a SCSI controller with five 1-GB drives. Configure the drives as a stripe set (without parity) using the available space on all drives.

    a. The solution meets the required result and both of the optional results.

    b. The solution meets the required result and one of the optional results.

    c. The solution meets the required result only.

    d. The solution does not meet the required result.

27. Which dialog is used to configure a network printer as a printer pool?

    a. Printers category of Network properties

    b. Ports category of Printer properties

    c. Pool property of Print device

    d. Spool property of Printer properties

28. Which of the following types of permissions provide the greatest degree of security?

    a. NTFS permissions

    b. FAT permissions

    c. Share permissions

29. Which type of user profile can be used to force a user to use certain desktop settings?

    a. Local user profile

    b. Roaming user profile

    c. Mandatory user profile

    d. Computer profile

30. Which of the following can be used to disallow access to the Find option on the desktop for any users of a certain computer?

    a. Mandatory user profile

    b. User policy

    c.   Computer policy

    d.   Local user profile

31. Which of the following computer types can be used for remote administration of a Windows NT Server computer? (select all that apply)

    a.   Windows 3.1

    b.   Windows for Workgroups

    c.   Windows NT Workstation

    d.   Windows 95

32. Which service or utility allows clients with NetWare client software to access shares on a Windows NT Server computer without additional client software?

    a.   CSNW

    b.   GSNW

    c.   FPNW

    d.   Migration Tool for NetWare

33. Which of the following protocols is an extension of the BootP protocol?

    a.   DNS

    b.   DHCP

    c.   TCP/IP

    d.   WINS

34. Which of the components of IIS includes support for the HTTP protocol?

    a.   Gopher server

    b.   WWW server

    c.   FTP server

    d.   DNS server

35. Which of the following utilities is used to configure the Internet Information Server?

    a.   IIS control panel

    b.   Internet Administrator

    c.   Internet Service Manager

    d.   Remote Access Admin

36. Which of the following TCP/IP ports is typically used for a web server?

    a.   21

    b.   70

    c.   25

    d.   80

37. You are running a web server on a Windows NT Server computer with 32 MB of RAM, a Pentium processor, and 2 GB of disk storage. Users are able to access web documents, but at busy times of the day some users report receiving an "access denied" error. What is the likely solution to this problem?

    a.   Add more disk storage

    b.   Increase the Maximum Connections value

    c.   Add more RAM

    d.   Increase the Connection Timeout value

38. Which of the following is a limitation of Personal Web Server (PWS) on Windows NT Workstation, but does not apply to Windows NT Server running IIS?

    a.   No Gopher support

    b.   No support for the HTTP protocol

    c.   Limit of 10 incoming connections

    d.   Limit of 2 GB of disk storage

39. Which of the following is a limitation of RAS in Windows NT Workstation but not in Windows NT Server?

    a.   Limit of 1 incoming connection

    b.   Limit of 10 incoming connections

    c.   Limit of 1 outgoing connection

    d.   Limit of 1 installed modem

40. A user running a word processing application is able to read files from the document directory, but is unable to save to the same directory. What is the most likely problem?

    a.   Network cable problem

    b.   User has no permissions for the directory

    c.   User has incorrect permissions for the directory

    d.   User's machine needs to be restarted

41. You are trying to install Disk Striping with parity on two 500-MB disk drives on the same controller and format them with the NTFS file system. You are unable to create the volume. What is the most likely problem?

    a.   Drives must be at least 1 GB

    b.   3 or more drives are required

    c.   NTFS is not supported

    d.   Each drive must have its own controller

42. Which Performance Monitor option can be used to write counter values to a file, establishing a baseline for performance?

    a. Alert

    b. Log

    c. Chart

    d. Report

43. When attempting to boot a Windows NT Server computer, a "Missing Operating System" message is displayed. What is the most likely problem?

    a. BOOT.INI file missing or corrupt

    b. BOOTSECT.DOS missing

    c. Boot sector corrupted or invalid

    d. NTLDR file missing

44. TCP/IP protocol counters for Performance Monitor are installed with which service?

    a. SMTP

    b. SNMP

    c. TCP/IP

    d. RIP for Internet Protocol

45. Which of the following capabilities are available in the version of Network Monitor included with Windows NT Server? (select all that apply)

    a. Monitor packets addressed to the local computer

    b. Monitor packets addressed from the local computer

    c. Monitor packets between two other computers

    d. Monitor other users of Network Monitor

46. You want to use Network Monitor to monitor traffic to and from a Windows NT Workstation computer, and capture the data on a Windows NT Server computer. Which service should be installed on the NT Workstation computer?

    a. Network Monitor Tools

    b. Network Analyzer

    c. Network Monitor Agent

    d. SMS

47. Which utility allows you to define a password for users of Network Monitor to capture and display packets from a workstation?

    a. Network Monitor Agent

    b. Network Monitor

c. Monitoring Agent control panel

d. SNMP Manager

48. Which Windows NT utility allows you to back up and restore the registry?

   a. REGEDIT

   b. REGEDT32

   c. BACKUP.EXE

   d. NTBACKUP.EXE

49. Which of the following utilities allows you to search the entire registry for a specific key or value?

   a. REGEDT32

   b. REGISTRY.EXE

   c. Server Manager

   d. REGEDIT

50. Which of the following protocols are supported by the RAS server? (select all that apply)

   a. TCP/IP

   b. PPP

   c. NetBEUI

   d. IPX/SPX

51. You are managing a network using a single master domain. The CENTRAL domain is the master. EAST and WEST domains contain resources, and are physically located across WAN links. Users in the EAST and WEST domains are complaining about slow logon times. You must choose a solution to improve logon times.

   Required Result: Improve user logon time for EAST and WEST.

   Optional Result: Reduce WAN traffic required for logons.

   Optional Result: Improve user logon time for the CENTRAL domain.

   Solution: Install two BDCs for the CENTRAL domain: one in the same physical location as the EAST domain, and one in the location of the WEST domain.

   a. The solution meets the required result and both of the optional results.

   b. The solution meets the required result and only one of the optional results.

   c. The solution meets the required result only.

   d. The solution does not meet the required result.

Answers to Questions

1. A. EAST and SOUTH are the trusted (user) domains.

2. C. Since two domains contain users, this would be the multiple master domain model.

3. C. A complete trust between five domains uses 20 trusts (5 * 4).

4. B. Trust relationships are created using the User Manager for Domains utility.

5. B. The trusting domain should be added to the list on the trusted domain first for the fastest synchronization.

6. A, C. Global groups and users can be members of a local group.

7. C. The WINS (Windows Internet Naming Service) service resolves NetBIOS names.

8. D. Services for Macintosh does not allow Windows clients to access files on Macintosh computers.

9. D. DHCP Relay allows DHCP to work across a router.

10. C, D. DHCP servers and WINS servers require a constant address, and should not use DHCP.

11. B. Decreasing the lease duration will make addresses available sooner after users log off, which should alleviate the problem.

12. B. The LMHOSTS file is a list of NetBIOS hostnames and addresses.

13. A. The HOSTS file is used for hostname resolution and is not used for NetBIOS resolution.

14. B, C. The HOSTS file and DNS are used in TCP/IP hostname resolution. The LMHOSTS file (choice A) and WINS (choice D) are used strictly for NetBIOS resolution.

15. A. The DNS name and address database is called a zone.

16. B. DNS can pass requests to WINS, which does not require a manually entered database.

17. C. Services for Macintosh allows Macintosh clients to access Windows NT resources.

18. C. Macintosh clients can access only files within a Macintosh-accessible volume.

19. B. Macintosh-accessible volumes can be created only on NTFS partitions.

20. A, B, D. Windows NT Server supports TCP/IP routing, DHCP forwarding, and IPX/SPX routing. NetBIOS (choice C) is a non-routable protocol.

21. A. The solution meets the required result and both of the optional results. Workstations on either subnet can use DHCP. Since a single DHCP server is in use, the 20 addresses can be distributed to any combination of nodes from the two subnets. A single DHCP server also provides centralized administration.

22. A, C. Static IP and IPX routing are supported by default. Dynamic routing requires an additional service (RIP for IPX or RIP for IP).

23. B. RIP for Internet Protocol should be installed to add dynamic IP routing support.

24. A, C, D. To function as a dynamic IP router, RIP for Internet Protocol should be installed. The computer will also need at least one more network card to be useful as a router. Only Windows NT Server includes the RIP for Internet Protocol service.

25. C. DLC is used primarily for communication with mainframe computers and networked printers.

26. A. The solution meets the required result and both of the optional results. A stripe set without parity provides fast read speed, improves write speeds, and would provide 5 GB of storage space.

27. B. The Ports category of the Printer properties dialog is used to configure a printer pool.

28. A. NTFS permissions provide the greatest degree of security.

29. C. A mandatory user profile can force the user to use certain desktop settings.

30. C. A computer policy can be used to disallow access to the Find option. While a user policy (choice B) can also restrict access to the Find option, this would affect one or more users rather than a certain computer.

31. C, D. Windows NT Workstation or Windows 95 can be used for remote administration.

32. C. FPNW (File and Print Services for NetWare) allows clients running NetWare client software to access Windows NT resources.

33. B. DHCP is an extension of the BootP protocol.

34. B. The WWW server in IIS uses the HTTP protocol.

35. C. The Internet Service Manager utility is used to configure IIS.

36. D. TCP/IP port 80 is typically used for an HTTP (web) server.

37. B. The Maximum Connections value in the WWW service properties dialog in Internet Service Manager limits the number of concurrent users.

38. C. PWS is limited to 10 incoming connections, as is NT Workstation itself.

39. A. Windows NT Workstation's RAS server is limited to one incoming connection.

40. C. Since the user is able to access the directory but cannot write files, incorrect permissions are the most likely problem.

41. B. Disk Striping with Parity requires a minimum of 3 drives.

42. B. The Log option in Performance Monitor writes counter values to a file.

43. C. This message usually indicates a problem with the boot sector.

44. B. The SNMP (Simple Network Management Protocol) service includes Performance Monitor counters for TCP/IP.

45. A, B, D. The version of Network Monitor included with Windows NT Server can monitor packets addressed to or from the local computer, and can monitor other users of Network Monitor. It cannot monitor packets between other computers (choice C).

46. C. Since the NT Workstation computer is being monitored but will not run Network Monitor, it requires the Network Monitor Agent service.

47. C. The Monitoring Agent control panel allows you to define a password for users of Network Monitor.

48. D. NTBACKUP.EXE allows you to back up and restore the local registry.

49. D. REGEDIT allows searches of the entire registry.

50. A, B, C, D. The RAS server supports TCP/IP, NetBEUI, and IPX/SPX, and the PPP dial-up protocol.

51. B. The solution meets the required result (improved user logon time for EAST and WEST) and one of the optional results (Reduce WAN traffic for logons). Since users of the CENTRAL domain are local to the PDC, the additional BDCs will not improve their logon time.

Highlighter's Index

Directory Services

Domains

One domain can support a maximum of 40,000 accounts (26,000 user accounts plus 26,000 computer accounts)

One BDC recommended for each 2000 users

Local Groups

Equivalent to groups in NT Workstation

Used to control access to a computer or domain resource

Can contain users and global groups

Global Groups

Available in NT Server domain model only

Used to group users with similar functions

Can contain users only

Can be made members of local groups on trusted domains

Trusted Domains

Trusts are one-way by default

Trusts are non-transitive (if A trusts B and B trusts C, A does not necessarily trust C)

Trusting domain: Contains resources to be shared

Trusted domain: Contains users who require access to resources

Helpful mnemonic: *Resources trust users*

For fastest synchronization, add trusting domain to list on trusted domain first

Trust Types

Simple (one-way) trust: One trusting domain, one trusted

Bidirectional (two-way) trust: Two domains; each is trusting and trusted

Complex trust: A combination of trusts between three or more domains

Single Domain Model

One domain, no trusts

Maximum of 40,000 accounts

Master Domain Model

Maximum of 40,000 accounts

One master (trusted) domain

One or more resource (trusting) domains

Each resource domain trusts master domain

Total trusts: One per resource domain

Multiple Master Domain Model

Maximum of 40,000 accounts per master domain

Two or more master (trusted) domains

One or more resource (trusting) domains

Two-way trusts between master domains

One-way trusts between each resource domain and master

Total trusts: (master domains) * (master domains - 1) + (resource domains * master domains)

Complete Trust Model

All domains are both trusted and trusting

Two-way trust between each domain and all other domains

Total trusts: (domains) * (domains - 1)

Advanced Network Configuration

DHCP Server

Assigns IP addresses dynamically from pool (scope)

Must create at least one scope

Addresses can be reserved for particular hosts

Managed with DHCP Manager utility

Can also dynamically assign gateway addresses, WINS addresses, etc.

WINS Server

Three methods of NetBIOS resolution: LMHOSTS file, broadcasts, WINS

Translates NetBIOS names to IP addresses

Configure with WINS Manager utility

DNS Server

Translates IP hostnames to IP addresses

Two methods of host name resolution: HOSTS file, DNS

Must create at least one zone (database) of names and addresses

Configure with DNS Manager utility

Services for Macintosh

Allows Macintosh clients to access NT files and printers

Allows NT clients to access Macintosh printers

Create Macintosh-accessible volume within NTFS volume with Server Manager

---

Internet Services

Multiprotocol Router (MPR)

Included with NT Server

Can route IP, IPX, Appletalk, relay DHCP

Static routing uses fixed (manual) routing tables

Dynamic routing uses protocol (such as RIP) to maintain route table

IP Routing

Static routing built into Windows NT

Use route command to manage static routes

Dynamic routing: Install RIP for Internet Protocol

DHCP Relay

Forwards DHCP requests between subnets

Can run on any Windows NT computer

Some routers already support DHCP (BOOTP) forwarding

IPX Routing

Static routing supported by default

Dynamic routing requires RIP for NWLink IPX/SPX Protocol

NetBIOS Broadcast Propagation option allows network browsing

Internet Information Server (IIS)

IIS 2.0 is included with NT Server

Supports WWW (HTTP), FTP, Gopher services

Configure with Internet Service Manager

Troubleshooting

Performance Monitor

Use to baseline server performance

Options: Chart, Alert, Log, Report

Install SNMP service for TCP/IP counters

Network Monitor

Can capture packets to/from local computer and broadcasts

Version included with SMS supports promiscuous (all packets) mode

Requires Network Monitor Agent on monitored computer

Requires Network Monitor Tools/Agent on monitoring computer

Can also scan network for other Network Monitor users

Server Optimization

Modify with Properties dialog for Server service

Minimize Memory Used (networks with 10 or fewer users)

Balance (networks under 64 users)

Maximize Throughput for File Sharing (64 users or more)

Maximize Throughput for Network Applications (for application servers)

Calculating Directory Services Database Size

User accounts: 1K

Global groups: 512 bytes plus 12 bytes per group member

Local groups: 512 bytes plus 36 bytes per group member

Computer accounts: 512 bytes each

Domain Controllers

32 MB of RAM supports 7,500 users maximum

64 MB of RAM supports 15,000 users maximum

128 MB of RAM supports 20,000 users maximum

One BDC recommended per 2,000 users

BDCs across WAN links improve performance

Optimize synchronization with ChangeLogSize and ReplicationGovernor values

PART 5

Windows 95

Exam Overview

Windows 95 is the most popular desktop operating system for Intel-based computers. Currently the most widely-used version of Windows, it is a 32-bit operating system with support for preemptive multitasking. Windows 95 has the same basic user interface as Windows NT 4.0.

Microsoft's MCSE Exam 70-064, *Implementing and Supporting Microsoft Windows 95*, covers the use of Windows 95 as a desktop operating system and network client. It includes information ranging from the basic features and installation of Windows 95 to its more technical aspects.

The Windows 95 exam is one of the two choices for the MCSE desktop operating systems requirement. The other choice, Exam 70-073, *Implementing and supporting Microsoft Windows NT Workstation 4.0*, is covered in Part 2 of this book. An exam for Windows 98 will be released by late 1998, but the Windows 95 exam is not currently scheduled to be retired.

The Windows 95 exam is generally considered to be one of the easiest MCSE exams, and the easier of the two desktop operating system exams. Even if you are experienced at using and supporting Windows 95, however, you should study this chapter. The exam covers many items, such as Windows 95's architecture and memory use, that you may not have run into.

In order to prepare for this chapter and the Windows 95 exam, you should be familiar with the concepts introduced in Part 1, "Networking Essentials." You should also have some real-world experience using and administering Windows 95 in a networked environment, and a basic background knowledge of MS-DOS and PC architecture.

Objectives

Need to Apply	_Reference_
Plan a Windows 95 installation.	"Planning the Installation" on page 332
Install Windows 95.	"Installing Windows 95" on page 334
Upgrade a Windows 3.x installation.	"Upgrading Windows 3.x" on page 336
Create a dual-boot system.	"Configuring Multi-Boot Systems" on page 337
Install network adapters, services, protocols, and clients.	"Installing Network Components" on page 339
Access network resources using drive mappings and mapped drives.	"Accessing Network Resources" on page 348
Configure Dial-up Networking.	"Dial-Up Networking" on page 349
Install hardware under Windows 95.	"Installing Hardware" on page 351
Partition hard disks and manage disk compression.	"Disk Configuration" on page 353
Backup data with the Backup utility.	"Backing up Data" on page 355
Configure shared files and printers.	"File Sharing" on page 356
Configure modems.	"Modems" on page 358
Remotely manage a Windows 95 computer.	"Remote Administration" on page 361
Use Net Watcher and System Monitor to monitor the computer.	"Monitoring Performance" on page 362
Correct disk problems with Disk Defragmenter and ScanDisk.	"Optimizing Disk Storage" on page 363

Windows 95

Study Guide

This chapter includes the following sections, which address topics covered on the Windows 95 MCSE exam:

Windows 95 Basics
Introduces Windows 95's features and its internal architecture and boot process, and provides an introduction to Windows 95's user interface.

Windows 95 Installation
Describes the planning required for an installation of Windows 95, the installation process, and special considerations such as multi-boot systems, upgrades, and automated setup.

Installing Network Components
Describes the network components of Windows 95 (protocols, services, adapters, and clients) and their use. This section also covers dial-up networking.

Managing Windows 95
Discusses various tasks involved in the administration of Windows 95: Hardware installation, disk drives, file sharing, printers, modems, user profiles and system policies, and remote administration.

Optimization and Troubleshooting
Describes methods of monitoring Windows 95's performance and introduces utilities used to optimize and troubleshoot the system. This section also describes several common Windows 95 problems and their solutions.

Windows 95 Basics

Windows 95, introduced in August 1995, is a 32-bit operating system that supports DOS, 16-bit Windows, and 32-bit Windows applications. Windows 95 is popular for stand-alone desktop machines and as a network client for Windows NT or other networks. A built-in peer-to-peer network system allows simple networks to be constructed using only Windows 95.

Windows 95 improves upon the previous version, Windows 3.11, with a variety of features, among them more stability, better multitasking, support for 32-bit applications, support for long filenames, more support for customization, a versatile desktop and file management system, and built-in support for dial-up networking.

The main alternative to Windows 95 is Windows NT Workstation. The latest version, NT Workstation 4.0, supports the Windows 95 user interface and runs most of the same applications. Windows NT Workstation has the following basic advantages over Windows 95:

- All components are 32-bit, improving speed on 32-bit processors.
- Multitasking is more reliable: DOS applications have separate memory areas by default, and 16-bit Windows applications can be configured to run in separate memory areas.
- Multiprocessing (two CPUs) is supported.
- Non-Intel CPUs (RISC) are also supported.
- Certain POSIX and OS/2 applications are supported.
- NT Workstation includes a great many security features missing from Windows 95.

Although Windows NT is more of an industrial-strength OS, Windows 95 does have certain advantages:

- Less expensive than Windows NT
- Requires less disk space and RAM
- Supports Plug and Play for hardware devices
- Supports a larger number of DOS applications
- Greater compatibility with Windows 3.1

On the Exam

For the exam, you should know the basic differences between Windows 95 and Windows NT Workstation, and the advantages of each. You may wish to review the description of Windows NT Workstation found in Part 2.

Windows 95 Architecture

Windows 95 has a complex architecture designed to support multitasking, multithreading, and multiple types of applications. The following sections examine the underlying workings of Windows 95.

X86 Architecture

Windows 95 was designed for Intel 386 and later processors, and is not compatible with any others. In order to understand Windows 95's components and workings, you should have a basic understanding of the architecture of Intel's x86 processors.

Intel 386 and later processors support two basic modes of operation:

- *Real mode* is the only mode supported by most DOS applications. In this mode memory is addressed in 64K segments, and limited to 16 segments: a total of 1 MB of memory. In DOS, memory is subdivided into 640K of conventional memory and 384K of high memory.

- *Protected mode* is supported by Windows 95, and under DOS by extended (EMS) or expanded (XMS) memory managers. In this mode all memory is addressed in a linear fashion, eliminating the 1-MB limit. Along with better memory support, this mode allows for multitasking support. This mode is also called Enhanced mode.

In protected mode, the x86 processor does not allow all applications to access all areas of memory. Instead, executable components use one of four processor protection modes, or *rings*. These are numbered from Ring 0 to Ring 3, and modeled as a set of concentric rings, with Ring 0 (the highest privilege) in the center and Ring 3 (the lowest privilege) on the outside.

Windows 95 uses two of the available rings:

- *Ring 0* is the most privileged mode. Execution at this ring is the fastest, and applications have direct access to memory and hardware. Since nothing prevents one application from writing over data used by another, Ring 0 is used only for trusted components: the OS itself and device drivers.

- *Ring 3* is the least privileged mode, but provides memory protection. While execution is slower, applications can be confined to their own address space. This ring also allows for the use of virtual memory, described later in this section. This mode is used for less critical operating system components and for user-run applications.

On the Exam

For the Windows 95 MCSE exam, you should know the difference between real and protected mode, and the difference between Ring 0 and Ring 3. You may also need to know which system components (described below) fit into each ring. Rings 1 and 2 are not used by Windows 95 and are not covered in detail on the exam.

Windows 95 Components

Windows 95 consists of a number of interacting components in both Ring 0 and Ring 3. The Ring 0 components include the base operating system and device drivers (described later in this section). The Ring 3 components are arranged as *virtual machines* (VMs).

Virtual machines are self-contained modules that support various functions of Windows 95. There are two basic VMs:

- The System VM, which supports 32-bit (Win32) and 16-bit (Win16) applications as well as basic OS functions

- MS-DOS VMs, which support MS-DOS applications. These VMs are started with their corresponding applications; each MS-DOS application has its own virtual machine.

The system VM is the main control center for Windows applications. It includes several components:

- The Kernel supports memory management and basic system services (file operations, memory management, and multitasking).

- The User module supports interaction with the user: the window-based interface, keyboard input, and the mouse.

- The GDI (graphics device interface) handles communication with the video driver for screen displays. Printing is also supported by the GDI.

- Win32 applications each have their own address space within the system VM, and can communicate with each other through the VM.

- Win16 applications share a single address space and can communicate with each other within this space.

Virtual Memory

Windows 95 uses a virtual memory model. Virtual memory serves two main purposes:

- *Paging*: Memory can be swapped, or paged, to a swap file on a hard disk. This allows for a greater amount of storage than physical memory alone. A system of *demand paging* is used to move the least recently used areas of memory to disk, making room for new storage. When an address within the swap file is requested, it is swapped back into physical memory.

- *Addressing*: Through this model, each 32-bit application is given access to what appears to be a 4-GB address space. A component of Windows 95 called the Virtual Memory Manager maps this virtual address space to actual memory and the swap file. 16-bit Windows applications share a 4-GB address space.

The 4-GB virtual address space is subdivided into areas for different uses, as listed in Table 5-1.

Table 5-1: The Windows 95 Virtual Address Space

Address	Purpose	Notes
0 MB–1 MB	MS-DOS applications	DOS applications are normally written to use this area of memory.

Table 5-1: The Windows 95 Virtual Address Space (continued)

Address	Purpose	Notes
1 MB–4 MB	16-bit Windows applications	Used only by address-dependent applications.
4 MB–2 GB	16- and 32-bit applications	This is the most frequently used area.
2 GB–3 GB	DLLs and APIs	These are components shared by Windows applications.
3 GB–4 GB	Device drivers	These are Ring 0 components.

On the Exam

You should know the address space divisions listed above for the Windows 95 exam. However, the exam does not cover technical details of memory management.

Drivers

Device drivers operate in Ring 0, and communicate with Ring 3 components (applications) to provide access to hardware devices. Windows 95 supports two types of device drivers:

- Protected-mode drivers, written for Windows 95; these usually have the VXD extension.

- Real-mode drivers, written for DOS; these usually have the SYS or EXE extensions.

Protected mode drivers provide better support for Windows 95 and multitasking, so they should be used whenever possible. Real mode drivers are sometimes necessary for using devices that were made for DOS, and do not include Windows-specific drivers.

The Registry

Windows 3.x used files with the *INI* extension to store settings for applications and the system. These included WIN.INI and SYSTEM.INI, used by the system, and a separate *INI* file for each application with configurable settings.

Windows 95 replaces *INI* files with a central database called the *registry*. The registry is a hierarchical database of keys, subkeys, values, and data that is used both by the operating system and by applications.

Along with centralizing the management of settings, the registry provides two important features: first, it's possible to remotely edit the registry of another computer. Second, the registry maintains separate settings for different users of the computer, allowing users to customize their settings without affecting other users.

The registry includes six main subtrees, described below. These are the same subtrees used in Windows NT's registry, although the contents of the subtrees vary between operating systems.

HKEY_CLASSES_ROOT

This key stores file associations, which specify the programs to be run when files with particular extensions are opened.

HKEY_CURRENT_USER

This key stores information about the current settings for the currently logged-in user.

HKEY_LOCAL_MACHINE

This key stores hardware-specific data such as drivers and interrupt settings, as well as software settings that do not change based on the current user.

HKEY_USERS

This key stores settings for each user in separate subkeys. When a user logs in, the appropriate subkey is copied to the HKEY_CURRENT_USER key.

HKEY_CURRENT_CONFIG

This key is used to store dynamic configuration information for the computer. This may be the same as the HKEY_LOCAL_MACHINE key, but may vary if a device was not attached to the system at the most recent boot.

HKEY_DYN_DATA

This key stores dynamic hardware information, specifying the current settings for removable disk drives, PC cards, and other hardware that can be changed without rebooting. This key is created dynamically in memory, and cannot be edited.

On the Exam

You should know the basic functions of each of these keys for the Windows 95 MCSE exam. In addition, you should know how to edit the registry and perform searches as described below.

You can edit the registry with the REGEDIT utility included with Windows 95. This utility is shown in Figure 5-1. REGEDIT allows you to access registry keys using a hierarchical display; in addition, the Find command under the Edit menu allows you to search for text in registry keys, values, or data. This utility is not able to check for errors in registry settings, so you should be careful when modifying registry values.

The registry is stored in two hidden files within the WINDOWS directory, USER.DAT and SYSTEM.DAT. It is automatically backed up each time Windows 95 boots to the USER.DA0 and SYSTEM.DA0 files. In the event of registry corruption, these files can be copied to USER.DAT and SYSTEM.DAT to restore the backup. This must be done in MS-DOS mode, since the files are open while Windows 95 is running.

Windows 95

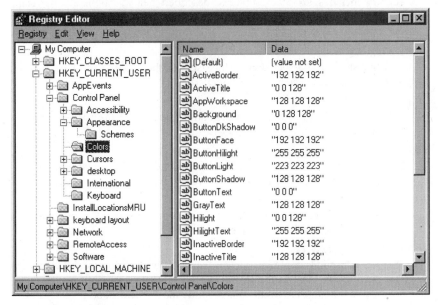

Figure 5-1: The Registry Editor utility

The Boot Process

Windows 95 has a reasonably simple boot process. Microsoft divides the boot process into four phases: bootstrapping, real mode boot, protected mode load, and desktop initialization. The following sections describe each phase in detail. Following these is a discussion of the MSDOS.SYS file, which can be used to customize the boot process.

On the Exam

For the Windows 95 MCSE exam, you should know the phases of the boot process and the files loaded in each phase. This information is also useful in troubleshooting the boot process, described in "Optimization and Trouble-shooting" at the end of this chapter.

Bootstrapping

The bootstrapping phase is handled by the computer's BIOS, and is performed the same way regardless of the operating system being loaded. At initialization, the BIOS initializes Plug and Play devices (described later in this chapter). It then loads the master boot record (MBR) from the primary hard disk and executes it.

Next, control is transferred to the boot sector. The IO.SYS file is then loaded to begin the operating system boot process. Both MS-DOS and Windows 95 use this file, although it serves a slightly different purpose in Windows 95.

Real Mode

The real mode portion of the boot process can be easily distinguished because it operates in text mode. Depending on the configuration of the computer, you may see the Windows 95 animated logo or a series of messages from drivers and TSR programs. (The Windows 95 logo is stored as LOGO.SYS on the boot drive).

This phase reads the MSDOS.SYS file (described later). It then loads the hardware-specific portion of the registry (SYSTEM.DAT) into memory. If compression is enabled, the DRVSPACE.BIN file is also loaded.

Finally, the CONFIG.SYS and AUTOEXEC.BAT files are read and executed, if present. These files are included for DOS compatibility, and are used to load real-mode drivers and set environment variables. They are not directly required by Windows 95.

Protected Mode

In this phase the CPU is switched to protected mode. The protected mode phase begins with the loading and execution of the WIN.COM file. This program loads VMM32.VXD, a device driver that handles several default devices. Any other defined device drivers are also started.

Next, the files that make up the system VM are loaded: kernel (KERNEL32.DLL), user (USER32.DLL), and GDI (GDI32.DLL). The video driver is also initialized, switching the display to VGA mode, or the appropriate mode set in the Control Panel.

Desktop Initialization

Finally, the shell (EXPLORER.EXE) is executed to display the desktop. This phase also executes any Windows programs that are defined to execute at boot time. These include the contents of the Startup group within the Programs group in the Start menu, as well as the following registry keys under the HKEY_LOCAL_MACHINE\SOFTWARE\Microsoft\Windows\CurrentVersion subkey:

- Run (programs listed here are run each time Windows 95 starts)

- RunOnce (these are removed from the registry after running; this is used for installation programs)

The LOAD= and RUN= entries, if any, in the WIN.INI file are also executed at this point. These are included for compatibility with Windows 3.x.

The Startup Menu

Windows 95 can optionally display a menu at the beginning of the real mode phase of booting. This option can be activated in the MSDOS.SYS file, described below; additionally, you can press F8 when the "Starting Windows 95" message appears to display the menu.

The startup menu includes the following options:

- Normal: The default boot mode, equivalent to the boot process when the menu is not displayed.

- Logged: The same as a normal boot, but a log of the boot process is displayed in the \BOOTLOG.TXT file.

- Safe mode: This mode loads a minimum of drivers (for example, the default VGA driver is used rather than the defined display driver). This mode is usually used to change settings to prevent a crash at boot time.

- Safe mode with network support: The same as safe mode, but with network drivers.

- Step-by-step confirmation: Prompts you for each step in the real mode phase of installation, including AUTOEXEC.BAT and CONFIG.SYS entries.

- Command prompt only: Skips the protected mode phase of installation and exits to the MS-DOS 7.0 command prompt.

- Safe mode command prompt only: Exits immediately to the MS-DOS 7.0 command prompt.

- Previous version of MS-DOS: Loads the previously installed DOS version. This option is only available if Windows 95 was installed as an upgrade.

The MSDOS.SYS File

Windows 95's boot options are stored in the MSDOS.SYS file. This file replaces the MSDOS.SYS binary file used in MS-DOS. It is a text file that can be used to change various settings used in the real mode portion of the boot process. All of these settings are optional; the default values are assumed if they are not defined.

This file is divided into two sections. The [Paths] section specifies options relating to disk directories, while the [Options] section includes various boot options. Table 5-2 describes the entries in the [Paths] section, and Table 5-3 describes the entries in the [Options] section.

Table 5-2: MSDOS.SYS Entries in the [Paths] Section

Option	Default	Description
HostWinBootDrv	C	The drive to boot Windows 95 from
WinBootDir	C:\WINDOWS	The directory for the Windows startup files (WIN.COM, etc.)
WinDir	C:\WINDOWS	The main Windows 95 directory

Table 5-3: MSDOS.SYS Entries in the [Options] Section

Option	Default	Description
BootDelay	2	Delay (seconds) to wait for function keys at startup
BootFailSafe	0	If set to 1, forces safe mode to be used at startup
BootGUI	1	Specifies that WIN.COM will be started; otherwise, the command prompt is displayed
BootKeys	1	Enables function keys (F8, etc.) at startup
BootMenu	0	Set to 1 to display the startup menu at every boot
BootMenuDefault	3 or 4	The default startup menu item

Table 5-3: MSDOS.SYS Entries in the [Options] Section (continued)

Option	Default	Description
BootMenuDelay	30	The delay (seconds) before the default startup menu item is selected
BootMulti	0	Enables the previous version of MS-DOS to be selected from the startup menu
BootWarn	1	Enables a warning before automatically entering safe mode
BootWin	1	Makes Windows 95 the default operating system
DblSpace	1	Loads DBLSPACE.BIN for disk compression
DoubleBuffer	1	Loads a double buffering SCSI driver
DrvSpace	1	Loads DRVSPACE.BIN for disk compression
LoadTop	1	Loads COMMAND.COM at the top of conventional memory
Logo	1	Enables display of the animated Windows 95 logo
Network	1	Enables the Safe Mode with Network Support option in the startup menu

---

On the Exam

You don't need to know all of the above flags for the MCSE exam. You should be familiar with the MSDOS.SYS file and its purpose, and the basic options such as BootMenu.

Using Windows 95

Windows 95's user interface is different from previous versions of Windows; the most noticeable change is that the desktop can contain program icons, and the Start menu replaces Program Manager. The following sections describe various components of the Windows 95 user interface.

The Desktop

The desktop is displayed when Windows 95 first loads. This consists of a background (configurable in the Display control panel, described later in this chapter), one or more icons, and the taskbar at the bottom of the screen. The taskbar includes three items:

- The Start button on the left side opens the Start menu.

- The middle portion of the bar displays buttons for currently running programs and open windows.

- The right-hand portion is the notification area, or tray. This area displays small icons for various services (such as a modem activity indicator) and an optional clock.

Windows 95

Icons displayed by default on the desktop include My Computer (opens a list of disk drives), Network Neighborhood (browses network resources), and Recycle Bin (a destination to drag files to be deleted).

The desktop is physically stored in a directory of the hard disk, typically \Windows\Desktop. Icons called shortcuts can be created on the desktop to link to applications or documents; actual files and folders can also be stored on the desktop. Shortcuts are indicated by an arrow in the lower left corner of the icon.

The Start Menu

The Start menu is Windows 95's main interface for running applications. Although applications can be run from desktop icons or from disk directories, most installed applications automatically create an icon in the Start menu. The Start menu includes these submenus by default:

Programs
> This is where most applications create icons or submenus, and where the applications included with Windows 95 are included. You can also create submenus directly under the Start menu.

Documents
> Displays a list of recently used documents. Selecting a document runs the associated application.

Settings
> Provides options for running the Control Panel (described below) and changing taskbar settings.

Find
> Searches for files, directories, or networked computers.

Help
> Displays the main Windows 95 help screen.

Run
> Opens a command-line window to run a program. Enter the path, the filename, and any command-line options. You can also specify a document filename (to be opened using its associated program) or a directory or UNC share name (to be opened in Explorer).

The Start menu is physically stored as a set of shortcuts and subdirectories in a folder on the disk, typically \Windows\Start Menu.

Windows Explorer

The main Windows 95 shell is EXPLORER.EXE, which is also run in separate instances to browse files or directories. Explorer has two display modes:

- A simple mode that displays a list of files only. This mode is used when you open the My Computer or Network Neighborhood icons. A typical display of the contents of a disk drive in this mode is shown in Figure 5-2.

- A two-column mode that displays a directory tree and a list of files. The Windows Explorer option in the Start menu uses this format.

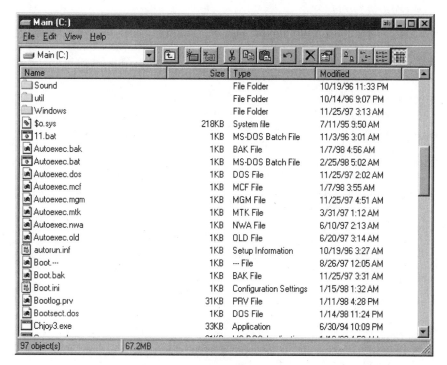

Figure 5-2: Explorer displays the contents of a disk

Creating a shortcut to a directory opens the one-column Explorer view. You can create an icon for a two-column view by using a command line such as the following:

```
explorer.exe /e,c:\windows
```

You can select *Options* from the View menu in any Explorer window to display three categories of options:

Folders

Choose whether items you open from the current Explorer window are displayed in the same window or a new window.

View

By default, MS-DOS extensions are not displayed in Explorer, and a variety of file types (such as DLL and SYS extensions) are not included in the listings. These options can be changed in this dialog.

File Types

While the previous settings are unique to particular Explorer windows, the settings in this dialog affect the computer globally. This dialog allows you to change the associations between file extensions and applications.

The Control Panel

Select *Control Panel* from the Settings menu in the Start menu to open the Windows 95 Control Panel. This is a set of icons displayed in an Explorer window, although it does not represent an actual disk directory. The following settings dialogs, called *applets*, are included in the Control Panel:

Accessibility Options
Provides options that may be useful for users with special needs. These options can be installed during the installation of Windows 95, or added using the *Add/Remove Programs* option, described below.

Add New Hardware
This opens the Add New Hardware wizard, which is able to search for new hardware or install drivers you specify. This is described in the "Managing Windows 95" section, later in this chapter.

Add/Remove Programs
Allows you to add or remove Windows components and other programs. The first tab of this dialog, Install/Uninstall, lists recently installed Windows 95 applications and allows you to run their uninstall programs. The second tab, Windows Setup, allows you to add and remove Windows 95 components. The third tab, Startup Disk, is described in the "Troubleshooting Common Problems" section of this chapter.

Date/Time
Allows you to set the computer's internal clock with the current time and date, and to set the local time zone.

Display
Allows you to change the desktop background (a wallpaper image, color, or pattern), select a screen saver, and modify the system colors and fonts. The Settings tab of this dialog allows you to change video adapter settings; use the Change Display Type button to change the display driver.

Fonts
Displays a list of currently installed fonts, and allows you to install or remove fonts. Windows 95 supports Truetype fonts as well as Windows 3.x style bitmap screen fonts.

Keyboard
Allows you to set the keyboard speed and repeat rate. You can also specify the language (keyboard mapping) and the type of hardware keyboard installed.

Modems
Displays a list of installed modems. This control panel is further described in the "Managing Windows 95" section, later in this chapter.

Mouse
Allows you to specify settings for the mouse, such as the speed of the mouse pointer. You can also choose custom mouse pointers.

Multimedia
Allows you to configure audio devices (sound cards), video playback, MIDI (music), and audio CD playing with a CD-ROM drive.

Network

Allows configuration of networking features. This control panel is described in detail in the "Installing Network Components" section, later in this chapter.

Passwords

Includes settings for user accounts and remote administration. These options are described later in this chapter.

Printers

Allows you to install, configure, or manage local or network printers. This control panel is described in the "Managing Windows 95" section, later in this chapter.

Regional Settings

Allows you to change the language used for screen displays in programs that support multiple languages, and to change region-specific number, currency, and time and date formats.

Sounds

Allows you to select sounds (stored in the Windows-standard WAV format) to be played when system events occur.

System

Allows you to modify system settings, such as drivers for hardware devices. This control panel was described in detail in "Windows 95 Basics."

On the Exam

For the Windows 95 MCSE exam, you should be familiar with all the above Control Panel applets, and should have experience using each of them to change Windows 95 settings.

Running Windows Applications

Windows 95 supports three types of applications:

- MS-DOS applications, running in a window or in full-screen mode
- 32-bit Windows (Win32) applications
- 16-bit Windows (Win16) applications

These types of applications are described in detail in the following sections.

Windows 95 Applications

True 32-bit Windows applications are supported within the Windows 95 System virtual machine. Each has its own virtual memory address space. Win95 applications also include a messaging queue, used to send messages between applications and the system.

Windows 95 applications fully support two features of Windows 95:

- OLE (Object Linking and Embedding) allows an object created in one application to be embedded in a document used for another application. For example, a spreadsheet could be included within a word processing document.

- DDE (Dynamic Data Exchange) supports data communication between applications. In addition, one application can send commands to control another application.

Windows 3.x Applications

16-bit (Windows 3.x) applications are also supported by the System virtual machine in Windows 95. These applications share a virtual memory address space and message queue, and can communicate with each other or with Windows 95 applications.

Because of the shared memory address, a 16-bit application that crashes can cause other currently running 16-bit applications to crash. Application problems such as these are discussed in the "Troubleshooting Common Problems" section of this chapter.

Running DOS Applications

While MS-DOS applications are not as sophisticated as Windows applications, Windows 95 includes a complicated subsystem to allow them to run and be as compatible with DOS as possible. DOS applications each have their own DOS virtual machine and their own virtual address space.

Since DOS applications in general were never meant to support multitasking, it is often necessary to specify particular settings to get an application to run properly. Windows 95 stores these settings in PIF (program information file) files. A default PIF file (DEFAULT.PIF) is used for programs without individual settings.

To set options for executing a program, right-click on the program and select Properties. A tabbed dialog of options is displayed; these options are discussed in the following sections.

Modifying a program's settings creates a PIF file in the same directory as the program, and with the first eight characters of the executable program filename as the PIF filename. You can also right-click on an existing PIF file to modify its settings. PIF files are displayed in Explorer with a shortcut icon, and described as "Shortcut to MS-DOS program."

On the Exam

These DOS application settings are emphasized on the Windows 95 MCSE exam. You should be familiar with the effects of all of the settings described below and have real-world experience using them to get MS-DOS applications to run properly.

General Settings

The options in this tab of the dialog describe the properties of the executable file or PIF file, including file type, parent directory, short filename (described in "Long Filenames" in this chapter), and modification date and time. You can modify the Read-only, Hidden, and Archive properties of the file.

Program Settings

This category of settings includes basic information about the DOS application and the way it will be executed. The following options are included:

Cmd line
> The command line to execute the program. This is usually the executable file name, including the directory path. Any command-line options supported by the application can be specified here.

Working
> The working directory for the application. This directory will be set as the current directory before starting the application. If not specified, the directory containing the application will be used.

Batch file
> An optional DOS batch file that will be processed before running the application. This can be used to set environment variables, create drive mappings, or implement other settings required by the program.

Shortcut key
> If desired, select a keystroke that can be used to start the application.

Run
> For programs that run in a window on the desktop, specify whether the window will be normal, minimized (displayed as an icon only), or maximized (enlarged to use the full screen).

Close on Exit
> If selected, the window will be closed when the MS-DOS program exits. Otherwise, it must be closed manually. Leaving this option unchecked is useful if the program displays information that you wish to read before clearing the display.

Advanced
> Displays the advanced program settings dialog (described in the next section.)

Change Icon
> Allows you to select an icon to represent the application. A default MS-DOS icon is used for programs without particular icons selected.

Advanced Program Settings

The Advanced button in the Program category of the MS-DOS properties displays the Advanced Program Settings dialog. This dialog includes advanced options that may be useful in getting difficult programs to run. The following options are included:

PIF name
Displays the name of the PIF file you are editing.

Prevent MS-DOS-based programs from detecting Windows
If selected, the MS-DOS application will be unable to detect the MS-DOS virtual machine it is running in. Some DOS applications automatically exit if they detect Windows; this setting prevents this, although the program may still be incompatible with Windows.

Suggest MS-DOS mode as necessary
When MS-DOS mode is used to run a DOS application, the GUI portion of Windows is exited and the application is effectively run under DOS 7.0. This allows stubborn applications to run, but does not allow for multitasking—all Windows applications are closed when switching to DOS mode. If this option is selected, Windows will detect DOS applications that attempt to directly access memory or hardware and suggest this mode.

MS-DOS mode
If selected, MS-DOS mode is used unconditionally for the application. This option also enables the remaining options, described below.

Warn before entering MS-DOS mode
If selected, a warning dialog will be displayed, giving you a chance to save information in Windows applications before exiting to MS-DOS mode.

Use current MS-DOS configuration
If selected, the drivers and settings in the AUTOEXEC.BAT and CONFIG.SYS files are used for this application.

Specify a new MS-DOS configuration
If selected, an alternate CONFIG.SYS and AUTOEXEC.BAT can be specified for the application.

Configuration
If the above option is selected, this button displays a dialog allowing you to select common CONFIG.SYS and AUTOEXEC.BAT settings. These are then added to the files for this application.

On the Exam

Since it basically exits Windows, MS-DOS mode should be used only as a last resort for stubborn applications. The memory and screen settings described below may help the application to run without using this mode.

Font Settings

The Fonts tab of the MS-DOS properties dialog displays a selection of fixed-width fonts that can be used to display the application in a window. (If displayed in full screen mode, the standard DOS font is used.)

The Available types option allows you to choose whether bitmap (screen) fonts, TrueType fonts, or both are available. The Font size dialog allows you to select fonts by size. A preview of the font is displayed in the lower portion of the dialog.

Memory Settings

The Memory tab of the MS-DOS properties dialog allows you to change the amount of various types of memory available to the application. The following settings are available:

Conventional memory
Set the total amount of conventional memory (memory below 640K) available to the program. The *Initial environment* option sets the amount of memory available to the program for environment settings.

Expanded (EMS) memory
Specify the amount of EMS memory to be made available to the program. EMS is the standard for using memory over 1 MB supported by memory managers such as EMM386.

Extended (XMS) memory
Specify the amount of XMS memory available to the program. XMS is an older standard that uses bank switching to provide access to memory over 1 MB.

MS-DOS protected-mode (DPMI) memory
Specify the amount of DPMI (DOS protected mode interface) memory to be made available. This is a new standard that allows DOS programs to use memory mapped by Windows 95.

On the Exam

The areas of memory described above are not literal; in other words, an MS-DOS program does not really have access to 640K of conventional memory. These memory amounts are made available from the DOS application's virtual 4-GB memory space.

Screen Settings

The Screen tab of the MS-DOS properties dialog includes options for the application's screen display. The following options are included:

Full-screen
If selected, displays the DOS application in full-screen mode, switching off the Windows desktop and GUI display as it is running. While the program is running, the Alt-Enter keystroke can be used to toggle between full-screen and window modes.

Window
Displays the DOS program in a window using the font settings specified in the Font tab. The number of lines available in the window is set by the *Initial size* option.

Initial size
> Sets the number of lines available in a DOS window. The default value is 25 lines.

Display toolbar
> If selected, a toolbar is displayed at the top of the MS-DOS application's window. This allows you to select font sizes and perform copy and paste operations.

Restore settings on startup
> If selected, any changes you make while running the program (such as changing the font or switching from full-screen to window mode) are remembered and used next time you run the program.

Fast ROM emulation
> If selected, a fast method is used to allow screen access from the MS-DOS program. This option can be turned off if the program is having display problems.

Dynamic memory allocation
> If this option is not selected, enough memory is allocated to allow the program to switch to graphics modes. If this option is selected, the memory not used by the current mode is available for use by other applications, and the program may be unable to switch modes.

Miscellaneous Settings

The final tab of the MS-DOS properties dialog, Misc, includes a variety of settings. This dialog is shown in Figure 5-3. The following categories of options are included:

Foreground
> If the *Allow screen saver* option is selected, the screen saver will be engaged if the system is idle, even if the DOS program is in the foreground. This may slow down the DOS program.

Background
> If the *Always suspend* option is selected, the application is suspended (paused) when it is minimized, or when another program is in the foreground.

Idle Sensitivity
> Specifies how closely Windows monitors the program's use of CPU resources. If Windows finds the program idle, it lowers its priority to allow more speed for other applications. The higher this setting, the more frequent the idle checks.

Mouse
> If the *QuickEdit* option is selected, the mouse can be used to highlight and copy text from the DOS window. If the *Exclusive mode* option is selected, the MS-DOS mouse drivers are used exclusively while the program is in the foreground, preventing the mouse from being used for other applications.

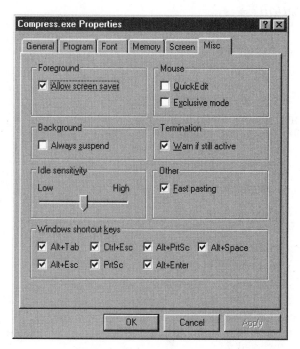

Figure 5-3: DOS Miscellaneous settings

Termination

If the *Warn if still active* option is checked, you are warned if you attempt to close the program's window before the DOS program exits. Not exiting properly may prevent the resources used by the application from being released.

Other

The *Fast pasting* option allows text to be quickly pasted from the clipboard into the MS-DOS application. This may not work for all programs.

Windows shortcut keys

This section includes options for the various shortcut keys used by Windows 95. Each selected key is available while the DOS program is in the foreground, making it undetectable by the DOS program. Keys can be deselected if the DOS program requires the use of the same key combinations.

Windows 95 Installation

Windows 95 includes a versatile installation program that can install Windows 95 on a new computer or upgrade an existing Windows 3.x installation. The sections below discuss the considerations to be made before installing Windows 95 and the installation process.

Planning the Installation

Before installing Windows 95, you should plan the installation by considering various factors: the hardware requirements, supported file systems, and network and security considerations. These are discussed in the sections below.

Hardware Requirements

Windows 95's hardware requirements are more demanding than Windows 3.x. The various requirements of the system are summarized in Table 5-4. You should perform any necessary upgrades on the computer before attempting to install Windows 95.

Table 5-4: Windows 95 Hardware Requirements

Item	Requirement
CPU	386 DX or higher (486 DX or higher recommended)
RAM	4 MB (8 MB recommended)
Display	VGA, Super VGA, or better
Hard disk	SCSI or IDE; 55 MB of space required for OS
Floppy disk	3.5", 1.4 MB
CD-ROM	SCSI or IDE (optional)
Network interface card	Most cards are supported; only required for networked machines

---

In the Real World

While Windows 95 officially requires 4 MB of RAM and Microsoft recommends 8 MB, I recommend 16 MB at the very least. Systems with 8 MB will be very slow when using all but the simplest application software.

Network Planning

Windows 95 supports two basic types of networks:

- Workgroup, or *peer-to-peer* networks, in which each workstation can share resources and handles its own user authentication. This type is best suited for small networks with 10 users or less.

- Domain, or *client-server* networks, in which one or more dedicated servers are used for resource sharing and network-wide user authentication. This type of network can handle large numbers of users.

For a new network, you should determine the type of network best suited to your needs. Windows 95 clients can log on to either type of network, but only a workgroup network can consist entirely of Windows 95 computers. If you are using a domain-based system, a Windows NT Server computer must be used as the domain controller.

File Systems

Windows 95 supports two main file systems:

- FAT (file allocation table) is the standard DOS file system.

- VFAT (virtual FAT) is an extended version of FAT supported by Windows 95 and Windows NT. This adds support for larger capacities, a larger number of files, and long filenames (described later in "Managing Windows 95"). VFAT is also accessible from DOS, but long filenames are not accessible.

Windows 95 does not support the NTFS file system supported by Windows NT. If you will be using Windows NT on the same computer as Windows 95 and need support for NTFS, you should leave room for a separate NTFS partition.

Another file system not supported by Windows 95 is HPFS (high-performance file system). This system is supported by OS/2 and by Windows NT 3.51 and earlier. Windows NT dropped HPFS support in version 4.0.

The Windows 95 installation program requires an existing FAT partition, which will be effectively converted to VFAT during the installation.

Planning File Sharing and Security

Windows 95 supports file and printer sharing: file system directories and printers can be shared, or made available across the network. A basic security scheme allows you to control access to these shared resources. Windows 95 also includes two basic security features:

- *User profiles*: Users can have their own settings for the computer, and an administrator can enforce settings.

- *System policies*: Certain portions of the operating system, such as the Run command and the Shut Down command, can be restricted from user access.

Windows 95

Each of these features is described later in this chapter. You may wish to review this information and plan which features will be used before installing Windows 95.

Installing Windows 95

The Setup (SETUP.EXE) program manages the installation of Windows 95. This program can be run from the Windows 95 CD-ROM or from a network share or local copy of the installation files. Setup can be run from either DOS or Windows 3.x, and will function the same way from either.

The actual installation process occurs in two phases: the real mode phase and the protected mode phase. These are described in the sections below.

Real Mode Phase

The real mode phase is performed in real mode, and can be recognized by the text-based (DOS) displays during this phase. This phase requires little interaction with the user. The following steps are performed:

1. The message "Setup is now going to perform a routine check of your system" is displayed. Press **Enter** to continue, and ScanDisk (described later in "Optimization and Troubleshooting") is run to check the drive for errors and cross-linked files.

2. Setup verifies that the CPU, memory, and DOS version are suitable for installing Windows 95, and checks the available storage space.

3. Setup attempts to unload any TSR programs currently resident to eliminate the possibility of conflicts.

4. Setup requires the use of an extended memory manager. If one is not already loaded, it is loaded at this time.

5. Setup searches for an existing Windows version. If found, a dialog is displayed suggesting that you run Setup from Windows. If Setup is run from Windows, the protected mode phase is executed in this version; otherwise, Windows 95 is loaded from the installation CD-ROM.

Protected Mode Phase

The real mode portion of Setup usually executes quickly. It then transfers control to Windows and switches the CPU to protected mode to continue the installation. The following steps are included:

1. A "Welcome to Windows 95 Setup" dialog is displayed. At this point the mouse driver is loaded, and the mouse can be used to select the remaining options. Press the Continue button.

2. Setup transfers control to the Windows 95 Setup Wizard. A license agreement is displayed; select *Yes* to agree to the conditions and continue the installation.

3. If a version of Windows 3.x is installed on the computer, you are asked whether to upgrade that version or install in a new directory.

4. The setup wizard scans the existing Windows directory (if any) and determines whether you have enough disk space to install Windows.

5. You are prompted for Setup options. You can set up in four ways: *Typical, Portable, Compact,* and *Custom.*

6. You are prompted for the product identification number included with the Windows 95 package.

7. You are prompted for a user name and company name for the computer.

8. If the *Custom setup* option was selected, the setup wizard prompts you whether to search for all hardware devices. By default, a diverse list of hardware is checked for. You can optionally modify the list to avoid crashes or conflicts.

9. Press Next to begin hardware detection. The detection process may take several minutes. This is the most common step for a system crash to occur; if it does, reboot and run Setup again to continue the process.

10. Specify whether three optional components should be installed: The Microsoft Network, Microsoft Mail, and Microsoft Fax.

11. Select the Windows 95 components to be installed. You can add or remove components later through the Add/Remove Programs control panel.

12. Select network components to be installed. Windows 95 networking is described in detail later in this chapter.

13. Specify a computer name (NetBIOS name), workgroup name, and optional description to identify the computer on the network.

14. A list of default settings for the keyboard, monitor, mouse, and other hardware is displayed. Press Next to accept the defaults, or Change to modify a setting.

15. Choose whether to create a startup disk. This disk can be used to reboot and repair the system in the event of a crash. If you select Yes, you must insert a blank formatted disk. You can create an updated startup disk later with the Add/Remove Programs control panel.

16. Press Next to begin copying files from the Windows 95 CD-ROM to the computer. This process may take several minutes.

17. When the setup process finishes, you are prompted to restart the computer. Press Finish to restart. Before the restart, the boot record is modified to run Windows 95.

18. When Windows 95 starts, setup continues and scans for Plug and Play hardware devices. You may be prompted for driver disks for some devices.

19. The final phase of setup sets up the control panel, the start menu, the help system, and the default MS-DOS settings. You are then prompted for time zone information.

20. You are prompted to restart the computer again. After Windows 95 loads this time, it can be used normally.

Setup.exe

setup [batchfile] [options]

While SETUP will work in most cases with no command-line options, various options can be used to modify the setup process. Except for those noted below, all of these options work either from DOS or Windows 3.x. A batch file can be specified to automate the installation, as described later in this section.

Options

/C

(DOS only) skips the loading of the SMARTDRV.EXE disk cache in the setup process.

/id

Skips the check for free disk space. (If the disk becomes full during the installation, the installation process will fail.)

/iL

(DOS only) loads a driver for a Logitech mouse rather than the default Microsoft driver.

/im

Skips the check for free memory. Setup should be run with a minimum of DOS drivers and TSR programs loaded.

/in

Skips the network portion of the setup process.

/iq

If specified, Setup does not check for cross-linked files.

/is

Skips the system check (ScanDisk).

/T:path

Specifies a path to be used for temporary file storage during the installation. Existing files in the specified path are deleted.

On the Exam

You should know all of these setup options for the Windows 95 MCSE exam. The batch option is described in detail later in this chapter.

Upgrading Windows 3.x

The Windows 95 installation automatically detects an existing installation of Windows 3.x, if any. You are prompted to choose whether to install Windows 95 in the same directory or a different directory.

If you install Windows 95 in the same directory, the following settings are copied to the Windows 95 installation:

*   Program groups (created as entries in the Start menu)

- WIN.INI and SYSTEM.INI settings, including Control Panel settings
- Network configuration (Windows for Workgroups only)

On the Exam

There are two different types of Windows 95 CD-ROM available: one for new installations, and one for upgrades. However, either can be used for a new install or an upgrade. The only difference is that the upgrade version requires proof that you own Windows 3.1: Windows 3.1 must be installed on the hard disk, or you must insert the first Windows 3.1 setup disk.

Configuring Multi-Boot Systems

Windows 95 can coexist with DOS, Windows 3.1, and one or more versions of Windows NT on the same computer. If you install the components in the correct order, a multi-boot configuration is created automatically. Considerations for multi-boot systems with each operating system are described below.

Windows 3.1 and DOS

Since Windows 3.1 is basically a DOS application, Windows 3.1 and DOS are treated the same way when creating a multi-boot system. To do this, first install DOS and Windows 3.1 if desired, then run Windows 95 Setup.

For multi-boot to work, you must specify a different directory for Windows 95 than the Windows 3.1 directory. After the Windows 95 setup, press **F8** when starting the computer to display the startup menu and select the *Previous DOS Version* option to run DOS or Windows 3.1.

You can also modify the MSDOS.SYS file to display the startup menu each type the computer boots, as described earlier in this chapter.

On the Exam

When you use a different directory to install Windows 95, settings are not copied from the Windows 3.1 installation. You can use the GRPCONV utility included with Windows 95 to convert Program Manager groups to the start menu, but some applications still may not run due to missing INI files or DLL files.

Windows NT

As with Windows 3.1, Windows NT and Windows 95 will automatically be set up in a multi-boot configuration if installed in the correct order. First install Windows 95, then install Windows NT Workstation or NT Server. Specify a different directory than the Windows 95 directory for the NT installation.

After Windows NT is set up, the NT boot manager will be displayed when you start the computer. Select the *Microsoft Windows* option to start Windows 95. If you installed Windows 95 over a DOS or Windows 3.1 installation as described above, you can still select that version from the Windows 95 startup menu.

On the Exam

Windows NT's boot manager can also be configured to list the two versions of Windows as separate options, eliminating the need for the Windows 95 startup menu. See Part 2 for information about the Windows NT BOOT.INI file.

Automated and Network Setup

Windows 95 setup includes support for an automated installation. In this type of installation, a batch file is used to specify all of the information that normally would be obtained through interactive prompts. The batch file is usually called MSBATCH.INF. Specify the batch file name on the command line when you run Setup to use an automated installation.

The MSBATCH.INF file includes a variety of settings corresponding to the information Setup usually prompts for. These are listed in the Windows 95 Resource Kit help file, included on the Windows 95 CD-ROM. Two utilities can also be used to create custom setup batch files:

- NETSETUP.EXE is intended for server-based installation. It can also create MSBATCH.INF files.

- BATCH.EXE is a simple utility that allows you to set options and creates the MSBATCH.INF file.

Both of these utilities are included with the Windows 95 Resource Kit, available separately from Microsoft. They are not included on the Windows 95 CD-ROM.

On the Exam

You don't need to know the exact MSBATCH.INF file options for the Windows 95 MCSE exams, but you should know how to start an installation using a batch file.

Removing Windows 95

The Windows 95 CD-ROM includes an UNINSTAL.EXE utility to remove an existing Windows 95 installation. Run this program from Windows 95 or DOS to remove most of the Windows 95 files.

Without the Uninstall utility, you can remove the directory you installed Windows 95 in (usually C:/WINDOWS), boot a DOS disk, and use the SYS C: command to restore the DOS boot sector.

On the Exam

The UNINSTAL.EXE utility does not work when you have upgraded an existing Windows 3.1x installation. One way to ensure that you will be able to remove Windows 95 is to copy the Windows 3.1 files (the WINDOWS directory) to another location, then upgrade to Windows 95.

Installing Network Components

The Network applet in the Control Panel, described earlier in "Windows 95 Basics," allows you to add and configure network components. This dialog can also be accessed by right-clicking on the Network Neighborhood icon and selecting *Properties*. The Configuration tab of this dialog is shown in Figure 5-4.

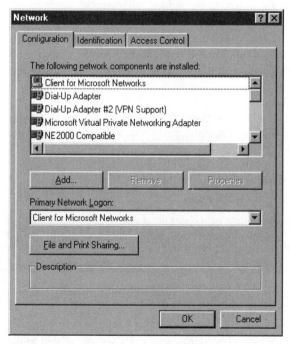

Figure 5-4: The Network control panel

Network components include network adapters, services, protocols, and clients; these are discussed in the sections below.

Network Adapters

Network adapters, also called network interface cards (NICs), are cards that install in a computer to interface it to the network. Network cards and the process of installing them are described in detail in Part 1 of this book.

Network adapters can be installed from the Configuration tab of the Network control panel dialog. Press *Add* to add a component, then select *Adapter* as the type of component to install. You can then specify a manufacturer and device to use a driver included with Windows 95, or use the Have Disk button to use a driver from the manufacturer.

Once an adapter has been installed, highlight it in the Network control panel and use the Properties button to display a dialog of settings for the adapter. This tabbed dialog includes the following categories of settings:

Driver Type
> Specifies the type of network driver in use: an enhanced (protected) mode driver using Microsoft's NDIS specification, a 16-bit real mode driver using NDIS, or a 16-bit real mode driver using Novell's ODI specification.

Bindings
> Each of the protocols installed on the computer is listed here. Select the ones that will be used with the adapter. By default, all protocol bindings are enabled.

Resources
> Specify an interrupt address (IRQ) and I/O (port) address for the adapter. This should match the settings on the card itself. Plug and Play network adapters are configured automatically.

Advanced
> Depending on the network adapter driver, one or more advanced settings may be listed in this dialog. For example, cards with a modifiable hardware (MAC) address use this page of options.

On the Exam

For the exam, you should have experience installing a network adapter in a Windows 95 computer. You should not need to know detailed IRQ information and other PC troubleshooting details. Detailed network adapter information is included in Part 1 of this book.

Network Services

Network services provide additional networking capabilities, usually related to file and printer sharing. The Configuration tab of the Network control panel can also be used to install services. The sections below look at the features of the most commonly used service, File and printer sharing for Microsoft networks.

File and Printer Sharing

Windows 95 computers can share files and printers with other computers in the workgroup or domain. To enable this feature, the File and Printer Sharing service must be installed.

To install file and printer sharing, select *Add* from the Configuration tab of the Network control panel. Select *Service* as the type of component to add. Select *Microsoft* as the manufacturer, and highlight the *File and printer sharing for Microsoft networks* service.

Once the service is installed, press the File and Print Sharing button in the Network control panel to display a dialog that enables the services. Check the file option, the printers option, or both. The actual process of sharing files and printers is described later in this chapter.

Network Browsing

Microsoft Windows networks maintain a list of network resources through a service called *browsing*. Various computers act as browsers to manage the resource list. This list is used when you open the Network Neighborhood window. The following types of browser may be included in the system:

Master browser
> This computer receives broadcasts from sharing computers and compiles them into a browse list. This list is then distributed to backup browsers.

Backup browsers
> These machines keep a backup copy of the browse list. When a client browses the network, a backup browser is contacted to provide the list of resources.

Potential browsers
> These are machines that can act as browsers, but are not currently participating in the browse process. All Windows NT, Windows 95, and Windows for Workgroups machines can be potential browsers.

Non-browsers
> These are machines that cannot act as browsers, but can make shares available and broadcast their lists to the master browser.

In a Windows NT network, Windows 95 machines usually act as potential browsers only. However, they are capable of acting as master browsers. If the master browser goes down, an election process is held to select a new master browser. Computers are selected based on their current browser type and their OS version (Windows NT has a higher priority than Windows 95).

The Browser service in Windows 95 is handled as part of the file and printer sharing service. To force a computer to act as the master browser, highlight *File and printer sharing for Microsoft networks* from the Network control panel. Select *Properties*.

The Browse Master option in this dialog can be set to *Automatic* (the default) to choose the browse master by election, or to *Enabled* to select this computer. Select *Disabled* to prevent the computer from being elected master browser.

Network Protocols

Windows 95 supports a variety of network protocols. These include NetBEUI, IPX/
SPX, DLC, and TCP/IP. The sections below describe each of these protocols in
more detail. Protocols can be installed from the Configuration tab of the Network
control panel; after installing a protocol, you must restart the computer to begin
using it.

NetBEUI

NetBIOS (Network Basic Input/Output Services), developed by Microsoft and IBM,
is a network service that supports a basic set of function calls used by network-
aware applications. NetBIOS can be used over any of the supported network
protocols. NetBEUI (NetBIOS Extended User Interface) is Microsoft's protocol built
specifically for use with NetBIOS.

NetBEUI has a low overhead compared with other protocols and is simple to
configure. However, it is not routable and supports a limited number of nodes, so
it is most useful for small networks. Since Windows 95 networking supports
NetBEUI by default, this is a simple protocol that can be used with Windows 95-
only networks.

If NetBEUI is not already installed on a computer, you can add it using the
Network control panel. Select *Add*, select *Protocol* as the type of component to
add, choose *Microsoft* from the manufacturers list, and choose *NetBEUI* from the
protocols list. Once NetBEUI is installed, its bindings and advanced settings can be
modified by selecting a NetBEUI entry and pressing the Properties button.

IPX/SPX

IPX (Internetwork Packet Exchange) and SPX (Sequenced Packet Exchange) are
protocols developed by Novell and supported by NetWare. Windows 95 includes
support for these protocols, which can be used to attach to NetWare servers or to
communicate with other Windows 95 and Windows NT machines using the same
protocol.

To install these protocols, select *Add* from the Network control panel. Choose Protocol as the type of component to install. Choose *Microsoft* from the manufacturers list, then choose *IPX/SPX-compatible Protocol*. After installing IPX/SPX, highlight its entry and select *Properties* to change settings related to these protocols. The tabbed dialog includes the following categories of settings:

Bindings
> Choose the clients and services that will be used with the IPX/SPX protocols. All of the items are selected by default. These are the same bindings you can modify from the service or client's Properties dialog.

Advanced
> This page includes a variety of advanced settings. In most cases the default values will not need to be changed. One exception is the Frame Type value. To support NetWare 3.11 and older servers, you may need to manually choose the Ethernet 802.3 frame type.

NetBIOS
> This page includes a single setting, which enables NetBIOS over IPX/SPX. This allows NetBIOS communications (such as those used in network browsing, described earlier in this chapter) over the IPX/SPX protocol.

DLC

DLC (Data Link Control) is IBM's protocol for mainframe communications. This protocol can be used with Windows 95 to communicate with these computers. More frequently, DLC is used to communicate with stand-alone print servers and network-ready printers (such as those made by Hewlett-Packard) that use DLC.

To install DLC, select *Add* from the Network control panel. Select Protocol as the type of component to add. Select *Microsoft* from the manufacturers list, and *Microsoft DLC* from the list of protocols. After DLC is installed, the DLC Properties dialog becomes available with the following categories:

Bindings
> Choose the clients and services that will be used with DLC. The default clients and services do not support this protocol, so this list will be empty until you install a service (such as that required for a printer) that supports DLC.

Advanced
> This category includes a wide variety of DLC communication options. These should not need to be changed unless required by the device you are communicating with.

On the Exam

For the Windows 95 MCSE exam you should only need to know how to install DLC and its basic description and purpose.

Windows 95

TCP/IP Basics

TCP/IP (Transport Control Protocol/Internet Protocol) is a suite of protocols in widespread use on the Internet. These are also the protocols used with UNIX systems. Windows 95 includes support for the TCP/IP protocol, which can be configured during installation or with the Network control panel.

You can opt to install TCP/IP during the Windows 95 installation or add it later using the Network control panel. To install TCP/IP, Select *Add*, select *Protocol*, choose *Microsoft* from the manufacturers list, and choose *TCP/IP*.

On the Exam

The following is a basic description of TCP/IP, which should be sufficient for the Windows 95 MCSE exam. TCP/IP is described in detail in Part 2.

Although TCP/IP requires more administrative attention than NetBEUI or IPX/SPX, it is efficient for large networks and is routable. A Windows NT computer with multiple network adapters can act as a TCP/IP router. Windows 95 does not have built-in support for routing.

TCP/IP Addressing

TCP/IP uses a system of *IP addresses* to distinguish between clients on the network. Each node has its own unique IP address. The IP address is a 32-bit number, expressed in dotted decimal format, such as 198.60.22.1. The address is divided into a network number and host number.

In configuring a TCP/IP client computer, you will need to know its assigned IP address and subnet mask. For networks connected to the Internet, these consist of a network number assigned by the InterNIC or an ISP and a host number assigned by the administrator. For private networks, network and host numbers can be assigned by the network administrator. Addresses can be automatically assigned by the DHCP protocol, described below.

On the Exam

You should be familiar with the names and descriptions of the following protocols, but you don't need to know their technical specifics for the Windows 95 exam. TCP/IP protocols are discussed in more detail in Part 4.

TCP/IP Protocols

The TCP/IP suite includes many protocols. The following are some of the protocols commonly used in Windows 95:

DHCP (Dynamic Host Configuration Protocol)
This protocol allows clients to be dynamically issued IP addresses from a pool of available addresses. Windows 95 can be configured to receive an IP address from a DHCP server. DHCP can also send information about WINS servers and other configuration details.

DNS (Domain Name Service)
Hosts on an IP network also have alphanumeric names corresponding to their IP addresses. These can be local names, such as *server*, or fully qualified names, such as *server1.company.com*. DNS is used to translate between host names and addresses.

WINS (Windows Internet Naming Service)
This is Microsoft's protocol for NetBIOS name resolution. WINS translates between IP addresses and NetBIOS names, described in Part 1.

SLIP (Serial Line Internet Protocol)
This is a protocol used for dial-up connections to servers. This is used by some Internet service providers and for connection to some UNIX systems.

PPP (Point-to-Point Protocol)
This is an alternative protocol for dial-up connections. PPP is newer and includes more sophisticated configuration and security features. In addition, while SLIP supports TCP/IP connections only, PPP can support other protocols.

PPTP (Point-to-point Tunneling Protocol)
This protocol is used to maintain virtual private networks, or VPNs. These are networks that use a large network (such as the Internet) as their transport. PPTP encrypts packets and sends them securely over the Internet to maintain a virtual WAN connection between computers in different locations.

TCP/IP Configuration

Once TCP/IP is installed, you can select one of its entries and select *Protocols* from the Configuration tab of the Network control panel to change TCP/IP settings. The TCP/IP Properties dialog includes a number of tabbed categories:

Bindings
Allows you to specify which network services will communicate using the TCP/IP protocol.

Advanced
This dialog includes an option that allows you to make TCP/IP the default protocol, along with other custom options.

DNS Configuration
Use the *Enable DNS* option to enable host name lookup via a DNS server. If enabled, you should specify the local computer's host and domain name, and one or more DNS servers to search.

Gateway
Specify the IP addresses of one or more gateways (routers). These will be used in the order they are listed to attempt to communicate with addresses not on the local network.

WINS Configuration

If the *Enable WINS Resolution* option is selected, a WINS server is used to translate NetBIOS computer names to IP addresses. Specify primary and secondary WINS servers and an optional scope ID (computers must have the same NetBIOS scope ID in order to communicate). You can optionally specify that a DHCP server (described below) will be queried to determine the WINS server address.

IP Address

If the *Obtain an IP address automatically* option is selected, a DHCP server is contacted to obtain an IP address. Alternately, select *Specify an IP address* and enter the IP address and subnet mask.

Network Clients

While Windows 95 can be used exclusively in small workgroup networks, it also functions well as a network client for larger networks. Client software is included with Windows 95 to act as a Windows NT or NetWare client; these clients are described in the sections below.

Windows 95 can act as a client for both systems at once, but one client must be specified as the primary client. To select this, use the pull-down menu labeled Primary Network Logon in the Network control panel's Configuration tab.

Windows NT

The Windows NT client is called Client for Microsoft Networks. This client can be used to log onto a Windows NT workgroup or domain. This is also the default client software used for Windows 95-only networks. The File and Print Sharing for Microsoft Networks service, described earlier in this chapter, requires the Client for Microsoft Networks to operate.

To install this client, select *Add* from the Network control panel's Configuration tab. Select *Client* as the type of component to add. Choose *Microsoft* from the manufacturers list, and *Client for Microsoft Networks* as the client. After restarting the computer, you can log onto the network.

Along with the client, you should install the appropriate protocols to communicate with the network. These can include TCP/IP, IPX/SPX, or NetBEUI, described earlier in this chapter.

Select *Client for Microsoft Networks* from the Network control panel and choose Properties to display the settings for this client. The following options are included:

Log on to Windows NT domain

If this option is selected, a Windows NT domain will be contacted to verify the username and password you enter at logon. If this option is not selected, workgroup networking is assumed.

Windows NT domain

Specify the Windows NT domain for the above option. You must have a valid username and password for the domain to log on. Specifying a domain here also makes the Windows 95 machine visible on network browse lists from machines logged into the Windows NT domain.

Quick logon

If this option is selected, mapped drives (described below) are not reattached each time you log on.

Logon and restore network connections

If this option is selected, mapped drives are reattached at each logon. This provides quicker access to the mapped directory, but may cause a delay during logon, particularly if the server is not currently available.

In addition to installing and configuring the client software, you will need to create a user account in Windows NT using the User Manager utility. Windows NT uses strictly user-level security. You will also need to set permissions (either share-based or NTFS-based) for resources the Windows 95 users need to access. For detailed information about Windows NT, see Part 2.

NetWare

The NetWare client included with Windows 95 is called Client for NetWare Networks. To install it, select *Add* from the Configuration tab of the Network control panel. Select *Client* as the type of component to add. Choose *Microsoft* from the manufacturers list and select *Microsoft Client for NetWare Networks*.

The IPX/SPX protocol, described above, must also be installed for communication with NetWare servers.

Once the NetWare client is installed, it can be selected as the primary network logon if a Windows network is not also in use. You can also select the client and press the Properties button to display the following options:

Preferred server

Choose a server to log onto. Client for Microsoft networks does not support logging into an NDS directory tree, as described below.

First network drive

Select a drive letter to be used as the first drive available for NetWare network and search drive mappings. Drive letters below the selected letter are restricted for use by Windows.

Enable logon script processing ·

If selected, Windows 95 will attempt to process the NetWare login script when you log on. Since these scripts are usually intended for DOS, they may not work properly under Windows 95.

Service Pack 1 for Windows 95 includes a new client for NetWare called Microsoft NDS Client. This client supports NDS (NetWare Directory Services), NetWare 4's central user and resource database. Novell's Client 32 for Windows 95 also supports NDS.

In addition to configuring the client software, Windows 95 users will require a user account on the NetWare server. NetWare uses user-level security, and no network resources are accessible without a valid username and password. Use the *SYSCON* (NetWare 3.x) or *NWADMIN* (NetWare 4.x) utility to create an account. You should also assign permissions for the resources that Windows 95 users will access. This can be done on a user or group basis.

A final feature of Windows 95's NetWare support is File and Print Sharing for NetWare. This service allows NetWare clients to access shared files and printers on the Windows 95 computer.

To install this service, select *Add* from the Network control panel, select Service, choose *Microsoft* from the manufacturers list, and choose *File and Printer Sharing for NetWare Networks*. The use of this service as a print server for NetWare is described in the "Network Printers" section later in this chapter.

Accessing Network Resources

Windows 95 integrates network resources into the file system for easy access by users or applications. Network resources can be browsed with the Network Neighborhood icon, referred to directly with UNC paths, or accessed from a mapped drive letter. These options are described in the following sections.

Network Neighborhood

Double-clicking the Network Neighborhood icon on the desktop opens an Explorer window that displays available network resources. A list of resources offered by computers in the local workgroup or domain is displayed, and the Entire Network option provides access to non-local resources.

UNC Paths

Universal naming convention, or UNC, is a standard for referring to network resources on the local network. A UNC path is similar to a file system path. The format of a UNC path is:

    \\servername\share

Servername refers to the server offering access to the resource, and *share* refers to the name of the shared resource. The path can continue to refer to subdirectories under the shared directory if access is allowed. File and printer sharing is described in more detail later in this chapter.

Mapped Drives

Right-clicking on the Network Neighborhood icon allows access to the *Map Network Drive* option. This allows you to define a UNC path to a network share and assign a local drive letter to the directory. Drives can be automatically mapped each time Windows 95 is started.

Drive letters can also be mapped from the command line (MS-DOS prompt) with the net use command followed by a drive letter and UNC. For example, this command maps drive X to the DOCS share on the West server:

```
net use x: \\West\DOCS
```

One benefit of mapped drives is convenience. A more important benefit is the fact that mapped drives become accessible to all programs, whether they use the 32-bit file selector or not. This allows some 16-bit Windows and DOS applications to access network directories.

Dial-Up Networking

Dial-Up Networking (DUN) is a Windows 95 service that allows a phone line and modem (or ISDN terminal adapter) to be used as a network connection. This can be used to dial into a Windows NT Server running RAS (Remote Access Service) or an Internet service provider (ISP).

DUN can be installed during the Windows 95 installation. If it is not currently installed, it can be added from the Add/Remove Programs control panel: choose the Windows Setup tab, choose *Communications* from the list, press the Details button, and check the box next to *Dial-up Networking*.

Once DUN is installed, a folder called Dial-Up Networking is listed in the My Computer window. Double-click this item to open the folder. The folder lists the currently defined DUN connections along with the Make New Connection option.

Creating a Connection

Select the *Make New Connection* option to start the DUN wizard, which prompts you for several categories of options to create the connection. These include the following:

1. Specify a name for the DUN entry, and select the modem to use for dialing. The process of installing modems is described later in this chapter.

2. Type the area code, telephone number, and country code for the computer you are dialing into.

3. Press the Finish button to complete the installation. You may now need to specify settings for the connection, as described below.

Connection Properties

Highlight a DUN entry, right click, and select *Properties* to display the Connection Properties dialog. This dialog allows you to modify the phone number and modem you selected when creating the connection.

Windows 95

You can press the Configure button in the properties dialog to display the TAPI modem properties, described later in this chapter. The Server Type button displays an additional dialog, shown in Figure 5-5, with details about the server described below.

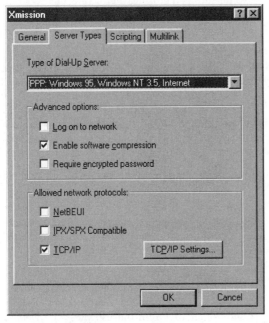

Figure 5-5: Server Types for a DUN connection

Type of Dial-up Server
> Specify the type of dial-up server protocol. The protocols supported by DUN are described in the next section.

Advanced Options
> These options address technical features of the selected protocol. Their settings depend on what the server requires.

Allowed network protocols
> The NetBEUI, IPX/SPX, and TCP/IP protocols are listed here. You can select which of these will be supported by the dial-up connection. Additionally, the TCP/IP Settings button displays the TCP/IP Properties dialog (described earlier in this chapter) to specify IP addresses and other options.

On the Exam

Questions about DUN are frequently seen on the Windows 95 MCSE exam. You should know all of the configuration details and features described above for the exam.

Dial-up Protocols

Windows 95's dial-up networking supports a variety of dial-up protocols. While each has its advantages and disadvantages, your choice of protocol will usually be based on what the dial-up server supports. The following selections are available:

PPP (Point-to-Point Protocol)
> PPP is a secure dial-up protocol that supports TCP/IP or other transport protocols. The PPP protocol is typically used for Internet providers and Windows NT 3.5 and later servers.

SLIP (Serial Line Internet Protocol)
> SLIP is a predecessor of PPP. It supports only TCP/IP data and does not support security. SLIP requires a script or terminal session to initiate a connection.

NRN (NetWare Connect)
> This is a proprietary protocol developed by Novell for their dial-up server product, NetWare Connect. You can use this option to access NetWare servers if they are equipped with dial-in software.

Windows for Workgroups and Windows NT 3.1
> This is a proprietary protocol supported by Windows for Workgroups and Windows NT 3.1. The protocol is a modified version of NetBEUI.

Managing Windows 95

The following sections address some of the day-to-day management that may be required for Windows 95. These include hardware installation, disk configuration, shared files, printers, modems, user profiles, system policies, and remote administration.

Installing Hardware

Windows 95 includes support for the Plug and Play specification, which allows hardware devices to be automatically detected, installed, and assigned computer resources (IRQs, I/O addresses, memory addresses, and DMA channels). In order for Plug and Play to work, three components must support the specification:

- The computer's BIOS must be Plug and Play compliant. The BIOS is responsible for detecting new and changed devices and informing the operating system of their presence and the resources they request.

- The operating system must support Plug and Play (as Windows 95 does). The OS assigns resources to the various devices and informs the BIOS and the devices of the resources they should use.

- Lastly, the devices (such as disk controllers, modems, and video cards) must support Plug and Play. A device informs the BIOS of the resources it needs and its available options (for example, a disk controller may support only IRQ 10 or IRQ 11).

Plug and Play Components

Within Windows 95, the Plug and Play specification is supported by a variety of components:

Configuration Manager
> This component supervises the Plug and Play process and receives information about configuration changes from the BIOS.

Bus Enumerators
> These services manage the various device attachment buses (ISA, PCI, and keyboard controller). These components are responsible for direct communication with the devices.

Resource Arbitrator
> This service manages the pool of available resources, and assigns them to devices. Legacy devices (those without Plug and Play support) are first assigned their specified resources, then Plug and Play devices are assigned resources based on their needs.

Registry
> The HKEY_DYN_DATA key of the registry, described earlier in this chapter, is used to store the current state of Plug and Play devices. The components above access the registry to obtain or modify the current configuration.

The Add New Hardware Wizard

In theory, Plug and Play devices will configure themselves automatically and prompt you to insert their driver disk when you start Windows. For devices that do not support Plug and Play, the Add New Hardware Wizard is provided. This wizard should be run after installing the physical hardware.

To access this wizard, select *Add New Hardware* from the Control Panel. Follow these steps to add hardware:

1. Press Next to begin the installation process.

2. Choose whether Windows 95 should attempt to detect the new hardware. This is the same process used during installation to search for non-Plug and Play hardware.

3. If you chose *Yes* above, a hardware search is performed and the detected hardware is displayed.

4. If you chose *No*, a list of available hardware types is displayed. Choose a category, a manufacturer, and a device. If the device is not listed and you have a driver on disk, choose the *Have Disk* option.

5. The driver is now installed. The driver disk or the Windows 95 installation CD-ROM may be required. The computer should be restarted to use the new device.

Device Manager

Device Manager is the second tab of the System control panel. This dialog displays a list of installed devices, divided into the same categories used by the Add New

Hardware wizard. Highlight an item and choose *Properties* to display or modify its settings.

Highlighting Computer and pressing the Properties button allows you to display devices by their resource usage. For example, Figure 5-6 shows a list of devices by their corresponding IRQs. This dialog is useful in resolving resource conflicts.

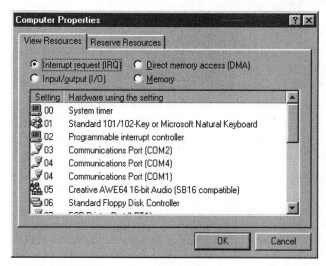

Figure 5-6: Device Manager displays devices by IRQ usage

Disk Configuration

As mentioned earlier in this chapter, Windows 95 supports VFAT, an extension of the FAT (file allocation table) file system used by DOS. Windows 95 supports the same partitioning scheme as DOS and adds support for long filenames. These are described in the sections that follow along with the built-in mechanisms for disk backups and disk compression.

Partitioning and Formatting

Windows 95 includes FDISK, a DOS program used for partitioning hard disks. To run this utility, type FDISK at the command prompt. This utility includes the following options:

Create DOS partition or logical DOS drive
    Creates a new primary partition, extended partition, or logical drive within an extended partition.

Set active partition
    Choose which partition is currently active (bootable).

Delete partition or logical DOS drive
    Deletes a partition or logical drive. All data on the partition is lost.

Display partition information
    Displays a list of partitions on the current disk drive.

Change current fixed disk drive

Choose a disk drive to modify partition settings for. Drives are numbered starting with zero.

To format a FAT partition with VFAT support, highlight the drive in the My Computer window, right-click, and select *Format*. You can optionally choose to copy system files to the disk.

Long Filenames

Any drive formatted with Windows 95 includes long filename (LFN) support. Long filenames are supported along with traditional DOS (8.3) filenames. Long filenames support the following features:

- Support for up to 256 characters (the practical limit is lower, since paths can contain a maximum of 260 characters).

- Support for spaces and punctuation characters: period, comma, semicolon, colon, and square brackets.

- Support for upper- and lowercase (files can be referred to without concern for case sensitivity).

Each long filename is stored in the VFAT directory along with a corresponding short filename for DOS compatibility. Windows 95 constructs short filenames with the first six alphanumeric characters of the filename, a tilde (~), and a number between 1 and 9. As an example, the Program Files directory under the Windows directory usually has a DOS filename of PROGRA~1. If an extension is used, its first three characters are used as the DOS extension.

In the Real World

Long filenames are stored in the FAT using several of the spaces normally used for short filenames. One potential issue is that there is a limit of 512 files in the root directory of a drive. Since a single long filename can use as many as 33 short filename entries, this limit can be reached quickly. Subdirectories do not have this limitation.

When LFNs are in use, you should not use any DOS utility (such as a disk defragmenter or directory sorter) that does not support long filenames. If you do, long filename information may be lost.

On the Exam

For the exam, you should know the features and limitations of long filenames and how to convert a long filename into its DOS equivalent.

Disk Compression

Windows 95 includes DriveSpace, a disk compression utility. (The Windows 95 Plus Pack includes a newer version of this utility.) Disk compression can compress an entire drive at a time, but not individual files.

To compress a drive, highlight the drive in Explorer and select *Properties*, then select the Compression tab. Select the Compress Drive button. You can also use a portion of the drive's space to create a compressed volume with a different drive letter.

Each compressed drive uses a host drive. This is a hidden drive that stores a single file containing the compressed data, usually called DRVSPACE.000 . If you use the Compress Drive button to compress the drive, a separate hidden host drive letter is created to store the compressed data. If you use the Create New Drive button, free space on the existing drive is used as the host for a new drive letter. In either case, you can adjust the portion of free space to be used as a host drive, allowing the remainder of the drive to be used for uncompressed files.

On the Exam

The Windows 95 swap file cannot be stored on a compressed volume. In addition, since a compressed drive is really a single file, one minor disk error can cause you to lose all of the files on the volume.

Backing up Data

Windows 95 includes a simple backup utility called Backup. This utility can be installed from the Windows Setup tab of the Add/Remove Programs control panel. Select the *Disk Tools* category, and select *Backup*. The Backup utility includes three tabbed dialogs:

Backup
Backs up the selected files or directories to the tape.

Restore
Restores one or more files from a tape backup set.

Compare
Compares an existing backup set with the contents of the corresponding files or directories.

Backup requires a tape backup device to work. The tape drive should be installed using the Add New Hardware wizard, described earlier in this chapter.

The Backup utility supports two types of backups:

Full Backup
Backs up all files in the backup set, and clears their archive bits to indicate that they have been backed up.

Incremental Backup

Backs up files that have been changed since the last backup. The archive bits are cleared, so each incremental backup backs up files changed since the last incremental backup or full backup.

In the Real World

You only need to know how to use the Backup utility for the Windows 95 MCSE exam. Since this is a limited program, you may wish to consider third-party software for backups. Most tape drives include more sophisticated and reliable backup utilities.

File Sharing

If you have installed the File and Printer Sharing for Microsoft Networks service as described earlier in this chapter, any directory or drive can be shared, or made available over the network. The following sections explain how to share and secure files.

User-Level and Share-Level Security

There are two basic types of security for Windows 95 shared files and printers:

- Share-level security (the default) uses individual passwords for each share.
- User-level security allow you to specify a computer to obtain a list of users from; this can be a Windows NT or NetWare server. You can then assign permissions to the shared resource for individual users or groups.

To select the security level, select the Access Control tab of the Network control panel, and select either *User-level* or *Share-level*. If User-level security is selected, a computer name or Windows NT domain name for the user list must be specified.

Configuring Sharing

To configure sharing, select a drive or directory, right click, and choose *Sharing*. The Sharing tab of the properties dialog is displayed. This dialog includes the following options:

Shared As

If selected, sharing is enabled for the resource.

Share Name

Choose a name for the share. This name is displayed in Network Neighborhood when browsing the network.

Access Type (Share-level)

If share-level security is in use, specify the access type (Read-only, Full, or Depends on Password).

Passwords (Share-level)

Specify a password for access to the resource. If the *Depends on Password* option is selected above, both Read-only and Full Access passwords should be specified.

If user-level security is selected, use the Add button to add a user or group to the permissions list for the resource. A complete list of users on the domain or computer that maintains the user list is displayed. You can add any user or group on the list to the Read Only, Full Access, or Custom lists for access to the resource.

The Custom option allows you to individually enable the following rights: Read, Write, Create, Delete, Change File Attributes, List Files, and Change Access Control.

On the Exam

You should have experience sharing resources and assigning permissions with both user-level and share-level security for the MCSE exam. You should also fully understand the difference between these access control methods.

Printers

Windows 95 includes versatile support for printers. Any number of printers can be installed, and printers can be shared in the same manner as disk directories. The following sections detail the process of installing and managing printers.

Installing a Printer

The Printers icon in the My Computer window can be opened to display a list of currently installed local or network printers. Use the *Add Printer* option to start the Add Printer wizard, used to install a new printer. Follow these steps to add a printer:

- Choose whether the printer is local (attached to the computer) or a network printer (attached to another computer or directly to the network).

- For a local printer, specify the printer type by choosing a manufacturer from the left column and a printer model from the right column. Use the Have Disk button to install a driver from disk.

- Choose the port the printer is attached to (COM1-4 or LPT1-3). For network printers, choose the network share that corresponds with the printer.

- Specify a name for the printer, and whether the printer will be used as the default printer for Windows 95.

Printer Properties

Once a local printer is installed, you can modify its settings. Highlight the printer's item in the Printers window, right-click, and select *Properties*. The following categories of settings are available:

General

Specify an optional description (comment) for the printer, and whether a separator page (banner) is printed between print jobs.

Details

This setting allows you to modify the printer port and driver, and specify timeout settings.

Sharing

Allows you to share the printer with other users, as described in the next section.

Paper

Choose the paper size and orientation currently loaded into the printer.

Graphics

Specify the graphics resolution and color dithering options.

Network Printers

The Sharing tab in the printer properties dialog allows you to share the printer. The sharing options are the same as those for file sharing, described in the previous section.

To add support to a Network printer to a Windows 95 workstation, choose *Network Printer* from the Add Printer wizard, and specify the UNC path to the network share. The driver for the printer is automatically installed based on the settings at the computer the printer is attached to.

Managing Print Jobs

Documents sent to the printer are stored as print jobs in a print queue. To display the queue, double-click on the printer's entry in the Printers window. You can then manage jobs with the menu options. For a local printer, these options can all be used from the computer attached to the printer; for a network printer, users have control over the jobs they have submitted.

The File menu includes a *Pause Printing* option, which prevents data from being sent to the printer. The *Purge Print Jobs* option removes all jobs from the print queue.

From the Document menu, the *Pause Printing* option pauses printing of the high-lighted document, and *Cancel Printing* removes the job from the print queue.

Modems

Windows 95 supports one or more modems, used to connect to phone lines for data transmission. Modems are used for the dial-up networking utility, described earlier in this chapter, and for other communication applications.

The TAPI (Telephony Application Programming Interface) subsystem of Windows 95 manages modems, and allows a single set of modem properties to be used from multiple communication programs.

Installing a Modem

Modems can be installed using the Add button in the Modems control panel. You can either specify a manufacturer and model for the modem or choose to let Windows 95 attempt to detect the modem. Once a modem is installed, choose Properties to change its settings. These include the following:

General
> Choose the port the modem is connected to (usually COM1-COM4), the modem speaker volume, and the connection speed. This is the speed between the computer and the modem; the actual connection speed depends on the remote modem.

Connection
> Choose the serial communication parameters (data bits, parity, and stop bits). You can also select whether dial tone detection is used and specify timeouts for unanswered calls and idle connections.

TAPI Settings

The *Dialing Properties* option from the Modems control panel allows you to specify TAPI settings:

Where I am
> Choose a location; multiple locations can be defined, especially useful for portable computers. Specify the area code and country code for the current location.

How I dial from this location
> Specify any dialing options for the location: dialing for an outside line, calling card dialing, call waiting, and tone or pulse dialing.

User Profiles and System Policies

Windows 95 supports two methods for managing user preferences, such as desktop and control panel settings:

* User profiles allow users to retain the settings they used in their previous sessions at the computer or network.

* System policies allow the administrator to mandate settings or restrict certain Windows 95 functions.

These features are described in detail in the sections below.

User Profiles

User profiles store a user's settings for later use. As mentioned earlier in this chapter, user profile information is stored in the HKEY_USERS registry key. User profile settings are managed from the User Profiles tab of the Passwords control panel. The following options are included:

All users of this PC use the same preferences
> If selected, user profiles are disabled.

Users can customize their preferences
> If selected, user profiles are enabled and the following settings become available.

Include desktop items and Network Neighborhood contents in user settings
> If selected, each user is given a separate desktop file under the \Windows\ Profiles\Username directory.

Include Start menu and program groups in user settings
> If selected, each user is given a separate Start Menu directory under the \Windows\Profiles\Username directory.

The user profile is stored in the USER.DAT portion of the registry. If profiles are enabled, each user has a separate USER.DAT file under the Profiles directory. Basic Windows 95 user profiles are called local user profiles. There are two other types of profiles:

Mandatory profiles
> A mandatory profile cannot be modified by the user. To make a profile mandatory, rename the user's USER.DAT file to USER.MAN after setting any desired settings. This prevents the user from saving changed settings.

Roaming profiles
> A roaming profile stores a user's settings on a server and is loaded regardless of the Windows 95 workstation the user logs on from. If Client for Microsoft Networks or Client for NetWare Networks is installed and user-level security is in use, profiles are stored in the user's home directory on the server (\LOGON for an NT server, or \HOME for a NetWare server). These can also be renamed to be mandatory roaming profiles.

On the Exam

Windows 95's user profiles are not compatible with Windows NT user profiles, described in Part 3 of this book. However, a user can have both Windows 95 and Windows NT profiles stored in the home directory.

System Policies

System policies allow an administrator to restrict user access to certain Windows features and prevent settings from being changed. You can create system policies using the System Policy Editor, included in the \Admin\Apptools\Poledit directory of the Windows 95 CD-ROM.

This utility allows you to create user policies for existing users or groups, and computer policies for specific computers. You can also specify a default user and default computer policy.

Each type of policy (user or computer) includes a hierarchical list of options. User policies include the following categories of options:

Control Panel
> Allows you to restrict access to the Display, Network, Passwords, Printers, and System control panels.

Desktop
> Includes restrictions for the desktop wallpaper and system color scheme.

Network
> Allows you to prevent users from modifying file and printer sharing options.

Shell
> Allows you to specify mandatory contents for the Start menu, desktop icons, and Network Neighborhood. You can also disable specific Start menu commands, such as *Run, Find,* and *Shut Down.*

System
> Allows you to disable the registry editor and the MS-DOS prompt. In addition, you can optionally specify a list of allowed Windows applications, preventing users from installing or running other applications.

Computer policies include these categories:

Network
> Allows you to mandate that user-level access control will be used, and require a valid username and password to start Windows 95. Additional items are available in this category depending on the network clients and services installed.

System
> Allows you to enable or disable user profiles and enable the use of the Run and Run Once keys in the registry, described earlier in this chapter.

On the Exam

Windows 95 system policies are similar to those used in Windows NT, but include some different options. You should know the above categories and the type of settings they contain for the Windows 95 MCSE exam.

Remote Administration

The Remote Administration tab in the Passwords control panel allows you to enable remote administration of a computer. If enabled, you can specify an administration password for share-level security, or a list of administrators for user-level security. (Some portions of remote administration require user-level security.)

Right-click on a computer in Network Neighborhood, select properties, and select the Tools tab to remotely administer the computer. The following tools are available:

Net Watcher
> This utility allows you to monitor network connections, and is described in the next section.

System Monitor
> This utility, also described in the next section, displays charts to monitor various system performance parameters.

Administer File System
> This option opens an explorer window displaying the computer's disk drives and printers. You can select the properties of an item to change its sharing options remotely.

In addition to these tools, the REGEDIT utility can edit registries for remote computers. To use this service, you must install the remote registry service. The installation files for this service are located in the Admin\Nettools\Remotreg directory of the Windows 95 CD-ROM. Use the Have Disk option from the Network control panel to install the service.

Once the remote registry service is installed, you can use the Connect Network Registry option from the Registry menu in REGEDIT to attach to the computer's registry.

On the Exam

Remote administration is a significant security risk, and should not be enabled without proper security. You should know all of the above details about remote administration for the Windows 95 MCSE exam.

Optimization and Troubleshooting

The following sections introduce utilities useful for monitoring the performance of Windows 95, utilities for optimizing disk storage, and a description of common problems.

Monitoring Performance

The following utilities allow you to monitor the performance of a Windows 95 computer:

- Net Watcher displays current network information.
- System Monitor tracks various performance parameters.

These are described in the sections below.

Net Watcher

The Net Watcher utility allows you to monitor the use of network resources on the local computer, or on a remote computer as described earlier in this chapter. It includes three display modes:

* A list of users currently attached to the computer and the number of shares and files they are currently using.

* A list of shared files and printers, including the users currently connected to them and the files in use.

* A list of files currently in use by remote users, including the user accessing them and the share they are accessed through.

System Monitor

The System Monitor utility allows you to display a chart of one or more system performance parameters, called *counters*, over time. The following categories of options are available:

File system
> Includes counters related to disk access, such as Reads/second and Writes/second.

Kernel
> Includes counters related to the core operating system: Processor Usage, Threads, and Virtual Machines.

Memory manager
> Includes counters relating to physical and virtual memory usage, such as Free memory and Swapfile in use.

In addition, categories are available for certain installed network clients, protocols, and services.

On the Exam

System Monitor is similar to the Chart option of Windows NT's Performance Monitor utility. You should know the basic usage of System Monitor and the basic categories of counters for the Windows 95 exam, but you do not need to know all of the individual counters.

Optimizing Disk Storage

Windows 95 includes two disk utilities that can be used to optimize and diagnose problems with disk storage. These utilities are both available from the drive properties dialog, and are described in the following sections.

Disk Defragmenter

Disk Defragmenter rearranges disk files to optimize the use of the disk. Choose *Defragment Now* from the Tools tab of the Disk Properties dialog to run this utility.

Disk Defragmenter first displays a dialog indicating the fragmentation of the disk. If the disk is over 10% fragmented, the dialog recommends that you defragment the disk. Press the Start button to begin the process, which may take several minutes depending on the size and fragmentation of the drive.

ScanDisk

Press the Check Now button in the Tools tab of the Drive Properties dialog to start this utility. ScanDisk checks the file allocation table (FAT) for errors, and is also able to scan the disk surface for errors. The following options are available:

Standard test
> Checks the FAT for errors, but does not scan the disk surface.

Thorough test
> Checks the FAT and scans the surface of the disk. The surface test may take several minutes.

Automatically fix errors
> If selected, ScanDisk attempts to repair any errors it detects. If this option is not selected, you are prompted at each error.

Troubleshooting Common Problems

Although Windows 95 is generally considered more reliable than Windows 3.x, it is susceptible to problems. The following sections describe some of the most common Windows 95 issues and their potential solutions.

On the Exam

For the Windows 95 MCSE exam, you should be familiar with all of the issues discussed in this section. More importantly, you should have real-world experience in troubleshooting a variety of problems with Windows 95.

Installation Problems

The Windows 95 setup process is rather involved, but is generally reliable. The most frequent setup problems occur as a result of hardware that is not 100% compatible with Windows 95 or problems with a previously installed version of Windows. The following tips may be helpful in solving installation problems:

- Be sure the computer meets the hardware requirements described in this chapter, particularly RAM and disk storage.

- During the installation, follow along with the steps of the setup process described earlier in this chapter. If a problem occurs in the Real Mode phase, it is most likely hardware-related or caused by a TSR program in memory.

- During the setup process, a file called SETUPLOG.TXT is created in the root directory of the boot drive. This file contains entries for various aspects of the setup process. Examining the last entries in this file may provide information about the problem.

- Three additional log files are created in the root directory of the boot drive during the first boot after installation: BOOTLOG.TXT logs the loading of modules and device drivers, DETLOG.TXT logs information related to device detection, and NETLOG.TXT logs the loading of network drivers.

- Some video drivers may cause the installation process to lock up, or cause problems with the boot process after installation. If this occurs, reinstall using a standard driver (i.e., VGA) and change the driver using the Display control panel after installation.

Boot Problems

Most Windows 95 boot problems can be solved with an understanding of the boot process, described earlier in this chapter. In addition, the following techniques may solve boot problems:

- Try booting in Safe Mode using the Startup menu. If safe mode loads correctly, the problem is most likely with a device driver.

- Reboot, and use the Startup menu to select the Logged option. This creates the BOOTLOG.TXT file in the root directory. The last entries in this file should suggest the cause of the problem.

- If you have a startup disk (boot disk), try booting using this disk.

- Run the Windows 95 Setup program to reinstall any corrupt or missing files.

Network Problems

If Windows 95 is unable to access a network resource, check the following items:

- Verify that the network connection is working. Try accessing a different resource or using the ping utility (TCP/IP) to test the connection to the server.

- Use the Device Manager tab of the System control panel to check that the driver for the network adapter is functioning correctly, and check IRQ and other resource settings.

- If TCP/IP is in use, run the WINIPCFG utility. This displays information about the TCP/IP configuration and may be helpful in resolving problems.

- If the user is accessing a shared resource under Windows 95, be sure the folder is shared correctly and that the password (if any) is correct. For Windows NT resources, check share and NTFS permissions.

- If the user is attempting to access NetWare resources, check for a frame type mismatch.

Windows 95

Printer Problems

If a user gets error messages indicating that a printer does not exist or is not responding, there is probably a network problem or sharing problem as described above. Check the following items in the event of a printer problem:

- Check the printer's print job list by double clicking on its entry from the Printers window. If jobs are not reaching the list, the problem is most likely the user's workstation or the network connection. If jobs are reaching the list but not printing, the problem is most likely with the printer or the computer it is attached to.

- If jobs are not reaching the printer's job list, check that there is adequate free space on the computer attached to the printer.

- For Windows NT or NetWare printers, verify that the user has the correct permissions to access the printer.

Hardware Problems

Problems with hardware in Windows 95 usually result in problems with the setup or boot process, as described above. If you have determined that hardware may be the problem, follow these suggestions:

- Try reinstalling the driver for the device. Obtain an updated driver from the hardware vendor if possible.

- Look at the Device Manager tab of the System control panel, and check whether the device is listed, and whether an error icon appears to the left of its name.

- If hardware is causing other problems, such as lockups or boot failures, try removing the driver for the hardware. If the other problems are resolved, you may need to replace the hardware or obtain an updated driver.

- If the hardware supports Plug and Play, make sure this feature is enabled in the computer's BIOS. For non-Plug and Play hardware, you may need to explicitly assign an IRQ in the BIOS setup program.

Suggested Exercises

The Windows 95 exam covers most of the features of Windows 95. To prepare for the exam, you should have as much experience as possible with all aspects of installing, using, and managing Windows 95.

A single machine running Windows 95 should be sufficient to prepare for this exam, although more than one machine will allow you to practice with a wider variety of features. If available, a Windows NT domain controller on the network is helpful for some aspects of the exam.

Performing the following exercises will help you prepare for the exam:

1. Install Windows 95 on a computer:

   a. Use the information in the *Study Guide* to determine if the computer meets the hardware requirements for Windows 95.

   b. If you will be attaching the computer to a network, install a network card. Be sure the settings (IRQ, etc.) will not conflict with other components of the computer.

   c. Perform the Windows 95 installation. As you install, follow along with the installation steps presented in the *Study Guide*.

   d. Because it's important to be familiar with the installation process, install Windows 95 several times in different configurations if possible.

2. Be sure you are familiar with all of the basic Windows 95 user interface elements: Explorer, the Start menu, the desktop icons, the Control Panel, and properties dialogs for drives, directories, files, and network shares.

3. Use the REGEDIT utility to browse and search the registry. Compare the list of subtrees shown with the list in the *Study Guide*.

4. Press **F8** at startup to display the Windows 95 boot menu. Try each of the options and observe the results.

5. Modify the settings for a DOS program. If possible, find a DOS program that has difficulty running under Windows 95 and modify whatever settings are needed to get it to run.

6. Install the network services and protocols described in the *Study Guide*, and observe their Properties dialogs.

7. If you have two Windows 95 machines on a network, share one or more folders from one machine and attempt to access them from the other machine. You will need to ensure that both machines are configured with the same protocols.

8. If you have two machines, configure one for remote administration and try the remote administration utilities described in the *Study Guide* from the other machine.

9. If you have access to a NetWare server, configure Windows 95 to log on to the NetWare network and access files on the server. Be sure to use the Microsoft Client for NetWare Networks, described in the *Study Guide*.

10. Configure a dial-up networking (DUN) phonebook entry for an Internet provider or other remote network.

11. You should have experience installing new hardware on Windows 95 computers, both Plug-and-Play and non-Plug-and-Play.

12. Compress a drive using DriveSpace. Copy a number of files to the drive and observe the amount of space they use. Uncompress the drive.

13. Run the Windows 95 Backup utility. If you have a tape backup device, back up a set of files.

14. Configure one or more printers (you can experiment with this without actual hardware printers). If you have two machines, share a printer on one machine and configure the other machine to print to it.

Practice Test

Test Questions

1. Which of the following is not a feature of Windows 95?

    a. Preemptive multitasking

    b. Multiprocessing

    c. 32-bit application support

    d. Long filename support

2. Which of the following are advantages of Windows 95 over Windows NT Workstation? (select all that apply)

    a. Plug and Play

    b. Lesser hardware requirements

    c. Higher speed

    d. Better DOS compatibility

3. Which Intel 386 processor mode is limited to 1 MB of memory?

    a. Real mode

    b. Protected mode

4. Which processor privilege mode used by Windows 95 is allowed direct access to memory and hardware?

    a. Ring 0

    b. Ring 1

    c. Ring 2

    d. Ring 3

5. Which virtual machine supports Windows 3.1 applications under Windows 95?

    a. System VM

    b. MS-DOS VM

    c. Win16 VM

    d. Win32 VM

6. Which of the following application types are supported by Windows 95? (select all that apply)

    a. 16-bit Windows

    b. 32-bit Windows

    c. POSIX

    d. DOS

7. Which of the following Windows 95 components supports screen displays and printing?

    a. User

    b. Kernel

    c. GDI

    d. Graphics VM

8. Which of the following statements are true of 16-bit Windows applications? (select all that apply)

    a. They share a 4-GB virtual address space

    b. They share a message queue

    c. They support the use of virtual memory

    d. They are run using the MS-DOS VM

9. Which portion of the 4-GB virtual address space is typically used by DOS applications?

    a. 0 MB–1 MB

    b. 1 MB–4 MB

    c. 4 MB–2 GB

    d. 2 GB–4 GB

10. Which of the following extensions is typically used for Windows 95 protected-mode device drivers?

    a. SYS

    b. DLL

    c. VXD

    d. OLE

11. Which of the following registry subtrees stores associations between document types and applications?

    a.   HKEY_CURRENT_CONFIG

    b.   HKEY_CLASSES_ROOT

    c.   HKEY_USERS

    d.   HKEY_DYN_DATA

12. Which of the following files are used to store the current registry values? (select two of the following)

    a.   USER.DAT

    b.   USER.DA0

    c.   SYSTEM.DAT

    d.   REG.DAT

13. The Windows 95 logo is displayed during which phase of the boot process?

    a.   Protected Mode

    b.   Real Mode

    c.   Bootstrapping

    d.   Desktop Initialization

14. Which phase of the boot process loads the USER32.DLL file?

    a.   Protected Mode

    b.   Real Mode

    c.   Bootstrapping

    d.   Desktop Initialization

15. Which key is pressed during the boot process to display the startup menu?

    a.   F5

    b.   F6

    c.   F8

    d.   F10

16. You have selected a new video driver on a Windows 95 computer. The new driver is not compatible with the video card, and causes the computer to crash as soon as Windows 95 starts. Which of the options in the Startup menu can be used to load Windows 95 and change the driver to a working driver?

    a.   Normal

    b.   Safe Mode

    c.   Step-by-step confirmation

    d.   Command prompt only

17. Which file should be modified to cause the startup menu to be displayed automatically when Windows 95 boots?

    a.   SYSTEM.INI

    b.   BOOT.INI

    c.   MSDOS.SYS

    d.   BOOT.SYS

18. Which control panel applet allows you to create a startup disk?

    a.   System

    b.   Add/Remove Programs

    c.   Startup

    d.   Passwords

19. Which control panel applet includes the option to choose between user-level and share-level security?

    a.   Network

    b.   Passwords

    c.   Shares

    d.   System

20. Which Windows standard allows one 32-bit application to send commands to another application?

    a.   DDE

    b.   OLE

    c.   VMM

    d.   TAPI

21. Which of the following application types dedicate a separate virtual address space to each application? (select all that apply)

    a.   16-bit Windows

    b.   32-bit Windows

    c.   MS-DOS

22. Which of the following MS-DOS application options may allow a program to run under Windows that does not work with the default settings? (select all that apply)

    a.   MS-DOS mode

    b.   Initial size

    c.   Memory settings

    d.   Prevent MS-DOS-based programs from detecting Windows

23. You are installing Windows 95 on a computer with 8 MB of RAM, a VGA video card, an IDE CD-ROM drive, and an IDE disk drive with 40 MB of free space. Which component will need upgrading before Windows 95 can be installed?

    a. RAM

    b. Video card

    c. CD-ROM

    d. Disk drive

24. Which network type should be used in a network of four Windows 95 computers?

    a. Workgroup

    b. Domain

    c. Client-server

25. Which of the following file systems are supported by Windows 95? (select all that apply)

    a. NTFS

    b. FAT

    c. HPFS

    d. VFAT

26. Which phase of the Windows 95 installation runs the ScanDisk utility?

    a. Real mode phase

    b. Protected mode phase

    c. Bootstrap phase

27. If you have an existing installation of Windows 3.11 and wish to install Windows 95 in a dual-boot configuration, which directory should Windows 95 be installed in?

    a. The same directory as Windows 3.11

    b. A new directory

    c. Either directory

28. If you wish to install Windows 3.1, Windows 95, and Windows NT in a multi-boot configuration, which should be installed first?

    a. Windows 95

    b. Windows 3.1

    c. Windows NT

    d. They can be installed in any order

Windows 95

29. Which programs in the Windows 95 Resource Kit can be used to create a batch installation file? (select all that apply)

    a. BATCH.EXE

    b. SETUP.EXE

    c. NETSETUP.EXE

    d. POLEDIT.EXE

30. Network adapters are installed from which control panel applet?

    a. System

    b. Device Manager

    c. Network

    d. Hardware Devices

31. Which of the following browser types can be run on a Windows 95 computer? (select all that apply)

    a. Master browser

    b. Backup browser

    c. Potential browser

    d. Non-browser

32. Which of the following network protocols is not routable?

    a. TCP/IP

    b. NetBEUI

    c. IPX/SPX

33. Which of the following protocols is typically used to support communication with a NetWare server?

    a. IPX/SPX

    b. TCP/IP

    c. DLC

    d. NetBEUI

34. Which of the following protocols is typically used for communication with network printers and print servers?

    a. IPX/SPX

    b. DLC

    c. TCP/IP

    d. NetBEUI

35. Which of the following protocols is *not* related to the TCP/IP protocol suite?

    a. DNS

    b. DHCP

c. SLIP

d. DLC

36. Which of the following services can translate between NetBIOS names and IP addresses?

    a. DLC

    b. DNS

    c. WINS

    d. NetBEUI

37. Which protocol is used to automatically assign IP addresses to TCP/IP clients?

    a. DLC

    b. DNS

    c. DHCP

    d. NetBIOS

38. Which of the following clients requires the IPX/SPX protocol?

    a. Client for Microsoft Networks

    b. Client for NetWare Networks

    c. Dial-up Networking

39. Which of the following is a valid UNC path for a share called DOS on a computer called Payroll?

    a. \Payroll\DOS

    b. \\Payroll\DOS

    c. Share:\Payroll\DOS

    d. \\DOS

40. Which of the following network protocols can be used with Dial-up networking? (select all that apply)

    a. TCP/IP

    b. DLC

    c. NetBEUI

    d. IPX/SPX

41. Which Plug and Play component assigns IRQs and other resources to devices?

    a. Configuration Manager

    b. Resource Arbitrator

    c. Bus Enumerator

    d. BIOS

42. Which control panel dialog can be used to remove an installed hardware device driver?

    a.   Configuration Manager

    b.   Device Manager

    c.   Add New Hardware

    d.   Add/Remove Programs

43. Which of the following is a valid DOS filename to correspond with the "System Files.data" long filename?

    a.   SYSTEM.FI

    b.   SYSTEM~1.DAT

    c.   SYSTEMFI.DAT

    d.   SYSTEM~1

44. Which of the following security levels requires the use of a Windows NT or NetWare server?

    a.   User-level security

    b.   Share-level security

45. Which Windows 95 service provides a common interface to modems for applications?

    a.   OLE

    b.   Modem Manager

    c.   TAPI

    d.   DDE

46. Which of the following could be used to prevent a particular user from using the Shut Down option?

    a.   Local user profile

    b.   Roaming user profile

    c.   User policy

    d.   Computer policy

Answers to Questions

1. B. Windows 95 does not support multiprocessing.

2. A, B, D. Windows 95 supports Plug and Play; has lower hardware requirements than Windows NT Workstation, and slightly better DOS compatibility.

3. A. Real mode is limited to the bottom 1 MB of memory.

4. A. Ring 0 is allowed direct access to memory and hardware.

5. A. The System VM supports Windows 3.1 applications.

6. A, B, D. Windows 95 supports Win16, Win32, and DOS applications.

7. C. The GDI (graphic device interface) supports screen displays and printing.

8. A, B, C. Win16 applications share an address space and message queue, and do support the use of virtual memory. They are run using the System VM, not the MS-DOS VM (choice D).

9. A. DOS applications typically use the first 1 MB of address space.

10. C. Protected mode device drivers typically use the VXD extension.

11. B. Associations between document types and applications are stored under the HKEY_CLASSES_ROOT subkey.

12. A, C. USER.DAT and SYSTEM.DAT store the current registry values.

13. B. The Windows 95 logo is displayed during the Real Mode phase of the boot process.

14. A. The Protected Mode phase of the boot process loads the USER32.DLL file.

15. C. Press the F8 key during the boot process to display the startup menu.

16. B. Safe Mode allows you to boot Windows 95 and change the display driver.

17. C. The MSDOS.SYS file can be modified to cause the startup menu to be displayed each time Windows 95 boots.

18. B. The Add/Remove Programs control panel allows you to create a startup disk.

19. A. The Network control panel includes the option to choose between user-level and share-level security.

20. A. DDE (dynamic data exchange) allows 16- and 32-bit Windows applications to send and receive commands.

21. B, C. MS-DOS applications and Win32 applications dedicate a separate virtual address space to each application. Win16 applications (choice A) share a single address space.

22. A, C, D. The *MS-DOS mode, Memory settings,* and *Prevent MS-DOS-based programs from detecting Windows* options may allow a DOS program to run under Windows 95. The *Initial Size* option (choice B) relates to window size and does not affect the application's ability to run.

23. D. Windows 95 requires a minimum of 55 MB of disk storage.

24. A. A workgroup network is well-suited to a network of four Windows 95 computers.

25. B, D. Windows 95 supports the FAT and VFAT (long filename) file systems.

26. A. The ScanDisk utility is executed during the Real Mode phase of installation.

27. B. For a dual-boot configuration, Windows 95 must be installed in a separate directory.

28. B. Windows 3.1 should be installed first, then Windows 95, then Windows NT.

29. A, C. The BATCH.EXE and NETSETUP.EXE utilities can be used to create a batch installation file.

30. C. Network adapters are installed from the Network control panel.

31. A, B, C, D. A Windows 95 computer can act as any of these browser types.

32. B. NetBEUI is a non-routable protocol.

33. A. The IPX/SPX protocol is typically used for communication with a NetWare server.

34. B. The DLC protocol is typically used for communication with network printers and print servers.

35. D. The DLC protocol is not related to TCP/IP.

36. C. The WINS service translates between NetBIOS names and IP addresses. DNS (choice B) performs a similar function, but translates between IP host names and IP addresses.

37. C. The DHCP protocol can be used to dynamically assign IP addresses to TCP/IP clients.

38. B. The Client for NetWare Networks requires the IPX/SPX protocol.

39. B. \\Payroll\DOS is the correct UNC path.

40. A, C, D. TCP/IP, NetBEUI, and IPX/SPX protocols can be used with Dial-up networking.

41. B. The Resource Arbitrator assigns IRQs and other resources to devices.

42. B. The Device Manager control panel dialog (part of the System control panel) can be used to remove an installed hardware device driver.

43. B. The short filename for "System Files.data" would be SYSTEM~1.DAT.

44. A. User-level security requires the use of a Windows NT or NetWare server.

45. C. The TAPI (Telephony Application Programmer's Interface) service provides a common interface to modems.

46. C. A user policy could be used to prevent a user from using the Shut Down option. A computer policy (choice D) can perform a similar function, but for a particular computer rather than a particular user.

Highlighter's Index

Windows 95 Basics

Windows 95 vs. Windows 3.x

More stability and better multitasking

Support for 32-bit applications

Long filename support

New, customizable user interface

Dial-up Networking

Windows NT Workstation vs. Windows 95

All 32-bit components

Better stability and better multitasking

Multiprocessor support (2 CPUs)

Supports RISC CPUs (Digital Alpha)

Some POSIX and OS/2 support

Better security

Windows 95 vs. Windows NT

Lower price

Lesser hardware requirements

Plug and Play support

Better compatibility with Windows 3.1

Better DOS compatibility

X86 Architecture

Real mode: Limited to 1 MB

Protected (Enhanced) mode: Full memory support, multitasking

Ring 0: Fastest execution; direct hardware and memory access; no memory protection

Ring 3: Memory protection; virtual memory; slower execution

Windows 95 Components

MS-DOS VM: Supports DOS applications

System VM: Kernel, User, GDI, Win32, Win16

Virtual Memory

Unused memory swapped to disk (demand paging)

4 GB address space:

> 0 MB–1 MB: DOS applications
>
> 1 MB–4 MB: Win16 applications
>
> 4 MB–2 GB: Win16 and Win32
>
> 2 GB–3 GB: DLLs and APIs
>
> 3 GB–4 GB: Device drivers

The Registry

HKEY_CLASSES_ROOT stores file associations

HKEY_CURRENT_USER stores control panel settings; loaded from user profile at login

HKEY_LOCAL_MACHINE stores hardware-specific data

HKEY_USERS stores default user settings and settings for each user profile

HKEY_CURRENT_CONFIG stores dynamic configuration information

HKEY_DYN_DATA stores dynamic hardware information

REGEDIT can edit, search, import, and export registry values

The Boot Process

Bootstrap phase: BIOS loads and executes MBR

Real mode phase: Loads MSDOS.SYS, SYSTEM.DAT, DRVSPACE.BIN, AUTOEXEC.BAT, CONFIG.SYS

Protected mode phase: Loads WIN.COM, kernel, user, GDI

Desktop initialization: Runs EXPLORER.EXE, applications in Startup group

Applications

MS-DOS: Each has separate DOS VM and memory space

Win16: All apps share a single VM, memory space and message queue

Win32: Each has its own VM, memory space, message queue

Installation

Hardware Requirements

CPU: 386 DX or higher (486 DX or higher recommended)

RAM: 4 MB (8 MB recommended)

Display: VGA, Super VGA, or better

Hard disk: SCSI or IDE; 55 MB of space required for OS

Floppy disk: 3.5", 1.4 MB

CD-ROM: SCSI or IDE (optional)

Network adapter (for networked machines)

Network Types

Workgroup (peer-to-peer) networks: Each workstation can share resources; each handles its own user authentication; best suited for small networks (10 workstations or less)

Domain (client-server) networks: One or more dedicated servers; centralized administration; any number of users; requires PDC (NT Server only)

File Systems

FAT: DOS standard; 2 GB maximum; 8.3 filenames

VFAT: Windows 95 and NT; 4 GB maximum; long filenames

NTFS: NT 4.0 and later; not supported by Windows 95

HPFS: OS/2 and NT 3.51 and earlier; no support in Windows 95

Installation Process

Real mode phase: Text-based; ScanDisk; checks hardware; unloads TSRs; Searches for existing Windows version

Protected mode phase: Loads GUI; performs installation

SETUP.EXE Options

/C: (DOS only) skips loading of SMARTDRV.EXE

/id: Skips the check for free disk space

/iL: (DOS only) loads driver for Logitech mouse

/im: Skips the check for free memory

/in: Skips the network portion of the setup process

/iq: Does not check for cross-linked files

/is: Skips the system check (ScanDisk)

/T:path: Specifies temporary file storage path

Network Components

TCP/IP
Named for Transport Control Protocol and Internet Protocol

Routable

Used for UNIX and the Internet

Main protocols: TCP (connection-oriented); UDP (connectionless)

IPX/SPX (NWLink)
Usually used for NetWare connectivity

Main protocols: IPX (connectionless); SPX (connection-oriented)

Routable

NetBEUI
Used to support NetBIOS

Low overhead

Non-routable; used for small networks

Clients
Client for Microsoft Networks

Client for NetWare Networks

File Sharing for Microsoft Networks

File Sharing for NetWare Networks

Dial-up Protocols
SLIP (Serial line Internet protocol): Simple; TCP/IP only; UNIX servers

PPP (Point-to-point protocol): Supports authentication and error control; TCP/IP or other protocol; NT servers

NRN: NetWare Connect (NetWare servers)

Windows for Workgroups and Windows NT 3.1 (proprietary protocol)

Managing Windows 95

Plug and Play
BIOS, OS, and devices must support Plug and Play

Configuration Manager supervises Plug and Play process; receives information about configuration changes from BIOS

Bus Enumerators manage device attachment buses; communicate with devices

Resource Arbitrator manages the pool of available resources; assigns them to devices

HKEY_DYN_DATA registry key stores current state of Plug and Play devices

Long Filenames

256 character limit

Short name: first six characters plus ~ (tilde) plus a number plus first three characters of extension

Cannot be used with DOS utilities that modify FAT

Backups

BACKUP.EXE included with Windows 95

Differential backup includes all of the files that have changed since the last full backup; does not clear archive bits

Incremental backup copies files that have changed since the last backup, whether full or incremental; clears archive bits

Security Levels

Share-level security (default) uses individual passwords for each share

User-level security uses user list from NT or NetWare server; can assign permissions to the shared resource per users or groups

User Profiles

Local profiles only work at a particular workstation

Roaming profiles stored on server; work at any Windows 95 computer in the network

Mandatory profiles are roaming profiles that cannot be modified by users

Remote Administration

Requires user-level security

Includes Net Watcher, System Monitor, Administer file system, Remote registry

Accessed from Tools tab of computer's Properties

Troubleshooting

Monitoring Performance

Net Watcher manages lists of shared resources and current users

System Monitor graphs performance counters over time

Disk Utilities

Disk Defragmenter rearranges files for optimum disk use

ScanDisk scans FAT and physical disk surface for errors

Index

Numbers

100BaseT, 43
10Base2 network, 42
10Base5 network, 43
10BaseT network, 42
16-bit Windows applications, 102
32-bit Windows applications, 102
70-058 exam, 5, 15–86
70-064 exam, 5, 309–383
   NT Workstation exam vs., 6–7
70-067 exam, 6, 187–252
70-068 exam, 6, 255–306
70-073 exam, 5, 89–184
   Windows 95 exam vs., 6–7
802 standards (IEEE), 24–26
802.2, 802.3 frame types, 124

A

/a option (NTBACKUP.EXE), 218
access to domains, 220
access control lists (ACLs), 143
Account Lockout option, 143
account policies, 143
accounts
   definition of, 19
   on PDC, 220
   for users, expiring, 221

accounts, user, 53, 139–144
   maximum number of, 258–259
   user rights, 144
   (see also users)
ACLs (access control lists), 143
Active Directory, 259
adapter entries (BOOT.INI), 114
adapters (see network adapters)
Adapters tab (Network panel), 203
Add/Remove Programs control panel,
   133
addresses
   high memory, 32
   I/O, 32–33
administration
   networks, 53–58
   remote, 227–228
   system policies, 224–227
   Windows NT Server, 219–228
administrative shares, 148
Administrator user, 139
Administrators group, 139
administrators, defintion of, 19
Advanced RISC Computing entries
   (BOOT.INI), 114–115
Advanced Setup option (Setup
   Manager), 118
advice for taking exams, 11
agents, SNMP, 155

browsers, 212
  browser election, 213
  Computer Browser service, 213
  types of, 212
browsing networks, 102, 212–213
bus topologies, 35
Bytes Total/Sec counter, 229

C

/C option (WINNT), 109
cable testers, 62
cables
  backbone, 35
  drop cables, 35
  RG-58/U, 42
  RG-58A/U and C/U, 42
  RG-8, 43
  troubleshooting, 61–63
  (see also networking)
callback option (RAS), 132
carrier sense, 26
CDFS file system, 106
CD-ROM
  booting Windows NT from, 107
  installing Windows NT from, 107
  problems, 159
cell switching, 53
centralization, 20
centralized processing, definition of, 19
certification programs, list of, 1–5
ChangeLogSize key, 285
CHAP protocol, 132
charting performance, 59, 154
choosing between MCSE exams, 6–7
circuit switching, 49
Clear All Events command, 153
Client Services for NetWare (CSNW), 122, 207
clients, 20
  definition of, 19
client-server networks, 20, 105
coaxial cable, 30
collision detection, 26
compact disc file system, 106
compatibility, hardware, 104
complete trust model, 264
complex trusts, 261
Computer Browser service, 213

computers
  adding to domain, 219
  crashes, 162, 286
  identifying with NetBIOS name, 54
  policies for, 142, 224–226
  viruses, 58
concentrators (see hubs)
configuring
  blue screen response behavior, 286
  DHCP Relay Agent, 273
  DHCP scopes, 267
  DHCP server, 266–268
  disks, 213–218
  DNS, 128
  DNS Server, 270
  Dr. Watson utility, 162
  IIS (Internet Information Service), 276
  Internet services, 272–278
  IP addresses, 127
  IP routing, 272–273
  last known good configuration, 156
  memory paging, 99
  multi-boot systems, 113–116
  NetWare server for GSNW, 208
  network cards, 60
  network interface cards (NICS), 32
  networking, troubleshooting, 230
  nodes, 61
  NT control panels for, 133–136
  NT Server domain network, 196–197
  NT Server networking, 194–196
  printers, 149–151
  PWS (Peer Web Services), 129
  RAS (Remote Access Service), 130
  RAS server, 210
  RIP for IPX, 274
  system backups, 215–218
  Windows NT Workstation, 133–151
  WINS service, 128, 268–269
connectionless network protocols, 45
connection-oriented network protocols, 45
connectivity
  devices for, 37–41
  over modems (see modems; RAS)
  troubleshooting, 60, 230
Console control panel, 133
continuing education, MCSE certification, 11

disks
    configuring, 213–218
    creating installation disks, 202
    ERDs (emergency repair disks),
        156–157
    installing operating system from, 107,
        196
    installing Windows NT from, 107
    Macintosh disk sharing, 271
    managing storage, 145–149
    monitoring drive activity, 229
    RAID, 57
    RAID (see also RAID)
    storage performance, 156
    swapping memory to (see virtual
        memory)
Display control panel, 134
display driver diagnostics, 158
[Display] section (UNATTEND.TXT),
    117
distributed processing
    definition of, 19
DLC (Data Link Control), 196
DLC protocol, 48
DMA channels, 32
DNS (Domain Name Service), 126
    configuring, 128
    configuring server, 270
    zones, 270
DOD Reference model, 46
Domain Admins group, 222
domain controllers, 196–197, 219,
    282–285
Domain Guests group, 222
domain master browser, 212
domain model, 20
domain networks, 105
    planning for (NT Server), 196–197
Domain Users group, 222
domains
    models, 262–265
    optimizing performance, 281–285
    security and, 219–220
    synchronizing, 284–285
    trusted, 259–262
    user/group access to, 265
DOS applications, 101
DOS operating system, booting, 100
DOS subsystem, 98

Dr. Watson utility, 162
drivers, promiscuous mode, 279
drives
    diagnostics on, 158
    monitoring, 229
    network, mapping, 103
DTES (data terminal equipment), 52
dual-boot systems, 113–116
/dump option (SYSDIFF), 119
dumps, memory, 286
DUN (Dial-up Networking), 50
duplexing, 56, 192
dynamic routers, 39
dynamic routing, 273

E
/e option (NTBACKUP.EXE), 218
/E option (WINNT, WINNT32), 109
editing the Windows NT Registry,
    137–138
electing browsers, 213
elective exams (MCSE), 3
    choosing, 7
EMI (electromagnetic interference), 27
emissions, 27
Enable Gateway option (GSNW), 208
Environment option (System control
    panel), 136
environment subsystems, 98
environment, diagnostics on, 158
ERDs (emergency repair disks),
    156–157
error control, 23
errors
    STOP (blue screen) errors, 162, 286
    Windows NT, 158–162
Ethernet, 41–43
    Switched Ethernet, 38
Ethernet networks, media access
        method of (CSMA/CD), 26
Event Viewer utility, 59, 152
exam 70-058, 5, 15–86
exam 70-064, 5, 309–383
    NT Workstation exam vs., 6–7
exam 70-067, 6, 187–252
exam 70-068, 6, 255–306
exam 70-073, 5, 89–184
    Windows 95 exam vs., 6–7

Maximum Password Age option, 143
/maxmem option (ARC entries), 115
MCP certification, 2
MCP+Internet certification, 2
MCSD certification, 4
MCSE certification, 2
  continuing education, 11
  core exams, 3, 5–6
  examination process, 6–11
MCSE program, ix, 1–12
  other resources for, xi
MCSE+Internet certification, 3
MCT certification, 5
media types, 27–31
medium priority, 101
member servers, 197
memory
  capturing activity data and, 280
  diagnostics on, 158
  disk partitions (see disk partitions)
  disk space problems, 159
  DMA channels, 32
  domain controller RAM, 282
  high memory addresses, 32
  managing disk storage, 145–149, 214
  memory dumps, 286
  minimizing usage of, 281
  monitoring, 229
  paging, 155
  virtual memory, 99, 155, 229
  Virtual Memory Manager (VMM), 98,
    99
memory counter, 60, 153
memory disk space, striping with parity
    and, 57
memory protection, 93
mesh topologies, 36
message switching, 49
microkernel (see kernel)
Microsoft
  certification programs, list of, 1–5
  network components, list of, 120
  Peer Web Services (see PWS)
Microsoft's Training and Certification
    Web page, xi
microwave networking, 31
migrating to Windows NT, 113
Migration Tool for NetWare, 208

Minimum Password Age option, 143
Minimum Password Length option, 143
MIPS processors, 95
mirror sets, 192, 214
mirroring, 56
mirroring disks, 192
mismatched network protocols, 61
modems, 50
  Modems control panel, 134
  RAS for (see RAS)
  Telephony control panel, 135
monitoring network traffic, 279–281
monitoring performance (see
    performance)
Mouse control panel, 135
moving files, 147
MS-CHAP protocol, 132
multi-boot systems, 113–116
multilink feature (RAS), 50, 130
Multimedia control panel, 135
multiple access, 26
multiple master domain model, 263
multiple-answer questions, 9
multi-port repeaters, 38
multiprocessing, 93
multitasking
  cooperative multitasking, 93
  preemptive multitasking, 93
multithreading, 93

N

names
  for network computers (NetBIOS
    names), 54
  WINS service, 55
  (see UNC pathnames)
NDIS (Network Device Specification),
    26
NetBEUI service, 48, 195
  RAS server and, 211
NetBIOS, 48, 205
NetBIOS names
  resolving, 269
  WINS service, 55, 268–269
NetWare connectivity, 121–124,
    206–210
  frame types, 123
  IPX/SPX protocols, 47, 122, 195, 207

PSTN (Public Service Telephone
    Network), 50
PWS (Peer Web Services), 128–130, 274

Q
questions, types of, 9–11

R
/r option (NTBACKUP.EXE), 218
radio networking, 31
RAID (Redundant Array of Inexpensive
    Disks), 57, 191–194
    hardware RAID support, 193
RAM of domain controllers, 282
RAM performance, 153, 155
RAS (Remote Access Server), 130–132,
    210–212
RAS (Remote Access Service), 50
    dial-up security, 131–132
    installing and configuring, 130
    phonebook entries, 131
rdisk entries (BOOT.INI), 114
realtime priority, 101
REGEDIT, REGEDT32 programs, 137
Regional Settings control panel, 135
registering for exams, 8
Registry
    editing, 137–138
    ERDs and, 156–157
reliability of network protocols, 45
Remote Access Admin utility, 211
Remote Access Server (see RAS)
remote administration, 227–228
removing WIndows NT, 116
repeaters, 38
    multi-port, 38
replacing damaged files, 157
ReplicationGovernor key, 285
Replicators group, 140
reports, performance, 60, 154
reserving IP addresses, 268
resolving NetBIOS names, 269
resource access problems, 160
resources for further reading, xi
resources, diagnostics on, 158
restoring data from backups, 217

retired exams, 12
RG-58 A/U cable, 42
RG-58C/U cable, 42
rights of users, 144
ring topologies, 36
RIP (Router Information Protocol), 39
RIP for IPX protocol, 274
RISC computers
    boot process on, 100
roaming user profiles, 142, 223
root Registry keys, 137
routable network protocols, 40
routers, 39–40
routing
    DHCP Relay Agent, 273
    IP routing, 272–273
    IPX routing, 274
    network layer for, 23

S
SAM (security accounts manager), 220
satellite microwave networks, 31
saving
    disk mirroring and duplexing, 56
    disk storage, 156
    fault tolerance (see fault tolerance)
    managing disk storage, 145–149
scenario questions, 10
scheduled activities (see automatic)
scheduling print jobs, 151
scheduling to take exams, 8
scope IDs, 55
scopes, DHCP, 267
scoring process, 11
SCSI Adapters control panel, 135
security, 138–145
    auditing, 53
    dial-up (RAS), 131–132
    events, monitoring, 152
    file sharing and, 148
    RAID (see RAID)
    SAM (security accounts manager),
        220
    SIDs (security identifiers), 220
    system policies, 142, 224–227
    user-level, 54
    Windows NT Server, 219–228

synchronization of domains, 284–285
SYSDIFF utility, 119
system backups, configuring, 215–218
System control panel, 135–136
system diagnostics, 158
system events, monitoring, 59, 152
system files, damaged, 157
system partitions, 100
system policies, 142, 224–227
System Policy Editor, 225
system troubleshooting, 161

T

/t option (NTBACKUP.EXE), 218
/T option (WINNT, WINNT32), 109
tape backups, 193
Tape Devices Control Panel, 135
/tape option (NTBACKUP.EXE), 218
Task Manager utility, 101, 153
T-carrier lines, 51
TCP protocol, 46
    counters for, 279
TCP/IP protocol, 46, 124–130, 195
    OSPF protocol, 39
    RAS and, 210
telephone system (PSTN), 50
Telephony control panel, 135
terminators, 35, 62
terminology, networking, 19
terrestrial microwave networks, 31
text-based phase (NT Workstation
    installation), 110, 199
thicknet, 43
third-party backup utilities, 217
threads (see multithreading)
time limit for exams, 8
timeout entry (BOOT.INI), 114
tips on taking exams, 11
Token Ring networks, 26, 43
    topologies, 37
    topology for, 36
tokens, 26
topologies, network, 34
    connectivity devices for, 37–41
traffic, network
    monitoring, 229, 279–281
    number of user accounts and, 259

Training and Certification Web page, xi
transceivers, 32
transmission media, definition of, 20
transport layer (OSI), 24
troubleshooting
    cables, 61–63
    connectivity, 60
    networks, 58–63
    NT Server networking, 229
    printing, 160
    STOP (blue screen) errors, 162, 286
    Windows NT, 285–286
    Windows NT errors, 158–162
    Windows NT Workstation, 156–162
trusts, 259–265
    models of, 262–265
    trusted domains, 259–262
    types of, 260
    user/group domain access, 265
two-way trusts, 261

U

/U option (WINNT, WINNT32), 109
UDF (uniqueness database file), 201
UDF files for installing WIndows NT,
    118
/UDF option (WINNT, WINNT32), 110
UDP protocol, 46
    counters for, 279
UNATTEND.TXT file, 117
unattended installation, 201
unattended installation files, 116
[Unattended] section
    (UNATTEND.TXT), 117
UNC pathnames, 54, 103
uninstalling Windows NT, 116
uninterruptible power supply (see UPS)
uniqueness database file (UDF), 118,
    201
uniquess, password, 143
universal naming convention, 103
unreliability of network protocols, 45
upgrading to Windows NT, 113
UPS (uninterruptible power supply), 58,
    194
    UPS control panel, 136

About the Author

Michael Moncur is a freelance author and consultant in Salt Lake City, Utah. He is the owner of Starling Technologies, a small company specializing in network consulting and web content development. Michael is certified as both a CNE and an MCSE, and is the author of several books on NetWare, NT, and the CNE and MCSE programs, including *NT Network Security* and *CNE Study Guide for IntranetWare* (Sybex/Network Press), and the upcoming *MCSE: The Electives in a Nutshell* (O'Reilly & Associates).

Colophon

Our look is the result of reader comments, our own experimentation, and feedback from distribution channels. Distinctive covers complement our distinctive approach to technical topics, breathing personality and life into potentially dry subjects.

The animal appearing on the cover of *MCSE: The Core Exams in a Nutshell* is an Asian elephant (*Elephas maximus*). Elephants are the world's largest terrestrial animals, striking not only for their great size (4–6 tons), but also their trunk. The trunk is used for both smell and touch, as well as for picking things up and as a snorkel when swimming. The most important use of the trunk is obtaining food and water. Another distinguishing feature is the tusks, modified incisors of durable ivory, for which man has hunted the elephant nearly to extinction. Like right- or left-handed people, elephants favor one tusk.

Elephants spend most of their day—up to 17 hours—preparing and eating their food, which consists of several hundred pounds per day of bamboo, bark, grass, roots, wood, and other vegetation. They generally sleep standing up for short periods. Elephants also take frequent baths in water or mud, and, when the weather is hot, fan themselves with their ears. They can trumpet loudly, and also often make a kind of relaxed purring or rumbling noise.

The lifespan of an elephant is about 40 to 50 years, though a few live into their sixties. They have keen hearing, and can learn verbal commands, increasing their popularity as circus stars and beasts of burden. Elephants have also been used in war, mostly notably by the Carthaginian general Hannibal.

Elephant cemeteries, where old and sick elephants congregate to die, are a myth. Experiments have proved that they are not afraid of mice, but do fear rabbits and some dogs. They have no natural enemies apart from man.

Edie Freedman designed the cover of this book, using a 19th-century engraving from the Dover Pictorial Archive. The cover layout was produced with Quark XPress 3.32 using the ITC Garamond font. Whenever possible, our books use RepKover™, a durable and flexible lay-flat binding. If the page count exceeds RepKover's limit, perfect binding is used.

The inside layout was designed by Nancy Priest and implemented in FrameMaker 5.5 by Mike Sierra. The text and heading fonts are ITC Garamond Light and Garamond Book. The illustrations that appear in the book were created in Adobe FreeHand 7 and Photoshop 4 by Robert Romano. This colophon was written by Nancy Kotary.

More Titles from O'Reilly

Windows NT System Administration

Windows NT in a Nutshell

By Eric Pearce
1st Edition June 1997
364 pages, ISBN 1-56592-251-4

Anyone who installs Windows NT, creates a user, or adds a printer is an NT system administrator (whether they realize it or not). This book features a new tagged callout approach to documenting the 4.0 GUI as well as real-life examples of command usage and strategies for problem solving, with an emphasis on networking. *Windows NT in a Nutshell* will be as useful to the single-system home user as it will be to the administrator of a 1,000-node corporate network.

Windows NT Desktop Reference

By Æleen Frisch
1st Edition January 1998
64 pages, ISBN 1-56592-437-1

A hip-pocket quick reference to Windows NT commands, as well as the most useful commands from the Resource Kits. Commands are arranged ingroups related to their purpose and function. Covers Windows NT 4.0.

MCSE: The Electives in a Nutshell

By Michael Moncur
1st Edition September 1998
550 pages, ISBN: 1-56592-482-7

A companion volume to *MCSE: The Core Exams in a Nutshell*, *MCSE: The Electives in a Nutshell* is a comprehensive study guide that covers the elective exams for the MCSE as well as the Internet requirements and electives for the MCSE+Internet. This detailed reference is aimed at sophisticated users who need a bridge between real-world experience and the MCSE exam requirements.

Essential Windows NT System Administration

By Æleen Frisch
1st Edition February 1998
486 pages, ISBN 1-56592-274-3

This book combines practical experience with technical expertise to help you manage Windows NT systems as productively as possible. It covers the standard utilities offered with the Windows NT operating system and from the Resource Kit, as well as important commercial and free third-party tools. By the author of O'Reilly's bestselling book, *Essential System Administration*.

Windows NT Backup & Restore

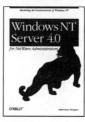

By Jody Leber
1st Edition May 1998
320 pages, ISBN 1-56592-272-7

Beginning with the need for a workable recovery policy and ways to translate that policy into requirements, *Windows NT Backup & Restore* presents the reader with practical guidelines for setting up an effective backup system in both small and large environments. It covers the native NT utilities as well as major third-party hardware and software.

Windows NT Server 4.0 for NetWare Administrators

By Robert Bruce Thompson
1st Edition November 1997
756 pages, ISBN 1-56592-280-8

This book provides a fast-track means for experienced NetWare administrators to build on their knowledge and master the fundamentals of using the Microsoft Windows NT Server. The broad coverage of many aspects of Windows NT Server is balanced by a tightly focused approach of comparison, contrast, and differentiation between NetWare and NT features and methodologies.

Windows NT System Administration

Windows NT SNMP

By James D. Murray
1st Edition January 1998
464 pages, Includes CD-ROM
ISBN 1-56592-338-3

This book describes the implementation of SNMP (the Simple Network Management Protocol) on Windows NT 3.51 and 4.0 (with a look ahead to NT 5.0) and Windows 95 systems. It covers SNMP and network basics and detailed information on developing SNMP management applications and extension agents. The book comes with a CD-ROM containing a wealth of additional information: standards documents, sample code from the book, and many third-party, SNMP-related software tools, libraries, and demos.

Managing the Windows NT Registry

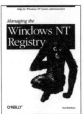

By Paul Robichaux
1st Edition April 1998
376 pages, ISBN 1-56592-378-2

The Windows NT Registry is the repository for all hardware, software, and application configuration settings. This is the system administrator's guide to maintaining, monitoring, and updating the Registry database. A "must-have" for every NT system manager or administrator, it covers what the Registry is and where it lives on disk, available tools, Registry access from programs, and Registry content.

Learning Perl on Win32 Systems

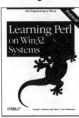

By Randal L. Schwartz,
Erik Olson & Tom Christiansen
1st Edition August 1997
306 pages, ISBN 1-56592-324-3

In this carefully paced course, leading Perl trainers and a Windows NT practitioner teach you to program in the language that promises to emerge as the scripting language of choice on NT. Based on the "llama" book, this book features tips for PC users and new, NT-specific examples, along with a foreword by Larry Wall, the creator of Perl, and Dick Hardt, the creator of Perl for Win32.

Windows NT User Administration

By Ashley J. Meggitt &
Timothy D. Ritchey
1st Edition November 1997
218 pages, ISBN 1-56592-301-4

Many Windows NT books introduce you to a range of topics, but seldom do they give you enough information to master any one thing. This book (like other O'Reilly animal books) is different. *Windows NT User Administration* makes you an expert at creating users efficiently, controlling what they can do, limiting the damage they can cause, and monitoring their activities on your system. Don't simply react to problems; use the techniques in this book to anticipate and prevent them.

Perl

Perl Resource Kit—Win32 Edition

By Dick Hardt, Erik Olson,
David Futato & Brian Jepson
1st Edition August 1998
1,832 pages
Includes 4 books & CD-ROM
ISBN 1-56592-409-6

The *Perl Resource Kit—Win32 Edition* is an essential tool for Perl programmers who are expanding their platform expertise to include Win32 and for Win32 webmasters and system administrators who have discovered the power and lexibility of Perl. The Kit contains some of the latest commercial Win32 Perl software from Dick Hardt's ActiveState company, along with a collection of hundreds of Perl modules that run on Win32, and a definitive documentation set from O'Reilly.

Perl

Perl Resource Kit—UNIX Edition

By Larry Wall, Nate Patwardhan, Ellen Siever, David Futato & Brian Jepson
1st Edition November 1997
1812 pages, ISBN 1-56592-370-7

The *Perl Resource Kit—UNIX Edition* gives you the most comprehensive collection of Perl documentation and commercially enhanced software tools available today. Developed in association with Larry Wall, the creator of Perl, it's the definitive Perl distribution for webmasters, programmers, and system administrators.

The *Perl Resource Kit* provides:

- Over 1800 pages of tutorial and in-depth reference documentation for Perl utilities and extensions, in 4 volumes.
- A CD-ROM containing the complete Perl distribution, plus hundreds of freeware Perl extensions and utilities—a complete snapshot of the Comprehensive Perl Archive Network (CPAN)—as well as new software written by Larry Wall just for the Kit.

Perl Software Tools All on One Convenient CD-ROM
Experienced Perl hackers know when to create their own, and when they can find what they need on CPAN. Now all the power of CPAN—and more—is at your fingertips. The *Perl Resource Kit* includes:

- A complete snapshot of CPAN, with an install program for Solaris and Linux that ensures that all necessary modules are installed together. Also includes an easy-to-use search tool and a web-aware interface that allows you to get the latest version of each module.
- A new Java/Perl interface that allows programmers to write Java classes with Perl implementations. This new tool was written specially for the Kit by Larry Wall.

Experience the power of Perl modules in areas such as CGI, web spidering, database interfaces, managing mail and USENET news, user interfaces, security, graphics, math and statistics, and much more.

Programming Perl, 2nd Edition

By Larry Wall, Tom Christiansen & Randal L. Schwartz
2nd Edition September 1996
670 pages, ISBN 1-56592-149-6

Coauthored by Larry Wall, the creator of Perl, the second edition of this authoritative guide contains a full explanation of Perl version 5.003 features. It covers Perl language and syntax, functions, library modules, references, and object-oriented features, and also explores invocation options, debugging, common mistakes, and much more.

The Perl Cookbook

By Tom Christiansen & Nathan Torkington
1st Edition August 1998
794 pages, ISBN 1-56592-243-3

This collection of problems, solutions, and examples for anyone programming in Perl covers everything from beginner questions to techniques that even the most experienced Perl programmers might learn from. It contains hundreds of Perl "recipes," including recipes for parsing strings, doing matrix multiplication, working with arrays and hashes, and performing complex regular expressions.

Perl in a Nutshell

By Stephen Spainhour, Ellen Siever & Nathan Patwardhan
1st Edition October 1998 (est.)
552 pages (est.), ISBN 1-56592-286-7

The perfect companion for working programmers, *Perl in a Nutshell* is a comprehensive reference guide to the world of Perl. It contains everything you need to know for all but the most obscure Perl questions. This wealth of information is packed into an efficient, extraordinarily usable format.

O'REILLY™

TO ORDER: **800-998-9938** • *order@oreilly.com* • *http://www.oreilly.com/*
OUR PRODUCTS ARE AVAILABLE AT A BOOKSTORE OR SOFTWARE STORE NEAR YOU.
FOR INFORMATION: **800-998-9938** • **707-829-0515** • *info@oreilly.com*

Perl

Learning Perl, 2nd Edition

By Randal L. Schwartz &
Tom Christiansen,
Foreword by Larry Wall
2nd Edition July 1997
302 pages, ISBN 1-56592-284-0

In this update of a bestseller, two
leading Perl trainers teach you to use
the most universal scripting language
in the age of the World Wide Web.
Now current for Perl version 5.004,
this hands-on tutorial includes a lengthy new chapter on
CGI programming, while touching also on the use of library
modules, references, and Perl's object-oriented constructs.

Advanced Perl Programming

By Sriram Srinivasan
1st Edition August 1997
434 pages, ISBN 1-56592-220-4

This book covers complex techniques
for managing production-ready Perl
programs and explains methods for
manipulating data and objects that may
have looked like magic before. It gives
you necessary background for dealing
with networks, databases, and GUIs,
and includes a discussion of internals to help you program more
efficiently and embed Perl within C or C within Perl.

Perl 5 Pocket Reference

By Johan Vromans
1st Edition February 1996
46 pages, ISBN 1-56592-187-9

This is the standard quick-reference
guide for the Perl programming language.
It provides a complete overview of the
language, from variables to input and
output, from flow control to regular
expressions, from functions to document
formats—all packed into a convenient,
carry-around booklet. Updated to cover Perl version 5.003.

Mastering Regular Expressions

By Jeffrey E. F. Friedl
1st Edition January 1997
368 pages, ISBN 1-56592-257-3

Regular expressions, a powerful tool
for manipulating text and data, are
found in scripting languages, editors,
programming environments, and
specialized tools. In this book, author
Jeffrey Friedl leads you through the
steps of crafting a regular expression
that gets the job done. He examines a variety of tools and uses
them in an extensive array of examples, with a major focus
on Perl.

Windows Software for the WWW

PolyForm™

WEB FORMS CONSTRUCTION KIT

By O'Reilly & Associates, Inc.
Documentation by
John Robert Boynton
1st Edition May 1996
Two diskettes & 146-page book
ISBN 1-56592-182-8

PolyForm™ is a powerful 32-bit web forms tool that helps you
easily build and manage interactive web pages. PolyForm's
interactive forms make it easy and fun for users to respond to
the contents of your web with their own feedback, ideas, or
requests for more information. PolyForm lets you collect,
process, and respond to each user's specific input. Best of all,
forms that once required hours of complicated programming
can be created in minutes because PolyForm automatically
handles all of the CGI programming for processing form contents. Requires Windows NT™ 3.51 or higher or Windows® 95.

Windows Software for the WWW

WebBoard™ 3.0

By O'Reilly & Associates, Inc.
Documentation by Susan B. Peck
& Jay York
1st Edition April 1998
CD-ROM & 368-page book
ISBN 1-56592-429-0

The new enterprise-class version of O'Reilly's live chat and multithreaded web conferencing system adds a score of enhancements sure to make it the discussion server of choice for the most active corporate intranets and public chat areas. WebBoard™ 3.0 builds on its predecessor's reputation for easy administration and customization with these new features: IRC chat, Microsoft SQL Server 6.5 database support, HTTP logging support, and mailing list support.

WebSite Professional™ V2.0

By O'Reilly & Associates, Inc.
Documentation by Susan B. Peck,
Judy Helfand & Mary Jane Walsh
September 1997
970 pages (2 Vols.)
Includes CD-ROM
ISBN 1-56592-327-8

While providing the latest innovations in web server technology, WebSite Professional™ 2.0 offers more options for creating dynamic sites than any other Windows web server. From programmability and publishing power to commerce and security, it is the most open, flexible, and robust web server on the market. Requires Windows NT™ 4.0 or Windows® 95.

Building Your Own Web Conferences™

By Susan B. Peck & Beverly Murray Scherf
1st Edition March 1997
270 pages, Includes CD-ROM
ISBN 1-56592-279-4

Building Your Own Web Conferences™ is a complete guide for Windows® 95 and Windows NT™ users on how to set up and manage dynamic virtual communities that improve workgroup collaboration and keep visitors coming back to your site. The second in O'Reilly's "Build Your Own..." series, this book comes with O'Reilly's state-of-the-art WebBoard™ 2.0 software on CD-ROM.

Building Your Own WebSite™

By Susan B. Peck & Stephen Arrants
1st Edition July 1996
514 pages, Includes CD-ROM,
ISBN 1-56592-232-8

This is a hands-on reference for Windows® 95 and Windows NT™ users who want to host a site on the Web or on a corporate intranet. This step-by-step guide will have you creating live web pages in minutes. You'll also learn how to connect your web to information in other Windows applications, such as word processing documents and databases. The book is packed with examples and tutorials on every aspect of web management, and it includes the highly acclaimed WebSite™ 1.1 server software on CD-ROM.

O'REILLY™

TO ORDER: **800-998-9938** • **order@oreilly.com** • **http://www.oreilly.com/**
OUR PRODUCTS ARE AVAILABLE AT A BOOKSTORE OR SOFTWARE STORE NEAR YOU.
FOR INFORMATION: **800-998-9938** • **707-829-0515** • **info@oreilly.com**

How to stay in touch with O'Reilly

1. Visit Our Award-Winning Site
http://www.oreilly.com/

★ "Top 100 Sites on the Web" —*PC Magazine*
★ "Top 5% Web sites" —*Point Communications*
★ "3-Star site" —*The McKinley Group*

Our web site contains a library of comprehensive product information (including book excerpts and tables of contents), downloadable software, background articles, interviews with technology leaders, links to relevant sites, book cover art, and more. File us in your Bookmarks or Hotlist!

2. Join Our Email Mailing Lists
New Product Releases
To receive automatic email with brief descriptions of all new O'Reilly products as they are released, send email to:
listproc@online.oreilly.com
Put the following information in the first line of your message (*not* in the Subject field):
subscribe oreilly-news

O'Reilly Events
If you'd also like us to send information about trade show events, special promotions, and other O'Reilly events, send email to:
listproc@online.oreilly.com
Put the following information in the first line of your message (*not* in the Subject field):
subscribe oreilly-events

3. Get Examples from Our Books via FTP
There are two ways to access an archive of example files from our books:

Regular FTP
• ftp to:
  ftp.oreilly.com
  (login: anonymous
  password: your email address)
• Point your web browser to:
  ftp://ftp.oreilly.com/

FTPMAIL
• Send an email message to:
  ftpmail@online.oreilly.com
  (Write "help" in the message body)

4. Contact Us via Email
order@oreilly.com
To place a book or software order online. Good for North American and international customers.

subscriptions@oreilly.com
To place an order for any of our newsletters or periodicals.

books@oreilly.com
General questions about any of our books.

software@oreilly.com
For general questions and product information about our software. Check out O'Reilly Software Online at **http://software.oreilly.com/** for software and technical support information. Registered O'Reilly software users send your questions to:
website-support@oreilly.com

cs@oreilly.com
For answers to problems regarding your order or our products.

booktech@oreilly.com
For book content technical questions or corrections.

proposals@oreilly.com
To submit new book or software proposals to our editors and product managers.

international@oreilly.com
For information about our international distributors or translation queries. For a list of our distributors outside of North America check out:
http://www.oreilly.com/www/order/country.html

O'Reilly & Associates, Inc.
101 Morris Street, Sebastopol, CA 95472 USA
TEL   707-829-0515 or 800-998-9938
       (6am to 5pm PST)
FAX   707-829-0104

Titles from O'Reilly

International Distributors

O'REILLY™

O'Reilly & Associates, Inc.
101 Morris Street
Sebastopol, CA 95472-9902
1-800-998-9938

Visit us online at:
http://www.ora.com/
orders@ora.com

O'REILLY WOULD LIKE TO HEAR FROM YOU

Which book did this card come from?

_____

Where did you buy this book?
❑ Bookstore   ❑ Computer Store
❑ Direct from O'Reilly   ❑ Class/seminar
❑ Bundled with hardware/software
❑ Other _____

What operating system do you use?
❑ UNIX   ❑ Macintosh
❑ Windows NT   ❑ PC(Windows/DOS)
❑ Other _____

What is your job description?
❑ System Administrator   ❑ Programmer
❑ Network Administrator   ❑ Educator/Teacher
❑ Web Developer
❑ Other _____

❑ Please send me O'Reilly's catalog, containing
a complete listing of O'Reilly books and
software.

Name _____   Company/Organization _____

Address _____

City _____   State _____   Zip/Postal Code _____   Country _____

Telephone _____   Internet or other email address (specify network) _____

Nineteenth century wood engraving
of a bear from the O'Reilly &
Associates Nutshell Handbook®
Using & Managing UUCP.

BUSINESS REPLY MAIL

FIRST CLASS MAIL   PERMIT NO. 80   SEBASTOPOL, CA

Postage will be paid by addressee

O'Reilly & Associates, Inc.
101 Morris Street
Sebastopol, CA 95472-9902